B.S.B.I. Conference Reports,

THE BRITISH OAK: ITS HISTORY AND NATURAL HISTORY

THE OAK TREE

The oak tree is very tall—
  it reaches out as if to clasp the sun.
The bark is prickly and jagged.
The roots spread in a curved pattern.
Where acorns have dropped new trees have sprouted.

The oak stands proud, haughty, majestic and grand.
Its ancient trunk is historical—
  the rings show it has probably stood
  on that single place for a hundred years.
The oak is abundant, growing mostly in forests.
It is timeless, our predecessor, it outlives us all.

SUSAN JONES, *Kingshurst Primary
School, Warwickshire at the
Royal Show, Kenilworth* 1973.

THE BRITISH OAK

ITS HISTORY
AND
NATURAL HISTORY

Edited by
M. G. MORRIS and F. H. PERRING

Published for
THE BOTANICAL SOCIETY OF THE BRITISH ISLES
by
E. W. CLASSEY, LTD.
PARK ROAD, FARINGDON, BERKSHIRE SN7 7DR

Copyright © 1974

THE BOTANICAL SOCIETY OF THE BRITISH ISLES

International Book No.
0 900848 78 2

Printed in Great Britain at the Pendragon Press, Papworth Everard, Cambridge

CONTENTS

	page
Preface	7
Conference programme	8
Introduction. E. W. JONES	11
A history of the taxonomy and distribution of the native oak species. A. S. GARDINER	13
Cytology and genetics of oaks. D. L. WIGSTON ..	27
Flandrian history of oak in the British Isles. SIR HARRY GODWIN and MRS J. DEACON	51
The oak tree in historic times. O. RACKHAM	62
Annual rings in modern and medieval times. J. M. FLETCHER	80
Growing oak. M. J. PENISTAN	98
Uses of oak, past and present. C. J. VENABLES	113
The oak and its legends. M. HADFIELD	123
Variation in oakwoods in Britain. R. C. STEELE ..	130
Nutrient cycles in oakwood ecosystems in NW England. A. H. F. BROWN	141
The reproductive characteristics of oak. M. W. SHAW	162
The effect of defoliators on tree growth. G. GRADWELL	182
Physiology of the oak tree. K. A. LONGMAN and M. P. COUTTS	194
Macrofungi in the oak woods of Britain. R. WATLING	222
The fungal pathogens of oak. J. S. MURRAY	235

The epiphytes of oak. F. Rose 250

Oak as a habitat for insect life. M. G. Morris .. 274

The galls on oak. A. Darlington 298

The importance of oak to mammals. G. B. Corbet .. 312

The birds of oak woodlands. J. J. M. Flegg and
    T. J. Bennett 324

Ecological aspects of oak woodland conservation
    D. T. Streeter 341

Appendix I
    Exhibits staged at the conference 355

Appendix II
    Excursion to Singleton Park 361

Appendix III
    Excursions to Sussex oak woods 363

Index 365

PREFACE

It is now becoming generally accepted that some of the most valuable conferences are those which bring together experts from a wide range of disciplines to discuss a topic of common interest but from a large number of viewpoints. It was for this reason that during 1970 the Botanical Society of the British Isles agreed to the suggestion that they should hold a conference devoted to a prominent species in our flora, of importance to the human race and to other plants and animals, and invite contributions on every aspect of its history and relationship with man. Having accepted this idea, British botanists did not take long to decide that the outstanding candidate for treatment of this kind was our most widespread and revered timber tree, the oak.

Some members of the BSBI may have felt that there could not be enough of interest for them in a programme devoted to one species: if so they were mistaken. With three years in which to prepare their papers contributors made enormous efforts to ensure that every item of relevance to their field was examined, and in several cases undertook research specifically for the conference, so that this report contains much original material. The Botanical Society is indebted to all the contributors for the efforts they made, which were undoubtedly the major factor in ensuring the success of the conference.

But they were not the only factor. The exhibition, which ran throughout the conference and was beautifully mounted by the exhibitors, was a fascinating demonstration of the importance of oak in subjects as diverse as church architecture and lichen habitats. It was noticeable that participants returned again and again to the exhibits.

This volume may help to explain the success of the conference to those who did not attend, including as it does an account of the exhibits and excursions and the text of all the papers given during the three days, excepting only the entertainment provided by Dr William Stearn who stood in at the eleventh hour, when ill health prevented Miles Hadfield from giving his paper. However, this volume can never completely reflect the success of the conference because much of that derived from the many new contacts made and ideas exchanged between experts from so many disciplines, and the consequences of these have only just begun. There can have been few other conferences which brought together so diverse a group of people who found they had so much in common, united as they were by a love of talking about, thinking about and feeling about oak.

Monks Wood Experimental Station,
Huntingdon
January, 1974.

M. G. MORRIS
F. H. PERRING

CONFERENCE PROGRAMME, 1973

held at

The University of Sussex

THURSDAY, 20th, SEPTEMBER

MORNING SESSION

11.00 Opening of Conference: Professor J. Sutcliffe, School of Biological Sciences, University of Sussex.

Introduction by *Chairman:* Dr E. W. Jones, Department of Forestry, University of Oxford.

11.15 Taxonomy and distribution.   A. S. Gardiner

12.00 Cytology and genetics of oaks.   Dr D. L. Wigston

12.45   Lunch

AFTERNOON SESSION

Chairman: J. R. Aldhous, Forestry Commission, Alice Holt.

14.00 Flandrian history of oak in the British Isles.
                    Sir Harry Godwin, F.R.S., and Mrs J. Deacon

14.45 The oak tree in historic times.   Dr O. Rackham

15.30 Annual rings in modern and medieval times.
                        Dr J. M. Fletcher

16.00   Tea

16.30 Growing oak.   M. J. Penistan

17.15 The uses of oak, past and present.   C. J. Venables

19.30   Dinner

EVENING SESSION

Chairman: J. R. Aldhous, Forestry Commission, Alice Holt.

20.45　The oak and its legends.　　　　M. Hadfield

21.15　The oak and the arboretum.　　　W. T. Stearn

FRIDAY, 21st SEPTEMBER

MORNING SESSION

Chairman: Dr S. M. Walters, Botany School, University of Cambridge.

9.00　Variation in oakwoods in Britain.　　R. C. Steele

9.45　Nutrient cycles in oakwood ecosystems in NW England.
　　　　　　　　　　　　　　　　　A. H. F. Brown

10.30　　　　　　　　　　Coffee

11.00　The reproductive characteristics of oak.　M. W. Shaw

11.40　The effect of defoliators on tree growth.　G. Gradwell

12.20　Physiology of the oak tree.　　　K. A. Longman and
　　　　　　　　　　　　　　　　　　　M. P. Coutts

13.00　　　　　　　　　　Lunch

14.45　Excursion to Open Air Museum, Singleton, near Chichester, Sussex.

19.30　　　　　　　　　　Dinner

EVENING SESSION

20.45　Film: The Major—the life and death of an oak tree.

SATURDAY, 22nd SEPTEMBER

MORNING SESSION

Chairman: Professor G. C. Varley, Hope Department of Entomology, University of Oxford.

9.00	Macrofungi in the oak woods of Britain.	R. Watling
9.40	The fungal pathogens of oak.	J. S. Murray
10.20	The epiphytes of oak.	Dr F. Rose

11.00	Coffee	
11.30	Oak as a habitat for insect life.	Dr M. G. Morris
12.15	The galls on oak.	A. Darlington

13.00	Lunch

AFTERNOON SESSION

Chairman: M. J. Penistan, Forestry Commission, Cambridge.

14.15	The birds of oak woodlands.	Dr J. J. M. Flegg and T. J. Bennett
15.00	The importance of oak to mammals.	Dr G. B. Corbet

15.45	Tea	
16.15	Ecological aspects of oak woodland conservation.	D. T. Streeter

18.30	Dinner

SUNDAY, 23rd SEPTEMBER

10.00 Day Excursion to Sussex oakwoods: Eridge Park, Nap Wood, Saxonbury Hill and The Mens.

INTRODUCTION

E. W. Jones

Department of Forestry, University of Oxford

The British people have a deep affection for their oaks; to take an example almost at random, the Edinburgh nurseryman William Boutcher in his 'Treatise on Forest Trees' (Edinburgh, 1775) describes it as 'This noble tree, the monarch of the woods, the boast and bulwark of the British nation'. Boutcher was not given to poetical outbursts; for him the ash is merely 'this useful, though not ornamental tree'. He was simply following the tradition of his time, and it would be easy to find half a dozen references to oak in similar terms by other writers of the period. British writers claimed that the superiority of the British navy over the French was due to the superiority of our oak timber over French timber, but this did not prevent French writers of the period referring in similar effusive terms to *their* oak as the finest in the world. And when we find German writers praising *their* oak as superior to that of all other countries, it becomes evident that the affection is general.

The basis for the British claim lay in the fact that the 'crooks' and 'knees' in the framework of a British man-of-war were made entirely from the naturally curved boughs of our widely spaced oak trees, whereas the French were obliged to use iron because their closely grown small crowned oaks did not yield enough large boughs. The British also believed that their oak timber was stronger and, in so far as it was usually faster grown because it was more widely spaced, there was probably some truth in this belief. But the high quality of Continental oak plants was also recognised. German and Polish oak brought down the rivers and sawn by wind-power at the ports was imported into Britain throughout the late middle ages and on into the 18th century, and was often preferred to English oak for furniture and panelling.

It is not difficult to appreciate the reasons why the oaks were held in such affection. They have a combination of properties—size, longevity, strength, durability and fissibility of wood, a high yield of fruit and of tannin, and an ability to coppice freely—which made them of exceptional utility amongst European trees; indeed there can be few plants other than those which yield staple foods which were so intimately related to the economy and the history of the people. Moreover a nation sees in the oaks qualities such as strength, endurance and dignity which it likes to see in itself.

The genus *Quercus* is very large, with about 450 species confined to the northern hemisphere but most of them in more southerly latitudes than Britain. Thus the Iberian peninsula has twelve species, the Balkan peninsula fifteen. By far the greatest concentration of *Quercus* species in the world is in Mexico, which has about 125 endemics together with a further 75 species which extend either northwards into the United States or southwards towards Colombia. Thus Mexico contains nearly half of the world's oaks. *Quercus* species are also abundant from the eastern Himalayas through southern China to Japan, and through Malaya, Java and Sumatra to the Philippines; in this region there are about 130 out of 175 Old World species, and they are often important dominants in montane forest in the tropics.

Thus the two oaks which we tend to regard as so typically British in fact form the northern outposts of a vast genus whose main territory is warm temperate and even tropical-montane. It is worth bearing this in mind when we consider their biology. In many ways they seem very ill-adapted to our cool-temperate climate, many of their behavioural traits being suited to warmer conditions. They come into leaf far too late to make full use of our growing season, and even then are often severely damaged by late frosts; the large fruits are readily killed by desiccation as well as frost, and germinate precociously. The ability of the seedling shoot when growing under adverse conditions to die back repeatedly whilst the tap root thickens and accumulates reserves until it is capable of making a long strong shoot in a single season is another feature frequent in trees of warm climates.

Entomologists agree that the oaks support the largest number of phytophagous insects of any single British plant species. *Acer pseudoplatanus,* the sycamore, supports a remarkably small insect fauna, and I have heard it suggested that this is because it is an exotic and its specific insect associates have not accompanied it to this country. But may not this difference between oak and sycamore be due to the oaks having associated with them the rich fauna of warm climates, whereas the sycamore, belonging to an exclusively cool-temperate genus, has associated with it the poor fauna of a cold climate? In many other respects the oaks are exceptional amongst the trees of central and north-western Europe, and many of their extraordinary features can be interpreted as inherited adaptations to warmer climates.

A HISTORY OF THE TAXONOMY AND DISTRIBUTION OF THE NATIVE OAK SPECIES

A. S. GARDINER

Merlewood Research Station, Grange-over-Sands

Introduction

The special part played by oak in the affairs of men is summed up very well by Rolfe[1]. He writes: 'Of all the trees, which are known to the naturalist, there is probably none, which appeals so strongly to the imagination, as the oak. It is so woven into our history and national life, that apart from its practical uses, it has earned a sentimental value, which is neither shared nor approached by any other tree'. But unfortunately, as in other cases, where man comes to regard certain wild animals or plants with a particular affection approaching a mystique, discussion of the relationship is seldom conducted without considerable dispute. It is hardly surprising, therefore, that an examination of the history of the classification and distribution of our two native species, Pedunculate oak, *Quercus robur* L. and Sessile oak, *Q. petraea* (Mattuschka) Liebl., reveals a story of confusion and disagreement.

Taxonomy

In ancient times, the Greeks, Romans and Macedonians had their own names for different oaks, which provided such botanists as Theophrastus and Pliny with a number of difficulties in resolving Latin and Greek terminology. Their problems are discussed by the pre-Linnaean naturalists such as Dalechamps[2], Parkinson[3], J. Bauhin[4] and Ray[5]. It is amongst these latter authorities that we find the earliest classifications of Pedunculate and Sessile oak, which became important supports for the taxonomies adopted by Linnaeus and later botanists.

Possibly the earliest separation of the two taxa, in a manner compatible with the modern concept of Pedunculate and Sessile oak, is that of the French botanist Dalechamps[2] (1586–7). Under the heading *Quercus* he describes several taxa to which he gave the name 'genera'. The Sessile oak he divided into male and female sub-units, *Platyphyllos mas et foemina,* the main differences being the size of the acorns. He describes the fruit-peduncles as short and thick. The Pedunculate oak, with larger acorns on long peduncles, Dalechamps classifies as his '*Quercus* genus 2', using the Greek name *Hemeris etymodris,* which he considered to be the equivalent of the *Robur* of the Latins. During the next decade in England, Gerard[6] described two oaks under the name *Q. vulgaris,* in his *Herbal* (1597), and named them the Common and the Wild oak. However, his description is rather too ambiguous to afford us a clear identification. A better picture is obtained from Parkinson (1640)[3]. Like Dalechamps, he describes the differences in fruit-peduncles, but in common with other botanists of the time, he considered gall formation an equally important feature.

A few years later, a major step forward was taken by the Bauhin brothers in Switzerland. Jean Bauhin (1650)[4] included both oaks in one taxon, which he designated *Quercus vulgaris brevibus ac longis pediculis*. His younger brother Gaspard Bauhin (1671)[7], however, treated them separately as *Quercus latifolia quae brevi pediculo est* (which he divided into male and female oaks) and *Quercus cum longo pediculo*. It is interesting to note that no mention is made by these authors of the characteristic differences in the leaf stalk. However, a remark by the English botanist Ray (1688)[5] indicates that some observers were aware of this distinction by that time. He writes: 'We are not able to postulate differences between these oaks unless we examine which leaves have stalks or otherwise' (original in Latin). But an unexplained anomaly appears in Ray's own classifications, which is remarked upon by Martyn (1792)[8]. In his *Catalogus Plantarum* (1677) Ray[9] equates Sessile oak, as defined by G. Bauhin, with *Quercus latifolia* Park. and *Q. vulgaris* Ger. and calls it the Common oak. Eleven years later in *Historia Plantarum* (1688) he adds the Pedunculate oak, as defined by G. Bauhin, to this description. However, in his *Synopsis* (1696)[10] he changes matters dramatically by treating the Pedunculate oak as synonymous with *Q. latifolia* Park. and *Q. vulgaris* Ger. and by elevating it in turn to the position of Common oak.

The advent of the Linnaean system of binomials, accompanied by a simplified Latin description, marks the beginning of the modern period of plant taxonomy. In Linnaeus's *Species Plantarum* (1753)[11] we find the earliest description of the Pedunculate oak, under the name *Quercus robur,* which complies with the present International Code of Botanical Nomenclature. The Latin description reads: *Quercus foliis deciduis oblongis superne latioribus; sinubis acutioribus; angulis obtusis.* However, it is necessary to comment, that this description by itself does not indisputably identify the Pedunculate oak. It is only when we examine the list of supporting authorities, in particular the citation '*Quercus cum longo pediculo.* Bauh. pin. 420', followed later by the words 'Habitat in Europa', that we see to which oak Linnaeus refers in his description. The dilemma is removed altogether when we consult the second edition of his *Flora Suecica* (1755)[12]. Here Linnaeus separates the Sessile oak as a variety β from his main species, citing G. Bauhin and Dalechamps as his supports. The accompanying list of Swedish habitats, which he gives for both taxa, also clearly indicates that he is distinguishing between Pedunculate and Sessile oak[13].

The first British botanist to adopt Linnaeus's classification of these two oaks appears to have been William Hudson in the first edition of his *Flora Anglica* (1762)[14]. A few years later a further taxonomic advance was made, in Britain on this occasion, with the publication of the eighth edition (1768) of Miller's *Gardener's Dictionary*[15]. Here, for the first time in the Linnaean era, the two oaks were separated as species and given distinctive binomials. Furthermore, Miller added the characteristics of the leaf-stalks to the description of the fruit-peduncles. But unfortunately, for reasons that time has obscured, he gave the binomial *Q. robur* to the Sessile oak, choosing a new name, *Q. foemina,* for the Pedunculate species. However, in our own country only Withering and Stokes (1787)[16] followed Miller's nomenclature, and British botanists soon returned to using names more compatible with Linnaeus's original choice. Matters were otherwise on the Continent, where Miller's confusing use of the binomial *Q. robur* was applied until the middle of the nineteenth century. In this form, occasionally with Linnaeus's name appended as authority, it appears in the works of Roth, Baumgarten, Willdenow and Reichenbach.

The next major contribution to this field in Britain was Martyn's *Flora rustica* (1792)[8]. In this work Martyn selected the binomial *Q. robur* for his species of the Common oak. He divided this into two varieties, *pedunculata,* the True British or Naval oak, and *sessilis,* the Sessile-fruited oak. Although he does not affirm it himself, it is probable that he took these epithets from Friedrich Ehrhart's *Beiträge*[17]. Ehrhart, a pupil of Linnaeus, published the names *Q. pedunculata* and *Q. sessilis* without description in 1790, *Q. pedunculata* being validated by Hoffmann in 1791[18]. Martyn also mentions the Durmast oak of the New Forest, which he distinguishes from his Sessile-fruited oak on account of differences in leaf-shape and colour, the texture and colour of the bark and his observation that 'The whole tree has much the air of the Chestnut and is of a freer growth than the true oak'. This putative distinction between Sessile and Durmast oak, the latter classified later as variety β of *Q. sessiliflora* by Smith (1804)[19], extended to the quality of the timber and was used in nineteenth-century arguments by the protagonists of Sessile oak against those who insisted that Pedunculate oak produced the better timber. The authors of modern works on timber, however, make no such distinction between Sessile and Durmast oak.

Four years after the appearance of Martyn's work, Richard Salisbury[20] returned both taxa to the species status, choosing the names *Q. longaeva* for the Pedunculate oak and *Q. sessiliflora* for the Sessile oak. From that time, until the rediscovery of the earlier *Q. petraea* (Mattuschka)[21] Lieblein (1784)[22] by Schwarz (1935)[23], Salisbury's binomial became the favourite choice of botanists describing the Sessile oak, and but for Schwarz's research would still be considered the first valid name. On the other hand, it is possibly due to Miller's use of *Q. robur* that Ehrhart's name for the Pedunculate species became so widely used. The prominence in the past of the names *Q. pedunculata* and *Q. sessiliflora* is still reflected in the literature of today, despite invalidation by the International Code of Botanical Nomenclature. Many botanists and others, in their publications, for the sake of clarity continue to cite them in parenthesis after their correct names. It is difficult to deny that they possess a certain aptness in meaning when used together, which possibly justifies their continued citation as synonyms.

The nineteenth century ushered in a period of extensive botanical and other biological interest, which is reflected both in the increased number of new journals, which started to appear at regular intervals, and in the many Natural History Societies and Field clubs, which were founded between 1830 and 1900. Botanists were made increasingly aware of the considerable ranges of variation within plant species and the possible existence of inter-specific hybrids. In a paper, read to an early meeting of the Botanical Society of Edinburgh in 1841 Greville[24] reported: 'I was under a strong impression that at least the two forms recognised as species under the names *Robur* and *sessiliflora* were really distinct. But I soon found that the ascribed characters were of little importance in rigid specific discrimination'. Further on in the same paper we read: 'It is impossible to define the general outline or circumspectio of the leaf, so as to distinguish any of the forms as species, as they run insensibly into each other'. The problem was not, however, confined to Britain. Botanists on the Continent sought to widen the strict definition of the species to include numerous varieties and forms; many of them are retained today by arboriculturists and nurserymen. At a local level, taxonomists appeared to rival one another in producing new names for the oaks in their own regions. Lasch in 1857[25] produced an extensive list of leaf and fruit-types of Sessile and Pendunculate oak and their intermediates found in the woodlands of Driesen in the Mark Brandenburg.

During the same period British botanists, like Greville, were apparently bedevilled, albeit unwittingly, by difficulties of quite a different origin. At some point during the first half of the nineteenth century, botanists, studying these two oak species, added the presence or absence of pubescence and stellate hairs on the underside of the leaf to their lists of distinguishing features. The first British botanist to do so appears to have been Professor D. Don in Leighton's *Flora of Shropshire* (1841)[26]. Unfortunately, this first attempt caused considerable confusion. Don's description of his intermediate oak is indistinguishable from an otherwise acceptable one for the Sessile oak. At the same time he created additional problems, by giving the slightly pubescent state of the underside of the leaves to the Pedunculate oak, and placing the glabrous condition with the Sessile species. These errors remained undetected, it seems, until 1910, when C. E. Moss[27] attempted to rectify the situation in his own authoritative paper. However, by that time Don's descriptions had achieved a wide acceptance and were reproduced in other works of major importance; Babington's *Manual of Botany* carried these descriptions, with only minor modifications, through ten editions up to 1922.

The occurrence of intermediates or putative hybrids between these two species stimulated Continental taxonomists to adopt a variety of names to describe the phenomenon. The earliest of these binomials is *Q. rosacea*, published by Bechstein in 1813[28]. Later, in 1816[29], he described a hybrid, using the binomial *Q. hybrida*, which was treated by some authorities as a synonym for *Q. rosacea*. However, in his later work Bechstein[30] appears to make a distinction between these two taxa. His description of *Q. rosacea* indicates that he is referring to the hybrid between Pedunculate and Sessile oak, but that for *Q. hybrida* embraces a hybrid, which resembles the Pedunculate oak, but gives us no direct information about the other parent. Bechstein's description of *Q. rosacea* was later criticised for its incompleteness by von Borbás (1887)[31], who drew attention to the fact that no mention is made of the presence of stellate hairs on the underside of the leaf. Whether his description is complete or not, it is perfectly clear to which hybrid Bechstein is referring in his description, and his binomial (as *Q.×rosacea*) must be regarded as the correct one for all nothomorphs of the parentage *Q.petraea× robur*.

In contrast with European literature there are only a few British references to this hybrid before the turn of the century, e.g. Bree (1836)[32], Hemsley (1877)[33] and Marshall Ward (1892)[34]. However, this apparent lack of interest was altered markedly by the appearance of Moss's classic paper in 1910[27]. His detailed description of both species and the hybrid, his rejection of the concept that they were both varieties of *Q. robur* and discussion of the nomenclature had lasting effect on their subsequent botanical treatment. Moss avoided the difficulty of choosing an acceptable trivial for the hybrid, which he describes simply as *Q. robur×sessiliflora*. In the same paper he provisionally added another species of oak to the British flora, namely *Q. lanuginosa* Thuiller, which he later removed from his list in the *Cambridge British Flora*[35].

A further minor advance in the classification of these two species was made by Harz[36] in 1885 and later, independently it seems, by Oelkers[37] in 1913; both workers noted that the fresh acorns of the Pedunculate oak bore longitudinal stripes of a brownish-green colour. A corresponding feature is absent in the Sessile species. This distinction, possibly because of its transient nature, seems to have remained outside the main stream of British botanical literature, until E. W. Jones[38] drew attention to it in his *Biological Flora* account in 1959.

During the nineteenth century a number of attempts were made to produce a systematic arrangement of the genus *Quercus*. Perhaps the best known of these is that of De Candolle[39], in which Pedunculate and Sessile oak are treated as subspecies of *Q. robur* L. De Candolle's system is reflected in British works of the same period, notably various editions of Bentham's *Handbook of the British Flora*. However, more recent arrangements, eg *Flora*

Europaea[40], have been influenced by the comprehensive work on oak systematics by Camus[41] and Schwarz[42].

Research in this century has demonstrated the existence of provenance differences in physiology and morphology[43] and the numerical techniques applied by Cousens[44] [45] [46] have enabled us to assess the extent of introgressive hybridisation. Little, however, has been added to the list of distinguishing features described in Clapham, Tutin and Warburg[47] and Jones[38] which enables a botanist in the field to discriminate more clearly between these two species. However Cousens found that many of these features were insufficiently described and allowed a wide variation in interpretation. At the same time he drew attention to a hitherto unstudied difference between the species in the folding of the leaves excised from opening buds, and suggested that these should be studied more closely.

One of the most important events in the recent history of oak taxonomy in this country is the nomenclatural change to the botanical name of the Sessile oak, which botanists were obliged to make under the International Code of Botanical Nomenclature. During the preliminary work on his monograph, Schwarz[23] became intrigued with the fact that, in terms of the most widely known literature, no botanist appeared to have described the Sessile oak as a sepetate species in the period between Miller in 1768, who misleadingly called it *Q. Robur* and Ehrhart in 1790, who gave it the name *Q. sessilis* without an accompanying description. Schwarz's research revealed otherwise and Salisbury's name, *Q. sessiliflora,* was found to have an antecedent in the *Q. petraea* of Mattuschka (1777) and Lieblein (1784), based on *Q. Robur* subsp. *Petraea* Mattuschka (1777). But there is no doubt that some botanists, including Schwarz himself, regard the necessity for such a change with regret since it forces us to drop a well-known and apt name for one whose meaning is obscure.

Distribution

Peats and sediments provide a pollen record, which indicates that oak has been dominant over large areas of the British lowlands for some 8000 years (see pps 51–61). It is also generally accepted that without the interference of man the main component of the vegatation cover would still be oak woodland. During the climatic optimum, approximately 5000 years ago, oak woodlands extended much higher into the hills, and oak boles, recovered from peat deposits, indicate that growth too was much more luxuriant. In more recent times the climate became warmer up to the time of the 12th century. During this period pannage was let out to owners of livestock, suggesting that at that time oak fruited regularly and in some abundance; today, there are longer intervals between good mast years.

Although there are notable exceptions, most botanists and foresters regard the Pedunculate and Sessile oak as native to the British Isles. However, it is almost impossible, in the present state of

FIGURE 1

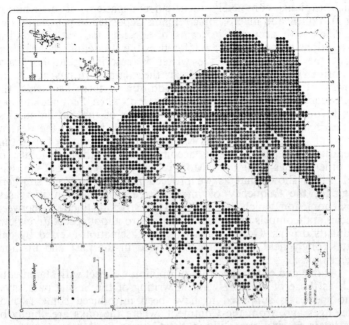

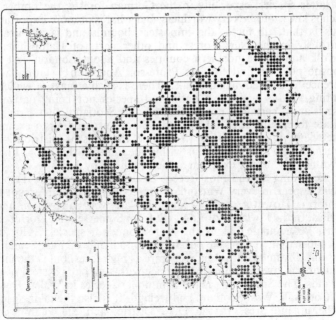

Distribution of native oak species in the British Isles

our knowledge, to write a history of the native oaks of this country, which explains completely their current pattern of distribution (fig 1). Pollen and macroscopic remains deposited in peat cannot be identified with accuracy in terms of species, and early botanical descriptions allow us to draw inferences but no definite conclusions about the species which the writer is describing; at least two authorities changed their minds in their later writings about the identity of the 'common oak'. In addition to these problems, the inadequacy of records of the long period, when Pedunculate oak was favoured silviculturally at the expense of the Sessile species, makes it impossible very often to distinguish between the descendants of former native oakwoods and the results of planting operations, the latter being accompanied by the possibility of the other species being used. More recently, the research of Cousens and others shows that as we proceed northwards from southern England, the frequency of introgressive hybridisation increases, a phenomenon which can obscure the strict distinctions between species and compels us, at the same time, to adopt speculative views about its origins. However, such is the fascination exerted by oak that strongly held views have developed in the past and in more recent times.

At one end of the spectrum of opinion we meet with statements, such as those of Rhind[48] who, in writing of the Sessile oak, says: 'The species is supposed to have been introduced some two or three ages ago, from the Continent, where the oaks are chiefly of this latter species, especially in the German forests, the timber of which is known to be very worthless. But what is of more importance to us is that, de facto, the imposter abounds and is propagated vigorously in the New Forest and other parts of Hampshire, in Norfolk and in the northern counties and about London'. At the opposite pole we find the late Professor Anderson[49] stating, with reference to the Pedunculate oak: 'There is such a mass of evidence pointing to this typically Continental species not being native of these islands, certainly not of Ireland and Scotland, that I do not hesitate to classify it as introduced'. Before proceeding to examine these views it is necessary to outline the present distributional pattern, and to accomplish this within the limits of this paper I have drawn heavily on the excellent summary given by Jones[38].

According to the most recent distribution maps (fig 1) both species appear in every Watsonian vice-county in Britain except the far north. However, their frequencies are very uneven in most districts. In the lowlands of England, from Somerset and Dorset east wards, Pedunculate oak is the more abundant species. It is also commoner than the Sessile oak in the woodlands of East Scotland, Ross and Cromarty. It is relatively rare as high forest but is the more frequent oak over hazel in the coppice-with-standards system of the lowlands. The Sessile oak is the commoner species in Wales, Devon and Cornwall, West Scotland and Ireland; it is also the main species of the upland areas in the Lake District and the Pennines. It frequently forms high forest, many areas of which were former stands of coppice. However, as Jones[50] points out, there are a number of disturbing elements in an otherwise simple pattern. Within the Pedunculate oak regions eg Hertfordshire and Kent, there are enclaves of Sessile oak, a situation, which he felt, might be reciprocated in the Sessile regions. During his own later investigations Cousens (pers. comm.) received the impression that the Pedunculate oak in Sessile regions was inserted, whilst Sessile in Pedunculate areas was residual.

Ecological studies have indicated differences in the habitat requirements of both species. There is a tendency displayed by the Pedunculate oak for basic soils rich in nutrients, which is linked to a preference for moist clays combined with a tolerance of waterlogging and even flooding. The Sessile oak, on the other hand, seems to prefer more acid soils, which are well drained, and this species, has a corresponding intolerance of flooding. These characteristics are to some extent reflected in the tendency of Pedunculate oak to occur in lower slopes and valleys and for the Sessile oak to be found on the upper slopes and hill tops. This general ecological picture, which is supported by the works of Tansley[51] and Fairhurst[52] and by Continental evidence, seems to have been widely accepted. It is however open to criticism. For example, Jones[50] states: 'Some writers have attempted to explain this distribution in terms of soil factors, but in some of the Sessile regions of the west there is no evidence at all of one species or the other showing any particular soil preference'. Cousens (pers. comm.) also does not accept the general interpretation, because the valley bottoms are obviously planted and therefore most likely to be of Pedunculate oak; also because there is a distinct absence of an ecotone, or border zone, between the two species, such as those observed in parts of the Continent and Scandinavia by Krahl-Urban[43] [53] and Johnsson[54], where hybrid forms are found more frequently than elsewhere.

Professor Anderson's case rested on the well-known preference, shown in the past by nurserymen for Pedunculate oak acorns, which are usually more easily stored and tend to produce larger plants in the early years of seedling growth. The fact that Sessile oak woodland, particularly in Scotland, was replaced by the other species through this practice and occasionally with negative results added weight to his theory[55]. He found additional support firstly in the fact that Sessile oakwoods are found over virtually the whole range of oak sites in Britain, and secondly from inferences drawn from early botanical treatises.

The little information contained in sixteenth and early seventeenth century botanical works is sufficient to allow us to speculate about which species was more abundant in former times; late seventeenth and eighteenth century literature, however, is decidedly contradictory. Gerard[6] describes both a 'common' and a 'wild' oak. His description of the 'common' oak is accompanied by a figure illustrating a specimen with stalked leaves and fruits. Of his 'wild' oak he says: 'The acorns are long, but shorter than those of the tamer oak; every one fastened in his own cup'. We can postulate that, by 'common' or 'tame' oak, Gerard is referring to those in cultivation, therefore planted and most likely the Pedunculate species. Following the same line of reasoning, his 'wild' oak with its shorter acorns is the oak of the forest and therefore the Sessile oak. However, in proceeding in this fashion we have to adjust slightly the meaning of the word common, in order to maintain the hypothesis that the Sessile oak was the more abundant species. For instance, Parkinson's[3] *Q. latifolia,* 'the broad-leafed oke', which he describes as 'This oke, which as I take it is the most common in our land' is probably the Sessile oak if his description is an accurate one. The characters, which he observed on the fruits, suggest that this is a reasonable assumption. In describing these, he says: 'The fruits or Acorns rising up in sundry other places, upon short stalks, two or three for the most part joyned together'. The next oak, which he lists, is *Hemeris sive Robur,* The Strong or Gall Oke, and of this tree he says: 'They flower and bear ackornes like the former, but not so plentiful and are greater, standing on longer stalks'. However, he does not make it clear whether he is referring in this case to a British oak, as further on he states: 'The first Oke is the most generall throughout the land, growing on high or low grounds indifferently, yet flourish best in a fruitefull ground: the other kinds that I can heare of, are not growing anywhere with us'. However, the next major English authority, namely Ray, places us in a quandary. In his first work (1677)[9] he unites synonymously Gerard's common oak, Parkinson's broad-leafed oak with the Sessile oak as described by the Bauhin brothers and calls it the common oak-tree; later (1688)[5] he adds the Pedunculate oak to this classification. In his third work (1696)[10] he drops the Sessile oak from this description, lists it quite separately and accords it a somewhat limited distribution. Although these changes are noted and later remarked upon by Martyn[8], no explanation for them is advanced by Ray himself. Miller, whose published works appeared some thirty years after Ray, offers us a reciprocal picture. In one of his early works[56] he puts forward a description for the common oak, which is almost identical to the one in Ray's third work[10]. However, some thirty years later he appears to have changed his mind because in the eighth and best-known edition of his *Gardener's Dictionary*[15], he makes the Sessile oak the common species. It is possible that the key to the puzzle set by Ray and Miller lies in different uses of the word common, but they leave us no clues; or that the distributional pattern of the two species had been so altered by planting that they found themselves in a situation which defied explanation.

By the turn of the eighteenth century, however, it seems fairly clear that the Sessile oak had become much less frequent in the south of England, which is indicated by remarks of Martyn[8], and later writers. Martyn, who expresses astonishment at Miller's classification, highlights an attitude unfavourable to Sessile oak, which seems to have gained ground particularly during the Napoleonic wars. He was in no doubt that the Pedunculate oak was, as he calls it 'the true British or Naval Oak'. This opinion is supported in other papers of the nineteenth century, where it appears that the buyers, employed by the Navy, preferred the curved stems of hedgerow-grown trees of this species to the straight stems of Sessile oak grown in woodlands. From this selective approach of the Naval timber surveyors the view that Sessile oak timber was inferior in other respects may have developed. Once such a view had become established it would be a relatively easy matter to expand it into one, in which the Sessile oak was regarded as 'the impostor'[48] and therefore not native but introduced. However, by 1840 a more rational attitude was beginning to appear, by which time such authorities as Bree[32] were pointing out that the Sessile oak was by no means rare in parts of England where it must be regarded as native. A number of the protagonists for the claims of both species came together at two meetings held by the Woolhope Naturalists Field Club in 1867 and 1868. Here a paper was read by the Reverend Henry Cooper Key[57] [58], which provoked a lively discussion on the merits of the timber of both species, the reasons for the scarcity of Sessile oak in southern England and the identity of the timber in historical buildings such as Westminster Hall. Both sides appear to have retained their original views, but from about this time onwards the theory that both species were native seems to have been generally accepted.

The question of the origin of species occupied the attention of naturalists during the early part of the nineteenth century culminating in Darwin's theories of evolution and natural selection. The concept that species were static entites was gradually overtaken by the proposition that they were convenient classificatory groupings, which often exhibited striking ranges of variation and occasionally intercrossed to produce fertile progeny. Cases of plant hybrids arising under natural conditions were reported more frequently, encouraging Focke to review the situation in his well-known *Die Pflanzen-Mischlinge* in 1881[59]. Hybrids between these two oaks were occasionally mentioned in the British literature, but the first paper, which dealt exclusively with the phenomenon did not appear until 1909; this was written by C. E. Moss[60]. His next and more comprehensive paper,[27] published the following year, had a greater impact, as older floras and handbooks revised after 1910 show a marked change in their descriptions of oak and oakwoods. There is no doubt that these descriptions contributed a great deal to the establishment of a popular concept that hybrids arose freely and frequently wherever Pedunculate and Sessile oak grew together. This view persisted for several decades until the publication, in 1941, of the results of Dengler's experiments[61]. These experiments, conducted over a period of ten years, illustrated that the cross was a difficult one to make under artificial conditions. He was led to carry them out in the first instance because he was convinced that the hybrid was by no means as frequent in nature as was generally believed. Additional support for this conviction was added by Jones[38] and Hadfield[62] from their field of experience in southern England. However, other regions of the distributional ranges of both species, where the frequency of intermediates is high, provoked botanists such as Weimark[63] and Johnsson[54] to seek other explanations. In Scotland, the confusing picture reported by Greville[24] was studied intensively by Cousens[44] [45] [46]. Using the techniques pioneered by Edgar Anderson[64] Cousens's studies indicate extensive introgression of the Sessile oak by the Pedunculate species, its increase northwards towards Scotland and the probable introgression of Pedunculate oak by another related species in glacial or pre-glacial times. The much greater introgression of Sessile oak in Scotland has probably been caused by the planting of the Pedunculate species and adds weight to Professor Anderson's theory that the species may not have been native to that country. His belief is indirectly supported by the generalization of Stebbins[65] that if two or more species meet in a changing environment, which is marginal for them, the frequency of hybrids may increase and result in a population which is strongly influenced by hybridization. However Stebbins also emphasises the converse, that if the same species exist in a stable habitat to which they are adapted, and if no ecological niches are available, hybridization will be minimal and will have little or no effect on the subsequent populations. In those parts of southern England therefore, where both oak taxa have grown for centuries under such conditions, it seems reasonable to suggest that both may be native to these areas and therefore indigenous to Britain.

Acknowledgements

For supplying a considerable amount of information and advice in the writing of the part dealing with oak distribution I am indebted to Mr J. E. Cousens of the Department of Forestry and Natural Resources, Edinburgh University. I am grateful to Mrs Audrey Eccles and Mr Richard Samways of the Records Office, Kendal for giving freely of their time to translating the Latin texts of the early literature and to my wife who dealt with the German references. My thanks are also owed to Mr M. V. Mathew and Mr D. V. Wilson of the Royal Botanic Gardens at Edinburgh and Kew respectively, to Prof. Dr T. Eckardt of the Botanisches Museum, Berlin, to Dr H. Conert of the Natur-Museum, Senckenberg, Frankfurt a. Main and Mr J. Beckett for providing access to library material.

REFERENCES

1. ROLFE, R. G. 'The Oak', *Country-side*, 1 (1905), 255
2. DALECHAMPS, J. *Historia generalis plantarum*, Lyon (1586–7)
3. PARKINSON, J. *Theatrum botanicum*, (1640)
4. BAUHIN, J. *Historia plantarum universalis*, Yverdon (1650)
5. RAY, J. *Historia plantarum*, 2 (1688)
6. GERARD, J. *The Herball*, (1597)
7. BAUHIN, G. *Pinax theatri botanici*, Basle (1671)
8. MARTYN, T. *Flora rustica*, 1 (1792)
9. RAY, J. *Catalogus plantarum Angliae*, (1677)
10. RAY, J. *Synopsis methodica stirpium Britannicarum*, (1696)
11. LINNAEUS, C. *Species plantarum*, 2, Stockholm, (1753)
12. LINNAEUS, C. *Flora Suecica*, ed. 2, Stockholm, (1755)
13. ULBRICH, E. 'Was ist Quercus Robus L.?', *Mitt. dt. dendrol. Ges.*, 34 (1924), 311–16
14. HUDSON, W. *Flora Anglica*, (1762)
15. MILLER, P. *The Gardener's Dictionary*, ed. 8, 1 (1768)
16. WITHERING, W. and STOKES, J. *A Botanical arrangement of British Plants*, 2, Birmingham, (1787)
17. EHRHART, F. *Beiträge zur Naturkunde*, 5, Hannover and Osnabrück (1790)
18. HOFFMANN, G. F. *Deutschlands Flora oder botanisches Taschenbuch für das Jahr, 1791*, ed. 1, Erlangen (1791)
19. SMITH, J. E. *Flora Britannica*, 3 (1804)
20. SALISBURY, R. A. *Prodromus stirpium in horto ad Chapel Allerton vigentium*, (1796)
21. MATTUSCHKA, H. G., GRAF VON. *Flora Silesiaca*, 2, Breslau and Leipzig (1777)
22. LIEBLEIN, F. C. *Flora Fuldensis*, Frankfurt am Main (1784)
23. SCHWARZ, O. 'Nomenclature of some British and German Oaks', *J. Bot., Lond.*, 73 (1935), 49–51
24. GREVILLE, R. K. 'On the botanical characteristics of the British oaks', *Trans. Proc. bot. Soc. Edinb.*, 1 (1841), 65–9
25. LASCH, W. 'Die Eichenformen der märkischen Wälder hauptsächlich der um Driesen', *Bot. Ztg*, 15 (1857), 409–20
26. LEIGHTON, W. A. *A Flora of Shropshire*, Shrewsbury (1841)
27. MOSS, C. E. 'British oaks', *J. Bot., Lond.*, 48 (1910), 1–8, 33–9
28. BECHSTEIN, J. M. 'Die Roseneiche, Quercus rosacea', *Sylvan*, (1813), 66–70
29. BECHSTEIN, J. M. 'Die Bastardeiche, Quercus hybrida', *Sylvan*, (1816), 63–4
30. BECHSTEIN, J. M. in *Forstbotanik oder Naturgeschichte der Holzgewächse*, 1 (1821), 214–216
31. BORBÁS, V. VON. 'Quercus erioneura', *Dt. bot. Mschr.*, (1887), 164
32. BREE, W. T. 'Further notices respecting British Oaks', *Gdnr's Mag.*, 12 (1836), 571–9
33. HEMSLEY, W. B. *Handbook of hardy trees, shrubs and herbaceous plants*, (1877)
34. MARSHALL WARD, H. *The oak: a popular introduction to forest botany*, (1892)
35. MOSS, C. E. *The Cambridge British Flora*, 2, Cambridge (1914)
36. HARZ, C. O. *Landwirtschaftliche Samenkunde*, 2, Berlin (1885)
37. OELKERS, T. 'Stiel und Traubeneichel', *Z. Forst-u Jagdw.*, 45 (1913), 18–45
38. JONES, E. W. 'Biological flora of the British Isles. Quercus L.', *J. Ecol.*, 47 (1959), 169–222
39. CANDOLLE, A. P. DE. *Prodromus systematis naturalis regni vegetabilis*, 16 (1864)
40. TUTIN, T. G., BURGES, N. A., HEYWOOD, V. H., VALENTINE, D. H., WALTERS, S. M. and WEBB, D. A. *Flora Europaea*, 1, Cambridge (1964)

41. CAMUS, A. *Les Chênes:monographie du genre Querus*, 1–3, Paris (1936–54)
42. SCHWARZ, O. 'Monographie der Eichen Europa und des Mittlemeer-gebietes', *Reprium nov. Spec. Regni veg. Beih.*, (1936–39)
43. KRAHL-URBAN, J. 'Trauben- und Stiel-eiche in Schweden', *Forstwiss. ZentBl.*, 70 (1951), 319–36
44. COUSENS, J. E. 'Notes on the status of Sessile and Pedunculate oaks in Scotland and their identification', *Scott. For.*, 16 (1962), 170–9
45. COUSENS, J. E. 'Variation of some diagnostic characters of Sessile and Pedunculate oaks and their hybrids in Scotland', *Watsonia*, 5 (1963), 273–86
46. COUSENS, J. E. 'The status of Pedunculate and Sessile oaks in Britain', *Watsonia*, 6 (1965), 161–76
47. CLAPHAM, A. R., TUTIN, T. G. and WARBURG, E. F. *Flora of the British Isles*, ed. 2, Cambridge (1962)
48. RHIND, W. *A History of the Vegetable Kingdom*, (1868)
49. ANDERSON, M. L. *The Selection of Tree Species*, Edinburgh (1950)
50. JONES, E. W. 'The Oaks in Britain', *Naturalist Hull*, (1943), 106–7
51. TANSLEY, A. G. *The British Islands and their Vegetation*, 1, Cambridge (1949)
52. FAIRHURST, H. 'The natural vegetation of Scotland: its character and development', *Scott. geogr. Mag.*, 55 (1939), 193–212
53. KRAHL-URBAN, J. *Die Eichen*, Hamburg and Berlin (1959)
54. JOHNSSON, H.' Ungdomsutvecklingen hos stjalek, druvek och rodek', *Svenska SkogsvFör. Tidskr.*, 50 (1952), 168–93
55. ANDERSON, M. L. *A History of Scottish Forestry*, Edinburgh (1967)
56. MILLER, P. *Catalogus plantarum officinalium quae in Horto Botanico*, (1730)
57. KEY, H. C. 'On the two species of the English Oak', *Trans. Woolhope Nat. Fld Club*, (1867), 178–84, 314–20
58. KEY, H. C. *Ibid*, (1868), 144–8
59. FOCKE, W. O. *Die Pflanzen-Mischlinge; ein Beitrag zur Biologie der Gewächse*, Berlin (1881)
60. MOSS, C. E. 'The hybrid oak in Yorkshire and other parts of Britain', *Naturalist Hull*, (1909), 113–14
61. DENGLER, A. 'Bericht über Kreuzungsversuche zwischen Trauben und Stieleiche', *Mitt. H. Goring-Akad. dt. Forstwiss*, 1 (1941), 87–109
62. HADFIELD, M. 'Random notes on British oaks', *Q. Jl For.*, 54 (1960), 141–145
63. WEIMARCK, H. 'Die nordiska ekarna', *Bot. Notiser*, (1947), 61–78, 103–34
64. ANDERSON, E. *Introgressive Hybridization*, London and New York (1949)
65. STEBBINS, G. L. 'The role of hybridization in Evolution', *Proc. Am. phil. Soc.*, 103 (1959), 240–8

CYTOLOGY AND GENETICS OF OAKS

DAVID L. WIGSTON

*Department of Biological Studies, Lanchester
Polytechnic, Coventry*

Introduction

The longevity of tree species, involving several years of seedling growth and a considerable period before first fruiting, complicates investigation of their cytology and genetics. Secondary thickening develops in the early stages of germination, and there are few tissue regions where satisfactory cytological and chromosome preparations can be made. The length of breeding experiments necessitates much reliance on circumstantial genetic evidence, such as assessment of viability and examination of variation in taxonomic status of individuals and populations.

Oaks are particularly difficult subjects. All tissues of *Quercus* species readily react to the presence of tannin[1], which interferes with preparations for cytological study, and is a particular difficulty in root and leaf tip examinations. In addition to problems of microtechnique, study of chromosome number and morphology is complicated by the homogeneity of karyotype throughout the genus. The variability of characters within *Quercus* species, and their similarity and range between species, further complicates genetic analysis by inference from taxonomic status.

Cytology of oak species

Oak species have not been much used for basic cytological investigation. Most references in the literature are associated with reproductive structures, particularly pollen grains. Unusual features of reproductive cytology and anatomy in oaks have been emphasised, such as the fusion of the base of the cotyledons forming an elongated petiole-like tube, superficially resembling monocotyledony[2], and occasional polyembryony. A condition rare in most plants has been reported in the genus; the outer integument of the ovule is fused over the nucellus, closing the micropyle except in the inner integument. This is attributed to chalazogamy, where the pollen tube tip passes directly through the ovule tissue, not the micropyle, penetrating the chalaza on the way to the embryo-sac[2].

A pollination phenomenom characteristic of the Fagaceae is a delay between pollination and final gametic union[2]. A gap of two months is common in oaks[3], the extremes being exhibited by *Quercus borealis* with some fourteen months between pollination and fertilisation[4], and *Q. velutina* where pollination occurs a year before the ovule is mature[3]. The delay is probably due to the intervention of unfavourable climatic conditions between pollination and fertilisation[2].

The most conspicuous and distinctive feature of the pollen grains of oaks is their possession of hyaline, wedge-shaped plugs embedded in their cell contents, radiating towards the furrows from the centre of the cell. Their function appears to be the rupture of the furrow membrane and to spread open the furrows when the grain is moistened[3].

The exine characteristics of oak pollen grains allow the genus, but usually not individual species, to be unambiguously identified in glacial and interglacial deposits[5] [6]. Spoel-Walvius[7] examined sections of pollen of *Q. robur, Q. petraea, Q. pubescens, Q. ilex* and *Q. coccifera* by phase-contrast microscopy. On the basis of exine construction the species were subdivided into a *Q. robur-petraea-pubescens* group and a *Q. ilex-coccifera* group, corresponding to the classification of Schwarz[8]. Erdtman et al[9] distinguished two pollen types within the *Q. robur, Q. petraea, robur × petraea* complex, on the basis of fine distinctions (of the order of 100 nm) of size, shape and wall structure measurements. However, it has not been definitely proved that these types are referable to either species and the authors tentatively define a *Q. robur*-type and a *Q. petraea*-type pollen.

Pollen viability, determined by cytoplasmic staining, has been used to circumvent the difficulty of extended breeding experiments in assessing the fertility of interspecific hybrids[10]. Abortive grains, accompanied by distortions and irregularities of grain form, have been reported in *Q. agrifolia* and *Q. velutina*[3].

The chromosomes of oak species

Most temperate woody genera, including *Quercus, Populus, Alnus, Ulmus, Acer, Viburnum* and *Vaccinium* have constant karyotypes[11]. All species of oak listed in the *Chromosome Atlas*[12] are diploid with 24 chromosomes, with the sole exception of *Q. dentata*, the Japanese silkworm oak, with 48 somatic chromosomes[13]. In polyembryonic individuals triploids have been reported[6]. Oak chromosomes are also exceedingly small and difficult to distinguish[11]. and it has not been possible to classify them in the symmetry-asymmetry scheme of Levitzky[14].

Chromosome morphology has been described in *Q. robur* and *Q. petraea*[6], and *Q. cerris, Q. suber* and *Q. × hispanica*[15]. The twelve haploid chromosomes of *Q. petraea* differ little from each other in size and shape, but it is reported that *Q. robur* has a group of four markedly smaller than the rest[6]. Caldwell and Wilkinson[15] examined karyotypes of *Q. cerris, Q. suber* and putative hybrids, including specimens of the 'Exeter Oak', *Q. × hispanica (Q. lucumbeana* Sw.) Every somatic metaphase complement examined had 24 chromosomes with a remarkable uniformity of morphology, with the exception of one specimen of the Exeter Oak believed to be a *Q. cerris × suber* F_1 hybrid (*Q. × hispanica*) in contrast to the majority of *Q. cerris-suber* segregates examined, which were F_2 or further blends. A characteristic idiogram, such as that of *Q. cerris* (fig 1a) has chromosomes ranging from one to four microns in length. The two shortest chromosomes have no apparent constriction, whilst the rest possess one or more. There are four chromosomes two microns in length with median constrictions only. A similar pair possess small satellites and another pair exhibit large satellites. Ten chromosomes, approximately three microns in length have one main and one secondary constriction, and the four largest bear two secondary constrictions. *Q. suber* (fig 1b) and most *Q. cerris-suber* (fig 1c) segregates show the same basic karyotypes. However, a specimen of *Q. × hispanica* (fig 1d) exhibited suppression of satellites on two chromosomes; the two remaining satellited chromosomes were not homologues, one satellite being large and the other small.

FIGURE 1

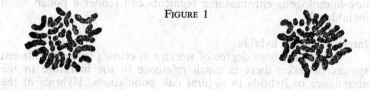

a: Quercus cerris
b: Q. suber

c: Q. cerris - suber
segregate

d: Q. x hispanica
(Exeter Oak)

Idiograms of oak karyotypes

Fertility of oak crosses

The absence of significant karyotype dissimilarity throughout the genus would imply a high degree of chromosome compatibility between any two parental species in crosses between oaks. Any major cytological difference, such as auto- or allopolyploidy, which could theoretically segregate and establish the constancy of a particular type, is lacking. However, high degrees of pollen sterility in presumed interspecific hybrids have been reported[10], and, in the results of experimental crosses between *Q. robur* and *Q. petraea* which have been published, figures of less than 2% of the cross pollinations setting fertile seed have been given[16] [17]. However Rushton[39] has recently achieved an increase in the success rate, up to 5%, when crossing British material.

Hybrids in which the chromosomes may appear to pair well at first metaphase, but are nevertheless sterile because the majority of pollen grains fail to develop, are not uncommon in other genera, as well as in *Quercus*[11]. This may be due to 'cryptic structural hybridity'[18], which assumes that parental species with similar karyotypes may differ with respect to many small rearrangements of chromosome segments. This results in looser pairing at pachytene, a reduction in chiasma frequency, and possible unpaired chromosomes at first metaphase due to chiasmata failing to form. Small numbers of such non-homologous chromosome segments can render a pollen grain inviable.

Interspecific oak hybrids

Despite the high degree of sterility in crosses between different species of oaks, there is much reference in the literature to the abundance of hybrids in natural oak populations. Hybrids of the indigenous British oaks, *Q. robur* and *Q. petraea,* have been reported from Scotland[19] [20], south-east England and Eire[21], the Midlands and Wales[10], north Lancashire[22], south-west England and the Lake District[23] (see pps 23 to 24). *Q. robur × petraea* hybrids have also been reported outside of the British Isles, including the Seine Valley[24], the Armoricain massif of Finistere[25], and Yugoslavia[21]. In Europe hybrids have been reported between *Q. robur, Q. petraea, Q. ilex* and *Q. lanuginosa*[6], and *Q. robur* with *Q. pedunculiflora* and *Q. conferta*[21] Other reported hybrids include *Q. cerris × suber* in both the natural and introduced parts of their range[15].

Variability of British oak species

Jones[27] takes the view that much of the variability of British oak populations is simply a manifestation of the normal infraspecific variation of *Q. robur* and *Q. petraea* and is not due to hybridisation as:—

(a) considerable genetical variation is normal in populations of trees such as oak, which are more or less self-sterile and reproduce only sexually, and

(b) it is more useful if names of species indicate groups of individuals that resemble each other in general appearance and behaviour, rather than individuals that resemble each other in some hypothetical ancestry.

Undoubtedly in many taxonomic situations the practicality of assigning a specific name to a population overrides other considerations. However, ancestry is usually inferred from comparison of appearance and behaviour, and the aims of taxonomy and phylogeny are not necessarily incompatible. A number of authors[20] [21] [23] have stressed the desirability of trying to distinguish between variation within the normal range of oak species and variation due to hybridisation, but the problem is confounded by the difficulty of distinguishing between natural and planted populations, and some believe that precise circumscription of species such as *Q. robur* and *Q. petraea* is impractical.

Provenances of oak[6] and other forest trees[28] show considerable variability and, in general, deciduous silviculture has not led to a narrowing of the genetic base characteristic of advanced cultivars of annual crops[29 30]. Difficulties of storage and transport of acorns suggest that import from outside the British Isles during the main period of oak planting from the sixteenth to nineteenth centuries was rare. Transport over long distances within Britain has been recorded[6], but it is probable that local natural populations would have, at least initially, provided the main source of acorns. Thus there would have been a partial redistribution of genotypes within British oak populations, possibly increasing variation in areas where some form of hybridisation was favoured. This would have produced patterns of variability naturally occuring elsewhere. Thus circumscription of the species and any hybrid range is not especially complicated by planting, although delimitation of planted populations is important in reconstructing the recent history of oak species.

Nature of oak variation

If variation among oak species were only infraspecific, the same range of variation would be expected in populations of a particular taxon in a given area. However, it has been shown that in some areas populations can be unequivocally ascribed to two or more *Quercus* species, whereas others show a range of intermediates.

Cousens[20] found that in Scotland although only the two native species, *Q. robur* and *Q. petraea* are involved, considerably more than half the fertile material at his disposal could not be diagnosed with confidence as belonging to either species; apparently *robur*-dominated woodlands exhibited such extreme variation that he concluded that this must, at least partially, be due to hybridisation. A few *Q. petraea* woods appeared to be relatively homogeneous, although showing wide infraspecific variation. Cousens[20 21] suggested that the variational patterns of *Q. robur* and *Q. petraea* could be accounted for by postulating:—

    (a)   limited interspecific hybridisation, and
    (b)   extensive introgessive hybridisation.

Introgression has been invoked by several workers finding a range of intermediates between two or more oak species, such as *Q. robur* with *Q. petraea*[10 22 23], *Q. lanuginosa*[24], *Q. pedunculiflora*[21] and *Q. conferta*[21] in Europe and Asia, and *Q. prinus* with *Q. alba*[26], *Q. margaretta* with *Q. gambellii*[31], *Q. dunni* with *Q. chrysolepis*[32], and the *Q. undulata* complex in North America[33].

Baker[34] has argued that some authors are too ready to offer introgression as an explanation of two forms connected by inter-mediates. Sometimes species are miscible in that extensive hybridisation between interfertile species or subspecies results in a complete series of transitions which may, at least locally, blend into one another without the spread of genes away from the initial area of hybridisation implied by introgression[35].

Introgression in oak species

In view of the controversy over postulated occurrences of introgression and the emphasis placed on the process in recent literature on oak species hybridisation, the evidence will be reviewed in detail. The essential characteristics of introgressive hybridisation are as follows[35 36 37]:—

1. Natural or artificial contact between closely related species which show a measure of reproductive (physiolo-gical) isolation.
2. Initial formation and establishment of F_1 hybrids between the species.
3. Relative intersterility of F_1 hybrids.
4. Relative fertility between F_1 hybrids and either parental species, favouring backcrosses.
5. Natural selection of favourable recombinant types, operating on establishment of seedlings and subsequent competition for environmental factors.
6. A resultant drift of genes away from the initial area of hybridisation towards one of the parental species.
7. An eventual formation of a population with taxonomic status attributable to one of the parental types, but exhibiting more variability than non-introgressed populations of the same species.

It is first necessary to comment on the possibility of introgression between species such as oaks with a partial fertility barrier. Oaks are very long-lived, and any hybrids established will be among many individuals of the parent species, so that backcrosses will be in the majority[38]. Thus the interspecific fertility barrier may be relatively unimportant if the hybrids are fully fertile with either parent[20]. It is also possible that reduced fertility will be little barrier to intro-gression if hybrids and backcrosses have any competitive advantage over parental genotypes[23].

The analysis of introgression in oaks

The analysis of possible introgression in populations can only practically be approached by examination of characters used in the assessment of taxonomic status, i.e. from a phenetic rather than a genetic standpoint. It is interesting to note that Anderson[37] contrasts the investigation of evolutionary processes from Mendelian genetic mechanisms, and the analysis of the role of hybridisation and mutation in evolution from examination of the variation patterns of populations, the latter procedure having led him to the concept of introgression. The technique of extrapolated correlates[36] is essentially reconstruction of population evolution from phenetic evidence.

The following techniques of phenetic analysis have been used in recent investigations of hybridisation in oaks:—
1. Theoretical species type analysis
2. Pictorialised scatter diagram analysis
3. Hybrid index calculation
4. Discriminatory analysis
5. Combination class analysis
6. Principal components analysis.

The applications of these techniques will be discussed with particular reference to the analysis of Q. robur × petraea introgression in south-west England[23].

Theoretical species type

Cousens[20] introduced the concept of the 'theoretical species type' (TST) as an empirical method for distinguishing between infraspecific and hybrid variability. A specimen with all qualitative character states under consideration in the diagnostic range for one species belongs to the TST. The TST for each species under consideration will vary according to the characters chosen for analysis. Table 1 shows the characters considered in the analysis of populations of indigenous oaks in south-west England. It may be assumed that in a pure stand of even highly variable species at least 50% of the individuals sampled would fall in the TST range of the species[23]. Also few non-TST specimens would be expected to depart by more than one or two character states from the TST definition.

A preliminary investigation of Dartmoor oak populations[23] suggested that Wistman's Wood and Steps Bridge wood provided pure stands of Q. robur and Q. petraea respectively. Over 50% of Wistman's Wood specimens sampled were TSTs, and few varied by more than one character state from the TST. For the Steps Bridge population less than 50% of the individuals were TSTs. The greatest single variable character was lobe-pair number, and over 40% of the non-TST individuals differed from the TST in being intermediate for lobe-pair number only. It appeared that a lobe-pair number of five, classified as intermediate, is in fact within the normal range of Q. petraea specimens, and if individuals differing from TST in this character only are regarded as TSTs, then well over 50% of the Steps Bridge individuals are TST specimens. The remaining individuals showed more variation than the Wistman's Wood population, but the majority differed from TST by one or two character states only.

These two populations serve to illustrate the range of infraspecific variability for selected characters in two species of oak.

Pictorialised scatter diagrams of oak populations

From table 1 it can be seen that analysis of leaf characters

Table 1

Taxonomic assessment of Q. robur, Q. petraea, robur × petraea, from leaf characters

Character	Diagnosis	Status	PSD Symbol
(a) Primary:			
Petiole percentage	9–20+%	Aff. petraea	
	0–8%	Aff. robur	
Leaf shape index	0–28	Aff. petraea	
	20–98	Aff. robur	
(b) Secondary:			
Nature of lobing	Deep, irregular	Aff. robur	
	Shallow, irregular/deep, regular	Intermediate	
	Shallow, regular	Aff. petraea	
Lobe-pair number	Four or less	Aff. robur	
	Five	Intermediate	
	Six or more	Aff. petraea	
Base of leaf	"strong" auricles	Aff. petraea	
	"medium" auricles	Intermediate	
	"weak" auricles	Aff. robur	
Large stellate hairs with ascending rays on midrib and in axils of main veins	Present	Aff. petraea	
	Absent	Aff. robur	
Small stellate hairs with appressed rays on the lamina	Present	Aff. petraea	
	Absent	Aff. robur	

provides two continuously variable and five coded characters. If the two continuous variables for each individual in a sample are plotted graphically, a bivariate scatter diagram results. Each coordinate can then be coded for the secondary (qualitative) characters, giving a pictorialised scatter diagram (PSD)[36] [40]. The scatter of points and their coding provides a visual description of the population from which the sample was obtained. The boundary range of TST specimens can be included, giving the TST scatter for both primary (quantitative) and secondary characters. The pattern of scatter can be interpreted in terms of taxonomic status and degree of hybridisation; different populations can be plotted and visually compared. If two species and their hybrids are examined, points for the two species should tend to concentrate in separate zones and show distinctive patterns of secondary coding, whereas intermediate specimens should have points lying outside and between the zones and show variable and intermediate patterns of coding.

Pure species and intermediate PSD distributions of sessile and pedunculate oakwood have been obtained from British and European populations[20] [21] [22] [23]. Fig 2 shows scatter diagrams of oak populations from south-west England illustrating Q. robur, Q. petraea, mixed and intermediate populations. Also included is the high level oakwood of Keskadale from the Lake District. This has formerly been described as Q. petraea[41] [42], but appears to illustrate partial intermediate status.

Hybrid index representation of oak populations

Calculation of hybrid index[36] [40] can be a useful method for visually and numerically describing complex populations where two species have hybridised and backcrossed to give plants of intermediate morphology. For each individual in a sample a numerical index is calculated which describes the degree to which the overall morphology of the individual is typical of one or the other species. Frequency distributions of these indices may be drawn as histograms. In an investigation of a mixed oak population in north Lancashire, Carlisle and Brown[22] calculated a percentage hybrid index (PHI) which allows a variable number of characters between individuals, and any number of characters may be used. Thus, whereas Carlisle and Brown used only four characters for PSD analysis, twenty were used for PHI analysis. The PHI frequency distributions showed differences between samples on slate (mainly Q. petraea), limestone (mixed Q. robur, Q. petraea and intermediates) and peat (Q. robur) sites within the woodland.

PHI analysis of leaf characters of selected oak populations from south-west England and Keskadale from the Lake District is shown in fig 3. The diagrams for Wistman's Wood (Q. robur) and Steps Bridge (Q. petraea) include analysis of spring and lammas growth, and leaf litter; reliable diagnoses of taxonomic status could be made on all types of leaf sample. Mixed and intermediate populations are also revealed. However, with a limited number of characters the

FIGURE 2

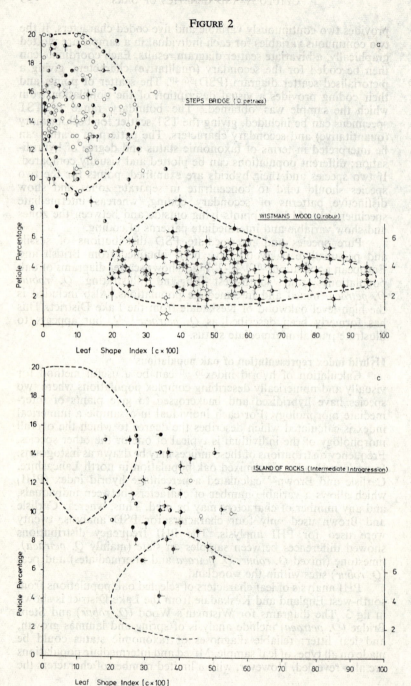

Pictorialised scatter diagrams of oak populations

FIGURE 2 (cont.)

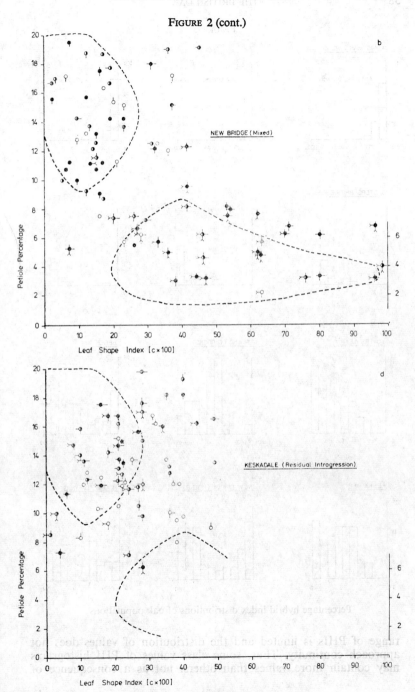

Pictorialised scatter diagrams of oak populations

FIGURE 3

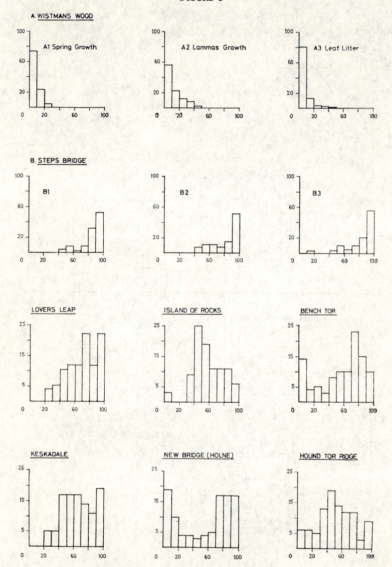

Percentage hybrid index distributions of oak populations

range of PHIs is limited and the distribution of values does not approach continuity. Thus, some class values of PHI histograms may contain more values than others, not as a consequence of hybridity but of the meristic nature of index values. The method is of less value than PSD analysis of oak populations by leaf characters, but when a large number of characters are used the method is superior.

Discriminatory analysis of oak populations

The variability of *Quercus* is such that a single specimen cannot be reliably assigned to a species or hybrid category on the basis of one character alone, and in the comparison of populations the ranges of a number of characters may overlap. In discriminatory analysis it is not individual character values but each set for two reference populations which provide the basis for distinguishing the taxa and assigning individual specimens to either taxon or hybrid category. What is required is the linear function of all observations— the discriminant function—that will distinguish, better than any other linear function, between the two reference populations on which the observations were made[43]. The discriminant function will also provide the lowest possible frequency of misclassifications of individual specimens. Mathematically the problem is maximising the ratio of 'between-group' to 'within-group' variances. For each population there is a group discriminant function, and for each individual within a population there is an individual discriminant function calculated from the individual character values. The group discriminant function provides a numerical expression of the taxonomic status of a population which can be used in areal analysis of taxonomic variation[23].

It should be noted that a group discriminant function only provides a measure of the mean variation in a population; it does not necessarily distinguish between a mixed and a hybrid population which may have the same group function. The distinction can be made on the basis of the frequency distribution of individual discriminant functions, which provides an analysis of the extent of variation within a population, clearly distinguishing between pure single species populations, mixed populations and those dominated by intermediate forms.

Fig 4 gives the frequency distributions of discriminant functions calculated on oak populations from south-west England and the Lake District. The preliminary analysis was performed on the two reference populations, Wistman's Wood (*Q. robur*) and Steps Bridge (*Q. petraea*). The populations were clearly distinguished, with *Q. robur* showing no greater variation than *Q. petraea* (in contrast to south-east England populations examined by Cousens[21]). Only two individuals, both from the *Q. petraea* population, would have been misclassified on the basis of the analysis.

Subsequent calculations on other populations revealed pure species, mixed and intermediate status. The intermediate populations show a drift of concentration of values towards the *Q. petraea* TST.

Ledig et al[26] utilised discriminatory analysis in the examination of the *Q. prinus, Q. alba, Q.×saulii* complex. The frequency distri-

FIGURE 4

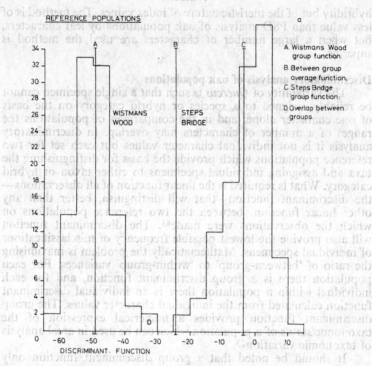

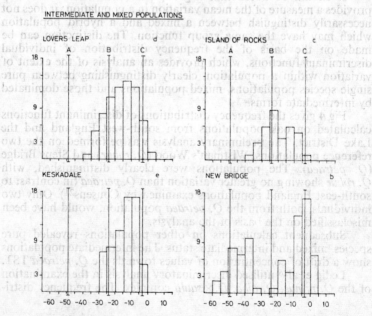

Distributions of discriminant functions of oak populations

butions of *Q. prinus* and *Q. alba* discriminant functions could be clearly distinguished. The frequency distribution of a putative *Q. prinus* × *alba* hybrid, identified as *Q.* × *saulii,* covered the range of both parental distributions with an intermediate bimodal concentration. The two modes suggested that the hybrid crosses with either parent, although the distribution was denser towards the *Q. prinus* parent.

It is important to note that in both examples of the application of discriminatory analysis to oak populations, the intermediate populations show a drift towards one of the putative parents, which is a prime characteristic of introgression[35][36][37].

Combination class analysis of oak populations

Cousens[20] drew attention to the problem of deciding the taxonomic status of specimens which show one character in the intermediate range between taxa; the specimen may lie within the normal range of variation of a taxon, but will not strictly 'belong' to it if the difference from theoretical status is in reality due to hybridisation. Cousens' technique of combination class analysis [20][21] allows examination of this problem, and is particularly deserving of wide application being an ingenious and powerful technique for analysing whether overlapping variation has at least an element of introgression.

Populations may be classified by grouping specimens with the same number of character states differing from TST, the groups being called secondary character combination classes. For leaf character analysis there are $3^2 \times 2^2 = 36$ possible combinations of

TABLE 2

Classification of secondary character combination classes

	Secondary character combinations						
Class:	I	II	III	IV	V	VI	VII
Character			Degrees of difference				
Combinations	Theoretical *petraea* combination	1	2	3			Theoretical *robur* combination
				3	2	1	
Possible	1	4	8	10	8	4	1
Actual	1	4	8	10	8	4	1

secondary characters, which may be classified according to their difference from each TST, giving seven combination classes (tables 2 & 3).

TABLE 3

Selected populations classified on the range and frequency of component secondary character combination classes in the samples

All figures expressed as a percentage of the total in the sample.

Category	Wood	I	II	III	IV	V	VI	VII
Q. robur dominated woods	Wistman's (litter)				2	9	17	72
	„ (spring)					6	28	66
	„ (lammas)			2	2	24	24	50
	Higher Piles Copse	2		5	7	16	18	53
	Black Tor Copse				8	16	35	41
	Lustleigh Cleave		2		3	10	27	58
	Woodbury			4	2	18	8	68
Q. petraea dominated woods	Steps Bridge (litter)	62	15	13	8	2	1	
	„ (spring)	50	27	13	6	4		
	„ (lammas)	52	17	22	5	4		
	Whitestone	67	17	11	5			
	Ausewell Rocks	60	11	19	8	2		
	Watervale (Lydford)	60	6	23	2	8		
	Head Barton	48	27	21	4			
Woods dominated by intermediates	Island of Rocks	11	23	29	23	14		
	Lovers Leap	19	32	22	18	5	3	1
	Keskadale	19	18	26	21	16		
Mixed woods with inter-mediates	New Bridge (Holne)	23	29	9	8	8	15	10
	Hound Tor Ridge	5	22	15	23	15	12	8
	Bench Tor	15	35	17	8	9	8	8

To assess the degree to which the variation within a combination class is due to infraspecific variability or to hybridisation, the range of variation for TST and non-TST specimens of the two primary quantitative characters used in PSD analysis may be compared[21]. The ranges should be similar if the departure from TST is simply part of normal variability, whereas if the bivariate means of the individual specimens of TST and non-TST combination classes are significantly different, hybridisation is indicated. If the means of each successive class from one putative parent to the other (classes I to VII for leaf character analysis of *Q. petraea* and *Q. robur*) are so distributed that they fall, in numerical sequence, on a curve linking the concentration centres of the two species, introgressive hybridisation may be inferred. Cousens[20] [21] found such an 'introgression path' in his combination class analysis of Scottish oak populations. In fig 5A bivariate means of combination classes for leaf character analysis of south-west England oak populations are plotted, and it can be seen that they fulfill the conditions for the interpolation of an introgression path.

The technique can be extended to individual populations[23]. If the bivariate means of combination classes within single populations are plotted, it can be seen whether the populations are stable or actually undergoing hybridisation. Stable populations should show randomly scattered means about and close to the population mean. Populations in a state of taxonomic change should have means directionally scattered along the introgression path. Both possible states can be seen in the plots of combination class bivariate means for individual oak populations (fig 5B–D). Populations undergoing taxonomic change include some, such as Hound Tor Ridge and Bench Tor, that are classified as mixed on the basis of PSD, PHI and discriminatory analysis. The scatter of points is strongly suggestive of active early introgression. Residual introgression is exemplified by the Lake District population, Keskadale, showing a relatively random scatter around the population mean with a distinct drift of scatter towards the *Q. petraea* TST. The direction of scatter in all of the populations revealing taxonomic change is towards *Q. petraea* as the assimilating species.

An essential feature of the complete introgressive process is that it is directive towards one of the parental species. The direction may be determined by:—

(a) intrinsic factors, as in the tendency for geneflow to proceed

FIGURE 5

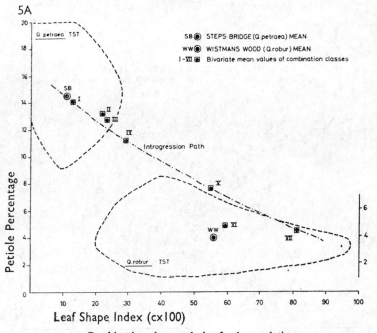

Combination class analysis of oak populations

FIGURE 5 (cont.)

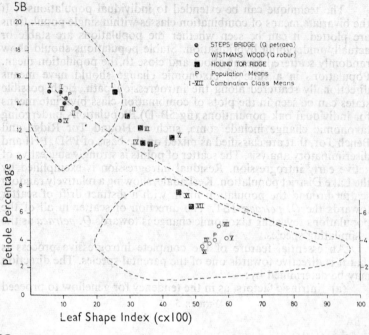

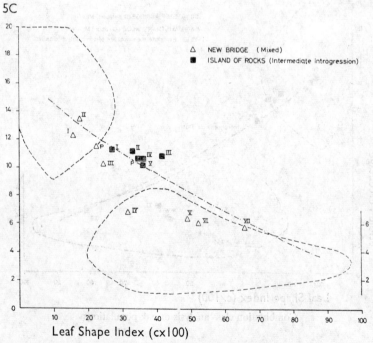

Combination class analysis of oak populations

FIGURE 5 (cont.)

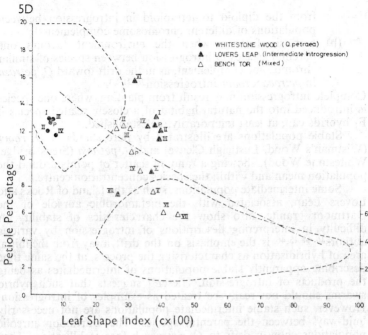

BENCH TOR (Mixed)
LOVERS LEAP (Intermediate Introgression)
WHITESTONE WOOD (Q petraea)

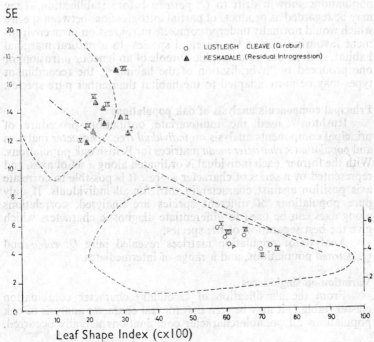

KESKADALE (Residual Introgression)
LUSTLEIGH CLEAVE (Q robur)

Combination class analysis of oak populations

from the diploid to tetraploid in introgression between populations of different chromosome complement[11];

(b) extrinsic factors, when the environment favours one parental species in introgression between species of similar chromosome complement, as in the drift toward *Q. petraea* in *petraea × robur* introgression[20][21][23].

Complete introgression may result from planting, where one species is introduced into the natural habitat of a closely related species if F_1 hybrids can, at least temporarily, be established.

Stable populations are illustrated by pure stands of *Q. robur* (Wistman's Wood, Lustleigh Cleave) and *Q. petraea* (Steps Bridge, Whitestone Wood), showing a random scatter of points around the population mean and within the species concentration centre.

Some intermediate populations, such as the Island of Rocks and Lovers Leap, associated with the metamorphic aureole of the Dartmoor granite, also show the characteristics of stability. A difficulty in interpreting descriptions of introgression by various authors[36][44][45][46] is the emphasis on the drift away from the initial area of hybridisation as characterising the process, at the same time describing apparently stable populations of intermediates as being the products of introgression. Hieser[47] suggests that such hybrid swarms should not really be treated as examples of introgression. However, such stable intermediate populations are not necessarily 'mid-way' between the parental species. The Dartmoor aureolic populations show a drift to *Q. petraea* before stabilisation. They may be regarded as products of partial introgression, between species which would normally undergo complete introgression in an environment favouring one of the parental species. In a natural marginal habitat, such as the metamorphic aureole of an igneous intrusion, or one produced by 'hybridisation of the habitat'[48], the recombinant types may be more adapted to the habitat than either pure species.

Principal components analysis of oak populations

Rushton[39] used the multivariate ordination procedure of principal components analysis on *individual tree × character* matrices and *population × character mean* matrices for British oak populations. With the former, each individual is ordinated along a set of axes, and represented by a series of character scores. It is possible to correlate axis position against character in turn for all individuals. If only pure populations of different species are analysed, correlations along axes can be used to differentiate diagnostic characters which give the best separation of the species.

Analysis of population matrices revealed pure *Q. robur* and *Q. petraea* populations, and a range of intermediates.

Variation on single trees

From the classification of secondary character combination classes (table 2) it may be seen that for leaf character analysis of oak populations all possible character combinations actually occurred.

Similar results, using a different range of characters, from Scottish populations led Cousens[20] to conclude that the secondary characters considered were homotypic and independently variable. However the extreme variation he found in other parts of the British Isles and Europe suggested polygenic control of both quantitative and qualitative[21] characters. From table 1 it can be seen that the qualitative leaf characters used are only qualitative in the sense that it is convient to code the character states in the absence of any useful quantitative measure. Auricle status, lobe-depth and regularity, and lobe-pair number are complex characters unlikely to be under the control of single allelic genes. In addition, although the presence or absence of a particular type of pubescence may be under the control of a single allele, when present its quantity and distribution may be polygenically governed.

In the early stages of the formation of a hybrid swarm strict qualitative characters tend to be 'linked' to the parent status, whereas polygenic quantitative characters react more swiftly to hybridity. PSDs of hybrid oak populations do not show any clear tendency for the variation of qualitative characters to be delayed in comparison with quantitative characters[20] [21] [23].

If the characters are under polygenic control, variation may be expected within single trees, whereas normal hybrids show little or no infra-individual variation. Examination of variation of characters on single trees from selected sites (fig 6) demonstrated that, for leaf characters, individual trees have as much variation as the populations from which they come, so that polygenic control of the leaf characters may be inferred.

Field analysis of the taxonomic status of oak populations
There are no truly diagnostic characters of sessile and pedunculate oaks that can, in isolation, be used to reliably assign an individual tree or population of oaks to either species or hybrid category.

Leaf characters (table 1) can be used for assessment of the taxonomic status of individual oaks and/or populations[23]. For rapid assessment, the calculation of leaf shape index, C, (table 1) is not suitable as this requires a computer program[23]; However, a rough analysis of ovate/obovateness can be obtained from the formula $F = W_3 - W_1/W_2$, where F is an index of leaf shape and W_1, W_2, W_3 are the widths respectively at 1/4, 1/2, 3/4, intervals along the length of the lamina from the base. For an ovate leaf W_1 and W_3 should be equal and the index will have a value of zero. For an obovate leaf W_3 will be greater than W_1 and the index will have a positive value. In practice it may be expected that aff. *petraea* specimens will not be perfectly ovate and a range of index values will be obtained, including some negative values (W_1 greater than W_3).

F can then be used with petiole percentage to provide coordinates for a pictorialised scatter diagram, which is the only reliable, relatively rapid method of taxonomic assessment. For individual

FIGURE 6

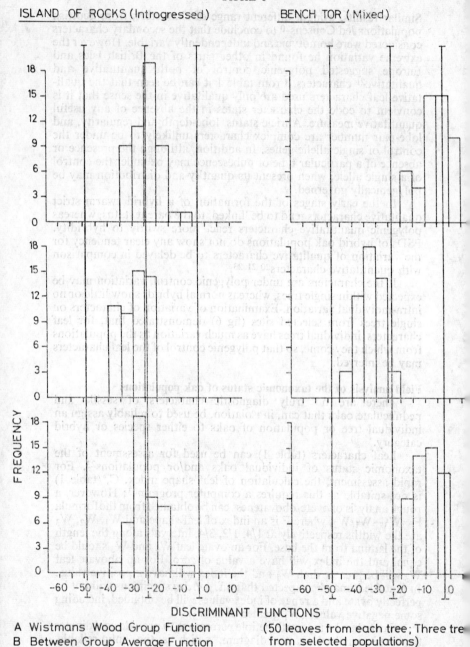

ISLAND OF ROCKS (Introgressed)   BENCH TOR (Mixed)

DISCRIMINANT FUNCTIONS

A Wistmans Wood Group Function   (50 leaves from each tree; Three tree
B Between Group Average Function   from selected populations)
C Steps Bridge Group Function

Variation on individual trees

trees fifteen or more leaves should be scored and plotted; for populations, twenty-five or more leaves should be collected over a large sample area (at least ten metres square) from either trees and/or leaf litter.

Reference scatter diagrams from populations or individuals of known taxonomic status would be needed for identification of species or hybrids from the field plots. The other techniques discussed in this paper are not suitable for field diagnosis, but should be applied after initial field identification for reliable assessment of taxonomic status.

Acknowledgements

I should like to thank Miss B. Livingstone for drawing the diagrams. Dr J. Wilkinson provided helpful discussion on oak chromosomes, and kindly allowed me to use his idiograms of oak karyotypes. Especial thanks are due to Dr M. C. F. Proctor who stimulated my interest in oak woodland and gave constant advice and support during my research on oak populations in south-west England.

REFERENCES

1. JOHANSEN, D. A. *Plant Microtechnique,* New York (1940), 85, 193
2. EAMES, A. J. *Morphology of the Angiosperms,* New York (1961), 179, 272, 310
3. WODEHOUSE, R. P. *Pollen Grains,* New York (1935), 373–9
4. SCHNARF, K. *Embryologie der Angiospermen,* Berlin (1929), 48–52
5. GODWIN, H. *The History of the British Flora,* Cambridge (1956)
6. JONES, E. W. 'Biological flora of the British Isles: *Quercus* L.', *J. Ecol.,* 47 (1959), 169–222
7. SPOEL-WALVIUS, M. R. VAN DER. 'Les characteristiques de l'exine chez quelques especes de *Quercus*', *Acta bot. néerl.,* 12 (1963), 525–32
8. SCHWARZ, O. 'Monographie der Eichen Europas und des Mittlemeergebietes', *Reprium nov. Spec. Regni veg. Beih.,* (1936–39)
9. ERDTMAN, G., BERGLAND, R. and PRAGLOWSKI, J. 'An introduction to a Scandinavian pollen flora', *Grana palynol.,* 2 (1961), 3–92
10. RUSHTON, B. S. 'Variation in Oaks', *Watsonia,* 9 (1972), 180–1
11. STEBBINS, G. L. *Chromosomal Evolution in Higher Plants,* Arnold (1971), 90–1
12. DARLINGTON, C. D. and WYLIE, A. P. *Chromosome Atlas of Flowering Plants,* London (1955)
13. SAX, H. J. 'Chromosome numbers in *Quercus*', *J. Arnold Arbor.,* 11 (1930), 220–3
14. LEVITZKY, G. A. 'The karyotype in systematics', *Trudy prikl. Bot. Genet. Selek.,* 27 (1931), 220–40
15. CALDWELL, J. and WILKINSON, J. 'The Exeter Oak—*Quercus lucumbeana* Sw.', *Rep. Trans. Devon. Ass. Advant Sci.,* 85 (1953), 35–40
16. PYATNITSKI, S. S. 'Gibridizacsiya Dubov', *Lesn. Hoz.,* (1939), 38–43
17. DENGLER, A. 'Berieht uber Kreuzungsversuche zwischen Trauben-und Stieleiche (*Quercus sessiliflora* Smith u. *Q. pedunculata* Ehrh. bzw. *Robur* L.)', *Mitt. H. Goring-Akad. dt. Forstwiss.* 1 (1941), 87–109
18. STEBBINS, G. L. *Variation and Evolution in Plants,* New York (1950), 222–5
19. COUSENS, J. E. 'Notes on the status of the sessile and pedunculate oaks in Scotland and their identification', *Scott. For.,* 16 (1962), 170–9

20. COUSENS, J. E. 'Variation of some diagnostic characters of the sessile and pedunculate oaks and their hybrids in Scotland', *Watsonia*, 5 (1963), 273–86
21. COUSENS, J. E. 'The status of the pedunculate and sessile oaks in Britain', *Watsonia*, 6 (1965), 161–76
22. CARLISLE, A. and BROWN, A. H. F. 'The assessment of the taxonomic status of oak (*Quercus* spp.) populations', *Watsonia*, 6 (1965), 120–7
23. WIGSTON, D. L. 'The taxonomy, ecology and distribution of sessile and pedunculate oak woodland in south-west England', *Unpublished Ph.D. thesis, University of Exeter,* (1971)
24. LIGER, J. 'Le chêne pubescent en Basse-Seine', *Révue Socs Sav. hte Normandie*, 43 (1967), 23–6
25. DIZERBO, A. H. 'Les chênes du Finistere', *Penn Bed*, 5 (1965), 140–2
26. LEDIG, F. T., WILSON, R. W., DUFFIEL, J. W. and MAXWELL, G. 'A discriminant analysis between *Quercus prinus* L. and *Quercus alba* L.', *Bull. Torrey bot. Club*, 96 (1969), 156–63
27. JONES, E. W. 'The taxonomy of British species of *Quercus*', *Proc. bot. Soc. Br. Isl.*, 7 (1968), 183–4
28. CALLAHAM, R. Z. 'Geographic variation in forest trees'. In Frankel and Bennet[30], (1970), 43–8
29. RICHARDSON, S. D. 'Gene pools in forestry'. In Frankel and Bennet[30], (1970), 353–66
30. FRANKEL, O. H. and BENNET, E. (eds) *Genetic Resources in Plants*, IBP 11 (1970), 7–18
31. TUCKER, J. M. and MULLER, C. H. 'A revaluation of the derivation of *Q. margaretta* from *Q. gambellii*', *Evolution*, 12 (1958), 1–17
32. TUCKER, J. M. '*Q. dunnii* and *Q. chrysolepis* in Arizona', *Brittonia*, 12 (1960), 196–217
33. TUCKER, J. M. 'Studies in the *Q. undulata* complex. I. A preliminary statement', *Am. J. Bot.*, 48 (1961), 202–8
34. BAKER, H. G. 'Taxonomy and the biological species concept in cultivated plants'. In Frankel and Bennet[30], (1970), 49–68
35. DAVIS, P. H. and HEYWOOD, V. H. *Principles of Angiosperm Taxonomy*, London (1963), 466–472
36. ANDERSON, E. *Introgressive Hybridisation*, New York (1949), 1–109
37. ANDERSON, E. 'Introgressive hybridisation', *Biol. Rev.*, 28 (1953), 280–307
38. STEBBINS, G. L. 'Role of hybridisation in evolution'. *Proc. Am. phil. Soc.*, 103 (1959), 231–51
39. RUSHTON, B. S. Personal communication, (1972)
40. ANDERSON, E. 'Hybridisation in American Tradescentias', *Ann. Mo. bot. Gdn.*, 23 (1936), 511–25
41. TANSLEY, A. G. *The British Isles and their Vegetation*, Cambridge (1947)
42. YAPP, W. B. 'The high level woodlands of the English Lake District', *N West. Nat.*, N series 1 (1953), 170–207, 370–83
43. FISHER, R. A. *Statistical methods for research workers*, Edinburgh (1936)
44. ANDERSON, E. and STEBBINS, G. L. 'Hybridisation as an evolutionary stimulus', *Evolution*, 8 (1954), 378–88
45. METTLER, L. E. and GREGG, T. G. *Population Genetics and Evolution*, Prentice-Hall (1969), 201–5
46. ZOHARY, D. 'Centers of diversity and centers of origin'. In Frankel and Bennet[30], (1970), 33–42
47. HEISER, C. B. 'Natural hybridisation and introgression with particular reference to *Helianthus*', *Recent Adv. Bot.*, 1 (1959), 874–7
48. ANDERSON, E. 'Hybridisation of the habitat', *Evolution*, 2 (1948), 1–9

FLANDRIAN HISTORY OF OAK IN THE BRITISH ISLES

SIR HARRY GODWIN and JOY DEACON

Sub-department of Quaternary Research
Botany School, Cambridge University

The nature of the evidence

Our reconstruction of the history of the oaks in Britain through the last ten thousand years depends upon the identification of remains recovered from various contexts, chiefly geological and archaeological, that allow reference to a recognizable period or have a quasi-absolute age in years. Oak may be recognized by timber, twigs, charcoal, bud-scales, leaves, fruit and cupules; these are found particularly in the frequent beds of oak-stools preserved in peat deposits of various kinds, where they represent either late stages in a natural vegetational succession from open fen, through carr to fen-wood with alder, birch and oak, or where they represent the natural forest vegetation of mineral soil overwhelmed by paludification and peat formation. We find oaks abundantly in such 'buried forests' and the bog-oaks, often stained black by the reaction of iron in the groundwater with tannins in the wood, have a deserved reputation for toughness. Those killed and entombed by the Fen Clay marine transgression in the East Anglian Fenland are often of huge dimensions: radiocarbon dating of their outer rings shows they were killed around 4,500 years ago, a date conformable with their association with neolithic artefacts. It has commonly happened that when rising sea-level has filled estuaries or lagoons with clays and silts, fresh-water fen has afterwards developed on the poorly-drained surface: this has in time become covered with fen-wood containing oaks. Given a shift in coastal conditions erosion may easily bring these soft alluvial beds once more to the open shore, where they constitute those 'submerged forests' or 'Noah's woods', that are taken popularly and often rightly as evidence of changing land- and sea-level. The British coasts are plentifully strewn with them and they are of very various ages, since fen-woods of all periods since the ice-age may be brought to exposure on the shore by the action of rising sea-level and coastal erosion. At Westward Ho! they are associated with a mesolithic flint industry, on the Essex coast with the Neolithic and in Lincolnshire with the Iron Age. Where the climate is sufficiently atlantic and hydrologic conditions are stable, the natural vegetational development may lead to acidification of the surface of the fen oak-woods, with replacement of oak by pine and finally the burial of all the woodland beneath the growing dome of *Sphagnum* moss in extensive raised bog. Evidence for this progression is easily traced both by the macrofossils and the pollen record, as for example

TABLE 1

Occurrence and utilisation of oak in radiocarbon years

(illustrated by typical sites)

	Site	Material	Significance	Age B.P.	Lab. Index
1.	Leman & Ower bank, N. Sea*	peat	substantial pollen fr., −120 ft (2.7m) O.D.	8415 ± 170 8742 ± 170 8196 ± 120	Q-105 Q-919 Q-982
2.	Red Moss, Lancashire	peat	first rise in oak pollen fr.	8354 ± 143	Q-422
3.	Broombarns, Perthshire*	oak	in peat below Carse Clay	6585 ± 130	Q-672
4.	Westward Ho!, Devonshire*	peat	fen oak growing in coastal peat—MESOLITHIC	6318 ± 134	Q-835
5.	Fawley, Hampshire*	oak	in peat at −25 ft (7.5 m) O.D.	6244 ± 140	Q-818
6.	Gatehouse of Fleet, Kirkcudbright	oak	in peat above Carse Clay	6026 ± 135	Q-380
7.	Ynyslas, Cardiganshire*	wood	oak in peat on shore	5898 ± 135	Q-382
8.	Ballynagilly, Co. Tyrone	oak	panel of house wall, NEOLITHIC	5168 ± 50	UB-201
9.	St. Germans, Norfolk*	oak	fenwood oak at −17 ft (5m) O.D.	4690 ± 120	Q-31
10.	Q. Adelaide, Ely, Cambridgeshire*	oak	trunk below Fen Clay	4495 ± 120	Q-589
11.	Arminghall, Norfolk	charcoal	oak from henge, NEOLITHIC	4440 ± 150	BM-129
12.	Wicken Fen, Cambridgeshire*	oak	trees below fen peat, NEOLITHIC	4605 ± 110 4380 ± 140	Q-130 Q-129
13.	Kileens Td., Co. Cork	oak	wooden trough, E or MID BRONZE	3715 ± 270 3510 ± 230	C-878 C-877
14.	Corlona, Co. Leitrim	oak	trackway	3395 ± 170	Gro-272
15.	Brigg, Lincolnshire	oak	monoxylous boat	2784 ± 100	Q-78
16.	Fiskerton, Lincolnshire	oak	monoxylous boat	2796 ± 100	Q-79
17.	North Ferriby, Yorkshire	oak	sewn plank boat	2700 ± 150	BM-58
18.	Nidons Track, Somerset	oak	morticed trackway timber, LATE BRONZE	2585 ± 100	Q-313
19.	Fordy, Cambridgeshire	oak	piles of trackway, LATE BRONZE	2560 ± 110	Q-310
20.	Shapwick Stn., Somerset	oak	monoxylous boat, IRON AGE	2305 ± 120	Q-357
21.	Teeshan, Co. Antrim	oak	crannog, EARLY CHRISTIAN	1970 ± 80	UB-266
22.	Tamworth, Staffordshire	oak	timber of defences, SAXON	1541 ± 80	Birm-58
23.	Kilmagoura, Co. Cork	oak	dendrochronological correlation, MEDIEVAL	725 ± 70	UB-317
24.	Mill Lough, Co. Fermanagh	oak	beam in crannog, MEDIEVAL	685 ± 80	UB-267

Sites asterisked show that the eustatic rise of ocean level was incomplete.

in the coastal forest-bed at Ynyslas and in the raised-bog sections of Borth Bog that lies just inland and indeed represents the former landward continuation of the shore deposits. The radiocarbon age of these trees is about six thousand years (table 1).

Of course macroscopic remains such as these are direct proof of growth in the locality, but they tend to be found only in special situations and somewhat sparsely. Such finds are supplemented by a wealth of artefacts made of oak timber by prehistoric man: oak was much employed in the construction of dwellings, trackways and palisades as well as in the manufacture of boats, looms, tubs, shields, hafts and so forth, and it has always been much used as firewood. The cultures represented by macroscopic identification of *Quercus* are as follows: Neolithic 21, Bronze Age 45, Iron Age 41, Anglo-Saxon 3, Norman 3, Medieval 5, figures that confirm the ancient prevalence and usefulness of the oak. Both as timber and as charcoal oak is very readily identifiable by its ring-porous nature, huge vessels and secondary rays, but one cannot refer such material to one rather than the other of the two present-day native species, *Quercus robur* and *Q. petraea*. Indeed very few records of any kind allow this differentiation, and this is certainly not possible with the pollen that provides our alternative source of historical evidence. Pollen of *Quercus* is wind-dispersed and its distant carriage precludes its use as evidence of local presence save when it is in high frequency in relation to that of other trees whose local presence is certain. The three-furrowed grains with a scabrate verrucate surface are readily recognizable, although they are much modified in appearance by the conditions of preservation and are rather subject to erosion. The rather low pollen-productivity of the tree leads to some under-representation of the genus in forest pollen-spectra although to a less degree than with the often associated limes, and the pollen-analyst has naturally to expect local over-representation in deposits that themselves actually contain the remains of oak woodland. These qualifications accepted, the very numerous long pollen-diagrams made throughout the British Isles, many embracing long stretches of time, afford us by far our fullest insight into the past status of oak in the vegetational history of this country.

The Pleistocene: interglacial events

The Pleistocene or Quaternary Period in which we live is strongly typified by the cold glacial stages and mild interglacial stages that have now succeeded one another for more than a million years. The number of such cycles is uncertain but recent geological study takes account of six cold stages in the British Isles, whilst a great deal is already known of the vegetational history of the three latest completed interglacials, the Cromerian, the Hoxnian and Ipswichian respectively. There is little doubt that at the present time we are within an unfinished interglacial stage, and in accordance with this we refer to the period since the last glacial stage in Britain (Weichselian or Devensian) as the Flandrian. The boundary between the two stages is to some extent arbitrary, but radiocarbon dates at the appropriate geological-biological horizon place it close to the convenient age of 10,000 years before the present, so that the lapse of the Flandrian so far has been what we may speak of as one decachiliad. Previous interglacials have been somewhat longer though of this order of duration, but they differed from the Flandrian in that they suffered hardly at all from the destructive attentions of man and so provide us with a most helpful control situation against which to view Flandrian events.

Studies of pre-Flandrian interglacials, especially in Britain, Denmark and the Netherlands have advanced so far that a common cycle of development is recognizable in them all. The cold glacial stage has frost-shattered unweathered soils moved by solifluction and melt water, with the ground covered with 'cryocratic' communities of plants, many of them arctic-alpine in present distribution growing in conditions of minimal competition with one another or shelter from the rigorous elements. The interglacial begins with a 'protocratic' stage of colonisation of the unleached soils by herbaceous and then by arboreal vegetation, with competition and shade increasing, and soils deepening and tending to become neutral. Thus we move into the 'mesocratic' stage of climax woodland upon slightly acid brown-earth mull soils, with widespread shade and root-competition that dominates all other plants and indeed all animal and human life within it. Finally there is the 'telocratic' stage that is envisaged as 'retrogressive' in a vegetational sense, with soils becoming heavily podsolised and acidic, bearing moor or heath and acidic woodlands, often coniferous in character with ericoid undergrowth on the leached forest soil. In time the telocratic communities give place to the cryocratic ones of the recurring glacial stage.

Turner & West[1] have used a basis of such a cycle for their fourfold division of recent interglacials into comparable chronozones as follows:

I *Pre-temperate zone:* forest of boreal trees such as *Betula* and *Pinus*.

II *Early-temperate (mesocratic) zone:* forest of deciduous mixed-oak woodland, typically with *Quercus, Ulmus, Fraxinus, Corylus* and *Alnus* on rich forest soils.

III *Late-temperate (oligocratic) zone:* mixed-oak forest declining in face of expansion of *Carpinus, Abies, Picea* and *Fagus* associated primarily with soil degeneration.

IV *Post-temperate zone:* forest of boreal trees, especially *Pinus, Betula* and *Picea* in stands becoming open and with damp ericaceous heath.

Taking Turner & West's divisions we have set out in fig 1 the mean frequency of oak pollen as a percentage of total tree pollen in the comparable sub-stages of the Hoxnian, Ipswichian and Flandrian. The correspondence is evident. Like the individual pollendiagrams from these periods, this histogram displays the great importance of *Quercus* in the two middle sub-stages, more especially in II, the early-temperate, before spruce and silver fir (in the Hoxnian) and hornbeam (in the Ipswichian) expanded in III. There is every reason to think that the species then concerned were *Quercus robur* and *Q. petraea* behaving, as von Post had always supposed, as major mediocratic indicators.

FIGURE 1

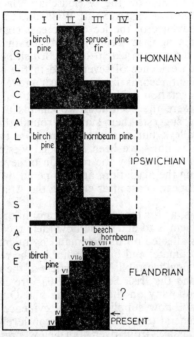

Histogram showing the mean frequency of *Quercus* pollen (as a percentage of total arboreal pollen including *Corylus*), through the three latest interglacials. The attribution of the Flandrian pollen-zones to the interglacial substages of Turner & West reflects the opinion of the present authors.

Within the Flandrian we have represented the mean pollen frequencies for *Quercus* in the successive pollen-zone system so fully developed for this time, but it has been adjusted to fit the sub-stages of the general scheme. Once again there is the rise from low values in sub-stage I to high values in II, but so far as we can judge, no subsequent decline, perhaps for causes associated with human interference, perhaps because of the minor competitive importance of other tree-genera. However that may be, it is evident that for the purpose of assessing the vegetational history of the oaks in the British Isles, we have to regard the Flandrian as an interglacial perhaps two-thirds completed. It is clearly nothing but misleading to think of it as 'post-glacial'.

The Flandrian decachiliad

1. *Origins.* We should make clear that we base our account of the Flandrian history of the British oaks upon the facts accumulated in the data-bank maintained by the Sub-department of Quaternary Research in the University of Cambridge[3] and already employed for compilation of the 2nd edition of the *History of the British Flora*[3].

At the maximum of the Weichselian glaciation ice-sheets extended as far south at least as South Wales and the South Pennines, whilst the last advance of the ice on the east coast was as late as only 20,000 years ago. It seems improbable that oak woodland survived within the present extent of the British Isles at these times for there is much evidence of severe cold in the area south of the ice-fields and plant records from outwash gravels and silts show open treeless vegetation with abundant arctic-alpine and steppe species. Where were the deciduous woodlands at this time then? Present evidence suggests their survival round the Mediterranean and in alpine valleys, but the question remains unanswered as to whether there may not have been a wooded western fringe on the continental shelf laid bare by the recession of several hundred feet in sea-level during the glaciation, and tempered by the Gulf Stream meeting the European coast after crossing the Atlantic south of the floating ice pack.

For the oaks, as for the mass of thermophilous plants, the first and crucial problem is to determine how their recolonisation of the British Isles was affected on the one hand by migration in response to ameliorating climate, and on the other by the restoration of sea-level that would finally establish the barriers of the English Channel, the North Sea and the Irish Sea against easy re-entry. Fortunately studies in palaeobotany on the one hand and Quaternary geology on the other have now supplied factual evidence of these events. The course of general (eustatic) rise in ocean levels has been dated by radiocarbon assay: from over 40m below present height some nine thousand years ago, at the opening of the Flandrian, there was a rapid rise in the next four thousand years to within 5m of present levels: subsequent changes were slow and small in degree. It is now quite certain from radiocarbon dated pollen diagrams that the rise in sea-level came too late to prevent wholesale re-establishment of the oaks within the British Isles (table 1). Pollen-analyses are now so numerous and widespread that we can, given care in interpretation, follow the history of the oaks in successive dated stages through the whole of the Flandrian period. It falls readily into three phases that can broadly be correlated with the standard pollen-zonation, with the major climatic periods and with radiocarbon dating; they are respectively the initial phase of migration and establishment, that of dominant mixed oak forests and finally the phase of progressive clearance and destruction by man.

2. *Migration and establishment* (10,000 *to* 9,000 *B.P.*). It is apparent from the pollen frequency maps of zones IV and V (fig 2)

FIGURE 2

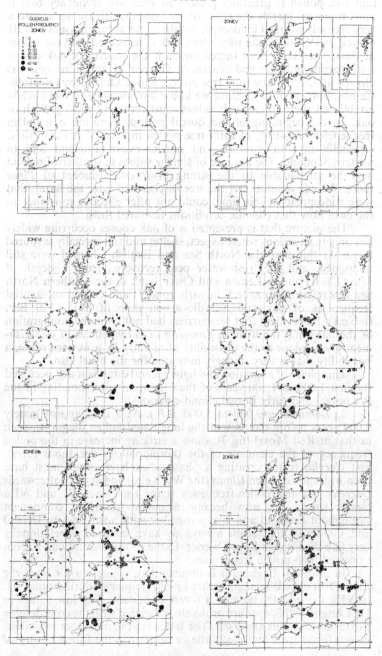

Pollen frequency of *Quercus* in the British Isles through the six pollen zones of the Flandrian, expressed as a percentage of the total arboreal pollen (including *Corylus*). (From Godwin[3])

that oak pollen is generally present in such low frequency that it must represent merely the effect of long distance air transport into a very sparsely wooded landscape. All the same, through zones I to III as well as IV and V, the sites where oak is registered, and the values at those sites have been increasing as if the sources of oak pollen were becoming larger and nearer. At Gosport (Hampshire) oak was already 10–20% of the total tree pollen, and at Old Decoy (Norfolk-Cambs. border) 5–10%. Since we know birch woodland was already established there, these high values must represent local growth of oak. In the beginning of the Boreal period, there are oak pollen frequencies of 5–10% of total tree pollen in zone V at many sites, especially in south-western and north-western England and in western Scotland. The absence of similar values in southern England may be attributable to the strong prior establishment of *Pinus* there. We can assume that the tree birches and later the hazel, that were widespread at this time, could not offer effective resistance to the oaks now that climatic conditions favoured them.

The picture that is presented is of oak copses occurring widely but only in situations where aspect, shelter and soil specially favoured them. At this time the North Sea and English Channel were still unflooded, and the fresh-water peat recovered from a depth of 37m (120 ft) on the Leman and Ower bank in the southern North Sea was referable to zone V or early zone VI and yielded substantial frequencies of oak and a radiocarbon date of 8415±170 B.P. (table 1). It is evident that sea-barriers had not hindered immigration of the oaks and the western grouping of early centres of establishment gives colour to the possibility of re-entry by a western route, a possibility that is very strongly indicated for the hazel also.

This phase of migration and light general establishment occupied the first 1,000 to 1,500 years of the Flandrian corresponding to the Pre-boreal and early Boreal climatic periods.

3. *Dominance* (9,000 *to* 5,000 *B.P.*). At a date approximately 9,000 years before the present the long dated pollen diagrams, such as that at Red Moss[4] (fig 3), show a striking increase in the pollen frequency of the elements of the thermophilous deciduous forest, first *Corylus* (often creating a phase when hazel scrub must have been widespread), then *Ulmus* (the Wych elm) and shortly afterwards *Quercus*. As the pollen-frequency maps for zones VI and VIIa clearly show, oak now became a major woodland component throughout England and Wales together with north-eastern Ireland and Galloway that seem always to have behaved vegetationally very like the English Lake District. In the rest of Ireland oak seldom exhibited high pollen frequencies.

In northern England it is notable that, whereas aside from the Lake District oak remains rather low in frequency during zone VI, in VIIa it evidently became a forest dominant. The low values in East Anglia in this zone are probably associated with the considerable expansion of *Alnus* and *Tilia*. The latter are the most thermophilous of our forest trees and play little or no part in the forest history of

FIGURE 3

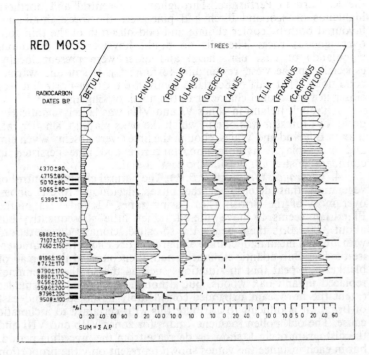

Arboreal pollen diagram from Red Moss, Lancashire, with radiocarbon datings for important pollen assemblage zone boundaries. The arboreal pollen total is inclusive of *Corylus* (after Hibbert, Switsur and West[4]).

Scotland or Ireland. The alder is not only responsive to warmth like the oaks but is strikingly dependent upon abundant soil moisture. At the opening of zone VIIa (the Atlantic period) c 7,500 to 7,000 years B.P. the alder exhibits so sudden, massive and widespread an increase in pollen frequency that it is only to be interpreted as a response to climatic shift that, over the oak forest territory, established alder thickets by streams and in wet swales wherever soils and slopes favoured water-logging. The resultant mosaic character of natural mixed-oak forest can still be seen here and there in Europe and North America but has been lost by clearance and drainage from most British woodlands.

As with northern England, so in Scotland the Atlantic period (zone VIIa) shows general increase in oak pollen frequencies over those of the Boreal (zone VI) but in neither are the mean values often more than 20% of the total tree pollen. This is not attributable to late arrival of the oak: we had its first expansion in Cumberland not long after 9,000 B.P. and there is a radiocarbon date of actual oak wood of 8354 ± 143 from beneath the Carse Clays in the valley of the R. Earn in Perthshire. Throughout the central and northern highlands of Scotland birch and pine were the forest dominants favoured both by cooler climate and podsolisation of the thin soils over igneous rock. There is no doubt however that deciduous woodlands of oak, elm, hazel and alder were present locally, especially in the west, responding to more fertile soil and warmer conditions. That part of Scotland south of the Clyde-Forth line was closer in vegetational character to the north of England.

Although Ireland in zones VI and VIIa was largely mantled by deciduous forest it was one in which the oaks played a smaller role than in England and Wales: though the limes were absent, Wych elm and hazel played a more important role and pine persisted in considerable strength outside the central plain.

4. *Clearances (from 5,000 B.P.)*. The natural climatic control of vegetation that determined the mixed deciduous forest climax over most of the British Isles during zones VI and VIIa of the Flandrian seems to have altered rather little subsequently, but about 3,000 B.P. there began the so-called 'climatic deterioration' with lowered mean temperature and greater oceanicity that characterise the final Sub-atlantic climatic period. It encouraged the spread of blanket-bog peat that in situations such as the southern Pennines replaced upland oak woods, but although beech, and to a smaller extent the hornbeam, expanded considerably in the south and east of Britain it is difficult to attribute this with certainty to a climatic cause. The oak pollen frequency maps for zones VIIb and VIII and the histogram of fig 1, show no decrease from the preceding period, but in each instance the values shown represent only the proportion of oak within the total spectrum of remaining forest, now greatly affected by quite other factors.

From about 5,500 B.P. there had begun a recognizable pattern of human modification of the natural forests. Early neolithic man thereabouts developed a system of selective clearance of trees specially suitable to provide leaf-fodder for pounded cattle. Elm was the tree most gathered and at this time it exhibits an extremely general recession in abundance: subsequently the limes were similarly affected. In a very large number of pollen diagrams we can trace the effects of temporary clearances with cultivation of cereals, abandonment and restoration of forest cover. The oaks were generally too tough for the polished stone axe and after temporary clearances they commonly increased. But of course cattle grazing the abandoned clearings or undergrazing the woodland would have retarded regeneration, as would fire, intentional or accidental, and this also often destroyed the top organic layers of the forest soils. As early as the Neolithic we know that clearing had established hazel coppice in oak woodland habitats. By the late Bronze Age human populations were larger, there was greater dependence on crops, and the tools of cast bronze were competent to fashion even oak, so that its worked timber is now encountered in trackways, the base-plates of houses and in both monoxylous and plank-sewn boats (table 1). By this time also the ox-drawn scratch plough had been introduced to be supplanted soon by the mould-board plough and then in Anglo-Saxon time by the true plough drawn by a team of oxen that could work even the heavy clay soils hitherto clad with intact oak woodland. In parallel was the advantage given to felling by the slip-eye iron axe. The land cleared by such means was increasingly devoted to sheep grazing rather than cattle-raising, especially afterwards within the great monastic estates, with correspondingly enfeebled forest regeneration. We find too in pollen diagrams such as that at Old Buckenham Mere, Norfolk evidence for selective felling of oak in Anglo-Saxon to Norman time, possibly for building in the nearby East Anglian capital, Thetford.

The pace and extent of disforestation have progressively increased by these means, inevitably affecting the oaks as major components of the prevalent deciduous forest. After dominating the temperate forest ecosystem for a million years the forest oaks have in five thousand years been subordinated to the destructiveness of man who has still to find, or even realise the need to find, an alternative equilibrium for the landscape he inhabits.

REFERENCES

1. TURNER, C. and WEST, R. G.   'The subdivision and zonation of interglacial periods', *Eiszeitalter Gegenw.*, **19** (1968), 93–202
2. DEACON, J.   'A data bank of Quaternary plant fossil records', *New Phytol.*, **71** (1972), 1227–32
3. GODWIN, H.   *The History of the British Flora.* Cambridge (1956), (ed. 2 in press)
4. HIBBERT, F. A., SWITSUR, V. R. and WEST, R. G.   'Radiocarbon dating of Flandrian pollen zones at Red Moss, Lancashire, *Proc. R. Soc.* B., **77** (1971), 161–76

THE OAK TREE IN HISTORIC TIMES

OLIVER RACKHAM

Corpus Christi College, Cambridge

Introduction

This paper deals with the part played by oak in the traditional management of woodlands, and also with oak as a non-woodland tree growing on land whose primary use is not the production of underwood or timber. Following the introduction of modern forestry over the last 250 years, it has in addition been grown as a plantation tree: this third aspect of oak is dealt with in a later contribution (pps 98 to 112) and will not be discussed here.

The history of woodmanship has seldom been critically studied (despite a long tradition of plagiarization) and it would be premature to try to summarize it for Britain as a whole. My observations are based chiefly on a study of Eastern England (fig 1), a region characterized by a high ratio of population to woodland, but no heavy industrial use of timber; by the early establishment of intensive woodland management and its conservative maintenance thereafter; and (in parts) by large numbers of non-woodland trees.

Summary of the woodland history of Eastern England[1] [2]

In prehistoric times (see pps 51 to 61) Eastern England was covered with a continuous forest of which oak formed a substantial part*. In some areas, forest clearance was early and complete; for instance, the Breckland and immediate environs of Cambridge were almost totally without woodland in the middle ages and probably much earlier. But even on heavy soils, by Domesday Book times the forest had been fragmented into scattered woods among farmland: the statistics, although notoriously uncertain of interpretation (see later), do not encourage the view that there was enormously more woodland in the region in 1086 than in 1945.

By the 13th century, when the earliest detailed documents appear, woodland had scarcity value. Woods varied in size from an acre or two to about 300 acres (120 ha) and were privately owned and sharply defined (often by boundary banks and ditches). Nearly all were intensively managed by what we should call a coppice-

---

* The only relevant pollen diagram published, that for Old Buckenham[3], is consistent with the historical account presented here, but owing to ambiguities of interpretation it adds little to our knowledge from other sources of oak in the last thousand years.

FIGURE 1

Eastern England, showing places named in the text.

with-standards system. The majority of the trees and shrubs (the *coppice*) were cut at intervals of 3 to 20 years and allowed to grow again from the stump; other trees (*standards*) were left standing for longer periods, forming an upper storey in the wood and producing larger timber. (Trees of a third type, *pollards,* repeatedly cut like coppice but at 6 to 12 ft (2 to 4m) above ground instead of near ground level, are characteristic of non-woodland sites and wood boundaries.)

Contrary to popular belief, the harvesting of woodland produce did not destroy the wood. When a man felled a tree, he expected it to be replaced, normally without artificial replanting. Woods were fenced to protect the new growth from grazing animals. They might occasionally be converted to arable (or vice versa), but woods (even small ones) are a remarkably stable feature of the landscape. The five woods of Barking (Suffolk), for instance, listed in 1251 in the *Ely Coucher Book*[4], are almost certainly still in existence (cf table 2) with approximately their original areas. The sinuous, and seemingly irrational, outlines of ancient woods often appear on the earliest large-scale maps (eg Chalkney Wood in 1598[5]) exactly as they are now. The survival rate of medieval woods varies: for instance it is very high in West Cambridgeshire and low in Norfolk.

This 'classical' system of woodland management is known from documents and buildings of the later middle ages. It was modified in various ways (in general less well documented) in succeeding centuries. In most woods the management system continued within living memory; but since 1945 there have been more rapid upheavals than at any comparable period in the past. At least half the woodland area has been converted to arable or forestry. Most of the remaining woods retain their historical continuity but are no longer managed. However woodmanship continues to this day, in very nearly its medieval form, in the Bradfield Woods (Plate II), and more or less modified in a few other places.

Function of oak in woodland management

In lowland England the growing of oak has most often been a by-product of some other activity. A wood normally yielded two products: wood or underwood (*boscus, subboscus*) mainly from coppice, and timber (*meremium*) from the standard trees. Underwood —poles used for fuel and many other purposes—was the main and regular product: the long-lived coppice stools, of a variety of species surviving from the prehistoric forest, ensured the wood's historical continuity. Oak appears to have been treated almost entirely as timber, although oak as underwood is a common practice in northern and western Britain[6].

Written evidence suggests that between half and three-quarters of the timber produced by woods went into buildings. Extant medieval buildings, therefore, contain a substantial sample of woodland timber. It is seldom possible to establish that a particular piece of timber came from a specified wood; buildings may indeed contain non-woodland or imported timber. These difficulties are less serious than they seem, because of the close relation between carpentry and woodmanship: a building system adapted to using small oaks implies a woodland system that regularly supplied them. We must avoid paying undue attention to the more expensive structures such as hammer-beam roofs, which may not be representative. The cheapest buildings will seldom survive.

The following conclusions are based mainly on the study of East Anglian buildings*, helped by written evidence.

1. Building timber is almost all oak (even where oak must have been brought from a distance). Elm[7], pine, etc., occur in undoubtedly medieval buildings, but are uncommon before the 18th century. Oak is the timber most often specified in documents and its supremacy in existing buildings cannot be wholly due to a higher survival rate. The wooden reinforcement of wattle-and-daub panels is sometimes split oak timber instead of the more usual hazel rods.

2. Early carpentry avoids lengthwise sawing, except for boards (some of which were imported from Continental manufacturers[8]). Each timber is a whole log squared: timbers of small scantling are got by choosing and felling small oaks. In the later middle ages there appears to be a gradual transition to the use of trees sawn lengthwise into two halves[7]. The modern practice of using larger trees and sawing them lengthwise into more than two becomes widespread in the late 16th century.

3. Medieval carpenters made more efficient use of their oaks than we do. They did not mind if the resulting timbers were waney (rounded at the corners through reaching the outside of the log) or crooked. Much skill was shown in accepting, and turning to good use, the irregular shapes inevitable in logs from a wild oak population (see p. 76)**.

4. Ordinary medieval buildings contain large numbers of small oaks—a principle which appears to be general in much of England. For the reasons given in the last two paragraphs, it is possible to determine how many trees went into a building and to a considerable extent their ages, shapes and sizes. Table 1 gives an analysis of some representative buildings. A farmhouse, typical of hundreds built in West Suffolk in the later middle ages, contains over 300 trees, half of them less than 9in (23cm) in basal diameter and only 1% of them exceeding 18in (46cm). Even a college (albeit a relatively poor one) used few oaks of more than 9in diameter. The many more flimsy buildings which have not survived presumably contained smaller trees still. Big oaks, by

---

* All the points mentioned in paragraphs 1 to 5 are also illustrated by the 14th to 16th century buildings from Hampshire and Kent in the Weald and Downland Open Air Museum, visited on a Symposium excursion (see Appendix II, p. 361).

** The deliberate *selection* of naturally-curved trees for special purposes (an essential feature of the cruck system used in other parts of the country) plays little part in the ordinary buildings of Eastern England.

modern standards, were used by kings (King's College Chapel, Cambridge) and by those builders who aspired to emulate kings.

5. Ordinary buildings contain few timbers more than 20ft (6m) long; those that are longer are usually crooked, knotty, and tapering where they reach into the crown of a tree that was not really long enough. Norwich Cathedral was an example of a structure (perhaps more common in the early middle ages) designed for large numbers of oaks with a reasonably straight length of as much as 28ft (8½m).

6. Medieval oaks were usually felled at between 25 and 70 years of age. Even the Falcon Inn, Cambridge, built c 1500 as the top hotel in town and framed no less than four stories high, turned out on recent demolition to be built entirely from oaks of less than a century's growth.

7. Timber was normally felled as occasion demanded and worked while still green.

Estate management accounts, notably those covering Gamlingay Wood[9] from 1279 to 1362 and Hardwick Wood[10] from 1342 to 1494, provide evidence of regular small fellings, mainly of oak, for maintaining buildings and machinery; of occasional heavy fellings[2] for new buildings; of transport over tens of miles to estates in the same ownership that had no wood; and of sales to owners who either had no wood or who had temporarily run out of a particular kind of tree. Information about the range of sizes of tree comes mainly from sales. The prices of Gamlingay and Hardwick oaks in the 14th century ranged from 0·30d to 20d each; there were also sales of oak stakes at from 0·23d to 0·30d. The more expensive oaks appear rarely. Allowing for the Black Death and changes in the value of money, it is clear that there was a range of at least 90-fold in the values of woodland oaks.

Occasional oaks existed which were much larger than those mentioned. The biggest timber on the Gamlingay estate was the windmill post. Three of these were bought between 1290 and 1342, costing from 18s to 25s 1d, more than ten times as much as the largest oak sold from Gamlingay Wood. The 17th century mill at Bourn, probably of similar size, has a post 23in (58cm) square. The Gamlingay post, being set in the ground like a gate-post (hence the frequent replacement), was probably at least 20ft (6m) long. Timbers of this size could not be got from the local wood but had to be bought in, perhaps from non-woodland sources (see p. 74). J. Saltmarsh has located nine places from which the timbers for King's College Chapel, some of which are roughly of this size, came. Only one source (Hales Wood) is known to have been a wood: the others were all parks, not necessarily woodland. The extreme size limit of available oaks is shown by the Octagon of Ely Cathedral, the grandest extant work of medieval carpentry (1328–42). The 16 struts on which the timber tower rests are meant to be 40ft long by

TABLE 1

Numbers and sizes of trees contained in various buildings

Trees are classified by basal diameter under bark, each class corresponding to twice the cross-section area of the previous class.

Class of tree	Basal diameter, in (cm)		House at Swaffham Prior, Cambs	Grundle House, Stanton, W. Suffolk	Corpus Christi College, Cambridge	Norwich Cathedral (main roofs)	King's College Chapel, Cambridge (main roof)
0	4½–6	(11–)	—	32	—	—	—
1	6½–8½	(16–)	38	140	1249	—	—
2	9–12½	(22–)	34	121	91	—	336
3	13–17½	(32–)	7	36½	60	675	48
4	18–25½	(45–)	—	3	—	—	107
5	26–36½	(65–)	—	—	—	—	42
Total trees			79	332½	1400	675	533
*Length and width of frame: ft (m)			40×16 (12×5)	67×20 (20½×6)	402×24 (123× 7½)	505×36 (154½× 11)	289×46 (88×14)

Swaffham Prior: small 3-celled house of the Great Rebuild (c 1600) in an area without woodland[43].

Grundle House: slightly larger than average class-B[44] house of c 1500 with open hall and two cross-wings.

Corpus Christi College: community house built 1352–78; of two storeys round a single court, stone outer walls but otherwise unostentatious.

Norwich Cathedral: non-decorative roof of great church, rebuilt c 1470 but typical of early middle ages[45].

King's College Chapel: ostentatious Perpendicular church roof built 1480–1512 (later concealed by vault)[46].

* *Dimensions given, in the case of buildings with more than one range, are the combined length and mean width of the ranges.*

The method of analysis and other details have been published elsewhere[7].

13½in square (12½m×34cm²), but with all England to draw on for the timber[11] the carpenter evidently had to make do with trees that did not meet this specification. All the struts taper rapidly at the top where they reach far into the crown of the tree; in six cases the design has been altered to use trees that even so were not quite long enough*.

To summarize, a normal wood contained a continuous range of sizes of standard trees from about 18in (45cm) basal diameter

---

* Particulars derived from inspection of the structure, there being no adequate published description.

downwards. They were mainly oak, up to 70 years old, and chiefly of the smaller sizes. The underwood, among which they grew, suppressed the branches up to about 20ft (6m) high and allowed them to form a crown above this height. They were managed on what we should regard as an irregular selection system in which demand rather than supply appears to have been the dominant factor. Plate III gives an impression of what such a wood must have looked like.

How closely spaced were the oaks? There are several records of heavy fellings. For instance, the 40 acres (16 ha) of the Merton College part of Gamlingay Wood supplied at least 561 trees of various sizes in 1333–37, and about 180 trees, mainly oaks, in 1358–59. The number of standard trees must have fluctuated enormously. Beevor's figures of 5 to 40 per acre (12 to 100 per ha) for various Norfolk woods in the 15th century[12] are probably a fair estimate of the range.

There is a popular tradition that the usual density of mature oaks in coppice was 12 to the acre (30 per ha) and that this wide spacing was a deliberate policy to promote the growth of natural bends for ship frames. Legend has much exaggerated the influence of the sea on woodland affairs: even in the Forest of Dean[13] and New Forest[14], where this influence was at its strongest, there is little or no evidence for such a policy. Neither shipbuilding[15] nor woodland records indicate more than occasional consignments of timber from Eastern England for the purpose, and most of this was from non-woodland sources[16]. The figure of 12 oaks to the acre does indeed appear in the statutes of woods (eg that of 1543[17]) which purported to regulate coppice-with-standards management naturally; but it is laid down as a minimum, and the penalties for infringement are not deterrent (as are those for failing to keep woods fenced in). Surveys of woods make it clear that the statutes were widely ignored, though a minimum of 12 oaks per acre is sometimes written into leases (at Gamlingay as late as 1768). The explanation given at the time for limiting the number of oaks in a wood was the obvious one that they interfered with the underwood*.

The evidence shows that we cannot expect historical continuity of *old* oaks in woodland (except perhaps in the boundary pollards round wood margins). Nor can we expect continuity of rotting wood as a habitat. Nothing of the felled oak was wasted; there are many records of monies received for *loppium et chippium,* bark, branches, dead wood, and even leaves.

Regeneration of oak in woods

It has long been appreciated[19] that oak seldom grows from

---

* An interesting case, relating to a region where, with a much higher ratio of wood to population than in Eastern England, there ought to have been less need to protect the coppice, is the recommendation in a survey of 1608[18] that some 6000 trees in coppices in the royal forests of Northamptonshire be felled 'for that they stand to the spoile of the underwood therein'.

seed in existing woods, though it does so freely outside woodland if protected from grazing. This appears to be a problem of the last hundred years: there is no suggestion that in former centuries any difficulty was found in replacing woodland oaks (else we should hardly find so many very small oaks sold). Oak does still regenerate freely in Bradfield and a few other West Suffolk woods in which acid soil appears to be a common factor. The recent decline of woodmanship is a partial explanation, for oak is a light-demanding tree and coppicing provided a succession of establishment sites that are now no longer available. However the date at which oak regeneration ceased in different woods does not correspond well with the end of coppicing.

Seed reproduction in oak is dealt with in a later contribution (see pps 162 to 181). In the past, the need for it was much reduced by vegetative reproduction from the stump. Oak coppices freely when cut up to at least 150 years' growth. The resulting shoots grow fast—up to 7ft (2m) high in the first season at Bradfield in recent years—and are much less vulnerable than seedling oak to damage by animals and to competition from underwood and herbaceous vegetation. Many of the existing oaks in ancient woods, originating mostly between 1780 and 1910[20], either have the remains of a stump at the base or, when felled, show the very wide first annual ring characteristic of a coppice origin. Medieval oak timbers, likewise, often have a curved butt with a wide first annual ring. Possibly the stakes and other very small oaks referred to in documents were the superfluous poles cut out in the operation of 'promoting' such stool-grown oaks to form the next generation of standards.

Changes in woodland management

The woodland system described is an efficient method of producing structural oak timber, given the need (in most cases) to subordinate timber to underwood production, the heterogeneity of wild oak populations, and the fact that many ancient woods are on sites too waterlogged to grow oak well. Early felling encouraged growth from the stump, making regeneration certain and rapid; it gave the flexibility needed to cope with the sudden demands of major building works; and it avoided the problems, such as heart-rots caused by *Laetiporus sulphureus* (Bull. ex Fr.) Murr. coming up from the stool or *Stereum gausapatum* (Fr.) Fr.[21] getting in through dead branches, which often develop if woodland oak stands beyond 100 years. The system was remarkably stable: it produced a sustained yield, both of oak and underwood, for at least 700 years. How was it affected by the vicissitudes of fashion and economics in the second half of this period?

I have estimated[7] that Grundle House, Stanton (table 1) represents the annual oak increment on about 290 acres (120 ha) of woodland. West Suffolk in 1500 was about $5\frac{1}{2}\%$ woodland. The average parish could have produced one such house about every $2\frac{1}{2}$ years if there were no other demands on its timber. The better-wooded areas seem to have been roughly self-sufficient in the medieval and sub-medieval periods with no great margin of surplus. Districts without woodland must have derived much of their timber from outside the region, including the Continent.

The following factors might be expected to upset the balance between production and consumption of oak.

1. *Intensive town building.* Lavenham and Wymondham survive of the many East Anglian towns that were rapidly rebuilt in timber between 1450 and 1650.

2. *The dissolution of the monasteries.* One would suppose that the release of timber from the demolition of monastic buildings, or the felling of monkish woods, ought to have reduced the demand for timber from other woods.

3. *The Great Rebuild.* The apparently unprecedented rate of house building, mostly timber-framed, in the countryside in the late 16th and early 17th centuries.

4. *The rise of the practice of sawing logs lengthwise.* This implies a transition period (perhaps spread over a century or more) in which oaks were allowed to grow larger than they had been previously*. It also makes it more difficult to use, without wastage, trees that are not straight.

5. *The decline of carpentry.* At the time of its greatest technological development in the later middle ages, carpentry was closely integrated with woodmanship. Its subsequent decline is described by Hewett[22] in terms of decreasing efficiency of jointing techniques; it manifests itself also in loss of the skill to exploit the natural properties of the material, and in increasing preoccupation with surface finish. Woodland oaks of the medieval type would have been regarded later as too crooked, knotty, or waney; large straight-grained trees, which carpenters still had the skill to use, presumably increased in value.

What effect did these factors have? Fig 2 shows the price of timber, mainly oak, at Cambridge (which had no local wood) during the 16th and 17th centuries, when the changes should have been most active. The price, in real terms, roughly doubled in 200 years, but the increase was confined to two periods. The sudden rise between 1540 and 1553 has no obvious explanation. The rise from 1575 to 1610 coincided roughly with the Great Rebuild: two West Suffolk men, Ryece[24] and Winthrop[25], complained at the time in general terms of a sho tage of timber, for which they blamed overconsumption. But Hammersley, in a recent study of Crown estates[26], has claimed that there was no serious *national* shortage of timber in

---

* In the Chilterns, minimum sizes for felling (albeit still comparatively small) were specified in certain woods from 1480 onwards[23].

the 16th and 17th centuries; a conclusion with which I concur, though with reservations about underwood and non-woodland trees.

A few surveys exist of trees in woods during this period of change. Little Bentley in 1598[27] is a model for the view that estates were temporarily exhausted by the Great Rebuild. Cowhey Wood was 59 acres (modern measure) 'wherin are but viij good tymber trees remayninge'; this and the other nine woods in the parish, total 430 acres (174 ha), mustered only 561 standard trees between them. The Barking woods (table 2) tell a different story. In 1607 they had a large, though variable, number of trees, which were much bigger than they would normally have been in the middle ages: the 1609 survey shows that a few trees were bigger still. A less accurate

FIGURE 2

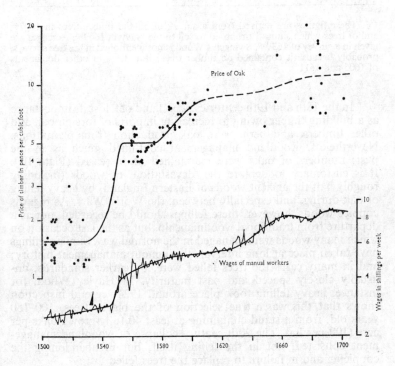

Prices of timber (mainly oak) at Cambridge in the 16th and 17th centuries. Each dot represents one transaction. As a rough guide to the value of money, the wages of manual workers (average of eight trades) are also given. Figures from Thorold Rogers[50], plotted on a logarithmic scale.

survey in 1605[28] shows that woodland trees in four other Suffolk parishes contained an average of from 5.2 to 6.7 cu ft per tree, little more than in medieval times.

TABLE 2

The Barking (Suffolk) woods in the 1600s

Name of wood (and modern spelling)	Acres	Timber trees, 1607			Naval trees, 1609	
		Trees	Trees per acre	Cu. ft per tree	Trees	Cu. ft per tree
Park	14	160	11.4	17·2	6	25.0
Tickley (Titley Hill)	4	40	10.0	18.8	—	—
Prestley (Priestley)	37	73	2.0	13.7	—	—
Swineside (Swingen's)	13	—	—	—	—	—
Boyney (Bonny)	82	1640	20.0	18.6	48	34.2

These figures are derived from a survey of all the timber trees in 1607[47] and of trees which James I proposed to sell to the Navy in 1609[48]. Acreages are given in a survey of 1639[49]. Swingen's Wood is not mentioned in the tree surveys, probably because it contained no timber trees; it appears in other documents of 1605 and 1611.

In the 18th and 19th centuries, woodland oak lost its importance as a building timber owing to increasing imports of foreign oak and other timbers, and perhaps to oak production from plantations. Nevertheless, woodland management continued much as in the past: numbers of oaks were maintained or increased (Plate III). It is customary to deplore the 'devastation' of woods (including roughly half the ancient woods of Eastern England) by heavy felling of oak during, and especially between, the World Wars. As regards coppice woods, however, these fellings should be regarded, not as a departure from traditional woodmanship, but as the last occasion on which many woods were managed in the normal way. Similar fellings have taken place at long intervals throughout management history; and in many cases the trees felled were, by earlier standards, unusually closely spaced and past maturity. In Hayley Wood, for instance, heavy felling took place around 1924; careful inspection shows that this was a true selection of the bigger trees, 100–150 years old, from a stand containing at least 40 fully-grown oaks per acre (100 per ha). The 20th century collapse of woodland management consisted, not in the felling itself, but in abandoning the coppicing and in failure to replace the trees felled.

Origins of woodland management

Throughout Eastern England, monastic cartularies and other documents of the 13th century take woodland management for granted as an established and fully-developed system. It must have had a long previous history of which little is known because few earlier documents survive.

Domesday Book (1086) takes little interest in woods. In Lincolnshire it states that about half the woodland acreage was *silua minuta*[29], presumably coppice. It hints at coppice-woods in West Cambridgeshire.

Elsewhere in the region, Domesday mentions woodland almost entirely in terms of the number of swine that it was supposed to feed. Commentators generally assume without argument that this was roughly proportional to the size of the wood, allowing perhaps for differences in the quality of woodland. But the matter is not so simple. Early sources[30] tell us that the pigs depended on the acorn crop, which varied enormously from year to year and often failed completely, as it does now. The assessment of a wood must have depended as much on the readiness of the local pig-men to gamble on a good acorn year as it did on the size of the wood. It is unrealistic to expect an objective equation (however approximate) between pigs and acres. In Eastern England the swine assessments, however arrived at, bear no relation to the *actual* pigs recorded in the same manors and probably reflect an obsolescent practice.

In about 100 cases the swine assessment decreased between 1066 and 1086. Round[31] attributed this to encroachment of arable on woodland, an explanation discounted by Lennard[32] who suggested instead the selective destruction of oak (and beech). The rise of woodland management, probably going on at this time, provides two further hypotheses. Either pigs were excluded from woods taken into management on the grounds that they damaged the stools; or the shift towards younger oaks so diminished the acorn crop that the pig-men abandoned this already erratic source of fodder and turned elsewhere.

Swine pannage is seldom mentioned in Eastern England, apart from Essex, after Domesday Book. At Little Bentley it went on as late as 1483[33] (perhaps not in woodland). In royal forests it lingered later still (to the present day in the New Forest).

Non-woodland oak

Apart from woods and plantations, oaks grow in hedges, in grassland and rough grazing of various kinds, and (less often nowadays) in fields and meadows. Traditionally, many (though not all) such trees are managed as pollards, which are familiar in many parks and in the unenclosed parts of Epping, Hainault, and Hatfield Forests. Occasionally pollards are so closely spaced as now to give the illusion of woodland.

Even in open-field parts of the country, hedgerow trees are recorded by the 14th century (eg Gamlingay 1356[9]) and existed in large numbers in the 16th century (as on the Gamlingay estate map of 1601[34]). In the other half of England, in which hedged fields existed early, 16th and 17th century estate maps[35] depict much larger numbers of hedgerow trees than there are now. Other types of non-woodland trees are of similar antiquity. The 'parkland' ecosystem of trees over grassland or heath* is shown in many early maps[36] and can sometimes be traced back further still. It is sometimes derived (as in parts of Hatfield Forest) from woodland in which grazing was allowed to prevent regeneration, and may revert to woodland if the grazing is removed. Staverton Park[37], although often misinterpreted as an unaltered fragment of prehistoric forest, illustrates these points.

It is probable that for centuries oaks have formed only an important minority among non-woodland trees. For instance, in 1608 there were 860 oaks among the 9036 decaying trees (perhaps pollards) in Havering Park[18].

Pollarding is definitely recorded at least by the 15th century[38]. It was practised in places where grazing animals made ordinary coppicing impracticable; or in order to provide long-lived trees of distinctive shape to mark boundaries; or as a means of allowing a tenant a loophole in a lease forbidding him to fell timber trees.

Pollarding prolongs the life of a tree: famous 'ancient' oaks are nearly all non-woodland trees, and many of them are pollards. Taking a rare opportunity to age pollard oaks from annual ring counts, I have shown that those of Christchurch Park, Ipswich— probably typical of old park pollards—originated shortly before 1580. Areas with large numbers of non-woodland trees may provide the historical continuity of old oaks which is lacking in woodlands.

There are many indications that non-woodland standard trees, especially in parks, were allowed to grow larger than in woods and were the main source of big timbers and of natural bends for use in shipbuilding[15]. For an early example, 80 trees confiscated by royal officials from the *wood* of Hasishey (now Alsa Wood) in 1274 were valued at 4d each, while oaks which they seized in the nearby Stansted *Park* were worth six times as much per tree[39]. A late example is illustrated by fig 3, which shows the larger sizes reached by non-woodland oaks in NW Essex in 1809 and the premium which big trees then commanded at auction. Growing oaks as long-rotation standards, or as pollards, is a natural reaction to the difficulty of replacing them on grazing land.

The origin and status of present-day oaks

Ecologists traditionally regard oak as in some sense the climax dominant tree of most of England. Existing semi-natural woods are treated, if at all possible, as variants of 'oak woodland'. This convention is based on the observations that nearly all such woods contain at least a few oaks; that oak occurred in large quantities in the prehistoric forest; and that many different non-woodland sites, left unmanaged for a few decades, succeed to oak-dominated scrub.

---

* In the middle ages the term 'park'—an enclosure for keeping deer—did not imply any particular form of vegetation.

FIGURE 3

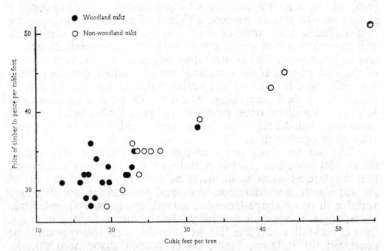

Size range of woodland and non-woodland oaks, and prices per cubic foot, in 1809. Compiled from an auction record relating mainly to trees in Ashdon and Radwinter[51]. Each point represents one lot of between 2 and 38 trees.

Human intervention has been a remarkably steady factor in many woods in Eastern England probably for a thousand years. What meaning can be attributed in these circumstances to 'oak woodland' and 'climax vegetation'?

In almost every ancient wood in the region, oak forms (or has formed in the recent past) the majority of the standard trees but hardly any of the underwood. This is so regardless of variations in soil and underwood composition, or of the suitability of the site for oak; it appears to have been the case throughout recorded history. Non-woodland trees, like underwood, are much more responsive to ecological and historical variation: oak is the commonest pollard in some places, but in others is replaced by elm, ash, hornbeam, or willow. The reproductive characteristics of oak on woodland and non-woodland sites might lead us to expect the opposite situation. Moreover, when woodland is unmanaged it does not remain dominated by oak for ever. On calcareous clays there is a succession[2] to woodland dominated by ash or elm. On acid sites oak would probably hold its ground longer, but would usually be succeeded in the end by birch. Sometimes these other trees kill the oaks by overtopping and shading; even if this does not happen, the existing oaks will eventually die without replacement. Only a hypothetical cyclical succession could bring the oak back.

The division into oak standards and underwood of other species does not depend on their biological suitability: it would work the other way round. It is determined by management policy.

Anyone with experience of woodmanship knows that he can control the composition of the standard trees by 'promoting' saplings or coppice shoots of the species desired, although if he decides to promote thin-barked species some of them may be damaged by sun-scorch and other extremes of temperature when the underwood shading their trunks is removed. He has much less influence over the composition of the underwood. If the standards are oak rather than ash, lime, etc., this must be because the timber value of oak (or its greater resistance to bark scorching) overrode all other considerations. With non-woodland trees, especially pollards, timber value was less important, sun-scorch unlikely to occur, and other factors were allowed to predominate.

The oak standards are thus the most artificial component of the ancient woodland ecosystem. But we would be wrong to conclude that they are as much an intrusion as larch or spruce. The oaks of ancient woods, and some non-woodland populations, are strikingly variable in trunk shape (straight, curved, or corkscrew), epicormic burrs, angle of branches and twigs, density and clustering of twigs, time of leaf-fall, etc. (Plate III). Most of this variation appears to be genetic[40]; for instance, variations of branch shape and attitude, which might otherwise be attributed to the environment of the tree when young, are usually repeated in the twigs. Moreover, there are some woodland oak populations, apparently genetically uniform, which do not show such variation. Except in one or two sites, the variation is all within *Quercus robur,* although occasionally one finds a tree with a single character of *Q. petraea.*

This variation strongly suggests that stands showing it are of wild origin. An oak population deliberately introduced from outside stock ought, as in a plantation, to be more uniform and to show some evidence of selection for timber quality. The uniform populations, which have straight clean trunks, show that this has happened in some woods, though even in such cases there are usually a few deviant trees from a wild stock which has not been completely suppressed.

I conclude that the prehistoric forest of Eastern England contained a highly variable population of *Q. robur* with a little *Q. petraea**. The existing woodland, and to some extent non-woodland, oaks are derived from this population. Replacement by coppice shoots, natural seed establishment, and planting (where necessary) from local stock maintained genetic continuity. With

---

* Eastern England is unusual in that *Q. robur* is the common oak throughout a very wide range of soil types. If the factors which have caused *Q. robur* to increase in highland areas at the expense of *Q. petraea* have also operated here, the surviving traces of the latter indicate a definite scatter of that species in the past. Anderson held the extreme view[41] that *Q. robur* was introduced to Britain by the medieval Cistercians; but it is hardly credible that in a few generations one oak should have so completely eliminated the other in a region with little Cistercian influence. Neither pollen nor micro-remains distinguish the two species, but Hadfield[42] points out that medieval representations of oak almost always depict *Q. robur* (see pps 127–9).

some recognizable exceptions, the establishment of plantation oak in the 18th and 19th centuries had little effect on the oaks of existing woods.

The term 'oak woodland' is often applied indiscriminately to any wood that happens to contain standard oaks. It draws attention to the most artificial feature of woods, and conceals their real ecological variation which is expressed in the underwood and ground vegetation. But although the oak has been singled out for special treatment down the centuries, many stands of oak may retain historical continuity with the pre-historic forest. Naturalists and others who urge the *planting* of oak as an answer to its conservation problems should remember that much of its beauty and interest, and part of its value as a habitat for plants and animals, lie in its irregularity and variability. The countryside will be poorer if the present heterogeneous oaks are replaced by uniform nursery stock from 'good' trees.

Acknowledgements

I wish to thank the custodians of archives which I have consulted, especially the Librarians of Merton College, Oxford and Pembroke College, Cambridge, and the County Archivists of Essex and East Suffolk. For opportunities to examine buildings I am indebted to Mr & Mrs D. P. Dymond of Grundle House, Mr D. Purcell and Miss C. Wilson (architects to Ely Cathedral), and Mr J. Saltmarsh of King's College, Cambridge. Mr Saltmarsh kindly allowed me to refer to his unpublished material. Dr D. E. Coombe, Mr Dymond, and Mrs S. Ranson made helpful comments on the draft of this paper. Part of the work was done in Cambridge University Botany School under a research project of the Natural Environment Research Council.

REFERENCES

ERO   = Essex County Record Office
ESRO = East Suffolk County Record Office
MCR   = Merton College (Oxford) Records
PRO   = Public Record Office
RCHM = Royal Commission on Historical Monuments

1. RACKHAM, O. 'The history and effects of coppicing as a woodland practice', in *The biotic effects of public pressures on the environment* (ed. E. Duffey), Monk's Wood Experimental Station Symposium, 3 (1967), 82–93
2. RACKHAM, O. 'Historical studies and woodland conservation', in *The scientific management of animal and plant communities for conservation* (ed. E. Duffey and A. S. Watt), Oxford (1971), 563–80. (Includes an account of the recognition of medieval woods in the field.)
3. GODWIN, H. 'Studies of the post-glacial history of British vegetation. XV. Organic deposits of Old Buckenham Mere, Norfolk', *New Phytol.*, 67 (1968), 95–107
4. British Museum: Cott. Claud. C. xi. Another copy: Ely Diocesan Registry (in Cambridge University Library) G/3/27

5. ERO: D/D Sm.
6a. EDLIN, H. L. *Woodland crafts of Britain* (ed. 2), Newton Abbot (1973)
 b. TITTENSOR, R. M. 'History of the Loch Lomond oakwoods', *Scott. For.*, **24** (1970), 100–18
7. RACKHAM, O. 'Grundle House: on the quantities of timber in certain East Anglian buildings in relation to local supplies', *Vernac. Archit.*, **3** (1972), 3–10
8. LATHAM, B. *Timber: its development and distribution*, London (1957)
9. MCR: 5342–5411 (and other Gamlingay records)
10. PEMBROKE COLLEGE, Cambridge: Hardwick records I 1–3
11. STEWART, D. J. *On the architectural history of Ely Cathedral*, London (1868)
12. BEEVOR, H. E. 'Norfolk woodlands, from the evidence of contemporary chronicles', *Trans. Norfolk Norwich Nat. Soc.*, **11** (1924), 488–508
13. HART, C. E. *Royal forest: a history of Dean's woods as producers of timber*, Oxford (1966)
14. TUBBS, C. R. *The New Forest: an ecological history*, Newton Abbot (1968)
15a. ALBION, R. G. *Forests and sea power: the timber problem of the Royal Navy 1652–1862*, Harvard (1926)
 b. CHARNOCK, J. *An history of marine architecture*, London (1800–2)
 c. HOLLAND, A. J. *Ships of British oak: the rise and decline of wooden ship-building in Hampshire*, Newton Abbot (1971)
16. PRO: E178/3785; E178/4564
17. Act of Parliament: 35 Hen VIII c 17
18. PRO: SP 14/42
19. WATT, A. S. 'On the causes of failure of natural regeneration in British oakwoods', *J. Ecol.*, **7** (1919), 173–203
20. RACKHAM, O. 'The history of Hayley Wood', in *Hayley Wood*, Cambridge (Cambs & Isle of Ely Naturalists' Trust) (in course of publication)
21. CARTWRIGHT, K. STG. and FINDLAY, W. P. K. *The principal rots of English oak*, London (HMSO) (1936)
22. HEWETT, C. A. *The development of carpentry, 1200–1700: an Essex study*, Newton Abbot (1969)
23. RODEN, D. 'Woodland and its management in the medieval Chilterns', *Forestry*, **41** (1968), 59–71
24. RYECE, R. *The breviary of Suffolk* (early 17th cent.; ed. F. Harvey, London 1902)
25. WINTHROP PAPERS, *Mass. Hist. Soc.*, **1** (1929), 295 ff
26. HAMMERSLEY, G. 'The Crown woods and their exploitation in the sixteenth and seventeenth centuries', *Bull. Inst. Hist. Res.*, **30** (1957), 136–61
27. ERO: D/DQ 16/1
28. PRO: E178/4548
29. DARBY, H. C. *The Domesday geography of Eastern England*, (ed. 3), Cambridge (1971)
30. Eg Huntingdonshire documents printed in: Neilson N. *Economic conditions on the manors of Ramsey Abbey*, Philadelphia (1898)
31. ROUND, J. H. 'Introduction to the Essex Domesday', in *Victoria County History: Essex*, **1** (1903), 333–426
32. LENNARD, R. 'The destruction of woodland in the eastern counties under William the Conqueror', *Econ. Hist. Rev.*, **15** (1945), 36–43
33. ERO: D/DB M122
34. MCR: C/17. Reproduced in part in RCHM, *West Cambridgeshire*, London (HMSO) (1968), Plate 29
35. Eg numerous examples reproduced in: *Catalogue of maps in the Essex Record Office, 1566–1855*, Chelmsford (1947, and supplements). See especially 1st suppl. Plate I (1952)
36. Eg examples from other parts of England reproduced in: Beresford, M. *History on the ground*, (ed. 2), London (1971)
37. PETERKEN, G. F. 'Development of vegetation in Staverton Park, Suffolk', *Fld Stud.*, **3** (1969), 1–39

38. ELAND, G. *At the courts of Great Canfield, Essex,* Oxford (1949), 54
39. *Rotuli hundredorum temp. Hen. III & Edw. I,* London, 1 (1810), 155
40. JONES, E. W. 'Biological Flora of the British Isles: *Quercus* L.', *J. Ecol.,* **47** (1959), 169–222
41. ANDERSON, M. L. 'The ecological status of Wistman's Wood, Devonshire', *Trans. bot. Soc. Edin.,* **36** (1953), 195–206
42. HADFIELD, M. 'The durmast oak in Britain', *Q. Jl For.,* **53** (1959), 197–205
43. Investigated by A. P. Baggs and O. Rackham: a note on its timber content appears in RCHM, *East Cambridgeshire,* London (HMSO) (1972), xxix–xxx, 123 (Swaffham Prior monument 8)
44. RCHM, *West Cambridgeshire* (1968), xlvi
45. Investigated (after demolition) by J. Fletcher and O. Rackham
46. RCHM, *City of Cambridge,* London (HMSO) (1959), 110–1
47. ESRO: HA1/BD/3/1
48. PRO: E178/4564
49. ESRO: HA1/BA/3/10
50. ROGERS, J. T. *History of agriculture and prices,* 3 & 4 (1872), 5 & 6 (1887)
51. ERO: B1002. Sale catalogue with printed details of numbers and estimated volumes of trees in each lot and pencilled notes of prices fetched.

ANNUAL RINGS IN MODERN AND MEDIEVAL TIMES

J. M. FLETCHER

*Research Laboratory for Archaeology and the
History of Art, Oxford University.*

Introduction

The annual rings laid down in trees reflect a number of environmental conditions, some relating to their site, others common to a wide region. Oaks are of particular value for dendrochronology since there are virtually no occasions on which the annual ring is absent and so the widths or densities of their rings may provide reliably dated information about the past.

In England it has often been assumed that the factors affecting the annual increments (or ring-widths) are so numerous and variable that similarities for trees in different woodlands, or even in the same woodland, would be rare. Our temperate climate, so different from the Desert States of the U.S.A. where dendrochronology has been so successful, was usually blamed for this state of affairs. As this assumption soon became a doctrine, there has been until recently almost no systematic work to study the ring-widths of English trees.

No such prejudice prevailed in the Scandinavian countries, where timber forms an important constituent of the national economy, or at the Universities of Tharandt and Munich where Professor Huber and his pupils pursued tree-ring research from 1938 onwards. In all, over 30 papers have been published from these Universities and other places in Germany on this subject. Two of the conclusions are relevant to this Symposium.

First, for the long-lived Spessart oak, a famous provenance of sessile oak (*Q. petraea*) growing in parts of Hesse and areas further to the south at altitudes above 200m, the pattern formed by the sequence of ring-widths is much the same for hilly terrain over a region which stretches 400km both from east to west and from north to south (fig 1). Further still to the west, the same pattern can apply in the Ile de France and eastern Normandy[1]; it has even been found in some English samples collected and examined in recent years by German dendrochronologists[2]. In the lowlands of north Germany the pattern is quite different.

The second concerns a mixed stand of oak, ash and alder[3] growing in the Forestry District of Geisenfeld, at an altitude of 365m on a plateau of terrace gravel near the Danube 70km north of Munich, where the average rainfall is 610mm (24in). Correlation

FIGURE 1

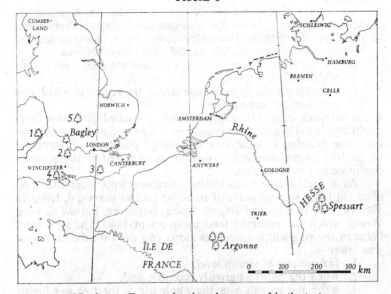

North-west Europe, showing places named in the text
Key to Woodlands/Forests
1 *Forest of Dean;* 2 *Little Cheseridge Wood;* 3 *Beechen Wood;*
4 *New Forest;* 5 *Hazelborough Forest*

coefficients (r) were calculated between the ring-widths of each species and five factors (which included precipitation, mean temperature, relative humidity at 14.00 hrs and potential evaporation), each expressed as monthly means. There were marked differences for the three species. For the oaks (about 115 years old) there were no outstanding large values of r, but factors contributing to wider rings were:

1. A warm October of the previous year.
2. A warm May, but not too warm July.
3. High precipitation in June.

It was noted that ash was more dependant on water conservation in the soil, particularly in springtime, than the other two species.

Over the past three years our research in dendrochronology at Oxford has been mainly concerned with measuring and matching the ring-widths of selected oaks which grew in south-east England between 850 A.D. and the present time. Previously, as part of a research programme in the Dept. of Forestry at Oxford, samples from English oaks formed a small part of a programme for measuring the densities of annual rings by X-radiography.

This contribution describes the work on recently felled oaks and then mentions briefly the ring-width curves obtained from Saxon times and some applications of our chronology for oak.

Recent growth

To study dendrochronology systematically in a relatively unexplored region, there are obvious advantages—availability, known dates of felling and known locations—to be gained by starting with recently felled trees[4] [5]. We started with two objectives:

1. To discover if there is one or more regional patterns to which oaks conform.
2. To estimate the approximate size of the region to which any common pattern applies.

From the work already done in Germany, it seemed likely that there might be one pattern for oaks growing in hilly woodlands and another for those growing in valleys or in isolated positions: furthermore better tree-to-tree correlation was to be expected if the samples conformed to strict criteria.

As a preliminary investigation, measurements were made on discs cut from various parts of trees, up to 160 years old, felled in 1969 or 1970 in a part of Bagley Wood, Berkshire, known as West Wood, which was common land up to about 1840. The agreement between the ring-width sequences along two radii on the same disc was lower—

1. for samples at stump level,
2. when the pith was grossly eccentric and,
3. when the growth over the whole life of the tree was highly irregular.

For the main part of the programme, we therefore limited measurements (a) to discs from the top of butt logs, the average height above ground being 4m, and (b) on each disc, to two radii the ratio of which did not differ by more than 1.5. Samples were taken from four sites on three estates. Two of the sites were in Bagley Wood: the others on the Eling Estate, Hermitage, Berkshire and on the Pilmer Estate, near Crowborough, Sussex. It will be noticed from the details in table 1 that the sites are on relatively high ground. The rainfall in Bagley Wood and its vicinity is known from records kept at and near Oxford. For the 150 years period from 1815 to 1964, it averaged 650mm (25½in) annually.

There are differences in the soil at the two Bagley Wood sites. In West Wood there is gravel of glacial origin overlying Kimmeridge Clay, giving a soil which dries readily and causes moisture stress, as evidenced by some drought cracks in larch in 1964; in Underwood, 2km away, the clay is much nearer the surface. The other Berkshire site, Little Cheseridge Wood, was a small isolated plantation of 8 acres (3ha) where the soil was a thin layer of clay on a chalky hillside facing south.

The choice of Sussex oaks was based on the availability of discs from butts being delivered to W. L. West & Sons Ltd of Midhurst. The trees came from Compartment 1 of Beechen Wood, a long narrow area which lies on a north slope where there is a light sandy silt from Hastings beds. This is an enclosed area, said to have been managed for some time as coppice-with-standards.

TABLE 1

Results on discs from oaks of slow to medium growth in certain Berkshire and Sussex woodlands

Sites	Altitude m	Trees sampled		Discs		Ring-widths	
		No	Approx. age years	Average underbark diameter cm	Average ring-widths mm	No of comparisons	Agreement W,%, s,%
Bagley Wood, Berkshire West Wood, SP 5002	115	6	140–160*	50	1.9	15	72 ±3.0
Bagley Wood, Berkshire Underwood, SP 5101	100	4	140–160	60	2.1	6	71 ±2.0
Eling Estate, Berkshire Little Cheseridge Wood, SU 5177	115	4	170	50	1.8	6	71.5 ±2.4
Pilmer Estate, Sussex. Beechen Wood, TQ 5231	100–140	6	165*	60	2.15	15	67.5 ±3.2

* Except for one, about 110 years old.

1. *Results for Berkshire and Sussex*

The average dimensions of the discs from the four sites are given in table 1. None of the oaks selected were of fast growth, the disc with the widest rings having an average ring-width of 2.5mm.

The widths of the annual rings, measured with a ×10 eyepiece to the nearest 0.1mm, where plotted on transparent semi-logarithmic paper which was identical in dimensions to that used by German dendrochronologists. As a measure of the agreement between two graphs, the percentage (W) of years in which the change in the widths in the same direction (an increase, the same, a decrease) was calculated either directly from the graphs or by our version of the Hamburg computer programme[6]. Between the two radii of a disc, the average value of W (for 20 trees) was 80%, the standard deviation, *s*, being ± 3.7%.

For each tree a single graph, the mean for the two radii, was made. Within each site, the agreement between each pair was then calculated. The means (table 1) lie between 67.5 and 72%. The value (69%) found for six oaks in a stand near Celle in Lower Saxony on the North German plain lies in the same range: there, however, the variation from the mean was greater $(s, \pm 6.5\%)$[4].

When the graph for a tree on one site is compared with that for a tree on a distant site, the agreement, is lower. Between the trees of West Wood (Bagley Wood) and those elsewhere, the means, each for 20 comparisons with 120–130 overlapping years, were:

Distance from Bagley Wood	Woodland	W, %	s, %
25km	Little Cheseridge	65	±3.0
120km	Beechen	63	±2.4

Mean curves From the graphs for individual trees, a mean curve was made for each of the four sites. The agreement between those for the two parts of Bagley Wood was 76.5%, so a further mean curve, for its ten trees, was made. This curve and those for the other two woodlands are shown in fig 2A. The agreements (W) between them are as follows:

	Little Cheseridge	Beechen
Bagley Wood	74%	68%
Little Cheseridge Wood	—	69%

In a similar study for Denmark[5] in which trees were sampled from ten stands, the mean of the 45 values of W was 67.5%, there being little variation with the distance apart (up to 220km) of the stands.

It will be noticed that the three curves of fig 2A show similarities (i) in the years (eg 1886, 1914, 1936, 1950) in which there are peaks; (ii) in the years (eg 1852, 1881, 1893 and 1938) which showed a marked decrease in width; and (iii) in the presence of deep and wide troughs (1839–45, 1860–6 and 1917–24).

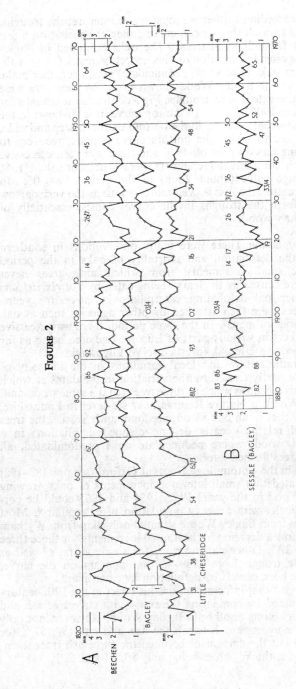

FIGURE 2

Ring-width plots. A. Mean curves for three woodlands in Berkshire-Sussex
B. Mean curve for four sessile oaks, Bagley Wood

Before proceeding further we must try to interpret the troughs. Though present on all three mean curves, they are absent on a few of the graphs for individual trees. The oaks examined in Bagley Wood provide most information on this aspect of restricted growth. Among the ten oaks (almost all pedunculate) which together make the mean curve for Bagley Wood shown in fig 2A there are wide variations in the extent of he troughs. Fig 3 contrasts the troughs for three trees from 1906 to 1938. In the top curve, it is shallow; in the middle one more marked; and in the bottom one both deep and wide.

For the tree to which the bottom curve applied, recovery to pre-1914 vigour was delayed till 1936 and there were ten successive years in which the annual increments were little more than 15% of their average value (about 2mm) in the period 1900–06. In terms of dry matter, the loss is even more serious as the very narrow rings which form the troughs in the curves consist essentially of low-density early wood.

Caterpillar defoliation There were many observations in southern England on the defoliation and mortality of oaks in the period 1917–24. The small increments, from which some trees never recovered, were caused by the leaves being eaten by *Tortrix viridana* (L.) and other oak-defoliating caterpillars in *successive* years. Weakened trees were then attacked by other agencies such as oak mildew and honey fungus[7]. In the same period, there was excessive mortality of oaks in various parts of Europe, one area being as far away as the pedunculate oak forests in NW Yugoslavia.

The sporadic nature and local variations in the intensity of defoliation are partly caused by the variation in the dates at which oaks flush. This can be as much as three weeks in the same woodland. In Roudsea Wood, a Nature Reserve near sea-level in Lancashire, it was noticed that in an oak wood, predominantly sessile, the trees which flushed relatively early or late escaped defoliation; in a nearby mixed wood, where pedunculate oaks predominated, all the resistant trees flushed late[8].

Research in the Entomology Dept. at Oxford (see pps 182–192) has demonstrated that small latewood increments of oaks growing in Wytham Wood in the years 1952, 1954 and 1965 could be correlated statistically with a heavy population of caterpillars[9]. Most of our samples from Bagley Wood, situated only 8km from Wytham Wood, also show a decrease in the annual increments for those three years (see fig 2A). Other narrow rings for single years, as well as the deep wide trough from 1839–45 that appears on the curve, may also have been caused by defoliation by caterpillars.

It was hoped that information on this effect in the 19th century would be obtained by comparing the ring-width curves of ash and oak felled near to one another in Bagley Wood. However, not only was there little agreement between the ash and oak (W, 57% for 1837 to 1971) but the agreement between the three ash trees themselves was slight, the W values being only 59, 64 and 68%.

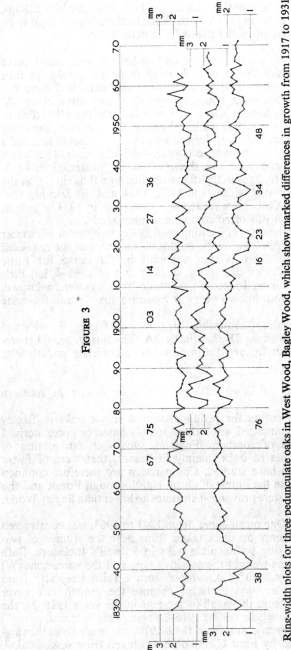

FIGURE 3

Ring-width plots for three pedunculate oaks in West Wood, Bagley Wood, which show marked differences in growth from 1917 to 1931

Any attempt to correlate, along the lines attempted by Elling[3], curves, such as those in fig 2A, with climatic effects would seem to be profitless on account of the effects from defoliation.

Curves for Sessile oaks A second and rather different mean curve (fig 2B) for Bagley Wood was obtained from the graphs for four trees, three out of four of which were sessile oaks and were not included in the ten trees, which formed the mean curve in fig 2A. One of these sessile oaks was a 120 year old tree recently felled in West Wood for which only a stump sample was available; the other two were 70 years old trees derived from coppice shoots in Laud's Copse in an area of abandoned coppice-with-standards. The fourth graph was the one with the shallow trough illustrated in fig 3.

Though the troughs in fig 2B are smaller than those in fig 2A the decreases in the ring-widths for 1952, 1954 and 1965 imply that attack by insects was present. The steep decrease in 1933, a year in which defoliation was often complete, confirms this.

Moisture stress, from the long spell of dry weather in the winter and spring of 1933-4, accounts, no doubt, for much of the restricted growth in 1934. This is also apparent in the curve for Little Cheseridge. But other dry spells, such as that of 1943-4, left little imprint on the curves. Indeed if the dates of the rings were unknown, interpretation from known years of moisture stress would be quite unreliable.

Years that were favourable for growth in Bagley Wood stand out more clearly in fig 2B than in fig 2A. The former would therefore be the better for any future attempt to correlate growth with climatic factors.

2. *Comparisons of Bagley Wood with other forests in southern England*

The mean curves for pedunculate and sessile oaks in Bagley Wood may be compared with others, mainly based on cores, derived for other parts of southern England. One such curve, that of Elphick[10], applies to oaks, mainly in Sussex, that were of faster growth than we have studied. Comparisons are therefore confined to certain trees in the Forest of Dean, Hazelborough Forest and the New Forest that were growing at altitudes no lower than Bagley Wood.

Forest of Dean One mean curve, from 1847 to 1968, was constructed from measurements on discs taken from near the stumps of two rather fast growing pedunculate oaks in Russell's Inclosure. Both ring-width graphs were of the sensitive type and the agreement (W) between them was 70%. A sample from a third tree, also from Russell's Inclosure, was excluded because the growth rate never fully recovered from the small increments in the years 1915-23, the average over the whole period 1915-70 being only 0.45mm.

A second mean curve, from 1839-1970, was made from the ring-widths obtained by Frau Giertz on cores taken from sessile oaks[2].

TABLE 2

Mean curves for Bagley Wood and other woodlands in southern England

Woodlands	Altitude m	No of trees	Approx. age years	Likely species	Years spanned	Average ring-width mm	Agreement (W, %) with Bagley Wood	
							Curve 1*	Curve 2†
Bagley Wood, (Curve 1), West Wood & Underwood	150	10	150	Ped.	1836–1971	2.0	—	81
Bagley Wood, (Curve 2), West Wood & Laud's Copse	160	4	110 & 70	Sess.	1881–1968	2.0	81	—
Forest of Dean, Russell's Inclosure	100	2	120	Ped.	1868–1968	2.7	68	65
Forest of Dean, Hadnock Speech House & High Meadow	40 180	3 3	150 185	Sess. Sess.	1868–1970	2.0	66	64
Hazelborough Forest, King Richard Copse	140	4	145	Ped.	1854–1968	1.6	67	70
New Forest, Salisbury Trench	120	5	200	Sess.	1903–1943	1.7	65	67

* Included in fig 2A   † Included in fig 2B

There were a number of differences between these two mean curves, the agreement for the period 1868–1968 being only 67.5%.

The year-to-year agreements between these two mean curves for the Forest of Dean and the two for Bagley Wood are given in table 2. They lie in the range 64 to 68%. Visual comparisons of the four curves suggest the following conclusions:

(a) Wide troughs, that is reduced growth in successive years, occur for the same periods, eg 1861–4, 1880–2, 1915–24, 1933–5 and 1954–6 in the two forests. Defoliation by caterpillars may have been largely responsible for these troughs. Yet severe effects were not always simultaneous: thus, in 1952 and 1965, such attack caused decidely narrow rings in the trees examined in Bagley Wood, but the rings in those years in the Forest of Dean were of average width.

(b) Late and severe frosts, such as that of mid-May 1935 which caused damage in both areas,[11] can affect the curves. The frost of May 1935 followed two successive years in which growth was already much reduced, primarily as a result of defoliation by caterpillars in 1933, but intensified by the dry winter and spring of 1933–4. Whereas in Bagley Wood the frost damage of May 1935 was insufficient to prevent an increase in the ring-width for that year, in the hilly terrain of the Forest of Dean, well-known for its frost-pockets, many of the ring-widths showed no increase. This applied particularly to the samples from the low-lying Hadnock Inclosure.

(c) Sessile like pedunculate oaks, are prone to show less growth in those years in which defoliation by caterpillars occurs, but the effect on sessile oaks is, on average, less severe, as has been noted previously[12].

(d) Years which stand out on the mean curves as favouring wide rings are 1865, 1883–6, 1914, 1917, 1925–8, 1945, 1950 and 1964. The relatively dry but warm summers of 1921 and 1943 produced wider, not narrower rings on trees at the higher altitudes in the Forest of Dean, where the annual rainfall (940mm, 37in) is considerably higher than in Bagley Wood.

Hazelborough Forest The tree-to-tree agreements (average, 72%) for four trees, all of slow growth, sampled in Hazelborough Forest are almost the same as the averages within the three Berkshire sites (table 1). There are fewer deep troughs in the Hazelborough curve, but those present (at 1916, 1919 and 1933–4) are for the same years and of similar magnitude to the troughs on the curve for the sessile oaks of Bagley Wood.

As in the higher parts of the Forest of Dean, the relatively high altitude of Hazelborough Forest seems to be responsible for reversing in certain years the usual pattern, the ring being wider in summers which are warm and dry. The peak on the ring-width curve of 1921 provides a striking example. Other peaks such as those for 1859, 1875, 1886, 1914, 1936 and 1950, coincide with those for Bagley Wood.

The New Forest The ring-widths reported by Jones [13] in 1947 were on cores taken (i) from 8 trees, about 300 years old, in an unenclosed area near Brook, and (ii) from 12 trees, in Salisbury Trench, about a mile away, an area enclosed and planted about 1700. The object of the investigation was related to the stag-headedness of oaks in the post-1920 period.

The tree-to-tree agreement for the cores was poor, partly no doubt because the growth rate of the various trees in the years before sampling had often been slow. The only graphs satisfactory for averaging were five for trees in Salisbury Trench. The average agreement between the 10 pairs of graphs was 69 %, but the variation about this average was considerable, s being $\pm 6.2\%$.

FIGURE 4

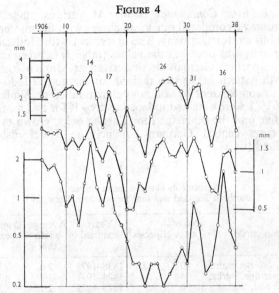

Regional ring-width curves for recent growth
Top: Southern Germany, Spessart oaks
Middle: ,,   England, Sessile oaks (curve B)
Bottom: ,,   ,,   Pedunculate oaks (curve A)

Details about the mean curve for these five trees are included in table 2. The overlap of only 40 years with the Bagley Wood curves is too short for agreement values to be statistically reliable. Of more significance is the similarity in all respects of the New Forest curve with the sessile oak curve for Bagley Wood over the period from 1916 to 1940. Their troughs from 1917 to 1926 are comparable, as are peaks at 1926, 1931, 1936 and 1939 and minima at 1933-4 and 1938.

3. *Mean curves for southern England*

The agreement values (64–70%, table 2) between the mean curves of the Forest of Dean, Hazelborough Forest and the New Forest are sufficiently good to justify using them, with our Berkshire–Sussex curves, to form two regional curves representative of slow growth in hilly woodlands in southern England. They are shown in fig 4 and consist of:

Curve A (mainly pedunduculate trees)	Total 24 trees: 20 in the Berkshire-Sussex woodlands and 4 in Hazelborough Forest.
Curve B (mainly sessile trees)	Total 15 trees: 4 in Bagley Wood, 6 in the Forest of Dean and 5 in the New Forest.

The agreement for the overlapping years, 1880–1968, is 78%.

Comparison with Continental curves At various stages of this investigation we compared our mean curves with the master chronologies published for Germany. The agreement with Hollstein's[14] for west Germany was poor but the values (table 3) between our curves and the important German curve derived at Munich[15] imply that the growth pattern in the two regions for the period 1830–1960 are affected to some extent by common climatic factors. Similar values (64 and 63%) were obtained independently [2][16] for two mean curves, one for five and the other for four English oaks, grown even more distant from central Germany, namely in Herefordshire and Cumberland (fig 1).

TABLE 3

Agreements between mean curves for southern England and that for southern Germany*

Mean curve	No of trees	Species	Years spanned	Average width mm	Overlap years	W %
Bagley Wood, Berkshire	10	Ped.	1838–1971	2·0	123	61†
Little Cheseridge, Berks.	4	,,	1824–1971	1·8	137	64†
Beechen Wood, Sussex	6	,,	1823–1972	2·15	138	58†
Berkshire-Hazelborough-Beechen (Curve A, Fig 4)	24	,,	1830–1971	2·0	133	64
Bagley-Forest of Dean-New Forest (Curve B, Fig 4)	15	Sess.	1880–1968	1·9	83	67

* Ends 1963. Average width for 1830–1963, 1.7mm. Although referred to here as the curve for southern Germany to be consistent with the phraseology used in northern Germany and elsewhere, this curve derived at Munich[15] is in fact based on the hilly region to the east of the Rhine in the central part of West Germany.
† Similar values were obtained between these three mean curves (fig 2A) and that for the woodland Les Islettes in the Argonne Forest (fig 1) results for which have been given by Hollstein[14] for the years 1856–1966.

The agreement between English oaks and the hilly parts of Germany to which the Munich curve applies seems to depend more on altitude and slowness of growth than on geographical proximity. The similarities and differences between our two curves for southern England and the Munich curve (believed to be almost unaffected by caterpillar defoliation) are shown visually in fig 4. Common years of maximum growth are 1867, 1875, 1903, 1914, 1927 and 1936. However, during the warm period in the early decades of this century, the strong growth that characterised the German curve was absent in southern England due to the defoliation by caterpillars that occurred here.

Correlation of the mean curve (24 trees) for Berkshire—Hazelborough—Beechen extends not only to the Continent (table 3) but to Yorkshire. The agreement with a [mean curve (10 trees) recently obtained for that area by Ruth Jones is 65% over the years 1830–1923.

To provide a model for the growth of oaks in southern (and probably central) England one can postulate two main groups:

(a) Fast-grown trees sited on rich and moist soils and at low altitudes with growth often limited as much by caterpillar defoliation as by temperature or moisture stress

(b) Trees of slower growth, present in woodlands on drier soils or at higher altitudes, also affected to a greater or lesser extent by caterpillar defoliation, but with their growth influenced

(i) by temperature on the moister sites, particularly in periods when the climate was cold; and

(ii) by moisture-stress on the drier sites, particularly in periods when the climate was warm.

In terms of the changing climate to which Lamb has drawn our attention[17], the relative roles of insect defoliation, temperature and moisture stress may well change in any one woodland not only from site to site, but from year to year, from decade to decade and from century to century.

Saxon oaks

Was the growth pattern of oaks growing in southern England in Saxon times different from that of the present time? Woodland management was almost non-existent but doubtless there were late frosts to cause defoliation. There may have been defoliation by caterpillars and the similarities with the growth pattern of Continental oaks may have been greater or less than for recent growth.

It is too early to suggest answers to these problems on the basis of the oak timbers of Saxon origin brought so far to the attention of dendrochronologists. Godwin measured 80 ring-widths on the large oak post which formed part of the burial compartment of the Sutton Hoo ship[18]. Lowther examined 11 samples of oak from Hamwih—the Saxon forerunner of Southampton—and made a floating chronology of 120 years[19], a chronology which he and

Schove attempted to date by meterological evidence[20]. In addition, there are oak timbers from the royal mill of Old Windsor which have been measured.

The number of samples from these do not approach in quantity the 4,000 pieces of oak excavated from the Viking trading post of Haithabu near Schleswig (fig 1). From measurements of about 30,000 ring-widths on 200 of the larger pieces, Eckstein was able to identify successive building stages over a period of 120 years[6].

Our own research in this period has so far been confined to the large Middle Saxon cistern found at North Elmham, Norfolk; to the Graveney boat; and to timbers from oaks which grew in Saxon times though used in the 11th or 12th centuries.

Five planks from the cistern provided a ring-width curve of 215 years for an oak felled in 832 ± 30 A.D. (by radiocarbon dating) at an age of about 240 years[21]. The rings in this curve lie mainly between 1 and 2mm but there are troughs, similar to those in recent growth, covering four to ten annual rings and with rings less then 1mm wide. Indeed this type of pattern is shown by the curve for the Graveney boat[22] that was built, not necessarily in England, about 900 A.D.

Oaks which had been growing during much of the late Saxon period were cut down in the Norman period for use in buildings and furniture. Of particular interest are two large chests[23] now in the muniment room at Westminster Abbey, both known to be late Norman by decorative features. They are so long that the lids are in two parts. For the 12½ft (3.8m) long chest, there is a board on the lid which shows 312 annual rings over a length of 41cm. These rings are dated by the Munich curve to the years 850–1161 (W, 63.2% for overlap of 291 years). For the mean curve for three trees used for this chest, the agreement with the Munich curve is surprisingly good (W, 68.5%, for the years 976–1161).

Applications

Because so much of the European research on the dendrochronology of oak has been done in Germany, many in England are unfamiliar with the applications already achieved[24].

They include the dating (i) of building phases in medieval cathedrals (Trier, Speyer and Schleswig), in churches, in belfries and in other buildings[1] [14] [25]; (ii) of the construction of the medieval boat recovered from Bremen harbour; and (iii) of the phases of the Viking settlement at Haithabu. In art history, various conclusions about the chronological order and attribution of panel paintings have been derived from measurements on the edges of such works of art by Dutch and other painters[24].

Similar material, the quarter-sawn boards used for Tudor panel portraits, have formed the main subject of our research. The presence of 200 or more annual rings from trees of relatively slow growth make many such panels ideal for dendrochronology. From portraits dated from 1533 to 1569 we have made a standard curve from which undated portraits by unknown artists have been approximately dated. Information gained from the dated paintings about the number of annual rings cut off in making boards free from sapwood, as well as observations on trees of recent growth, agree with the findings of Hollstein[14] that the number of sapwood years is about 25 for oaks of 200–250 years.

Further developments

The results presented above deal with the *widths* of annual rings because German experience indicated that their study offered most promise for finding some reproducible pattern for oaks grown in southern England.

However, there are characteristics of the annual rings of oak which can usefully supplement ring-widths. One that we have noticed concerns an abnormality in the early wood vessels, normally from 0.3 to 0.4mm diameter. For occasional years the growth rings on boards derived from places far apart show few such large vessels but mainly small ones of less than 0.2mm diameter (Plate IV). This abnormality has been detected for 1433 A.D. on boards from 11 trees, though absent on boards from another 8 trees. Other years for which it has been noticed for several trees are 1344 and 1450.

Finally, a chronology based on late wood densities may prove useful in due course to supplement ring-widths in the dating of the fast grown timber used in buildings. Hitherto there has been no reliable dating of the density sequences derived for medieval oak at Oxford[26]. There is now the possibility that some of these can be matched against the standard ring-width curve that is being built up for southern England from panels and chests.

Acknowledgments

This research has been carried out with a grant to the University of Oxford from the Leverhulme Trust Fund. Mr F. S. Walker, Mrs Cholmondeley Tapper and Mrs Margery Mills have participated in much of it. Various owners of woodlands have permitted samples to be taken, while the foresters Mr H. Doman, Mr L. O. Birch and Mr M. C. Fletcher have assisted us in obtaining them and Mr P. Franklin and Mr I. Gourley of the Dept. of Forestry in cutting and polishing them. Our work in the Muniment Room at Westminister Abbey was facilitated by the Keeper, Mr N. H. MacMichael.

We are grateful to Frau V. Giertz of Munich for giving us numerical values for the southern German curve from 832 to 1963, this period covering years beyond those for which values have been published: also for the loan and permission to use results for sessile oaks in the Forest of Dean.

Helpful information and assistance has been received from members of the Dept. of Forestry at Oxford, in particular Dr E. W. Jones, Mr E. C. Dawkins, Miss J. Howse, together with Mr H. Wright, Mrs Ann McShane, Mrs Janet Jones and Miss Linda

Roberts of the computing section: also from Mr C. G. Smith of the Dept. of Geography.

REFERENCES

1. HUBER, B. and GIERTZ-SIEBENLIST, V. 'Central European dendrochronology for the Middle Ages', in Berger, R. (ed.) *Scientific Methods in Medieval Archaeology*, Univ. California Press, (1970), 201–21
2. BERGER, R., GIERTZ, V. and HORN, W. 'Can German tree-ring curves be applied in France and England?', *Vernac. Archit.*, **2** (1971), 3–6
3. ELLING, W. 'Untersuchungen über das Jahrringverhalten der Schwarzerle', *Flora*, **156B** (1966), 155–201
4. BAUCH, J., LIESE, W. and ECKSTEIN, D. 'Über die Altersbestimmung von Eichenholz in Norddeutschland mit Hilfe der Dendrochronologie', *Holz Roh-u. Werkstoff*, **25** (1967), 285–91
5. BARTHOLIN, T. S. 'An investigation of the possibility of dendrochonological dating of oak in Denmark', *Forst. ForsVaes. Danm.*, **33** (1973), 215–41
6. ECKSTEIN, D. and BAUCH, J. 'Beitrag zur Rationalisierung eines dendrochronologischen Verfahrens und zur Analyse seiner Aussagesicherheit', *Forstwiss. ZentBl.*, **88** (1969), 230–50
7. ROBINSON, R. L. 'Mortality amongst oak', *Q. Jl For.*, **21** (1927), 25–7
8. SATCHELL, J. E. 'Resistance in oak to defoliation by *Tortrix viridana*', *Ann. appl. Biol.*, **50** (1962), 431–42
9. VARLEY, G. C. and GRADWELL, G. R. 'Defoliation by caterpillars and timber production from oak trees in England', *11th Int. Congr. Ent.*, **2** (1962), 211–14
10. ELPHICK, G. P. *Sussex Bells and Belfries,* Chichester (1970), 210–20
11. DAY, W. R. and PEACE, T. R. *Spring Frosts* (ed. 2), *Bull. For. Commn, Lond.*, **18** (1946)
12. OSMASTON, L. S. 'Mortality amongst oak', *Q. Jl For.*, **21** (1927), 28–30
13. JONES, E. W. 'Climatic fluctuations 1890–1939', *Nature, Lond.*, **160** (1947), 479
14a. HOLLSTEIN, E. 'Jahrringchronologische Datierung von Eichenhölzern ohne Waldkante', *Bonnes Jb.*, **165** (1965), 12–27
   b. HOLLSTEIN, E. 'Die Abhangigkeit des dendrochronologische Datierung von Holzart, Holzqualitat und Konservierung', *Mitt. Bund-Forsch Anst. Forst-u. Holzw.*, Reinbek bei Hamburg, no 77 (1970), 31–42
15. HUBER, B. and GIERTZ-SIEBENLIST, V. 'Unsere tausendjährige Eichen-Jahrringchronologie durchschnittlich 57 (10–150)-fach belegt', *Sber. öst. Akad. Wiss. Abt.*, I, **178** (1969), 32–42
16. CHARLES, F. W. B. 'Dendrochronology', *Timb. Trades J.*, 1971 (30 Oct): Suppl. *Forestry and Home-Grown Timber*, 14–19
17. LAMB, H. H. 'Britain's changing climate', in Johnson, C. G. and Smith, L. P. (eds) *The Biological Significance of Climatic Changes in Britain*, Inst. Biol. Symposium, **14** (1965), 3–31
18. GODWIN, H. 'Timber from the Sutton Hoo Ship-burial', *Antiqu. J.*, **20** (1940), 200–1
19. LOWTHER, A. W. G. 'Saxon Timbers', *Proc. Hamps Fld Cl. Arch. Soc.*, **17** (1949–52), 129–33
20. SCHOVE, D. J. and LOWTHER, A. W. G. 'Tree-rings and Medieval Archaeology', *Med. Arch.*, **1** (1957), 78–95
21. WADE MARTINS, P., FLETCHER, J. and SWITSUR, R. 'North Elmham', *Current Arch.*, **4** (1973), 22–8
22. EVANS, A. C. and FENWICK, V. H. 'The Graveney Boat', *Antiquity*, **45** (1971), 89–96

23. RCHM,   *Westminster Abbey*, London (HMSO) (1924), 51
24. BAUCH, J. 'Anwendungen der Jahrringanalyse', *Angew. Bot.*, **45** (1971), 217–229
25. ECKSTEIN, D., BAUCH, J. and LIESE, W. 'Aufbau einer Jahrringchronologie von Eichenholz für die Datierung historischer Bauten in Norddeutschland', *Holzzentralblatt*, **96** (1970), 674–6
26. FLETCHER, J. M. and HUGHES, J. F. 'Uses of X-rays for density determinations and dendrochronology', *Bull. Fac. For. Univ. Br. Columbia*, **7** (1970), 41–54

GROWING OAK

M. J. Penistan

Forestry Commission, Cambridge

Introduction

'The monarch oak, the patriarch of trees
Springs rising up, then spreads by slow degrees
One hundred years he grows, one more he stays
Supreme in state, then in one more decays.'

after Dryden

It may seem strange to those who are dismayed at the preponderance of conifers in the renewed British woodland and forest that foresters in the Forestry Commission and elsewhere have experience of oak growing and that research into this is still carried out. As someone who has had a small part to play in growing oaks for timber and in conserving oakwoods as an environment, even in cutting back oaks to conserve a grassland environment, it is only right to acknowledge the example and instruction of many foresters in England and Wales and Scotland, both Commission and private men in the woods, and to thank the silviculturists of the Forestry Commission for data given, published and otherwise, from their experiments.

In preparing this contribution some reference has been made to earlier practitioners, to Evelyn[1], Haddington[2], Cobbet[3] and Brown[4]. It is remarkable how little practice has changed over three centuries. What follows is a personal assessment of practice and attempts to show how the oak grower should set about his task today.

TABLE 1

Area of oak woodland in Britain

Forestry Commission Census of Woodlands, 1965–7

Country	High Forest	Standards-over-coppice	Scrub	Total
England	140.9 (348.7)	9.8 (24·3)	15.1 (37.2)	165.8 (410.2)
Wales	13.9 (34.5)	—	15.0 (36.9)	28.9 (71.4)
Scotland	11.1 (27.5)	—	8.6 (21.6)	19.7 (49.1)
Total	165.9 (410.7)	9.8 (24.3)	38.7 (95.7)	214.4 (530.7)

Figures given are 1,000s of ha (1,000s of acres)

The growing stock

The Forestry Commission Census of Woodlands, 1965–7[5] gives these data. Oak (*Q. robur* and *Q. petraea*) occupies 13% of British high forest, behind Scots pine (*Pinus sylvestris* L.) 20% and Sitka spruce (*Picea sitchensis* (Bong) Carr.) 20%. It still ranks first in England (23%), is fourth in Wales (9%) and eighth in Scotland (2%). The areas occupied are given in table 1.

The area of oak worked actively as coppice is negligible at 160ha (400 acres) in Britain. The total oak woodland areas are still considerable, but the high forest age class distribution is far from normal; see table 2. Most standards-over-coppice are also old, as is much of the scrub.

TABLE 2

Age class distribution of oak high forest

Forestry Commission Census of Woodlands, 1965–7

Country and Conservancy	PW/FC	Planting Year Classes					
		1961+	1941–60	1921–40	1901–20	pre-1901	Total
England NW	PW	—	(1.0)	(0.9)	(3.4)	(40.3)	(45.6)
	FC	(0.1)	(0.8)	(0.2)	(0.2)	(0.8)	(2.1)
		(0.1)	(1.8)	(1.1)	(3.6)	(41.1)	(47.7)
NE	PW	—	(0.4)	(0.7)	(2.0)	(11.9)	(15.0)
	FC	—	(0.2)	(0.2)	(0.1)	(0.5)	(1.0)
		—	(0.6)	(0.9)	(2.1)	(12.4)	(16.0)
E	PW	—	(1.2)	(2.0)	(2.5)	(39.1)	(44.6)
	FC	(0.1)	(4.4)	(3.6)	(0.5)	(0.8)	(9.4)
		(0.1)	(5.6)	(5.6)	(3.0)	(39.9)	(54.0)
SE New	PW	(0.3)	(1.3)	(2.0)	(9.9)	(92.6)	(106.1)
	FC	(0.1)	(1.1)	(0.7)	(1.0)	(9.5)	(12.4)
		(0.4)	(2.4)	(2.7)	(10.9)	(102.1)	(118.5)
SW Dean	PW	—	(1.4)	(6.7)	(11.6)	(77.2)	(96.9)
	FC	(0.2)	(4.4)	(1.6)	(1.0)	(8.2)	(12.4)
		(0.2)	(5.8)	(8.3)	(12.6)	(85.4)	(109.3)
England	PW	0.1 (0.3)	2.1 (5.3)	5.0 (12.3)	11.9 (29.4)	105.6 (261.1)	124.6 (308.4)
	FC	0.2 (0.5)	4.4 (10.9)	2.5 (6.3)	1.1 (2.8)	8.0 (19.8)	16.3 (40.3)
		0.3 (0.8)	6.5 (16.2)	7.5 (18.6)	13.0 (32.2)	113.6 (280.9)	140.9 (348.7)
Wales	PW	— (0.1)	0.2 (0.6)	0.2 (0.5)	1.1 (2.7)	10.6 (26.3)	12.2 (30.2)
	FC	— (0.1)	0.6 (1.5)	0.1 (0.2)	0.2 (0.6)	0.8 (1.9)	1.7 (4.3)
		— (0.2)	0.8 (2.1)	0.3 (0.7)	1.3 (3.3)	11.4 (28.2)	13.9 (34.5)
Scotland	PW	— (0.1)	0.1 (0.3)	0.1 (0.3)	0.5 (1.3)	9.7 (24.0)	10.4 (26.0)
	FC	— —	0.1 (0.3)	0.1 (0.2)	0.2 (0.6)	0.2 (0.4)	0.6 (1.5)
		— (0.1)	0.2 (0.6)	0.2 (0.5)	0.7 (1.9)	9.9 (24.4)	11.0 (27.5)
Great Britain	PW	0.2 (0.5)	2.5 (6.2)	5.3 (13.1)	13.5 (33.4)	125.9 (301.4)	147.4 (364.6)
	FC	0.2 (0.6)	5.1 (12.7)	2.7 (6.7)	1.6 (4.0)	8.9 (22.1)	18.5 (46.1)
		0.4 (1.1)	7.6 (18.9)	8.0 (19.8)	15.1 (37.4)	134.8 (323.5)	165.9 (410.7)

PW=Private woodlands   FC=Forestry Commission woodlands

Figures given are 1,000s of ha (1,000 of acres)

Two points can be stressed: the vast majority (81%) of the growing stock is older than 65 years, and the area of the younger stands is greater in the Forestry Commission forests than in private woodland, though both are minute in terms of the whole and imposed economic policy may have reduced the area of the Forestry Commission holding, but not greatly.

It would be useful to look at the age of the very large proportion of the pre–1900 growing stock, the youngest stands of which are a mere seventy years old. About two thirds of this area is in the 1861–1900 class and one third older[6]. Fig 1 shows diagrammatically the age class distribution of native oaks in Britain.

FIGURE 1

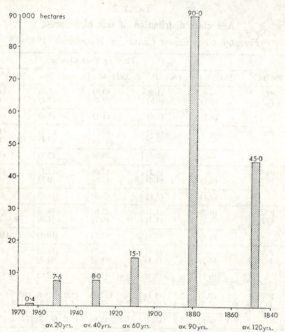

Age and area distribution of oak high forest.
Forestry Commission census of woodlands, 1965–7

While Dryden's original verse gives a three-century span to each of the stages of the growth of oak, my modified lines at the beginning of this paper use a sylviculturally more accurate span for each of 100 years. It can be said that 40,000 ha (100,000 acres) of the growing stock are no longer rising up and that 80,000 ha (200,000 acres) are coming to the end of that stage. Further it must be borne in mind that almost all the oakwoods have been combed through for good quality timbers: the number of really good quality stands of oak is very small. The 1947–9 census showed only

565 ha (1,400 acres) as elite. At present the Forest Tree Seed Association has only nine registered seed stands, a different classification, and probably of a much higher standard. There has not been much recent interest in registered seed, though in 1973, under European Economic Community rules, all seed must be from a registered source of good quality, and the woods on the 1949 list need to be looked at again. There are still, however, many good quality, straight, vigorous trees of reasonable age in Britain, not necessarily in woodlands but in the policy woodlands of mansion houses, and our growing stock, although ageing, is by no means completely moribund. While the young stands are a very small proportion of the growing stock there is still the prospect of managing them and conserving them for future supplies of seed, while the development of tree banks and seed orchards makes it possible, as well as desirable, to ensure the future of oak planting material of the highest quality.

Oak as a hedgerow tree

Hedgerows are aptly described as linear woodland and hedgerow trees can be said to be standards over linear coppice. They certainly were managed in the same way; enough saplings or tellers being selected to grow on to timber at each hedge laying and the stock of trees being managed to secure a succession of timber. Just as oak has been the commonest timber tree in coppice, so it is in hedgerows, even though it has no suckering habit, as has elm.

The Forestry Commission took a census of hedgerow and park timber in 1950–51[13] and again in 1965-67[5] . Both were systematic strip samples and results have only been published by countries (see table 3).

TABLE 3

Quantities of hedgerow timber by countries in millions of cubic metres 1951
(millions of Hoppus cubic feet)

	England	Wales	Scotland	Great Britain
All species	2.05 (55.7)	0.38 (10.8)	0.26 (6.7)	2.69 (73.3)
Percent of Total	84	11	5	100
Percent oak in Total	31.4	31.2	24.2	31.0
Order of occurrence	1st	1st	2nd to beech (25.7%)	1st

The results in 1965-67 were of the same order except in SE England, where the area of woodland lost to housing resulted in a large increase in the volume of hedgerow and park timber, much of which would be oak. Size class distribution by volume was broken down to species in 1950-51 only. Oak is less well represented in the smaller size classes.

No differentiation was made between the two native species. It can be assumed however, that *Q. robur* is in most cases the hedgerow tree with *Q. petraea* occurring only as relict woodland standards in the Welsh marches.

The 1965-67 report made a comparison between the distribution of hedgerow trees by size classes for the two censuses as follows:

Year	Saplings	Small	Timber Classes Medium	Large	Total	Shorts	Total
1951	31	18	22	22	62	7	100
1965-67	23	28	23	22	73	4	100

While the medium and large classes correspond, there has been a substantial movement from saplings to small timbers with no compensating replacement of saplings. This does not augur well.

The 1951 Report gives in discussion oak as the principal tree with ash in the north-west of England, though it does poorly compared with elm and sycamore in the industrial areas. It dominates the hedgerows of the Cheshire Plain. In the lowland of the north-east there is much good oak, with ash, sycamore and beech. It was the chief tree in the midland vale where clay is heavy and in Norfolk and Suffolk but in the midlands gives way to ash on the wolds and elm in alluvial areas. It predominates in the south-east and south-west except on calcareous sites and loamy vale soils.

The Census reports give no data on health. A rather homespun sample[14] taken in summer 1972 in eastern England showed oaks to be deteriorating to a greater extent than other species. The oak in Norfolk particularly is in a bad way. However, oak more than most species survives with a good deal of dead timber in the crown, though it cannot be considered, any more than much other hedgerow timber, to be a particularly long term feature of the landscape. Nevertheless, the present growing stock is a large and useable resource, but as in woodland oak, it is an ageing one (see table 4).

While recruitment of oak in hedgerows is rare, it colonises in the absence of rabbits the wide verges of lesser country roads in clay areas among the strong growth of thorns, and there is scope for its acceptance and husbanding there.

The form of oaks

In the past oak has been used chiefly in Britain for construction work. While it is present in beams of large span in cathedrals, much of it was relatively short and stout. Certainly, in its use for ships a shorter bole and massive crown was favoured. More or less free growth as standards over coppice provided what was needed and stocking in such places as the Forest of Dean was open to secure this form. The large-scale reafforesting of the Dean from 1820 to 1850 to produce naval oak misfired in the face of iron ships and since then production of a longer bole and less crooked limb has been favoured. At the present day it is these oaks with longer stems which meet the

TABLE 4

Status of oak hedgerows in counties in East England, July 1972

County	% Oak			All species			% Oak of total trees	Most plentiful other spp.
	Good	Stag-headed	Dead	Good	Stag-headed	Dead		
Lincoln	73	21	6	87	11	2	8	Ash 32%
Rutland	65	23	12	85	10	5	10	Ash 58%
Huntingdon	58	39	3	70	28	2	11	Elm 46%
Northampton	54	43	3	85	14	1	7	Elm 41%
Oxford	80	18	2	89	11	1	12	Elm 44%
Buckingham	82	17	1	90	10	—	13	Elm 42%
Hertford	61	34	5	82	15	3	21	Elm 32%
Cambridge	66	30	4	89	10	1	10	Poplars etc. 43%
Norfolk	27	66	7	49	45	6	52	Elm 14%
Suffolk	72	25	3	82	15	8	31	Elm 34%
Essex	85	12	3	80	11	9	21	Elm 43%
All counties	56	39	5	80	17	3	20	Elm 33%

demand for oak timber in Europe. These are the trees sought by the forester for registration as seed sources for the production of high-quality wood: straight grained, well figured and of reasonable girth. The tendency to greater height growth, longer bole and simpler, more straight-branched crown in *Q. petraea* makes it preferable in current conditions.

Collection of mast

Oaks bear their first good crops when between 40 and 80 years old and are in full production when between 80 and 120 years. Today the mast of *Q. petraea* is preferred. The acorn is often smaller than in *Q. robur* which may well have been preferred traditionally for its heavier cropping for pannage. Mast is collected from the ground below trees of good quality—from stands which must in future be registered under EEC rules. The usual method is to spread tarpaulins, or to rake the ground clear of litter. Care in collecting is obviously well worth while. Hand picking avoids further cleaning and helps storage. Woodpigeons and rodents collect the seed at the same time, and jays, in addition to eating some, plant others. Hessian slung hammockwise off the ground provides protection against animals where mast is of special value.

The mast is produced in quantity fairly regularly, though there are occasional blank years such as 1972. *Q. robur* is a better producer than *Q. petraea*. Good yields occur every two to four years in *Q. robur* and three to five years in *Q. petraea*. It should be transported in open-woven hessian sacks and tipped onto a concrete floor under cover until it can be sown.

The mast of *Q. petraea* may number between 130 and 500 per kg (60 and 220 per lb), that of *Q. robur* between 110 and 450 per kg (50 and 200 per lb)[7].

Nursery practice

1. Storing the mast

If immediate sowing is not possible acorns can be stored through the winter. Mast will heat if stored in quantity so should be regularly turned. It should be protected from rats and mice, and from the weather. They will often 'chit' or sprout the radicle, but this is no disadvantage.

2. Sowing and seedbed management

It is best to sow as soon as possible after collection in a normal light nursery soil of good fertility and pH 5.5 to 6.5. Acorns should be covered with 5cm (2in) of soil but are vulnerable at this depth to mice and pheasants. However there is a traditional method of protection which has proved completely successful in extensive sowings at Savernake and can be generally recommended (see Plate IV). Prepare beds about 1m wide (the inside track of a small tractor) by ploughing or throwing up soil from the alleys. Cuff off 5cm (2in) of soil. Sow the acorns at about 300 to the metre run (250 to the yard) and cuff back the soil to give 5cm cover. The finished bed should then be covered with a 6mm ($\frac{1}{4}$in) layer of sawdust and a further 10cm (4in) of soil dug out of the alleys between the beds and spread over the sawdust. This masks the presence of acorns to birds and mice. In late April the mast should be tested for the full emergence of the radicle and, when this is 5cm (2in) long, the top cover should be cuffed off to the sawdust, leaving the bed ready for the emergence of the apparently naked plumule.

3. Seedling management

By the end of the growing season the seedbed should yield some 180 seedlings per metre run 20–30cm (8–12in) high. They should be protected against late spring frost in this first season by lath cover into June. They may need spraying with 4kg in 1,000 l of water per ha of colloidal sulphur (3pt in 100 gall) on both sides of the leaves to control oak mildew (*Microsphaera alphitoides* Griff. & Maubl.) which can weaken seedlings (or transplants). *Q. robur* is more susceptible than *Q. petraea*. At the end of the first growing season the plant will have a 30cm (12in) tap root.

4. Planting stock

Practice varies. In clean, recently felled ground, strong one year seedlings with intact taptoots which can be expected to continue development after planting are preferable. The root of a two-year seedling below its 20–30cm (8–12in) or more stem will be broken (with some difficulty) in lifting. It is preferable to undercut two year stock early in the second season. This will produce a stout plant for less clean ground. Otherwise a transplanted one year seedling after a season's growth will produce a good 30cm (12in) high stem on a truncated but regenerating tap root and fairly fibrous system as well. The well developed tap root of oak makes the plant relatively hardy in movement and it survives planting well. Larger stock, up to 60–75cm (24–30in) must be transplanted annually to provide a compact, fibrous root system. Oak should rarely be planted as anything larger than 75cm (30in) and half that height is better, and very much cheaper. Feathers and standards are for landscape and ornamental work.

Direct sowing

This can be done when large quantities of mast are available and has taken the form of setting acorns close together along furrows ploughed at planting line distances, 1.5m (5ft) apart and ploughing back the slice. The large quantity apparently defeats the acorn feeders and long lines of very closely spaced small trees result. When the need to use mast of good provenance to the best effect is recalled, line sowing in woodland is wasteful.

The tending of young plantations

Apart from protection against wildlife, young oaks need help against competition from swamping weed growth and a degree of shelter from spring frosts. Discreet weeding is necessary to ensure full vigour in the first two years. Plants tend to become bushy at this stage and the traditional treatment of cutting back to ground level in winter is well worthwhile, a straight vigorous shoot resulting which will usually hold its own with woody regrowth.

With vigour thus ensured, side shade and side competition, provided the crown is open to full light, will stimulate height growth while the tree 'springs rising up'. A study of the development of oak saplings in natural regrowth shows this and is the foundation of the New Forest saying that 'the thorn is mother to the oak'. So is birch further north, as well as other woody plants less palatable to browsing animals. Shrub willows, *Salix caprea* L. and *S. atrocinerea* Brot. can be overpowering, however, and while the skill in tending oak involves chiefly knowing how little release is needed, it is obviously unwise not to keep an eye on competing growth.

Once the canopy has been formed, oak almost completely supresses ground vegetation. Smaller twigs, close to the stem, with no heart die quickly and tend to fall away on their own. Larger branches leave rotting stubs and these may need pruning from the best-formed predominant trees which are being grown on, particularly on free-grown stems.

While oak in the thicket stage appears to respond well in form and to some extent height from competition, this tolerance begins to lessen with height and from 7.5m (25ft) onwards, the long crown necessary to vigorous growth begins to decrease. At some 10m (33ft) it is necessary to give more space to the crowns of better trees by thinning if growth is to be maintained and particularly for the crown/root balance to be kept. The style of thinning, therefore, is at first a crown thinning, giving space for the maintenance in depth of crown as well as its lateral extension. For continued balanced growth a limited number of predominants is favoured—not more than 150 to the ha (60 per acre), this number being reduced as soon as possible to 100 to the ha (40 per acre), by sixty years, when there should be little need for further thinning. Should the crowns be compacted and reduced through competition, and the lower crown level pass up the stem faster than the crown extends upwards, subsequent thinning leads to the formation of adventitious stem shoots—epicormic branches, an undesirable feature in timber and an unsatisfactory contributor to growth. The forester must, therefore, so thin as to avoid this undesirable reaction by the tree. It is thought by some that tendency to epicormic production is inherited. Certainly some vigorous individuals are less prone and *Q. petraea* is generally less prone than *Q. robur*. The best seed sources tend to have reached their excellence from better vigour and tolerance of competition and therefore seem to have less tendency to epicormic branching.

Productivity

The need to maintain the vigour and production of the best stems in an oak stand of diminishing tolerance results in wider spacing and lighter stocking. Oak is not a rapid grower in height compared with other broadleaves and most conifers. This and its lighter stocking results in lower productivity. This is seen in table 5 which shows height growth for the maincrop after thinning of the average productivities in British private woodlands[8]. Oak and beech are least productive and oak takes longest to reach its maximum productivity in terms of volume production alone. This low productivity and the knowledge that oak responds to competition in youth has led throughout the history of replanting in Britain to the

TABLE 5

Height growth of some trees of average productivity in British private woodlands at thirty, forty and fifty years

Species	Average yield class	Maincrop height in metres		
		30 years	40 years	50 years
Pseudotsuga menziesii, Douglas fir	14	17.9	22.8	26.5
Thuja plicata, Red cedar	12	11.8	15.5	18.4
Picea abies, Norway spruce	11	11.7	15.1	18.7
Pinus nigra subsp. *laricio,* Corsican pine	11	12.7	16.3	19.3
Pinus sylvestris, Scots pine	8	10.3	13.5	16.3
Larix decidua, European larch	7	13.9	17.1	19.6
Larix kaempferi, Japanese larch	9	15.4	18.5	20.8
Fagus sylvatica, Beech	6	11.4	14.6	17.1
Quercus spp., Oak	4	9.6	12.3	14.5
Quercus spp., Oak (better sites)	6	12.2	15.4	18.1

use of 'nurse' trees which provide side shade. There was an old Scots saying 'Larch will buy the horse, oak the saddle'. The trees attendant on the oak were the European conifers, Scots pine (*Pinus sylvestris* L.), Norway spruce (*Picea abies* (L.) Karsten) and European larch (*Larix decidua* Mill.). These have a more compatible height growth with oak then have the American conifers, though the columnar habit of Western red cedar (*Thuja plicata* D. Don) and Lawson cypress (*Chamaecyparis lawsoniana* (A. Murray) Parl.) is less aggressive than the firs, spruces and hemlocks. Table 5 is not an absolute comparison but shows well enough how stands of oak need release from over-topping by nursing species comparatively early in their life.

Observation and calculation indicates a desirable final stand spacing of oak of not more than 100 stems per ha (40 stems per acre) at a spacing of 10m (33ft): plantations of oak and a matrix of compatible nurses maturing or at least reaching saleable size quickly should be laid out with this in mind (see fig 2). The most productive, with least oak, would consist of groups of nine or sixteen small plants at 12m (40ft) centres in a conifer matrix. A safer pattern would prescribe double the number of groups suitably disposed. A solution providing a broadleaf middle-aged stand is to use lines or bands of oaks alternately with bands of conifers. It is desirable to have at least three rows in each band and in the early stage of tending, a whole row of nurses can be removed, while the oak band can grow on and provide scope for selection of the best stems at wide spacing. From the point of view of fine timber production a limited number of oaks of chosen proved provenance would suffice. To provide landscape or habitat more oaks are desirable and bands preferable, though this can waste a fine provenance unduly while it is in short supply. Larches, being rapid early growers easily marketed and attractive in landscape are good nurses, particularly European larch of chosen provenance. Japanese larch (*L. kaempferi*) or hybrid larch (*L.×eurolepis*) need to be separated by a 'blank' line from the oak bands. On a standard inter-row spacing of 2m oaks would be planted 1m apart in the lines, there would be a gap of 3–4m then three or four lines each 2m apart of nurses planted 2m apart down the lines, giving 12m centre to centre between oak rows. Another possibility is to plant only the middle line of the 12m oak band. There is some evidence that as good a nursing effect results, provided the middle, planted row is closely spaced. The choice of nursery or matrix trees has been discussed by Darrah and Dodds[9]. In addition to compatible height growth, a discreet branching habit is needed. In this respect, Norway spruce, Western red cedar and Lawson cypress are prefereable to the pines.

The Forestry Commission has a number of experiments to test the production of pure oak plantations at a range of spacings and in mixture with conifers, chiefly European larch. These show best form at closer spacings up to 1·4m × 1·4m (5ft × 5ft) at thirty five years, with a fall in height at this spacing; 2·0m × 2·0m (6ft × 6ft)

FIGURE 2

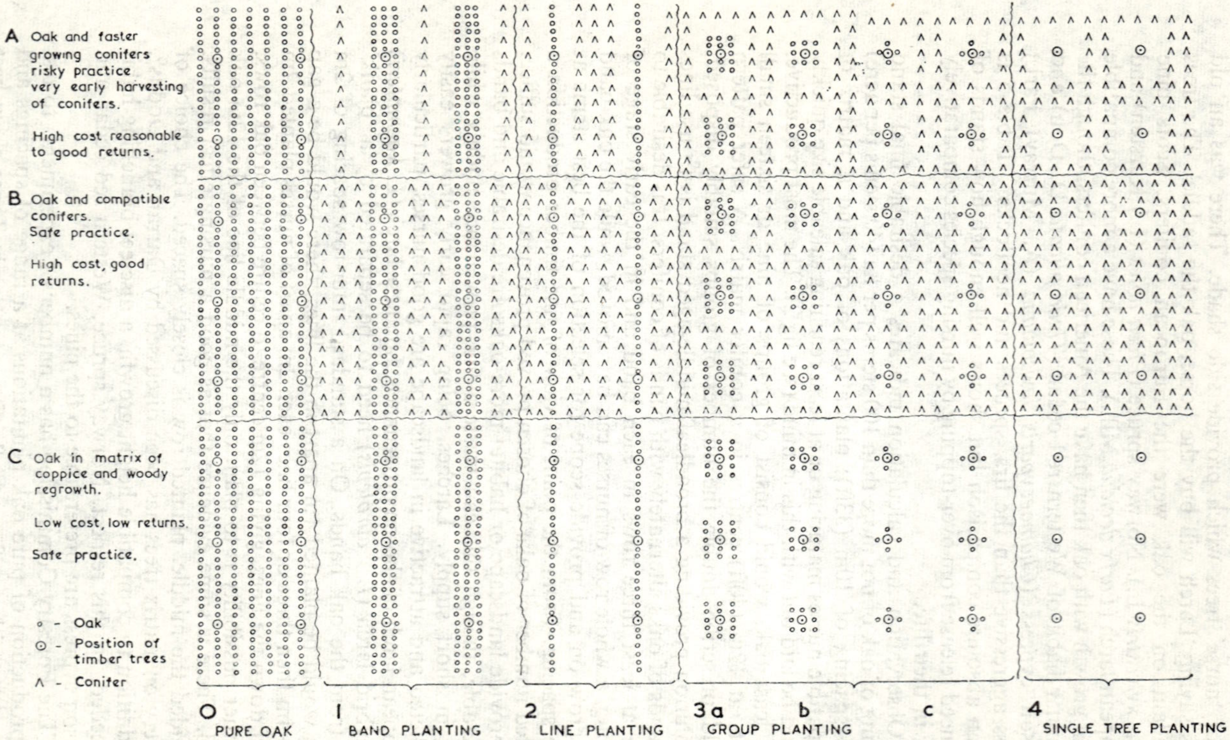
A Oak and faster growing conifers risky practice very early harvesting of conifers.
High cost reasonable to good returns.
B Oak and compatible conifers. Safe practice.
High cost, good returns.
C Oak in matrix of coppice and woody regrowth.
Low cost, low returns.
Safe practice.
∘ - Oak
⊙ - Position of timber trees
Λ - Conifer
0 PURE OAK
1 BAND PLANTING
2 LINE PLANTING
3a b c GROUP PLANTING
4 SINGLE TREE PLANTING

The options open to the grower of oak form (0) pure planting, to (4) single tree planting at mature tree spacing, with matrices of (A) conifer nurses of fast, incompatible rates of growth, (B) conifer nurses of slower, compatible rates of growth, and of (C) coppice and adventitious broadleaf trees and shrubs. Roughly to scale with mature trees at 100 metre spacing. Preferred options for the forester are B1, B2b and B2c for greater production, and C3a, C3b and C3c for safe results, low input and least spacing shows better girth, however, but poorer form. At age thirty five group plantings at 100 to the ha (40 per acre) of oak have had almost all of the larch removed leaving good stands of oak developing.

Free growth

In present day conditions of expensive money, treatments to reduce the time for oak to reach a useful size have attracted experimentation. Oak timber from standards grown above coppice in relatively free growth is known to be of good quality. Free growth has been studied since 1950 by the Commission but the basic observations by Hummel were published in 1951[10] and it is worth summarising four of his findings:

1. Timber height in free-grown oak is usually low and green pruning is essential.
2. The average crown diameter in feet (C) of free-grown oaks is equal to twice the breast height quarter in inches (G) plus a constant of 4, i.e. $C=2G+4$. This relationship is independent of height and age. In metric terms this is about $C_m = 0.2D_{cm}+1.2$ (where D=diameter).
3. Free-grown oaks may reach 25in quarter girth at breast height—81cm (32in) diameter in 100 years on exceptional sites and 65cm (26in) on favourable ones. The current growth culminates long after 100 years—rotations could be 150 years.
4. A very small number of young trees per acre is enough to give full stocking at maturity. Twenty six trees on a favourable site (Quality Class II, metric yield class 5) will completely cover the ground at maturity.

Three sets of plots in the Welsh marches at Crumbland, Tintern, and in Hampshire at Alice Holt and Micheldever established in 1950 and 1956 have enabled these conclusions to be reached[11]. 'While volume production is reduced, the value of the stand is increased and the reduced time to achieve saleable sizes is a distinct advantage financially'. Lorraine Smith[13] has confirmed that the yield from investment in conventionally managed oak plantations is less than 3% and this figure is only reached when complementary revenue is included. Extra revenue is independent of free growth treatment which will increase the financial yield. The investment in pruning to 7m and the reduction of early returns they estimate will yield 4%. Apart from pure stands, which are likely to be rare, it is considered that free growth of oak can be practised in any reasonable stocked pole-stage stand with sixty well-spaced vigorous straight oaks per ha (25 per acre). 'The woods managed on free growth techniques are unlikely to be noticeably different in their external appearance... Internally, the sight of well-spaced, well-grown trees should please at least all true foresters while the increased light to the forest floor could well ensure a more prolific shrub and small tree layer,... which is likely to be welcomed from the point of view of wildlife habitat.'

A final possibility is the use of spontaneous woody regrowth of any species following felling as a matrix for group replanting of oak. This has the advantage of a low initial input of resources but the disadvantage of a very small return for many years, and is no more rewarding than the conventional group or band mixtures which cost more but yield more. The discounted expenses exclusive of management expenses are respectively £308 and £375 per ha over 120 years, and the discounted revenues £10 and £85 in recent calculations in East England, though these have not taken Hummel's calculated growth into account.

Protection

Young stands of oak are browsed by rabbits and deer. The first have been controlled without exclusion in many cases since the myxomatosis outbreak, and there has been much natural extension of oak by jay-planting in uncultivated and ungrazed grass and heath. Deer can in most circumstances be controlled by planned culling, but in some cases, as with rabbits, expensive excluding fences are needed. Grey squirrels very seriously damage oak by stem barking when their populations are high after a good breeding season Defoliation by caterpillars is endemic, particularly in *Q. robur* but is rarely damaging (see pps 182–192). The relatively thick leaves of *Q. petraea* are more resistant. Frosting will stunt oak plants and frost hollows must be avoided. Oak is host to many fungi and most of these are saprophytic, needing some predisposing condition of ill-health or ill-management before they are damaging (see pps 235–248). The most serious of these is the heart rot, *Stereum gausapatum* (Fr.) Fr., which reduces the timber value of trees with well developed crowns which are later partially killed by competition.

Stand forms

This paper has been concerned chiefly with the creation and management of even-aged stands of maiden trees, or apparently maiden trees. Many sessile oaks of good form in maturity, particularly in the upland west and north have been 'stored' or singled from vigorous coppice. A study of such stands will show quite often a population of trees of age-steps equal to the coppice rotation, probably twenty years. The best current growth rate is invariably on the best-crowned trees of whatever age and one doubts whether the selections made at intervals after the first have ever had much chance to grow. Certainly they are unable to react quickly to further growth if the pre-eminent trees are felled. There appears to be no future for economic oak coppice and only 160ha were picked up in the sample census of 1967. Similarly, all-aged stands *with a close canopy* are unlikely in the future. The all-aged open stocking of standards-over-coppice, too, would appear to have little future beyond the examples carefully and rightly maintained by nature conservationists, unless the re-establishment of oak by spaced groups, subsequently managed for free growth, permits partial harvesting and restocking in larger woodlands. Even here the likely need to protect new stands against browsing would favour larger stands rather than very small plots of new trees.

Natural regeneration

To obtain natural regeneration the forester needs copious seed (to overfeed animals) of desirable quality, a receptive seedbed, a ready market for timber and much skill and patience. There have been some signal successes in Britain; Blakeney Walk in the Forest of Dean, for instance in the early 1900s, yielded many ha of seedlings after a record mast and is now a fine oakwood. Cultivation of a seed bed by controlled pannage is still possible in the Forest of Dean and the New Forest, but the regeneration of oak naturally is today incidental to restocking: patches being welcomed by foresters and used, but not awaited in patience over a decade.

Sites

The extent of oakwoods in hill country is now so limited that, whether it be scrub or of good form, there is good cause for conserving and regenerating it for the landscape and above all for the habitat it provides. Where grazed and consequently rendered stagnant, regeneration is impossible and the control of browsing is essential. All sites can well be managed on a low input basis, but consideration must be given to restoring vigour by introducing good strains of *Q. petraea*. In some cases genetic considerations might preclude this. Some very acid sites with a past history of coppice working which has led to the removal of all but the leaves of the crop for charcoal, stakes, spars, bark and faggots, with a subsequent gleaning by sticking women, have become 'oak sick'. Oakwood conservation projects here could well include nutrients. In lowland country, too, site would seem to be less important than maintaining what is left. Oak will grow on most sites of reasonable soil depth, say over 30cm (12in). Frost hollows should be avoided. However, the need would appear to be to restore the growing stock in areas where growth will be faster rather than slower and where the relatively expensive stock of good provenance will flourish. In times of high money cost all forestry will not yield commensurately with the going rate of interest, and must be subsidised. Good productivity can be got at relatively low cost with conifers on comparatively poor upland sites. The small patches of steeper land unhandy to plough in lowland Britain which in the past has often produced the finest oak should carry a proportion again. Similarly, woodland in the clay vales, notoriously expensive to stock productively, and much of other lowland wood, whether on primary unploughed sites or not, should have its proportion of oak planted. This should be oak capable of producing high quality wood as well as forming a landscape and a habitat. We shall hardly be able to replace the vast area of aging oak which is our present heritage but we should devote to oak growing, to the conserving of oak sites as productively as possible, a proportion of every oak wood or stand where it exists today, and particularly where it flourishes.

Growing oak is a stately business. It is a good subject for the silviculturist, quick to take form, slower to mature. We are unlikely to produce it in quantity in future, but we can and shall produce quality which, a hunderd years from now, or less, is certain to be admired and valued for itself as well as for the habitat it provides for all life, man included.

REFERENCES

1. EVELYN, JOHN. *Silva, A Discourse of Forest Trees*, (1664)
2. HADDINGTON, THOMAS, SIXTH EARL OF (1761), *Forest Trees*, ed. Anderson, M. L., (1953). London and Edinburgh
3. COBBETT, WILLIAM. *The Woodlands*, (1825)
4. BROWN, JAMES. *The Forester*, ed. Nisbet, John, (1894)
5. Forestry Commission. *Census of Woodlands, 1965–7*, (1970)
6. Forestry Commission. *Census Report No. 1, Census of Woodlands 1947–9, Woodlands of Five Acres and over*, (1952)
7. ALDHOUS, J. R., *Nursery Practice*, Forestry Commission Bulletin No. 43, (1972)
8. Forestry Commission, Planning & Economics Branch, Management Services Division. *Analysis of Growing Stock in Forestry Commission and Private Woodlands*, (1971), Table 15
9. DARRAH, G. V. and DODDS, J. W. 'Growing broadleaves in mixture with conifers', *Forestry*, 49 (1967), 220–9
10. HUMMEL, F. C. *Forestry Commission Report on Forest Research for the Year ending March 1950*, (1951) 65–6
11. JOBLING, J., PEARCE, M. L. and SMALL, PAMELA A. 'Free growth of oak', in *Broadleaves in British Forestry*, Forestry Commission Bulletin, (1974) (at press)
12. LORRAINE SMITH, R. 'Economic problems of growing hardwoods in Great Britain', Paper to British Association for the Advancement of Science, Section K*, Leicester 1972
13. Forestry Commission. *Census Report No. 2, Hedgerow and Park Timber and Woods under Five Acres 1951*, (1953)
14. Forestry Commission. 'A Hedgerow Tree Survey in East England Conservancy 1972', a circulated report by East England Conservancy

PLATE I

Above

An overturned oak in the fen oak-wood growing over deep peat at Calthorpe Board, Norfolk: other standing oaks in the background. Overthrow is facilitated by the shallow horizontal growth of roots above the high water table.

Photo: *H. Godwin*

Below

Trunk of a 'bog-oak' that grew in the Neolithic Period on the Jurassic clay of the Fenland basin near Ely, Cambridgeshire. Its long unbranched bole shows that it developed in high forest. It was entombed by peat that formed as incipient marine transgression caused water-logging. Its radiocarbon age is 4495 ± 120 years.

Photo: *John Slater*

PLATE II

A manorial wood of Bury St Edmund's Abbey, still managed as in the middle ages. Oaks, of mixed ages from about 70 years downwards, are scattered in underwood of many different species which is cut on an average rotation of 11 years. Felsham Hall Wood (Bradfield Woods). Photo. *O. Rackham*

PLATE III

A typical stand of oak in ancient woodland, revealed by cutting the underwood. The oaks are mostly between 100 and 200 years old. There has been little or no felling or replacement for 50 years. About 20 oaks per acre. Note the extreme variation (which exists also in Felsham Hall Wood) in habit and shape, trunk burrs, density of twigs, time of leaf-fall, etc. Hayley Wood. Photo. *W. H. Palmer*

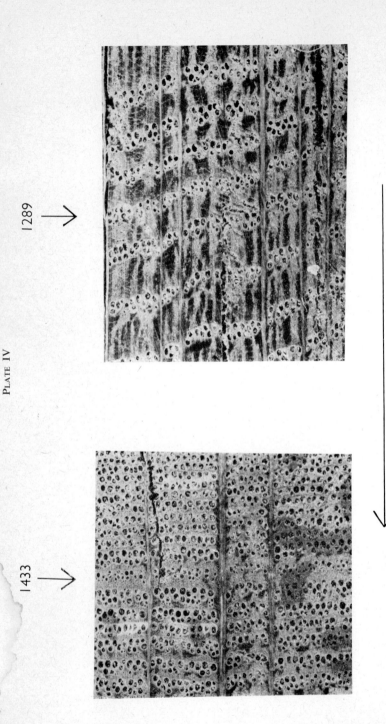

PLATE IV

1289 →

1433 →

Direction of growth

Edge of Door A9 of Cupboard of c 1518 made for Corpus Christi College, Oxford showing early wood with small vessels for the years 1289 and 1433 A.D. *Clarendon Laboratory, Oxford* *Photo.*
magnification × 6

PLATE V

Sowing acorns—Savernake Forest 1960

Drills have been drawn down a 1 metre wide seedbed by a tractor whose wheels form the alleys. Acorns have been sown 5 cm apart in the drills at 5 cm depth. The drills are then closed by rakes and the bed rolled by hand. A thin layer of sawdust is then spread over the bed and a further 10 cm of soil is dug by hand from the alleys and spread over the sawdust. This is enough to deter birds and mice. When germination begins in spring, the 10 cm layer is cuffed back into the alleys, down to the sawdust level, and the acorns can develop. Photo. *M. Penistan*

PLATE VI

Heterophylly in a variety of oak. Shoot from 20 year old tree of *Q. petraea* var *laciniata,* showing narrow, irregularly incised leaves on the first flush, while the second flush leaves are normal (apart from damage to the 4th and 6th leaf). Note also the abscission layer at the base of the first flush. (From H. L. Späth[210]

PLATE VII

Above

Oak mildew, *Microsphaera alphitoides,* on oak leaves showing the white, mainly external mycelium.

Below

Oak mildew, *Microsphaera alphitoides*. Enlarged view of surface of diseased leaf showing ascocarps (c × 20). The latter vary from about 30–100μ in diameter.

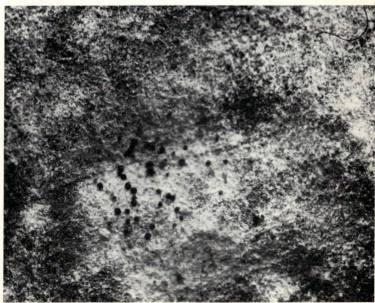

Photos: *Forestry Commission*

Plate VIII

Oak dieback: hedgerow specimens of *Q. robur* in Norfolk showing type of die back described by Young (1965).

Photo: *Forestry Commission*

USES OF OAK, PAST AND PRESENT

C. J. VENABLES

Castletown Sawmills, Stafford.

Oak in the past

As I am not an historian nor an architect I can only speak to you on the uses of oak timber past, present and future from a life times experience as a homegrown-timber merchant—first of all sawing and preparing native oak for repairs, restorations, alterations to and additions to old buildings, ships, and wind and water mills—then sawing oak for the many uses for which it was the accepted raw material from the turn of the century right up to the second world war—and now sawing, seasoning and machining oak for the purposes for which it is now being used and for which I see a steady demand in the future.

My childhood days were spent in the timber yard. We lived in one of the houses within its boundries. It was divided into two by what was then a country lane which has now become a busy thoroughfare. On the south side of this lane was the sawmill built in 1883 after the previous mill had been burnt to the ground in 1882. In front of the mill there was roughly three acres of land on which were piled the logs drawn in by horses and steam engines to meet the requirements of the sawmill producing timbers for railways, canals, road vehicles, collieries, farm buildings and fencing. About 75% of this was oak. On the other side of the lane was another three acre yard on which were dumped large oak logs of all sorts of shapes. Some of them had been there as long as I could remember, for it was the custom then to attach the greatest importance to the length of time the logs had lain unsawn in the round. Stock taking was an unknown exercise in those days but my grandfather and my uncle knew practically every log as an individual and when orders came in for large, long or curved timbers for restoration or extension work in churches or historic buildings they knew pretty well where to go to find the right logs for the job. It was often a hard days work with men and horses with chains and pulley blocks and jacks to extract the logs from the piles and draw them up to the sawmill particularly if they happened to be at the bottom covered by other large logs whose weight had pushed them right into the ground. Practically all these logs had been felled in the early spring and stripped of their bark for tanning. There were in Stafford in those days over 20 shoe factories; all family businesses, small by modern standards. They were dependant for their oak tanned leather on the two tanyards who looked to my grandfather for their supplies of oak bark for curing the hides. The ring of sapwood on these logs had long since rotted away and to the uninitiated they looked like piles of rubbish through which grew blackberry brambles and beneath which free range hens reared their own clutches of chicks and our own variety of surface nesting rabbits enjoyed protection. But the heartwood was as sound as ever and though the moisture content was still high a great deal of maturing and stabilisation had taken place. Nevertheless when large sections were sawn out of these old trees surface cracks would develop due to surface shrinkage as surely but perhaps not as quickly or as deeply as if they had been sawn from recently winter felled trees.

This led me to wonder if our forefathers, like many specifiers of oak today, asked for beams to be sawn from logs felled 6–8 years and to be free from heart and sapwood and knots. A lifetime of experience inspecting old oak framed buildings and examining members that through one cause and another have had to be replaced convinced me that they did not. They went out into the forest and selected the smallest trees that would roughly square up to the required dimensions with the minimum of adzing or sawing. Nor did they select the cleanest butts. They would thus produce a beam with the heart right down the centre. The inevitable knots would be smaller, from a smaller diameter tree. These knots would in any case only penetrate halfway through diminishing in size to nothing at the heart. The knots would also serve to prevent the equally inevitable drying cracks from running too far from end to end and for this very reason sound knots and burrs would be welcomed. For timbers not exposed to the weather they did not exclude sapwood. In other words they accepted the trees as they grew making full use of their pecularities in their use of individual pieces and in their over all design. For wind braces and crucks and similar curved members trees would be selected of approximately the right shape and they would be split down the heart in the forest immediately after felling (when splitting is comparatively easy) so that perfectly matching opposite members were obtained. The curved members required in building wooden ships were similarly selected but undoubtedly these were hauled to the saw-pit at the shipyard or the timber yard for conversion. In many cases beams and posts for framed houses in addition to being roughed out to size in the forest clearing would also be mortised and tennoned there and in many cases the whole buildings or sections of it would be erected there and then knocked down for transport to, and erection at, the building site.

The limitations of English oak as well as its hardness, strength and durability soon became known to our forefathers whose obsevation of the natural phenomena around them must have been very acute for them to have developed their techniques as they did. They would soon realise that while the sapwood was hard and durable if not exposed to the weather it would rapidly deteriorate under alternate wettings and dryings and particularly in contact with the soil at ground level.

So, eventually, crucks were not dug into the ground and framed buildings were based on large dimensioned sills laid on masonary or stonework well above ground level wherever possible. They would never have dreamed of setting oak fence posts in concrete right up to ground level. Also great care was taken with weathering and guttering. Hence the large overhang of the gables and the large projection of the rafters on the roof. All these features lent themselves to decoration by the wood carver and in the barge boards they were really able to let themselves go.

They would realise too that no power on earth could restrain the shrinkage as large beams dried out. They would come to appreciate that tangential shrinkage was greater than radial shrinkage and that end shrinkage was practically negligible. They knew that drying splits would develop on the tangential surface along the medullary rays towards the heart, and that if they made a tangential saw cut in an oak log on a hot summers day surface checks would develop at once which would close up in the next shower of rain and open up again in the sun or in a dry atmosphere. Consequently framed buildings were so designed as to accommodate shrinkage and timbers used for interior fittings were quarter sawn from large butts to ensure the minimum of movement and to avoid surface checks and splits. Later alterations involving the cutting of load bearing members or their complete removal have led to the distortion in the frames in many old buildings.

Added to this, failure particularly in recent years, to keep gutters and spouts clear led to wet penetrating into the inevitable cracks right into the hearts of the large members and into the joints, providing ideal conditions for dry rot and other forms of decay and then, eventually, death watch beetle.

The craftsmanship of the millwright as seen in the few surviving wind and water mills was developed to a fine art. Here again we find the use of natural curves where curves were required and the toleration in very large members of knots of very considerable size provided they were in such a place as not to weaken or cause distortion.

The wooden walls of old England too were not only things of beauty but masterpieces of utilisation of all the crooked shapes which an uninhibited oak tree can produce. In my Company's timber yard you can still see a pile of bent and crooked oak logs to which some of the few remaining wooden boat builders come for knees and crooks. Old building restorers too come for replacements for windbraces and other curved members.

Just before the First World War when part of Bristol University was being built the builders foreman carpenter spent quite a lot of his time at our sawmill watching the conversion of the large members required in the roof trusses there. This was a happy liaison for he knew where the inevitable knots, catspaws and cracks could be tolerated without weakening or affecting the strength or the decorative role of each member. Incidentally when Bristol suffered one of its more severe blitzes during the Second World War I happened to be on fire watching nearby and saw those same timbers charred and black still supporting the roof while many adjacent steel framed buildings collapsed leaving a tangled mass of twisted girders.

The high calorific value of oak as a fuel must have been well known to our forefathers. They would have learnt too that the steady heat of red glowing gleed was hotter and better for most purposes than high rising flames. From this the preparation of charcoal was the next step and many oak forests on the Welsh borders, in the midlands and near London were worked on a short coppicing rotation for fuel. In my own native Staffordshire we have the remains of charcoal fired glass furnaces sited in suitable glades of such forests to take advantage of prevailing winds where in the middle ages refugees from the continent set up their glass works. The charcoal was burnt under turves alongside the glass kilns. It was burned in this primitive way right up till the Second World War when production had to be supplemented by sectional iron furnaces that could be taken down and moved from forest to forest where suitable cordwood and small diameter poles were available.

The changing use of oak

Perhaps I have dwelt too long on the more distant past. Let us now consider the role of English oak from the industrial revolution right up till the Second World War. Take for instance the wheelwright's craft. The slender spokes in those beautiful carriages, cart and wagon wheels, were split out by hand from selected butts of tough oak, the knaves or hubs cross cut as sections from logs of suitable diameter drilled through the heart and stored for months of seasoning before finally turned to size. Then the dressed spokes were driven firmly into the mortice holes and iron hoops white hot from the forge were driven tightly onto either side of the hubs. As these cooled they shrank and closed up all drying cracks and tightened the hub onto the shanks of the spokes. Similarly when the felloes had been fitted to the circumference at the outer end of the spokes the whole wheel was pulled together tightly by the outer hoop. This too was driven on tightly while white hot and the crackling and spluttering and charring that took place as the hoop cooled and contracted was pleasant to watch, to smell and to hear.

All through the first war my Company had two men cleaving oak spokes for artillery wagon wheels. After that war one of them went on cleaving spokes and, from the off falling smaller pieces, ladder rungs, for many years. The other man switched over to splitting and dressing cleft oak fencing rails and pales. When they retired they were not replaced. Oak spokes were no longer required and cleft oak fence pales are now only produced by one or two specialist firms.

I have spent some time on wheels for the wheel is the most important part of transport. But in addition the greater part of the under frames of road vehicles was made of oak. And, of course, the frames of all railway wagons were made of oak as were colliery tubs for transporting the coal from the face to the shaft. The canals used large quantities of oak in lock gates as well as in the barges. And, of course, it was the ambition of most folks to be able to afford to be buried in an oak coffin. Oak was used extensively on the farms not only in gates and fencing but in cow stalls, hay racks, stables and in feeding troughs. So you can see that every piece of oak that came to the sawmill could be used for some very important purpose and our sawyers became very expert in making the very best use of every tree. One must remember too that a very large proportion of the trees came in from parks and hedgerows and as barbed wire was unknown all the shorter members of wagon frames and all the coffin boards were produced from these short butts. For the railway wagon solebars and siderails and the long planks required for canal barges larger woodland trees were necessary.

Apart from the fact that metal wheels had replaced wooden ones this general pattern of oak usage continued right up until the Second World War. Between the wars railway companies had experimented with steel framed wagons and long steel frames on bogies at each end began to replace the coupled pairs of old single bolstered wooden framed trucks which had been used for carrying long lengths. By 1938 steel frames, and in fact all metal bodies, had become a serious threat to the oak wagon scantling trade but war-time iron shortages and the great demand for war equipment caused the railway companies to go back to the wooden wagon for all except long loads. At the end of the war, as soon as iron and steel supplies became available, wooden framed wagons went out for ever.

At the same time metal frames were replacing wooden frames in all types of road vehicles. Metal replaced wood in colliery tubs, canal barges were lying unused and dilapidated in all the canal basins and the lock gates were no longer kept in first class repair. Furthermore an oak coffin was no longer a status symbol—a car in the family counted more than an oak suit for poor old Dad— and for a while obechi began to replace even the poor mans elm. Concrete and iron posts competed with wood, and wire of various types competed with fence rails. New farming techniques and standards of hygiene ousted timber from stables, pigsties and cowsheds. Concrete and metal barns and silos replaced the old timber barns.

It is difficult for anyone not intimately connected with the timber trade—particularly the native timber trade, to appreciate the complete revolution that had taken place in the decade after 1945. It was a revolution that was seen to be coming in the 1930s but so delayed by war-time conditions that the whole native timber trade had been lulled into a false sense of security. When I was president of the Home Timber Merchants' Association soon after the war, I was pressed to lead deputations to the Minister of Transport asking him to insist on the continued manufacture and use of timber framed railway wagons—to go to the Minister of Agriculture to press for priorities for timber in gates, fences and farm buildings. It was, of course, as useless as King Canute's exhortations to the tides on the sea shore.

Up till 1945 there had been plenty of work for all the small local sawmills throughout the country producing goods vital to the essential industries of the country. Now wood (and native timber in England was 70% oak) had lost for ever its hitherto most stable and biggest markets and was having to compete with other materials in almost all other fields. Meanwhile the supply position of oak logs had completely changed. Ever since the fire of London we had to depend more and more on imported timber. It was cheaper to bring sawnwood by sea from Baltic ports to London than to haul it from forests in the midlands. Eventually timber from all over the world was coming into the country and we were able to buy the cream of the forest production of the world, the lower grades being consumed locally or burnt as forests were cleared for agriculture. By 1914 we were importing 90% of our requirements. As demand was good this did not vitally affect the home timber trade. It did keep prices down and this meant low prices for standing trees. The outbreak of the First World War restricted our imports to bare necessities and all out efforts were made to increase the production of home grown timber resulting in severe overcutting of our woodlands. This led to the setting up of the Forestry Commission in 1919 to build up and maintain a supply of native timber (softwoods) against another emergency. Between the two wars the drain on our native woodlands continued to be severe. Large blocks of hardwoods mostly oak were sold to meet death duties and in cases where estates were broken up for the same reason, buyers cashed in on the woodlands rather than maintain them on a sound sylvicultural basis of selective fellings.

The Second World War led to still greater overcutting of forests already depleted by one war and by a complete lack of forest policy for private woodlands in the interwar years.

By the end of World War II our traditional oak forests were in a sad state. Furthermore the government's forest policy to encourage the growing of softwood in place of hardwoods first for strategic reasons, as softwoods constitute a very high percentage of our requirements, and later for economic reasons, as softwoods showed a quicker return, led to the clearing not only of low grade oak stands but also of many stands of thriving young oak to make way for Douglas fir and larch. Very few private landowners on whom the supply of oak trees is largely dependent were able to resist the pressure to go over to softwood planting. This led to the flooding of a diminishing market with large quantities of inferior and small diameter oak trees with a consequent depression of prices. Many sawmills among them some of very long standing were forced out of business. In fact today there are fewer members in the Home Timber Merchants' Association of England and Wales than there were in the Midland Section alone at the end of the war. This small remnant consists of those sawmillers who did not hang on to the pattern of the trade as it used to be but looked forward to things as they were going to be.

The future for oak

It had always been a cause of grief to me to see our most beautiful figured oak going into coffins to be seen for a few days only. I grieved too during the war when working for the government timber production department as I watched one of the Royal Engineers Forestry Corps sawmills cutting railway sleepers out of beautiful cherrywood, yew and cedar as well as oak. One of the sad consequences of war. Before the war orders had come in regularly from Railway Companies and collieries so that sawmills had no time to stop and wonder at the beauty of our native woods—their bright and lively grains and textures, the endless varieties of shades of colour and grain in every species.

Practically the whole of the Forestry Commission's research and experiments were devoted to conifer growing and oak was regarded as a luxury that no one could really afford to grow. Consequently there is now, and there will be for years to come, a shortage of first quality oak trees in Britain, with difficult marketing conditions for the lower grades. This shortage of first grade oak logs is not confined to Britain. It is common to the whole of Europe, the USA and Japan, the principal oak growing areas of the world.

At this stage however it is very important to face up to the difficulties not only in the growing of oak (see pps. 98–112) but also to the problems of converting and seasoning oak and preparing it and machining it for modern uses particularly in centrally heated buildings. However I would like to make one general observation on the growing of oak. The view still held in France and Germany that the more slowly it is grown the better it is for high grade joinery and for veneers is, in my experience, quite false. I have yet to meet a veneer cutter who does not welcome a very quickly grown tree with 5 or 6 rings to the inch of diameter and he will pay the same price for it as for one whose growth has been restricted to 15 or 20 or even more rings to the inch. The important thing is even growth. It is uneven growth that produces difficulties in seasoning and stability. As sale prices per cu ft depend more upon large diameter than long length the forester should aim at a butt length of 10–20ft (3–6m.) putting on even growth as quickly as possible. As I have just said it is not within my terms of reference to enlarge upon this but I would like to add that oak should be felled in the winter and not put up for sale with restrictive clauses as to removal that make winter felling impossible.

Modern extraction and haulage equipment make the movement of high grade oak butts economically viable over long distances to get them to the specialist mills now engaged in their conversion. The handling of these butts in the sawmill is facilitated by modern lifting and conveying systems. But the intrinsic difficulties of oak remain. First of all there is a definite ring of 2–3in width of sapwood all round the tree. In converting to a 'sap free' specification this means an additional waste factor of 10–20%. Now in my opinion properly dried sapwood—particularly if it is kiln dried—is no defect. If it is not properly dried it falls a prey to decay or to the Powder-post beetles, *Lyctus* spp. In fact specifications of American and Japanese oak timber say 'sound sapwood no defect.' The next problem encountered is the wandering heart, which in a timber like oak usually means that unless it can be well boxed in large sections the central core of 6–10in diameter is waste too. These are waste factors peculiar to the conversion of oak.

If one starts to saw an oak log through on a hot summers day no power on earth will prevent almost immediate surface checking on the outer tangential cut. Though a subsequent shower of rain will close up these checks they will immediately reopen in further seasoning either in the kiln or the log pile or in the carpenters shop. Therefore, one is limited by the weather when converting good oak butts.

The fashion for white oak, that is oak in its natural colour not treated with ammonia or any of the other agents that produce brown or almost black wood, means that careful handling at every stage of conversion is essential. If two oak boards are left lying together as they come off the saw surface staining, impossible to eradicate later, will commence over-night. Overdo the humidity in the kiln and blotchy discolouration results. Even pockets of moisture in the middle of a pile of boards in stick for air drying will start colour deterioration. Now this colour difficulty is not peculiar to oak. In fact everyone realises that it occurs in sycamore and beech. The point I want to make is that handling sawn oak for high class work needs just as much care.

The seasoning of oak presents further problems. It is one of the world's most difficult woods to dry. Go too fast and distortion and cracking ruin the timber. Go too slow and the cost in interest and storage space are likely to ruin the operator.

My own Company had hoped by the installation of the very latest type of drying kilns to reduce the outlay in idle capital and invaluable yard space locked up in piles of oak for one, two or three years on stick. We have been disappointed. Whereas we can dry ash, elm, sycamore or beech in a matter of weeks from sawing from the log, we are reconciled to holding oak for at least 6 months for 1in, 1 year or more for 2in and up before we attempt the final kiln drying essential to meet conditions in centrally heated buildings. Even so the degrade is far greater than in any of our other native woods. Experiments with so called electronic drying have proved equally disappointing and the Platten drying on which the junkers Danish Beech Strip Flooring is based while suitable for beech, sycamore and maple has proved quite unable to cope with oak. But we have not given up trying. We are in close contact with timber drying research throughout the world and may one day achieve a breakthrough. Meantime woe betide the man who goes into high grade oak conversion unaware of these difficulties.

What are the answers to these difficulties? How are we dealing with English oak now and what are the prospects for the future? For without question, rightly handled and rightly used it is unique in its beauty, durability and variety.

First of all veneered plywood, or blockboard can replace solid boards in the large surfaces required in cupboards, tables and other furniture. Even in veneers English oak still stands out as different in its variations of grain and texture from European, American or Japanese oak. Solid boards are costly but very many people think it is worth paying extra money for solid wood in articles of furniture or house fittings that they are going to live with.

Design should aim at using the smallest possible dimensions that can be easily dried. In this connection some of the war-time utility ranges of household furniture are examples of pleasing articles made out of readily available wood. My wife and I still sleep on a bed with war-time utility ends in English oak and most of our bedroom furniture is of the same vintage. The beautiful oak chairs produced for Coventry Cathedral are built from pieces of very small dimensions. One sees in them the master's hand of Sir Gordon Russell who also guided war-time furniture design.

Wall and ceiling cladding, spandrills and doors can be made of narrow 'V' jointed boards easily dried and if rightly fixed easily adapting to changes in humidity and temperature. Newel post and handrails can be made up out of components of a maximum of 2in thick. In fact our fathers and our grandfathers were adepts at this method of building up large sizes 100–150 years ago.

In reproduction furniture, in restorations, in repairs and in additions to old buildings, in the replacement of old doors, cupboards and stairs the inclusion of sound knots, burrs, grain deviations and sound hearts will add to the beauty and charm, and even a certain amount of distortion, provided this has been catered for in the design, can add effect.

Other timbers will have their periods of popularity. They all have peculiar individual properties and beauties but none of them will ever finally oust our native oak. Its good to live with. Every passing change of light and shade is reflected in it and shows up unsuspected little gems of grain. Familiarity increases ones attachment to it. To discerning people who spend their work days with tubular steel and plastics the evening and weekend welcome of one's English oak will increase as days go by.

Out of doors my lapped paled oak fence 45 years old and moved four times has matured to a nice silvery grey and is as beautiful as a piece of furniture. Main road oak fencing with morticed posts and rails are still in great demand for servicability and harmony in the countryside. The pergola of sawn oak shows ones roses and clematis to best advantage.

Oak limbs and small rough trunks can now be chipped and with balanced surfacings of softwood chips make first class man-made boards. Altogether I see a bright future for the worlds most beautiful timber. But grow it, tend it, convert it and use it with a full understanding of its rugged vagaries.

THE OAK AND ITS LEGENDS

Miles Hadfield

Dillons Orchard, Wellington Heath, Herefordshire

Introduction

There are only two trees that in the past have played an important part in what might be called the sociological aspects of British life. These are the oak and the hawthorn. Oak and thorn in their various early forms provide the origins for more place names than any other kinds of tree, and this is also true of references to trees as boundary markers in the Anglo-Saxon charters. Grundy[1] showed that eighty-two individual trees or small groups of trees are named in the Saxon charters of Worcestershire. Twenty-three of them are thorns and twenty oaks; the remainder is of a dozen or so other native species. It seems possible that the cult of the thorn, which involved localised trees such as the Glastonbury thorn which must not be damaged, and also the species generally with the still strongly held belief that hawthorn flowers must not be cut and brought in the house, arose because solitary thorn trees of great age and distinctive character are to this day found in open spaces and are valuable landmarks.

This need to give supernatural authority to outstanding trees also applied to oaks that were, often in a land of dense forest, important landmarks, place marks, or public meeting places—religious or secular. Even today, many an old oak in an open space at the centre of a village carries the notices of Women's Institute or other local meetings. These prominent oaks centuries ago gave their names to many places, with names having a variety of origins and meanings.

Oak in place names

If one works through a volume such as *The Concise Oxford Dictionary of English Place Names*—note the restriction to English, even though oaks are very common in Wales—probably the commonest oak element is the Old English *ac*, meaning oak, as the first or second element in a name, usually with *-ton*, tun meaning anything from an enclosure to a homestead or village. There are several Actons in Shropshire and Staffordshire with proper names attached, such as Acton Round. In Norfolk Acle comes from *acleah*, an oak wood, while in Lancashire *acton* takes the form of Aighton.

Aike in Yorkshire is *ac* unattached, very unusual. In other places, *ac* changes to the termination *ock,* such as Matlock in

Derbyshire, the oak where a moot was held, and Hodsock in Nottinghamshire, Hod's oak. In quite a few places names which started off with *ac* have now ended up as oak, such as the several that are now Oakleigh. *Ac* also becomes *ag,* such as Agden (Yorkshire), the oak valley.

The dative singular of *ac, aec,* is found, somewhat disguised: Each (Kent) and Eachwick (Northumberland) both mean 'of oaks'.

The old Scandinavian *eik* for oak appears not very obviously in Aigburth (Lancashire), oak hill; Eagle (Lincolnshire), oak wood; Eakring (Nottinghamshire), oaks forming a ring; Greenoak (Yorkshire) with a puzzling literal meaning of green oak—one perhaps that held its leaves very late; and Thornock, (Lincolnshire) meaning 'thin oak'.

Langobardic *fereha* meaning 'oak' turns up at Firle (Sussex) while the British *derva* and the Welsh *derw* both meaning oak come into England with such names as Derwent and Darent.

It is indeed unfortunate that the place names of England and Wales connected with oak and their origins and situations have not been the subject of annotated maps as that prepared by Brown[2] showing the location of 83 place names based on thorn. We might learn a great deal from it. However, for oak place names are of minor importance compared with other aspects.

Oak and Mistletoe

We had better start off with the legend of mistletoe oaks and the druids. The first adequate account in English is found in *The Historie of the World, Commonly called the Naturall Historie of C. Plinius Secundus* (23–79 A.D.) in Philemon Holland's translation, dedicated to Sir Robert Cecil and published in 1601. The text is as follows:

'And this you must thinke, that the Misselto is not to be taken for the fruit of a tree, and therefore, as great a wonder it is nature, as any other.

It is remarkable that when on trees that shed their leaves it is always green in winter.

It is seen in greatest plenty on the oak.

Moreover, set or sow this Misselto which way soever you will, it will never take and grow: it cometh only by the mewting of birds, especially of the Stockdove or Quoist, and the Blackbird, which feed thereupon, and let is passe through their bodie. And this is the nature of it, unless it be mortified, altered and digested in the stomacks and belly of birds, it will never grow.... The male beareth a certain graine or berry: the female is barren and fruitless. But sometimes neither the one nor the other beareth at all'.

Then follow instructions for making bird lime 'for to catch poor birds by their wings' using walnut oil. Pliny continues:

'....I cannot overpass one thing thereof used in France: The Druidae (for so they call their Divineurs, Wise men, and the state of their Clergie) esteem nothing more sacred in the world, than Misselto, and the tree whereupon it breedeth, so it be the Oke. Now this you must take by the way, These Priests or Clergiemen chose of purpose such groves for their divine service, as stood only upon Okes; nay they solemnize no sacrifice nor perform any sacred ceremonies without branches and leaves thereof, so as they may seeme well enough to be named thereupon Dryidiae in Greeke, which signifieth as much as the Oke-priests. Certes, to say a truth, whatsoever they find growing upon that tree over and beside the owne fruit, be it Misselto or anything else, they esteem it as a gift sent from heaven, and a sure sign by which that very god they serve giveth them to understand, that he hath chosen that peculiar tree. And no marvale, for in very deed Misselto is passing season and hard to be found upon the Oke; but when they meet with it, they gather it very devoutly and with many ceremonies: for first and foremost, they observe principally that the moon be just six days old (for upon that day they begin their months and new yeares, yea, and their severall ages, which have their revolutions every thirtie years) because she is thought then to be of great power and force sufficient, and is not yet come to her halfe light and the end of her first quarter. They call it in their language All-Heale (for they have an opinion of it, that it cureth all maladies whatsoever) and when they are about it gather it, after they have well and duly prepared their sacrifices and festivall cheare under the said tree, they bring thither two young bullocks milke white, such as never yet chew in yoke at plough or wain, and whose heads were then and not before bound, by the horne: which done, the preist arraied in a surplesse or white vesture, climbeth up into the tree, and with a golden hook or bill cutteth it off, and they beneath receive it in a white soldiours cassocke or coate of armes: then fall they to kill the beasts aforesaid for sacrifice, mumbling many oraisons and praying devoutly, That it would please God to bless this gifte of his to the good and benefit of all those to whome he had vouchsafed to give it. Now this persuasion they have of Misselto thus gathered, That what living creature soever doe drinke of it, will presently become fruitfull thereupon: also, that is a sovereign countiepoison or singular remedie against all vermine. So vaine and superstitious are many nations in the world, and oftentimes in such frivolous and foolish things as these'.

No one, so far as I know, has ever suggested that Pliny was referring to an English practice. He seems to have been a mixture of enterprising journalist, accurate reporter and the comic professor of literature. For instance, he believed that lilies came up from the liquor that dropped from their flowers, acutely noted that nothing his compatriots could do would improve the quality of the black mulberry, and carelessly got himself choked to death by the fumes of Vesuvius as its lava smothered Pompeii.

It is assumed that Pliny's anecodote refers to the Celtic period. Powell[3] tells us that these persons in our islands had their gods of oak and beech (the latter at that period of limited distribution) and personal names connected with wood (generally) particularly yew and alder. Sacred trees, woods and groves were the homes of tribal deities, but tree forms were not used in their art and in those parts of our islands where the heritage of the Celts remained longest, the mistletoe has never grown.

Of sacred groves, we have in Book IV of John Evelyn's *Sylva* (1664) thirty-two pages on the subject—a shattering display both of ancient learning and prose which, alas, does not help us.* A little later from John Ray's *Historia Plantarum* (1686) we learn that mistletoe is rare on oak.

Apparently, there was for long a body of learned persons which did not believe that mistletoe grew on oak in England. J. C. Loudon in his *Arboretum et Fruticetum Britannicum* (1838) records that until 1831 when it was cut down there was an oak near Ledbury bearing mistletoe which was believed to have acquired it from a willow nearby which was loaded with it. However, in the grounds of Eastnor Castle not far off was another oak in which there were several plants of mistletoe, one of which was of great age and vigour, its branches occupying a space nearly 5ft in diameter.

'The mistleto on the oak grows with greater vigour, and has broader leaves, than that which has grown with the apple; and its stem does not form that swelling with its junction with the oak, that it does on most other trees. Of these facts we had ocular demonstration from a large and handsome specimen sent us in March, 1837, by Mr. Beaton**; and which, in order that the fact of the mistletoe growing on the oak might no longer be doubted by botanists or gardeners we exhibited on April 4th, 1837, at the meeting of the Horticultural Society, and of the Linnean Society, held on that day'.

This oak with mistletoe still occurs (1973) at Eastnor.

Oak and medieval life

Subsequent publications, such as the *Golden Bough* [4] give us no help about an oak-mistletoe cult in Britain, but that there

---

* The late Roland E. Cooper, a great authority on the mythology of trees had a letter in the *Quarterly Journal of Forestry* of January 1959 enquiring if any reader could refer him to information he needed about these ancient groves. He remained unanswered.

** The gardener of the neighbouring estate of Haffield

existed often a deep, mystical symbolism involving Britain's oaks is at once seen from their use in medieval ornamentation in our churches.

This use takes several forms. I was first particularly made aware of one type by the remarkable series of telephotos taken by the late C. J. P. Cave reproduced in his *Roof Bosses in Medieval Churches* [5]. Again and again the decoration of these consists of oak leaves—apparently a relic of old pagan traditions discreetly placed high up in the roof. Likewise, they are found in another secretive feature—the undersides of misericords. Foliated masks of 'green men' are not uncommon as decorations on capitals and realistic if formalised oak leaves, almost invariably with accurate representations of acorns, are found in every English cathedral* and many churches. The remarkable fact is that almost always they are unmistakebly Pedunculate, with the angular growth of that species untypical of the Sessile kind.

An interesting exception to this rule is displayed by the very realistic representation of *Q. petraea* in Claydon church, East Suffolk, carved on bosses, showing foliage and acorns. I had never found that species in the district; for example, the ancients oaks in Staverton Thicks not far away are Pedunculate.

Further my brother lives near Claydon in an old house where all the oaks along his drive are Pedunculate in all their details. I had known these oaks for ten years when one day I noticed a silvery sheen on the underside of the leaves of a small number They were dense with stellate down. This was not present on other oaks around the house or in the district, with one exception a few miles away. Whether there is a remote connection between the carving in the church and those trees in the drive remains a problem.

The often secretive use of oak in medieval church decoration on so large a scale and the appearance of strange oak-men in medieval times suggests that some protective mumbo-jumbo surrounded the trees for practical purposes.

Another reason for a cult of the oak is well seen from the Domesday Book where woodland, excluding the royal forests, is virtually described in terms of what it would produce: fuel, charcoal and, above all, the number of pigs an area would support. As Rackham (p.73) has already pointed out the acorn crop on which the pigs fed varied enormously from year to year. It seems probable to me that the fact that the Pedunculate oak produces a heavier crop of acorns more frequently than the Sessile oak would not have been lost on the people who would naturally have chosen to depict the species which was of greatest importance to them in their carvings.

From Norman times, the finest oaks were probably preserved in royal forests. So no doubt it was safer to put representations of the

---

* The remarkable and precisely accurate botanical sculpture in Southwell Minster includes oak, but forms an exceptional subject on its own.

oak, and oak-lore of the good old days, where they would only be seen by the common people staring round in rather bad taste up above their heads or under their seats.

Modern legends

Some of the legends about oaks are of relatively recent origin. The more one wanders about and examines oak trees in the British Isles the more one realises that the geographical distribution and particularly the ecological conditions under which the two species grow as cited in standard works rank as one of the legends of fact if not of theory.

One can find specimens of each species of the same vigour, size and age growing side by side in various degrees of density in the west and midlands of England, in East Anglia and in the Welsh hills. Doubtless this is often due to planting by man: the effect in detail of the vast felling of oak woods which began in the time of Henry VIII and the beginnings of replanting under Burleigh in the reign of Queen Elizabeth I have still to be studied. However there is ample evidence to show that many of our oak woods have been planted or replanted by man, not necessarily always with the original species.

Once Pedunculate oak has been introduced into an area features of its reproduction give it greater opportunities to spread than Sessile oak. The acorn of _Q. petraea_ is difficult to detach from the tree until it becomes free from its almost stemless cup, when for the most part it falls to the ground to lie or be picked up entire (not a very easy job). On the other hand the acorns of _Q. robur_ are firmly attached to a long stalk which can be snapped off the tree to provide a convenient handle to carry them by (This point was noticed by Michael Dryton (1563–1631) in his poem in which Oberon picks up an acorn on its stalk to lay about his enemy Pigwiggin, as with a club).

I have a Pedunculate oak tree at the bottom of my garden and in the autumn numbers of jays fly into it, collect something and fly off vigorously out of sight. Writers tell us how the life-cycle of the jay, particularly its habit of collecting acorns and distributing them, is concerned with oakwoods. I guessed that the jays might be snapping off acorn stalks, usually carrying two acorns a journey, and putting them into store. This operation took place when the acorns were still firmly embedded in the cups; it was certainly completed with great expedition. Its effectiveness in distributing the seed at such a comparatively early, green stage of its development seemed a little dubious. However, by chance I was sent some sprays of cultivars of _Q. robur_ in early September with unripe green acorns from which I had to cut the cups to sow. They germinated normally.

It seems to me that the Pedunculate oak has always had an enormous advantage over the Sessile in effectively establishing itself over a far wider range and doing so more rapidly whatever the conditions of soil, climate etc. First, it fruits earlier in life and more regularly, and secondly the fruit is carried in far greater numbers over much wider distances avifically.

Conclusion

The reasons why *Q. robur* in the British Isles had far greater importance to man than *Q. petraea* can be easily displayed by summarising what has been said above.

First, as a more regular producer of a natural food in autumn for our once most valuable animal, the pig, of which practically every part is edible or usable and suitable for storing. In the Domesday Book woods are often given in terms of swine measurement. For example, in Shropshire entries we are specifically told that a wood was for fattening swine (*porcis incrassandis*).

Or in Spenser's *Shepheards Calendar* (1579):

> 'There grew an aged tree on the greene,
> A goodly oke sometime had it bene
> With armes full strong and largely displayed......
> Whilome had been the king of the field
> And mochell mast to the husband did yielde,
> And with his nuts larded many swine'.

To some extent the beech is also a mast tree, but particularly in the past, it covered a relatively small area of our woodlands.

Another quality of the Pedunculate oak which gives it for the Englishman great superiority over the Sessile was the immensely strong naturally angled and curved branching system which provided the crucks in the timber-framed houses and the huge timber arches as for example in Westminister Hall, and the timber-framed house turned upside-down which was the framing of our ships. We have no other tree which provides all these.

Finally there is the rapid 'avificial' dissemination of the Pedunculate acorns which it seems to me gave it an enormous advantage over the Sessile in effectively establishing itself over a far wider range and doing so more rapidly whatever the conditions of soil or climate.

REFERENCES

1. GRUNDY, G. B. *Saxon Charters of Worcestershire*, Birmingham Archaeological Society (1931)
2. BROWN, P. W. F. Map of England and Wales showing location of place names based on thorn. Unpublished. See *Folklore*, 70, 417
3. POWELL, T. G. E. *The Celts*, Thames and Hudson (1958)
4. FRAZER, SIR J. G. *The Golden Bough*, Macmillan, (1890)
5. CAVE, C. J. P. *Roof Bosses in Medieval Churches*, Cambridge (1948)

VARIATION IN OAKWOODS IN BRITAIN

R. C. STEELE

Natural Environment Research Council, London

Extent and distribution of oakwoods

The pollen record[1] shows that oak rose to dominance in British forests in the Boreal period, some 7–8,000 years ago, and oakwood was the predominant woodland type until recently. In the past two or three decades oak woodland has been superseded as the most common type by woodland of Scots pine (*Pinus sylvestris* L.) and Sitka spruce (*Picea sitchensis* (Bong.) Carr.). Oak woodland still occurs on a substantial scale and is still widely distributed (see pps 98–100). Appendix 1 shows how privately-owned oakwoods were distributed in 1965–67. Comparable figures are not available for Forestry Commission oakwoods but these amounted then to about 10% only of the total area of oakwood.

Privately owned oakwood occurs in every county in England and Wales, and all the mainland Scottish counties except Bute, Clackmannan, Kinross and Caithness. The first three of these counties contain small areas of state-owned oakwood and it is only Caithness which is recorded in 1963–67 by the Forestry Commission as having no oakwood. McVean and Ratcliffe [2], however, in a reconstruction of the distribution of woodland types prior to the onset of large-scale human forest clearance show small areas of oakwood in the south of Caithness. Thus oakwood has probably occurred in all the counties of England, Scotland and Wales (except for the outlying Scottish islands) within the present climatic period.

The relationship between the distribution of oak and climate, soil and altitude are dealt with elsewhere (see pps 18–24), sufficient to note here that oakwoods occur on a very wide range of soils and that up to about 300m (1,000ft) altitude the climate over most of Great Britain does not prevent the growth of oak.

Types of oak woodland

Nearly every native tree is associated with oak as are most of our native shrubs, and the majority of woodlands herbs also occur in oakwoods. Species lists of oakwoods would thus include nearly all our woodland plants. Distinctions between oakwoods based on the relative abundance of oak and other tree and shrub species can mislead because all our oakwoods have been managed to a certain degree and management has favoured some species at the expense of others. The species composition of the field layer to some extent and the relative abundance of these species to a greater extent is also influenced by the management which the tree and shrub layer has undergone as well as by soil, climate, topography, altitude and geography. How then can we classify and describe oakwoods when they are found under such a wide range of soils, climates and altitudes and have often undergone considerable modification as a result of intensive management?

The references at the end of this contribution contain descriptions of different types of oakwood in Britain and the accounts and references in Tansley[3] are particularly valuable and comprehensive. The most useful general published classification and description of oakwoods is given by Jones[4] which is based on nutrient and water supply. This classification, on which the following account is based, provides reference types only and within each type there is considerable variation and there is a continuous gradation linking these types.

A. MOST NUTRIENT-DEFICIENT SOILS, USUALLY PODSOLS OR GLEY-PODSOLS ON HIGHLY SILICEOUS ROCKS

Oak   *Q. petraea*
Associated trees and shrubs   *Betula* spp
                                       Ilex aquifolium
                                       Sorbus aucuparia
                                       Frangula alnus (in south)

1. Drier soils	2. Damper soils	3. Wet sites
Vaccinium myrtillus	Species under A1	*Molinia caerulea*
Deschampsia flexuosa	*Molinia caerulea*	*Juncus acutiflorus*
Calluna vulgaris	*Blechnum spicant*	*Viola palustris*
Carex ovalis	*Dryopteris carthusiana*	*Hydrocotyle vulgaris*
Galium saxatile		*Lotus uliginosus*
Melampyrum pratense		*Ranunculus flammula*
Potentilla erecta		*Sphagnum* spp

B. BASE-DEFICIENT SOILS BETTER SUPPLIED WITH NUTRIENTS THAN A. (ie low-base status Brown Forest Soils rather than podsols)

Oak   *Q. petraea* on lighter soils
                                       Q. petraea and *Q. robur* on heavier soils
Associated trees and shrubs   *Betula* spp
                                       Carpinus betulus (often coppiced)
                                       Castanea sativa (often coppiced)
                                       Crataegus monogyna
                                       Ilex aquifolium
                                       Prunus padus (in north)
                                       Salix caprea
                                       Sorbus aucuparia
                                       S. torminalis (on heavy soils in central and southern Britain)

1. Drier lighter soils	2. Heavier damp soils	3. Wet sites
Holcus mollis	*Rubus* spp	*Agrostis stolonifera*
Pteridium aquilinum	*Salix atrocinerea*	*Deschampsia cespitosa*
Anthoxanthum odoratum	*S. caprea*	*Ranunculus flammula*
Conopodium majus	*Anemone nemorosa* (esp.	*Lychnis flos-cuculi*
Digitalis purpurea	in coppiced woods)	Many species from A3
Endymion non-scriptus	*Luzula pilosa*	Some from C3
Galium saxatile	*Molinia caerulea*	
Lonicera periclymenum	*Stachys officinalis*	
Luzula multiflora	*Succisa pratensis*	
L. sylvatica (in west)	The rarer plants include:	
Oxalis acetosella	*Convallaria majalis*	
Teucrium scorodonia	*Hypericum androsaemum*	
	Pulmonaria longifolia	
	Ruscus aculeatus	

On more fertile sands
and loams and in coppiced
woodland also:
Anemone nemorosa
Corydalis claviculata (in west)
Euphorbia amygdaloides
Lamiastrum galeobdolon
Moehringia trinervia
Silene dioica
Stellaria holostea

C. BASIC SOILS OR SOILS RICH IN NUTRIENTS

Oak
                                  Q. robur
                                  Q. petraea (in west and north)

Associated trees and shrubs

Acer campestre	*Populus* spp
Betula spp	*Prunus avium*
Cornus sanguinea	*P. spinosa*
Corylus avellana	*Rhamnus catharticus*
Crataegus monogyna	*Salix* spp
C. laevigata (central	*Sorbus aria*
and SE England)	*S. torminalis*
Euonymus europaeus	*Tilia cordata* (mainly central and southern
Fraxinus excelsior	Britain)
Ligustrum vulgare	*Ulmus glabra*
Malus sylvestris	*Viburnum lantana*
Populus tremula	*V. opulus*

Most native trees and shrubs occur in these types of woodlands.

1. Well-drained sites	2. Heavy basic clays and loams	3. Sites with copious and freely moving water
Arctium minus	As for C1	*Alnus glutinosa*
Arum maculatum	*Ajuga reptans*	*Carex riparia*
Brachypodium sylvaticum	*Allium ursinum*	*Epilobium hirsutum*
Bromus ramosus	*Angelica sylvestris*	*Eupatorium cannabinum*
Campanula latifolia	*Calamagrostis epigejos*	*Humulus lupulus*
(in north)	(in more open areas)	*Mentha aquatica*
C. trachelium (in south)	*Carex pendula*	*Populus* spp
Circaea lutetiana	*Colchicum autumnale*	*Salix* spp
Cynoglossum officinale	*Filipendula ulmaria*	
Fragaria vesca	*Iris foetidissima*	
Galium aparine	(southern England)	
Geranium robertianum	*Paris quadrifolia*	
Helleborus spp	*Primula elatior* (local in	
Hypericum hirsutum	East Anglia)	
Lathraea squamaria	*P. vulgaris*	
Mercurialis perennis	*Ranunculus ficaria*	
Sanicula europaea		
Tamus communis		

D. WOODLAND ON DEEP PEAT

Oak   *Q. robur* (but never abundant)

Associated trees and shrubs

Alnus glutinosa	*Ribes nigrum*
Betula spp	*R. sylvestre*
Crataegus monogyna	*Salix atrocinerea*
Frangula alnus (in England and and Wales)	*Solanum dulcamara* *Viburnum opulus*
Rhamnus catharticus (mainly in southern and eastern England)	

Fen peats   More acid peats

Calystegia sepium	*Erica tetralix*
Carex acutiformis	*Molinia caerulea*
C. paniculata	*Myrica gale*
Cladium mariscus	
Filipendula ulmaria	
Iris pseudacorus	
Lychnis flos-cuculi	
Lysimachia vulgaris	
Lythrum salicaria	
Phragmites communis	
Solanum dulcamara	
Symphytum officinale (only in eastern England)	
Thelypteris palustris	
Urtica dioica	

Two oakwood types of particular interest are the western oakwoods, which contain 'oceanic' species and a high proportion of epiphytes, and high-level oakwoods which are also rich in epiphytes.

1. Western oakwoods

Much of Britain has an 'oceanic' or 'Atlantic' type of climate which is generally equable and characterised by well-distributed rainfall, high atmospheric humidity and small diurnal and annual temperature ranges. Species such as *Vaccinium myrtillus, Ilex aquifolium* and *Endymion non-scriptus* thrive under these conditions, as do the so-called 'Atlantic' bryophytes. This 'Atlantic' element of the bryophyte flora needs a moist atmosphere, and woodlands provide very favourable habitats for them. Ratcliffe[5] has written a full account of the ecology of Atlantic bryophytes. Many species form mats which cover stumps, logs and the sloping bases of surface roots while others are more strictly arboreal and clothe the trunks and limbs of trees; rotting logs are also the habitat for other bryophytes. Most of the bryophytes characteristic of wooded localities are not confined to them and may also be found where shade and humidity are maintained but Ratcliffe records that he has not yet found *Sematophyllum demissum* except under trees. In Scotland the tree trunks of these western woods also often bear a profusion of lichens, including such large foliose species as *Lobaria pulmonaria, L. laetevirens, Sticta fuliginosa* and *Parmeliella plumbea* but these are much scarcer in the west of England and Wales. This aspect of oakwoods is described in detail elsewhere (see pps 250–272).

Some of the oakwoods of North Wales are famous as the richest British localities for Atlantic bryophytes outside south-west Ireland and oakwoods in the Lake District and western Scotland are also very rich in species. An important requirement of these Atlantic bryophyte species-rich woodlands seems to be continuity of woodland cover and a lack of excessive disturbance of this cover.

2. *High-level oakwoods*

Woodlands on Dartmoor and in the Lake District provide examples of oak under extreme conditions.

The Dartmoor examples consist of three small woodland fragments of which Wistman's Wood is the best known. These isolated but apparently natural woods are of *Q. robur* which is surprising as the oakwoods flanking Dartmoor are of *Q. petraea*. Wistman's Wood consists of three main blocks of trees with some smaller clumps and totals about 3.5 ha (9 acres) with an altitude range of 365m to 420m (1200–1380ft).

Wistman's Wood was thought to be degenerating but Archibald[6] shows that it is increasing in area and that the trees are now growing quite vigorously. This woodland contains a large number of epiphytes including 23 liverworts, 42 mosses and 31 lichens many of which occur on the trunks and branches of the oak. In addition there are seven species of vascular plants growing as epiphytes:

Polypodium vulgare   *Dryopteris dilatata*
Luzula sylvatica   *Oxalis acetosella*
Sedum anglicum   *Sorbus aucuparia*
Vaccinium myrtillus

The luxuriant epiphytic growth in Wistman's Wood appears to be declining due partly perhaps to the increased growth of the trees and the raising of the canopy with a reduction in humidity.

Examples of *Q. petraea* at high altitude are seen in the Birkrigg and Keskadale Oaks in Cumberland in the Lake District. These lie between 349m and 425m (1150–1400ft) and between and 303m and 455m (1000–1500ft) respectively. As in Wistman's Wood the trees are stunted and bryophytes are abundant.

Effects of management on oakwoods

1. *Oak species*

The distribution of *Q. robur* and *Q. petraea* has been much confused by man's activities, especially as *Q. robur* has usually been favoured when planting woodlands. The national distribution of oak has been investigated but little seems to have been recorded on the effects on the flora of changing the species of oak in an oakwood. Preliminary work by Fairbairn[7] shows that *Q. petraea* casts a deeper shade and also tolerates more shade than *Q. robur*.

Jones[4] quotes work which indicates that the leaves of *Q. petraea* decay much more slowly than those of *Q. robur*. The effects of these features on the other plants of an oakwood do not appear to have been studied.

2. *Succession from abandoned land*

The development of oakwood on abandoned arable land on the area known as Broadbalk Wilderness has been described by Tansley[3]: Before 1882 the soil, a heavy loam, carried a wheat crop every year but in that year the wheat was not harvested, and allowed to seed. By 1914 a dense oak-hazel thicket with much bramble had developed and also contained *Hedera helix, Arum maculatum, Sanicula europaea* and *Viola odorata* in the centre with *Geum urbanum, Brachypodium sylvaticum, Mercurialis perennis, Heracleum spondylium, Arrhenatherum elatius, Stachys silvatica* and *Urtica dioica* around the margins. By 1938 the woody species also included Field maple, sycamore and ash with dogwood, hazel, hawthorn, holly, privet, blackthorn, elder and goat willow. The field layer was dominated by ivy. Indeed an abundance of ivy in the field layer of an oakwood seems to indicate a recently created woodland.

The development of oakwood from abandoned pasture has also been described by Adamson[8] and Salisbury[9].

3. *Grazing and pannage*

Grazing and pannage, the feeding of stock on mast, are other management practices which affect the composition of oakwoods. Allowing stock into a woodland in the autumn to eat the acorns is not now often done although the practice still continues in the New Forest using pigs. The effects of pannage on woodland composition are not known. Grazing of oakwoods continues on a considerable scale in the uplands and the general effect, especially when sheep are grazed, is to convert a herb-rich field layer into one dominated by grasses, which vary with the soil conditions. On the dry, base-poor brown earths of upland oakwoods the abundant grasses include *Agrostis tenuis, A. canina, Anthoxanthum odoratum* and *Deschampsia flexuosa* and in wetter situations *Molinia caerulea* is abundant. Bracken is often much more widespread in woodlands grazed by sheep than in their ungrazed counterparts. Ungrazed woodlands may contain a greater abundance of species such as *Vaccinium myrtillus, Luzula sylvatica, Potentilla erecta* and sometimes a luxuriance of ferns including *Dryopteris dilatata, D. filix-mas, D. pseudomas* and *Thelypteris limbosperma. Lonicera periclymenum* is also often abundant in ungrazed woods on poor soils with *Corydalis claviculata* in rocky places.

Heavily grazed oakwoods on soils of intermediate or good fertility also show this dominance of grasses but usually with a greater abundance of grazed down forbs than under more acid soil conditions. Tall forbs are especially sensitive to grazing so ungrazed woods have a higher representation of such species than grazed woods. The grazing of lowland woodlands is not now a very usual feature but it occurred through much of the 19th century and sufficient documentary evidence probably exists which when combined with field studies, will enable us to know in more detail the effects of grazing on the flora of lowland oakwoods. Some studies have been initiated, for example the effects of Fallow deer (*Dama dama*) grazing on the oxlip (*Primula elatior*) in Hayley Wood in Cambridgeshire by the Cambridgeshire and Isle of Ely Naturalists' Trust.

4. *Silvicultural practices*

There are seasonal changes in the floristic composition of the field layer of oakwoods on the better soils between early spring and the middle of summer which correspond with decreasing light intensity as the canopy develops. Species such as *Endymion nonscriptus, Ranunculus ficaria, Anemone nemorosa,* and *Allium ursinum* put on rapid vegetative growth and flower early in the year then die down and almost disappear above ground. They are followed by later flowering species such as *Conopodium majus, Circaea lutetiana* and *Geum urbanum.* Some species flower early but persist vegetatively right through the summer, eg *Primula vulgaris, P. elatior* and *Mercurialis perennis.* These pre-vernal and vernal flowering plants are favoured by the traditional English method of managing oak as standard trees in the silvicultural system known as coppice-with-standards. The coppice usually consisted of hazel often with ash and, depending on local conditions, Field maple, Small-leaved lime, Sweet chestnut, elm, beech, hornbeam, birch and sallow may also have formed the coppice. In parts of the north and west oak itself was coppiced often in extensive and relatively pure stands. Before the mature coppice is felled the field layer is usually scanty because of the dense shade cast. After felling there is a great increase in the pre-vernal and vernal flowering species which react rapidly to the increased light. The spectacular displays of gregarious species such as bluebell, primrose, oxlip, wood anemone and lesser celandine are a feature of coppice oakwoods on the better soils. The coppice herbs are of three main types: those which colonise clearings and spread rapidly after coppice cutting and persist through the shade phase; those which are shade tolerant and colonise dense stands of coppice when they become just light enough to allow the development of a field layer; and others which depend for their abundance on the absence of taller, more aggressive plants.

5. *Felling and planting*

Oakwood bryophyte and lichen communities are particularly sensitive to felling. Many of the bryophytes, especially the Atlantic species already mentioned, need the shade and high atmospheric humidity conferred by the tree canopy and the more sensitive species soon die out when the tree or shrub layer is lost. This may not matter for common or rapidly spreading species as they may be able to recolonise cleared areas when conditions become suitable again but for the rarer species, whose capacity to spread appears at present to be very limited, recolonisation after complete clearance may not occur. By contrast many of the vascular plants of an oakwood do not appear to be severely affected by felling if the wood is immediately regenerated, especially if the clear-felled areas are not too extensive. Clearances of oakwoods for agriculture have commonly been made in the past and, at a later date, many of these cleared areas have been replanted with trees, sometimes oak. The flora of such re-established woodland is usually much poorer in species than the flora of a long established woodland. Detailed studies of the relationship between the flora of old established and recently created woodland are of considerable interest and are being made by O. Rackham and G. F. Peterken among others. Dense young plantations of oak, as with most species of tree, have a very small number of vascular plants and where much loose leaf litter persists throughout the year bryophytes too may be practically absent.

REFERENCES

1. GODWIN, H. *The History of the British Flora,* Cambridge (1956)
2. MCVEAN, D. N. and RATCLIFFE, D. A. *Plant communities of the Scottish Highlands,* Monographs of the Nature Conservancy no. 1, London (HMSO) (1962)
3. TANSLEY, A. G. *The British Islands and their Vegetation,* **1,** Cambridge (1949)
4. JONES, E. W. 'Biological flora of the British Isles, *Quercus* L.', *J. Ecol.,* **47** (1959), 169–222
5. RATCLIFFE, D. A. 'An ecological account of Atlantic bryophytes in the British Isles', *New Phytol ,* **67** (1968), 365–439
6. ARCHIBALD, J. F. *A management plan for Wistman's Wood Forest Nature Reserve,* The Nature Conservancy (1966)
7. FAIRBURN, W. A. 'Preliminary light-intensity study under sessile and pedunculate oak', *Forestry,* **27** (1954) 1–6
8. ADAMSON, R. S. 'The woodlands of Ditcham Park, Hampshire', *J. Ecol.,* **9** (1922), 114–219
9. SALISBURY, E. J. 'The ecology of scrub in Hertfordshire,' *Trans. Herts. nat. Hist. Soc. Fld Club,* **17** (1918), 53–63

APPENDIX I

Distribution of privately-owned oakwoods by counties and woodland type

(hectares)

Areas derived from figures kindly provided by the Forestry Commission

ENGLAND	Private				
	High Forest	Coppice-with-Standards	Coppice	Scrub	Total
Bedfordshire	1,013	—	—	54	1,067
Berkshire	3,477	26	—	117	3,620
Buckinghamshire	1,345	—	—	123	1,468
Cambridgeshire	265	—	—	3	268
Cheshire	1,686	—	—	234	1,920
Cornwall..	5,835	—	—	807	6,642
Cumberland	951	—	—	848	1,799
Derbyshire	1,168	—	—	205	1,373
Devonshire	15,375	—	—	767	16,142
Dorset	2,025	296	—	156	2,477
Durham ..	678	—	—	191	869
Essex	1,512	—	—	200	1,712
Gloucestershire ..	2,262	473	28	142	2,905
Hampshire	12,274	687	—	958	13,919
Herefordshire	3,671	33	—	448	4,152
Hertfordshire	2,416	—	—	49	2,465
Huntingdonshire	470	—	—	—	470
Isle of Wight	405	—	—	41	446
Kent	6,753	3,365	18	1,050	11,186
Lancashire	3,791	1,176	—	534	5,501
Leicestershire	810	—	—	23	833
Lincolnshire	1,435	—	—	109	1,544
London ..	1,711	40	—	299	2,050
Norfolk ..	4,378	188	—	139	4,705
Northamptonshire	829	—	—	22	851
Northumberland	1,518	—	—	356	1,874
Nottinghamshire	1,391	—	—	52	1,443
Oxfordshire	1,740	—	—	29	1,769
Rutland ..	—	—	—	55	55
Shropshire	3,423	—	—	883	4,306
Somerset	3,771	—	—	1,230	5,001
Staffordshire	1,426	—	—	207	1,633
Suffolk	2,749	379	—	75	3,203
Surrey	5,152	104	—	1,238	6,494
Sussex	12,445	2,795	25	388	15,653
Warwickshire	2,068	—	—	76	2,144
Westmorland	1,636	—	63	114	1,813
Wiltshire	4,247	267	—	437	4,951
Worcestershire ..	2,814	—	—	492	3,306
Yorkshire E.R. ..	370	—	—	32	402
N.R...	1,531	—	—	904	2,435
W.R...	2,098	—	—	968	3,066
Total	124,924	9,828	134	15,055	149,942

APPENDIX I (cont.)

SCOTLAND	Private		
	High Forest	Scrub	Total
Aberdeenshire	48	87	135
Angus	228	36	264
Argyll	1,280	4,206	5,486
Ayrshire	924	224	1,148
Banffshire	—	13	13
Berwickshire	357	51	408
Bute	—	—	—
Caithness	—	—	—
Clackmannanshire	—	—	—
Dumfriesshire	629	247	876
Dunbartonshire	406	403	809
East Lothian	122	131	253
Fifeshire	60	—	60
Inverness-shire	672	1,081	1,753
Kincardineshire	20	—	20
Kinross-shire	—	—	—
Kirkcudbrightshire	729	961	1,690
Lanarkshire	271	126	397
Midlothian	179	279	458
Moray	92	6	98
Nairnshire	41	19	60
Peeblesshire	30	—	30
Perthshire	2,584	260	2,844
Renfrewshire	20	—	20
Ross & Cromarty	60	243	303
Roxburghshire	164	21	185
Selkirkshire	38	52	90
Stirlingshire	1,097	—	1,097
Sutherland	73	24	97
West Lothian	62	—	62
Wigtownshire	131	83	214
	10,317	8,553	18,870
Unsurveyed	202	202	404
Total	10,519	8,755	19,274

APPENDIX I (cont.)

WALES					Private		
					High Forest	Scrub	Total
Anglesey ..	..	..	..	..	110	—	110
Breconshire	..	..	..	..	1,142	1,996	3,138
Caernarvonshire		..	..	..	671	753	1,424
Cardiganshire	..	..	..	..	330	1,623	1,953
Carmarthenshire		..	..	..	605	3,528	4,133
Denbighshire	..	..	..	..	1,464	912	2,376
Flintshire ..	..	..	..	..	573	278	851
Glamorgan	..	..	..	..	791	1,150	1,941
Merionethshire	..	..	..	..	2,174	1,516	3,690
Monmouthshire ..		..	..	..	1,144	104	1,248
Montgomeryshire		..	..	..	1,641	1,357	2,998
Pembrokeshire	..	..	..	..	411	1,008	1,419
Radnorshire	..	..	..	..	1,175	691	1,866
Total	..	..	..	..	12,231	14,916	27,147

NUTRIENT CYCLES IN OAKWOOD ECOSYSTEMS IN NW ENGLAND

A. H. F. BROWN

Merlewood Research Station, Grange-over-Sands

Introduction

Studies of the processes and functioning of ecosystems form one way in which we can increase our understanding of the natural environment, and hence the impact of man's activities on it. Such a whole ecosystem approach may include studies of production or the flow of energy through the system, but both of these processes are dependent on the availability of nutrients which, in most cases, is dependent in turn on their being recycled. An important approach, therefore, is to determine and evaluate the cycle of major plant nutrients, together with the losses and gains for the entire ecosystem. Those losses and gains which occur naturally, ie nutrients leached from the ecosystem through the soil into the rivers on the one hand, or gained in rain, dust etc on the other, are also part of a cycle, although a very much larger one in which materials circulate between the land, rivers, oceans and atmosphere.

The cycle (within ecosystems) consists of the uptake of nutrients mainly in simple inorganic form from the soil or atmosphere; the, at least partial, incorporation of these nutrients into more complex organic materials within the plants, some of which are retained as current production of roots, stems, branches and shoots; and the return of the remainder to the soil surface, by the leaching action of rainfall, as litter fall, or through death of the plants. On becoming re-mineralised, the nutrients in this dead organic material are again taken up by the vegetation. Additionally, there is normally a subsidiary cycle via secondary producers, ie plant-eating animals, either vertebrate of invertebrate which in turn provide food for predators. Unassimilated materials (faeces) and, subsequently, the dead bodies of the animals also join the organic debris. Nutrient-cycling is the major expression, within the ecosystem, of the inter-action between plants and soils, and is also of significance in the formation of the soil itself. Arguably, therefore, it can be considered the most important single basis for analysing an ecosystem, although a combination of approaches is necessary for the fullest under-standing.

Studies on this theme have been carried out at Merlewood since it was established as the Nature Conservancy's first research station 20 years ago. Oakwood, using the term in a fairly broad sense, was selected as the ecosystem on which to concentrate such studies, being the typical local native woodland, and the presumed climatic climax. It thus provided a good base-line against which more disturbed or artificial ecosystems could later be compared. Because Silurian slates and Carboniferous limestone both occur within the neighbourhood of Merlewood it has been possible to study the two contrasting oakwood systems which these geological formations support. The two types are exemplified by the two main research areas: Bogle Crag on slate, and the Carboniferous limestone site of Meathop Wood, which is a main woodland site within the International Biological Programme. Earlier studies had been made at Roudsea Wood National Nature Reserve where, interestingly, the slate and limestone occur side by side in the same wood. The present paper attempts to present a very general picture of the cycle of nutrients in oakwoods based on the complementary studies made at these two main sites, and will briefly draw comparisons between them and with other woodland ecosystems. In order to facilitate such comparisons, and for the sake of simplicity, the above-ground data only are considered. Similarly, only the net annual changes will be examined, although of course, there is much seasonal variation in nutrient flow and some cycles can occur over a shorter time than one year. A detailed account of the Meathop work, including studies of the below ground components, is currently being prepared[1].

Site descriptions
1. Bogle Crag
Bogle Crag Wood (9.3 ha, 23 acres) part of the Forestry Commission's Grizedale Forest in NW Lancashire, is 90–140m (290–460ft) above sea level, with a western aspect. The soil is a well-drained, acid brown earth, with a mean pH of 4.5 and a moder humus, overlying Silurian slates and mud-stones of the Bannisdale series. Mean annual rainfall is 171cm (67.5in). Apart from small flushed areas, the woodland is dominated by a single-storey high forest (but derived from former coppice) of Sessile oak (*Quercus petraea*) with a few scattered birch (*Betula* spp). At the time of the studies (1961–1965), the trees were in the main about 80 years old (although varying from 40–120 years) with 158 trees/ha. The canopy was 90–95% closed. The ground flora mainly consists of Wavy hair-grass (*Deschampsia flexuosa*) and bracken (*Pteridium aquilinum*) [This woodland corresponds with the A1 to B1 type described by Steele (p. 131).—Ed.]
2. Meathop Wood
Meathop Wood (c. 45m, 150ft, above sea level) is a research area, which is part of a larger area (40ha, 100 acres) of woodland on the outcrop of Carboniferous limestone, with terraces and small scarps, known as Meathop Fell. On the south side, the wood is within about 300m of the estuary of the R. Kent (Morecambe Bay) The terraces are covered with a variable, but mainly shallow, layer of glacial drift, giving rise to a brown earth with mull humus and a pH (4.1–7.5) which varies markedly, mainly with the depth of soil

and hence the influence of the underlying limestone. Mean annual rainfall is 124cm (48.5in).

Meathop is a mixed deciduous woodland; oak, ash and birch of varying age, dominate the upper canopy, with smaller proportions of sycamore, Wych elm and other tree species. A variable, but usually well-developed, under-storey is present, consisting of hazel with some hawthorn, ash and calcicole shrub species. The ground layer is species rich, but is dominated by *Mercurialis perennis, Rubus vestitus* and *Brachypodium sylvaticum* together with *Endymion non-scriptus, Anemone nemorosa, Oxalis acetosella* and many other herb species. Studies started in 1965, and are still continuing. [This woodland type falls into the B2 to C1 categories of Steele (p. 132).—Ed.]

The components of the cycle

Although information on transfers from soil to roots, and subsequently to the various parts of the trees, is not available in detail, the remaining components of the oakwood cycle may now be examined in more detail. Full descriptions of the methods used at the two research sites are given elsewhere (Carlisle et al[2] [3] [4] for Bogle Crag; Satchell[1] for Meathop) and will not be repeated here. All sampling, however, was related to units of known area such that by combining weights (or volumes in the case of water) with the concentrations of nutrients given by chemical analysis, the absolute quantities of nutrients per unit area of woodland (kg/ha) could be determined for the various components.

1. *Nutrients retained in tree increment*

Information on the nutrients retained in the net increment of the trees is dependent on first establishing the dry weight increment of the stand. This is conveniently done by determining increases, over a period of say 5 years, in total stand biomass the latter being obtained from the relationship (derived from felling sample trees) between the girths of all trees in a given area and their dry weights. Chemical analysis of the various biomass components enable the total nutrients present in the stand to be calculated, together with the additional quantities retained annually. Data are presented in tables 5 and 6. Shrub data for Meathop are included with the trees, as will be the case throughout this paper; no shrubs were present in the sampled areas of Bogle Crag.

2. *Litter fall*

The most obvious route of return between trees and the forest floor is by the autumn leaf fall. There are, however, many other types of litter which provide additional transfer paths, some very appreciable. In the spring, the bud scales and catkins fall, together with a number of young leaves, especially in windy weather. Later the peduncles with or without acorns, add to the litter, and, throughout the year, dead branches, twigs, fragments of bark and other materials contribute considerable quantities of litter. All these litter fractions can be sampled using suitable collecting vessels;

TABLE 1

The quantities of nutrient elements in different types of oakwood litter falling annually: Bogle Crag and Meathop
(Kilograms/hectare)

Part of tree	Dry weight		N		K		Ca		Mg		P	
	Bogle Crag	Meathop	Bogle Crag	Meathop	Bogle Crag	Meathop	Bogle Crag	Meathop	Bogle Crag	Meathop	Bogle Crag	Meathop
Leaves	2126	3251	21.1 (51.3%)	39.5 (54.4%)	6.3 (59.9%)	17.2 (68.2%)	16.8 (70.4%)	57.0 (74.2%)	2.7 (70.8%)	8.6 (71.1%)	0.92 (42.0%)	2.26 (52.1%)
Twigs and branches	1163	1776	7.7 (18.8%)	12.8 (17.6%)	1.6 (15.0%)	3.2 (12.7%)	4.2 (17.5%)	14.2 (18.5%)	0.5 (13.7%)	2.1 (17.35%)	0.39 (17.8%)	0.72 (16.6%)
Miscellaneous debris	568	709	12.3 (29.9%)	20.3 (28.0%)	2.6 (25.0%)	4.8 (19.0%)	2.9 (12.1%)	5.6 (7.3%)	0.6 (15.5%)	1.4 (11.6%)	0.88 (40.2%)	1.36 (31.3%)
Total	3857	5736	41.1	72.6	10.5	25.2	23.8	76.8	3.9	12.1	2.19	4.34

Percentages of the total for each element per site given in parentheses.

Note: Some of the Meathop data are provisional and subject to revision in Satchell[1] different types of litter were collected in containers appropriate to the size of the litter materials. Samples must be removed frequently from the collecting vessels to avoid changes in nutrient content through leaching, respiration or decomposition. Dry weights of these various types of litter, together with chemical analyses, for each month throughout the year, permit their role in the nutrient cycle to be assessed. Results are given in table 1 which demonstrate the significance of the non-leaf litter, and in particular, the role of the miscellaneous debris in the phosphorus cycle. The monthly data also enable the importance in the cycle of the litter falling in spring and summer to be seen. Bogle Crag data presented in table 2 suggest that more P, and almost as much N and K, are returned to the forest floor in the litter of spring and summer as fall in the period of main autumn leaf fall. Only small amounts return in winter litter.

TABLE 2

Seasonal pattern of litter fall nutrients: Bogle Crag
(Kilograms/hectare)

Season	N	K	Ca	Mg	P
Spring and Summer (April–September)	18.4 (45%)	4.5 (43%)	6.5 (27%)	1.21 (31%)	1.19 (55%)
Autumn (October-December)	21.6 (53%)	5.9 (56%)	17.1 (72%)	2.63 (68%)	0.94 (43%)
Winter (January-March)	1.0 (2%)	0.1 (1%)	0.2 (1%)	0.03 (1%)	0.04 (2%)
Total	41.0	10.5	23.8	3.87	2.17

Percentages of total for each element in parentheses.

3. *Leachates*

A less conspicuous pathway for nutrient return is that resulting from the action of rainfall. Chemical analysis of rainwater shows that it has a small, but ecologically significant, content of plant nutrients (table 3). However, a comparison made of rainfall collected above the woodland canopy or outside the wood with that sampled beneath the canopy, shows that in dripping through the tree leaves, twigs and branches (throughfall), rainwater is considerably enriched in the bases K, Ca and Mg. Conversely, inorganic N is regularly removed from the rainwater, and in some months total N (ie inorganic+organic), together with P, are also reduced, probably by micro-organisms in the canopy, or possibly through foliar absorption (fig 1). The rain which runs down the main branches and the trunks (stem flow) is even richer in base elements. A good deal of this enrichment, but not all, is due to the leaching of nutrients out of the canopy, mainly from the foliage, but possibly in part from micro-organisms present on the foliage, but derived directly or indirectly from the trees' tissues and therefore part of the cycle.

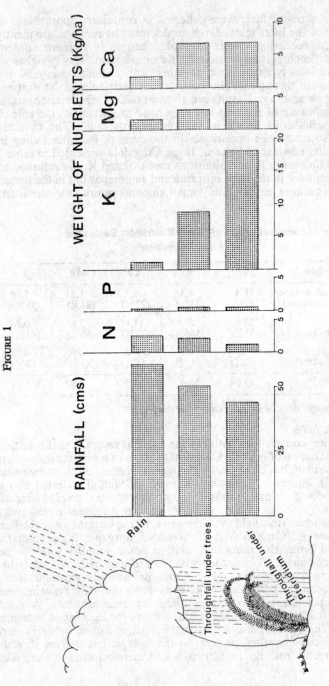

FIGURE 1

Quantities of nutrients (kg/ha) in rainwater above and beneath the canopy at Bogle Crag Wood, NW England, for the period July–October inclusive.

A proportion of the enrichment, however, has a quite different source, being derived by the washing from the tree crowns of particulate matter, aerosols and dust, which have been 'filtered' from the atmosphere by impaction on the canopy, (ie matter which is additional to the similar material removed from the atmosphere in the rain, and which is largely responsible for the nutrient content in ordinary rainfall). This widely reported phenomenon has been discussed by White and Turner[5]. The practical value of trees for filtering particulate matter from the air, including radioactive particles and other pollutants has been studied in Germany[6] [7]. In the present context, we clearly need to be able to distinguish between throughfall enrichment due to nutrient circulation and that resulting from impaction, which represents additional income to the ecosystem. Within the Meathop Wood Research programme, White has developed a method for obtaining a weekly sample through the year of the particles trapped on filter-paper discs, simulating leaves, exposed to air movements but shielded from rain. The equipment used, together with other meteorological instruments, was supported on a tower at mid-canopy level. A factor was obtained to convert quantities recovered from simulated leaves to estimates of the amount caught on the actual leaves present in a given area of woodland canopy[5]. The results given in table 3 suggest that nutrient income from the impactation of aerosols on the woodland canopy is comparable with that in the rainfall.

TABLE 3

Atmospheric income of nutrient elements: Meathop
(Kilograms/hectare)

	N	K	Ca	Mg	P
Rainfall ..	5.9 (+N fixation)	3.2	6.9	5.4	0.23
Aerosols ..	—	3.4	1.8	8.4	0.12
Total ..	5.9+	6.6	8.7	13.8	0.35

4. *Ground flora*

The role of ground flora has been assessed by periodic harvesting throughout the year. It parallels in most respects the role of the tree; nutrients are taken up and returned annually by adding to the litter, although some would also be retained if a steady state had not been reached (ie if annual biomass were increasing). In both research sites it has been assumed that the latter is not the case and that all uptake in the herb layer is recycled. The quantities involved are given in table 4. Materials are also leached from ground flora by the rain. In studies at Bogle Crag, the enriched throughfall from the tree canopy was shown to be further enriched after passing over bracken fronds. These data were obtained by allowing newly emerged fronds in the spring to grow through slits in the polythene floor of a number of frames. Subsequently, the rachides were sealed into place with an inert sealing compound. The natural slope of the ground facilitated collection of waters from the lowermost corner of each frame. The results are demonstrated in table 4 and fig 1, and show the appreciably increased cycling of magnesium and potassium which results, but that little extra calcium was cycled in this way.

TABLE 4

Nutrient elements cycled by leaching from bracken and in its litter: Bogle Crag

(Kilograms/hectare)

	N	K	Ca	Mg	P
Bracken litter ..	12.9	6.9	4.0	1.3	0.89
Leached from bracken ..	−0.3	9.4	0.1	1.0	0.09

5. *Herbivores*

The litterfall and leaching pathways by which nutrients are returned to the forest floor, appear to be essential or 'obligatory' parts of the cycle. A 'non-obligatory' route is provided by herbivores and any associated carnivore food-webs. Despite the great diversity of different animals, especially invertebrates, associated with oak— or perhaps because of it, in that their diversity inhibits the build-up of over-large numbers—the quantitative role of animals in the nutrient cycle is usually small and hence has been omitted from the main nutrient cycle tables and diagram. At Meathop, the numbers of defoliators appear to have been consistently very low. On slate sites in the district however, populations of *Tortrix viridana* build up from time to time, possibly related to the markedly reduced species diversity amongst trees and other plants on such sites compared with the woodlands on limestone. At Bogle Crag, there was a moderately severe defoliation by the larvae of *Tortrix* in 1961 but only low numbers in the other years during the period under study (1961–1965). The role of such defoliation in the nutrient cycle was studied by sampling the frass falling to the ground, and by obtaining a converstion factor in order to relate the weight of frass to the weight of foliage consumed. Numbers of leaves eaten were also sampled. The effects of such defoliations are discussed later.

6. *Litter decomposition*

Nutrients falling to the forest floor in the litter cannot, for the most part, re-enter the uptake cycle again until they are made available (mineralised) by the activities of the decomposer organisms. The decomposition stage, therefore, is a critical one without which litter would accumulate indefinitely, nutrients would remain organically 'locked up' and unavailable, and the soil conditions become radically altered—as happens when excessive raw humus formation occurs or, more extremely, with peat formation. On the other hand, the drawn out processes of mineralisation provide a regulatory mechanism whereby nutrients are provided continually and steadily for re-use, and, in the main, prevented from being washed out of the ecosystem. It has been shown that woodlands can be very efficient at retaining their nutrients, the latter being rapidly lost into streams and rivers if the forest is cleared[8].

The bulk (80–90%) of the decomposition is carried out by micro-organisms[9], ie bacteria, fungi and actinomycetes. However, their normal role appears to be at least partly dependent on the catalytic effects of soil animals, whose feeding activities aid decomposition in a number of ways[10]. The resulting food-web is of great complexity and involves very many species, but the more important organisms in base-rich oakwoods are earthworms (Oligochaeta), springtails (Collembola), millipedes (Diplopoda) and nematode worms. In more acid sites, such as Bogle Crag, earthworm activity is markedly reduced, but springtails and mites assume greater importance; the importance of fungi relative to bacteria also increases. Because of the essential role of decomposers in ecosystem functioning and because of the complexity of the process, this aspect of ecosystems in general has probably received greater attention than any other. Details of such work are outside the scope of this paper but, for Bogle Crag, studies limited mainly to the role of fungi, have been published by Hering[11, 12]; the fuller information for Meathop is given in Satchell[1].

In contrast to the nutrients returning in the litter fall pathway, where availability for re-use is delayed to a greater or lesser extent, those falling to the forest floor by leaching are immediately re-usable either by the trees and other plants themselves or by the micro-organisms in the litter. These leached nutrients may thus serve these organisms in their vital role of litter decomposition by providing a rapidly utilisable nutrient source. Similarly, the soluble carbohydrates, mainly sugars resulting from the honey-dew of aphids which are also washed from the canopy in the summer[13 14], may furnish them with a readily assimilable energy source.

Nutrient uptake and cycling

Having presented information on the various parts of the cycle, the overall picture obtained (table 5 and fig 2) can now be considered and discussed. Net annual uptake consists of the sum of materials retained, together with those returned in the cycle. Gross uptake will be greater if shorter term cycles or movements within the tree take place during the year, as indeed appears to be the case. For example, during the growing season, there are variations in the absolute nutrient content of the foliage. At Bogle Crag, phosphorus content reached a maximum in May-June, followed by peaks for nitrogen and potassium and magnesium in late June, whereas calcium content behaved quite differently and continued to rise until the autumn. Apart from this last element, the absolute quantities of these nutrients have considerably lessened by the time the leaves fall, partly through the leaching losses already referred to, but also through a process of nutrient conservation whereby

FIGURE 2

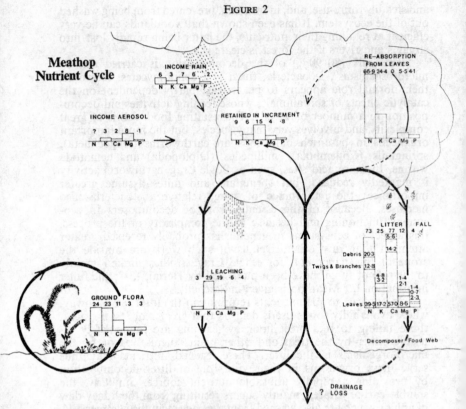

Meathop Nutrient Cycle

Quantities involved (kg/ha/year) in the above-ground nutrient cycle at Meathop Wood, NW England.

materials are translocated back into the tree before leaf fall and do not therefore enter the external cycle. This 'internal cycle' is especially marked in the case of phosphorus and nitrogen. The maximum foliar levels and the amounts which are re-absorbed in this way (allowances having been made for leaching) for Meathop are shown in the table and figure. Although the full data are not available for Bogle Crag, there are strong indications that this process is even more marked for phosphorus and nitrogen but less so for potassium and magnesium[5]. The quantities of nitrogen re-absorbed are so large (at Bogle Crag equivalent to almost half the total nitrogen in the above-ground biomass) as to lead to the speculation that some may be translocated out of the tree entirely, via root exudates.

Large amounts of nutrients are required by the tree leaves for their development anew each spring and for their subsequent activity as the ecosystem's principal energy-fixing zone. The foliar peaks for nitrogen, potassium and magnesium coincide with the period in

TABLE 5

Net annual quantities of nutrients taken up and recycled: Bogle Crag and Meathop
(Kilograms/hectare)

	Dry weight		N		K		Ca		Mg		P	
	Bogle Crag	Meathop	Bogle Crag	Meathop	Bogle Crag	Meathop	Bogle Crag	Meathop	Bogle Crag	Meathop	Bogle Crag	Meathop
(1) Retained in above ground increment (estimated from stem data at Bogle Crag)	1326	3964	2.5	9.2	1.9	5.9	1.5	14.6	0.25	3.8	0.29	0.78
As % of total uptake (7)			(5.6%)	(10.8%)	(6.3%)	(9.9%)	(3.8%)	(13.2%)	(2.4%)	(23.0%)	(9.6%)	(14.1%)
(2) Cycled in all types of litter	3857	5736	41.1	72.6	10.5	25.2	23.8	76.8	3.9	12.1	2.19	4.34
(3) Cycled in leachates (no allowance for aerosols at Bogle Crag)			0.9	3.3	17.5	28.5	14.2	19.3	6.2	0.6	0.55	0.40
(4) Cycled in ground flora (no allowance for ground flora leaching at Meathop)	1470	1031	12.6	24.3	16.3	23.0	4.1	11.0	2.3	3.3	0.98	2.66
(5) Maximum leaf content			105.4	97.2	24.2	46.9	26.3	47.5	6.6	10.3	6.6	6.45
(6) Resorption from leaves				66.9		24.4		0		5.5		4.09
(7) Total net tree uptake (1)+(2)+(3)			44.5	85.1	29.9	59.6	39.5	110.7	10.35	16.5	3.03	5.52

Note: Some of the Meathop data are provisional and subject to revision in Satchell[1].

mid-summer when the amount of daylight available for photosynthesis is also at a maximum. At this time, the leaves contain high proportions of the total nutrients present in the vegetation; at Bogle Crag, 61 % of the nitrogen, 52% of the phosphorus and somewhat smaller proportions of the other elements[15]; because of the greater total biomass relative to foliage at Meathop, percentages for this site (derivable from tables 5 and 6) are lower. At both sites, these peak requirements of the leaves are greater than the net quantities cycling in the case of nitrogen and phosphorus—again emphasising the internal cycle—and are a high proportion of the cycled potassium and magnesium. Conversely, considerably more calcium is cycled than is apparently required by the leaves.

Annual retention by the trees in their new growth is also shown. Most of these retained materials are incorporated into the sapwood and bark. The latter is rich in most elements, especially calcium, 75% of the total calcium present in Bogle Crag in the above ground vegetation being in the bark. Although the new extension shoots (1 year twigs) are also rich in nutrients, their dry weight biomass, and hence absolute nutrient content is small.

1. *Nitrogen*

Nitrogen is taken up by the trees as a whole in greater amounts than any other element at Bogle Crag, and is exceeded only by calcium on the limestone site of Meathop. At both sites, nutrient uptake by the leaves was greatest for nitrogen. Very little of this leaf N is leached out and only about a third of it falls in the leaf litter, the larger portion returning to the tree; an amount approaching that in the leaf fall, however, also falls in the non-leaf litter. This large internal cycling of nitrogen has already been referred to; it is also reported to be a marked feature of some grassland systems[16]. In the ground flora, nitrogen, is again taken up more than other elements, but is only about a quarter of the maximum tree uptake. The reduction of the nitrogen content of the throughfall in some months compared with incident rainfall has already been noted. There was further diminution of nitrogen in the bracken leachate at Bogle Crag.

At the same time, large quantities of nitrogen from the air are added to the system by nitrogen-fixing organisms. This probably includes appreciable amounts on the leaves, with even more fixed in the soil. Thus, at Meathop, preliminary results suggest that 109kg/ha is fixed annually, compared with only 12kg/ha lost in drainage. Insofar as nitrogen is not a normal constituent of soil parent material, ecosystems in general must be dependent on acquiring nitrogen through income by fixation or otherwise; the accumulation of nitrogen appears to be especially marked however in woodlands, and Duvigneaud and Denaeyer-De Smet[17] quote high figures for this phenomenon in a wide range of forest types. Nitrogen does not appear to be a limiting factor, even at Bogle Crag, judging from studies of the nutritional requirements of oak on these soils[15][18].

2. *Potassium*

Potassium shows a marked contrast with nitrogen in its behaviour in the cycle. This very mobile element is easily washed from the tree by rain, and the leaching pathway accounts for more than half the potassium cycle in the trees. Of the smaller remaining portion falling as litter, about two-thirds is in the leaf fall. The significance of the ground flora in the potassium cycle is greater than for any other element. At Meathop, the ground flora provided more of this element in its litter than fell in the tree leaf fall, and indeed almost as much as fell in all types of the tree litter (cf tables 1 and 5). The studies in bracken at Bogle Crag showed that, for this species at least, as with the trees, potassium was leached out of it during the summer in larger quantities than fell in its litter.

3. *Calcium*

Although leaf uptake is dominated by nitrogen, at Meathop uptake by the trees as a whole is greater for calcium than for any other element. Even at the base-poor Bogle Crag site, the total vegetation biomass contains more calcium than any other element, three quarters of which is in the bark of the trees. Unlike other elements, calcium also continues to accumulate in the foliage, well past the period of maximum leaf weight and activity, and indeed until leaf fall; leaf fall is the major pathway of return for calcium. Calcium differs from other elements also in the quantities lost in the drainage water. Several studies quoted by Duvigneaud and Denaeyer-De Smet[17] show that drainage losses of nutrients from forest ecosystems are all very small except for calcium; data from Meathop support this finding. The very large accumulation of calcium in the bark and in the senescent leaves and the removal of calcium in the drainage water, suggest that calcium is present in the system and is taken up in amounts greater than those required for metabolic activity. It is tempting to speculate that, far from needing to conserve this element, stratagems are employed, even on an apparently base-poor site such as Bogle Crag, to remove calcium from the cycle. Apparent luxury uptake is even more marked at Meathop.

4. *Phosphorus*

Of the macro-nutrients under discussion, phosphorus is present in much the smallest amounts, both in total, and circulating in the ecosystem. In other respects, it largely parallels nitrogen, with an efficiently conservative cycle. Phosphorus is held closely in the metabolising leaves; little is leached out and in some months none at all. The young, rapidly expanding leaves require relatively large amounts of phosphorus in the spring but, as with nitrogen, a marked internal cycle operates in which two thirds of this peak quantity is re-absorbed before leaf fall. The leaf litter contains only half the total litter fall phosphorus, much of the remainder being in the miscellaneous debris fraction which includes the phosphorus-rich catkins and budscales falling in spring. Although very little is washed out of the foliage when living, there is evidence that phosphorus is lost relatively quickly after the leaves have fallen. The phosphorus content of Bogle Crag litter was reduced by 60% in just six weeks from leaf fall, a proportion only exceeded by the mobile element potassium. This apparently quick mineralisation of phosphorus may enable the roots to re-absorb it during late autumn, possibly aided by mycorrhizas, before their activity declines in the winter, thus ensuring its re-cycling. The fact that a somewhat greater proportion of the phosphorus which returns both as litter (see table 2) and as leachate[3] does so during the spring and summer, will similarly aid retention of this element within the cycle.

At Meathop, lysimeter studies suggest that the amounts of phosphorus lost by soil drainage are so small as to be more than balanced by atmospheric income. Nevertheless, experiments carried out into the nutrition of oak seedlings at Bogle Crag suggested that this site is deficient in phosphorus as far as seedlings are concerned, and hence perhaps for the ecosystem as a whole.

Ecosystems compared

A comparison of Bogle Crag and Meathop can be made from the above-ground data presented in table 5. Although it can be seen that Bogle Crag had consistently lower figures for nutrient quantities than Meathop, reflecting the lower productivity both of woody material and foliage, the differences cannot solely be explained in this way. The *proportions* (shown as percentages in the table) of the total annual uptake which are retained within the tree increment are also consistently lower at Bogle Crag. If a further comparison is made with comparable data taken from Duvigneaud and Denaeyer-De Smet[17] for mixed oakwood at Virelles, Belgium, a site yet more productive than Meathop, the proportions withdrawn are greater still, with 31% of the nitrogen uptake, 22% potassium, 31% calcium, 28% magnesium and 35% of the phosphorus uptake being retained in the above-ground increment. These increased proportions are achieved however without an increased absolute uptake, except for calcium; magnesium uptake is very similar to Meathop, that for nitrogen, potassium and phosphorus somewhat less. A possible interpretation is that although absolute uptake of nutrients may, on the poorer sites, be similar to or even greater than that for the better areas, the proportions which the system can afford to remove from the cycle into increment is low. Conversely, correspondingly higher proportions (or even absolute amounts) are needed for cycling in order to keep the system functioning under adverse site conditions

Ecosystems may also be compared on the basis of the distribution of the total nutrient capital between the various parts—total vegetation biomass, including roots, the undecomposed litter and the reserves in the soil. Data for Bogle Crag being incomplete, only Meathop and Virelles are compared here, in table 6. The proportions of the total 'available' capital (ie excluding the non-exchangeable fraction in the soil) present in the vegetation and litter are also shown as percentages. Whilst figures for nutrient distribution at the two sites are in general very comparable, differences

TABLE 6

Comparison of nutrient distribution in Meathop (Westmorland) and Virelles (Belgium from Duvigneaud and Denaeyer-De Smet[17])
(Kilograms/hectare)

	N		K		Ca		Mg		P	
	Meathop	Virelles	Meathop	Virelles	Meathop	Virelles	Meathop	Virelles	Meathop	Virelles
Annual retention in increment	24	30	13	16	30	74	6.1	5.6	1.7	2.2
Tree biomass	716	495	416 (56%)	296 (56%)	828 (43%)	1204 (8%)	145 (60%)	97 (37%)	44.1 (52%)	39
Ground flora biomass	22	38	16 (2.1%)	46 (8.6%)	8 (0.4%)	44 (0.3%)	3 (1.2%)	5.4 (2.0%)	2.1 (2.5%)	5.1
Undecomposed litter	180	44	49 (6.6%)	17 (3.2%)	237 (12.2%)	107 (0.7%)	24 (9.9%)	5.1 (1.9%)	7.6 (8.9%)	1.9
Soil 'available'*			249 (34%)	157 (30%)	840 (43%)	13600 (89%)	64 (26%)	151 (57%)	29.4 (35%)	920
Soil 'non-available'	5550	4480	24100	26600	1440	119400	15600	6310	969	
Total 'available' capital	743	532	743	532	1943	15029	242	264	84.8	

Note: Root data are included in the biomass and increment figures. Some of the Meathop data are provisional and subject to revision in Satchell[1].

* Extractable in ammonium acetate, pH 7, at Meathop (except P for which an isotopically exchangeable figure was determined). Virelles data given as exchangeable quantities.

occur reflecting, on the one hand, differences in available bases (potassium, calcium and magnesium) in the two soils and, on the other hand, the apparently greater rate of litter decomposition at Virelles. These differences apart, the broad picture provided by both these mixed oakwoods is similar to that found in other temperate deciduous woodland. Between about a third and two thirds (37–60%) of the total 'available' nutrient capital is locked up in the roots, stems and branches of the trees (except for calcium at Virelles). Smaller amounts are immobilised in litter, although these are still significant, especially if seen in relation to the requirements for the annual increment, which they generally exceed. These proportions may be contrasted, on the one hand, with the northern coniferous forests and, on the other, with tropical rain forests. In the northern forests, the proportions of the nutrient capital in the undecomposed litter can be at least as high as, or even considerably higher than, those in the biomass owing to a much slower rate of litter decomposition[19]. Conversely, in the tropical rain forest, most of the nutrient capital is in the biomass; there is virtually no litter accumulation because of its extremely rapid decomposition; and because of the high rainfall the major pathway for the return of nutrients to the forest floor is in fact by leaching[20].

Effects of perturbations

The prospect of understanding or predicting the effects of 'perturbations', or disturbances, on an ecosystem is one of the objectives of whole-ecosystem studies. It is therefore appropriate to see whether the present information is at least sufficient to produce hypotheses, in two cases which appear relevant in this context.

1. *Defoliation by* Tortrix viridana

Although the role of herbivores in the oakwood nutrient cycle appears to be small under normal circumstances, it is worthwhile considering their significance on those occasions when appreciable defoliation does occur. In his studies of *Tortrix viridana* defoliation at Roudsea Wood, which contains both slate and limestone woodland, Satchell[21] noted that severe defoliation was restricted to the areas of slate. This is probably also true for the southern Lake District generally, and may relate to the species poverty of these woodlands on acid soils. The virtually pure oak on many of these sites is almost certainly an artefact deriving from the former high value of oak which was favoured either by planting or otherwise[22]. These woods are therefore relics of a former commercial monoculture, prevented by grazing from becoming more diverse, and of which Bogle Crag is typical.

At this site, 1961 was a year of moderately severe defoliation by *Tortrix* in which 27% of the mean number of leaves or 25% of the mean leaf area in the sample plot were eaten by the larvae in May–June. A new flush of leaves was produced in early July, although sampling suggested that this replacement was about 10% less than the initial defoliation. Potential for photosynthesis was therefore reduced not only during the period of larval activity, and in particular during the long days of midsummer which are likely to be of special importance[23], but also to some extent for the remainder of the season.

TABLE 7

Comparison of nutrients which would be removed in defoliation, with those retained in annual increment: Meathop

(Kilograms/hectare)

	N	K	Ca	Mg	P
Annual increment requirement (including root-growth) ..	24	13	29	6	1.7
Leaf content at seasonal max.	97	47	47	10	6.4

Defoliation may however be even more severe, with many trees made completely leafless[24]. The reduction in oak increment following defoliation which has been demonstrated by a number of authors (eg Varley and Gradwell[23]) may not be solely due to the reduction in photosynthesis. Defoliation occurs when both the weight of leaves and their nutrient content are at or near the seasonal peak; the internal circulation of nutrients already referred to—especially important for nitrogen and phosphorus—is thereby entirely prevented. Replacement of this foliage in the new flush of leaf expansion, therefore represents a considerable drain on the trees' reserves of both organic materials and nutrients. The significance of this loss of reserves can be judged if the defoliation losses are compared with the requirements for nutrient retention in the trees' annual increment. Although absence of root data prevents such a comparison being made for Bogle Crag, the Meathop results in table 7 show that the loss of leaves (at the seasonal maximum) would remove the equivalent in nitrogen and phosphorus, and almost the equivalent for potassium, of the amounts required in four years total annual tree increment. It may be significant that Varley (quoted in Carlisle et al[2]) found that artificial defoliation in May of a small oak tree, produced virtually no stem increment for at least three years.

Defoliation by *Tortrix viridana* can occur for several years in succession once its numbers have built up sufficiently[21]. Even though materials remain within the system the repeated replacement of leaves during such outbreaks is nevertheless likely to make demands on the trees' nutrient reserves very much greater than can be supplied by re-cycling, with concomitant increment loss, unless mineralisation and uptake rates can both be increased several-fold.

Rafes[25] has pointed out, on the other hand, that some partially compensatory mechanisms may be associated with defoliation, including the possibility that the decomposition of litter might be speeded up both by the addition of easily mineralised nutrients in the frass, and by the extra insolation resulting from the reduced canopy.

2. The effects of cropping

Phosphorus supply and its circulation appear to be key factors in the oakwood ecosystems and, as far as Bogle Crag and other slate sites are concerned, where increment is very low, deficiency in phosphorus is possibly a main factor limiting growth. This very low productivity has in the past inhibited foresters from retaining oak on such sites. Although there may well be a variety of reasons for such slow growth, it is none the less of interest to see whether any light is thrown on the problem by examination of a somewhat speculative nutrient balance-sheet which it is possible to derive from existing data.

Natural losses of nutrients by drainage are small and tend to be more than balanced by income. These woods are not natural, however, and have been managed for centuries, with nutrient removal in the produce. Although such cropping would occur only at intervals—long or short depending on whether standards or coppice were removed—it may be assumed to be on average equivalent per year to the annual increment. It must be further assumed that nutrient retention in the increment of a coppice stand is similar to the figures available for high forest; and that the existing data for foliage adequately represent those for the foliage which would be present at the end of a coppice cycle (when the canopy would be at least as dense). The Bogle Crag data are given in table 8 and suggest that, if the stems only are harvested—the most likely situation today under high forest conditions—an annual cropping loss equal to the increment is more than balanced by atmospheric income. In former times, however, and especially under a coppice system,

TABLE 8

Mean annual atmospheric income, and possible mean annual cropping losses of nutrients: Bogle Crag

(Kilograms/hectare)

	N	K	Ca	Mg	P
(1) Atmospheric income*	(N-fixation)	5.8	8.5	14.5	0.40
(2) Retention in stem increment	1.2	1.0	1.0	0.10	0.10
(3) Retention in stem and branch increment	2.5	1.9	1.5	0.25	0.29
(4) Leaf content at seasonal maximum	105.4	24.2	26.3	6.6	6.6
(5) 1/14 × (4) (Mean leaf removal in 14 year coppice cycle)	7.5	1.7	1.9	0.5	0.5
(6) Maximum possible removal in coppicing (3)+(5)	10.0	3.6	3.4	0.75	0.79

* includes a notional figure for aerosols taken from Meathop data

the branch-wood was also utilised and the quantities of nutrients so removed are also shown in the table. Most of the Lake District woods were in fact coppiced, providing a variety of produce. Oak was the most valuable species; partly through the variety of uses to which all sizes of its wood could be put, including the manufacture of enormous quantities of charcoal required in the iron-smelting industry; and partly because of the high value of its bark, used in tannery. Because bark-removal and the splitting of the stems or branches necessary for many of the other uses were both much easier after the sap had risen in the spring, oak was the last species to be cut, some, if not all being left until May, June or even early July[26]. By this time, therefore, not only would the trees have been in leaf but, as was noted earlier, the nutrient content of the foliage at least, if not the tree as a whole was approaching its maximum. All parts of the felled trees were almost certainly removed from the site; there is evidence that even the foliage and twigs were burnt in special pits or cauldrons to provide potash which was used in the manufacture of the soft-soap or lye required for cleansing the fleeces or fulling the cloth in the extensive local wool industry[26]. Potash was also produced by burning bracken, which has a high potassium content. On the basis of a 14-year coppice cycle (records give a range of 12–16 years) an additional average annual loss would result from foliage removal, shown in line 5 of table 8. Although some of the high foliar nutrient content in spring may result from an internal redeployment of materials and not be due solely to uptake, it is apparent that delay in cutting until May-June would have led to a marked increase in nutrient loss, especially of phosphorus, which could have exceeded the income for this element. These losses may have been increased even more by burning bracken if it was present in the woodlands in worthwhile quantities. In the context of the above remarks it is noteworthy that most of Bogle Crag Wood is almost pure oak; that it was managed as coppice until about 1880; and that bracken is a dominant component of the ground flora. Dependent, therefore, on the rate at which nutrients in the soil are made available by weathering of the soil parent material, or by other release phenomena, the possibility exists that the relatively intensive cropping systems of the past have built up a phosphorus deficit within ecosystems like Bogle Crag. Even small losses in drainage might significantly influence the balance in such circumstances. On the other hand, the inherently more fertile soils of the limestone may have been able to withstand cropping losses which, because of higher productivity, would have been correspondingly even greater.

Conclusion

In the moist climate of north-west England where shortage of water can rarely be an important factor, the productivity of an ecosystem will be largely dependent on nutrient availability, which in turn partly depends on nutrient cycling. However, the very limited comparisons between oakwood ecosystems which have been made here suggest that the rate of nutrient cycling is not related in any simple manner with productivity. Data from more sites are necessary however, before this point can be clarified; indeed, only by studying a range of sites will it be possible to understand more fully the significance of nutrient cycling in ecosystem functioning.

At the same time it is clear that the functioning of an ecosystem is also dependent on factors which appear unimportant in nutrient cycling terms. For example, the limited significance of herbivores and other animals in the nutrient cycles of most forest systems[27] inadequately reflects their role in such ecosystems. They almost certainly play an important part in influencing woodland structure and dynamics by selective feeding (for example of seedlings and apical meristems), by seed dispersal, and no doubt in a variety of subtle ways, the importance of which is quite other than via nutrient cycling.

Nevertheless, a sufficiently useful model of the ecosystem can be derived from nutrient cycling studies to demonstrate their contribution to an overall understanding of how the system functions; to help in understanding the effects of management; and in generating hypotheses for a variety of problems.

Acknowledgements

I am most grateful to a number of colleagues at Merlewood, in particular Mr E. J. White and Dr J. E. Satchell, for making available the results from Meathop Wood prior to publication elsewhere. I also wish to thank Mr J. N. R. Jeffers and Dr Satchell for their constructive criticisms of the text.

REFERENCES

1. SATCHELL, J. E. (ed., in prep.). *The Ecology of Meathop Woods*
2. CARLISLE, A., BROWN, A. H. F. and WHITE, E. J. 'Litter fall, leaf production and the effects of defoliation by *Tortrix viridana* in a sessile oak (*Quercus petraea*) woodland', *J. Ecol.*, **54** (1966), 65–85
3. CARLISLE, A., BROWN, A. H. F. and WHITE, E. J. 'The organic matter and nutrient elements in the precipitation beneath a sessile oak (*Quercus petraea*) canopy', *J. Ecol.*, **54** (1966), 87–98
4. CARLISLE, A., BROWN, A. H. F. and WHITE, E. J. 'The nutrient content of tree stem flow and ground flora litter and leachates in a sessile oak (*Quercus petraea*) woodland', *J. Ecol.*, **55** (1967) 615–27
5. WHITE, E. J. and TURNER, F. 'A method of estimating income of nutrients in catch of airborne particles by a woodland canopy', *J. appl. Ecol.*, **7** (1970), 441–61
6. HERBST, W. 'Baum und Waldgegen radioaktive atmosphärische Beimengungen', *Allg. Forstz.*, **13** (1960), 194–5
7. BLUM, W. 'Der Wald als Aerosolfilter', *Forst-u. Holzwirt*, **20** (1965), 220–3
8. LIKENS, G. F., BORMANN, F. H., JOHNSON, N. M., FISHER, D. W. and PIERCE, R. S. 'Effects of forest cutting and herbicide treatment on nutrient budgets in the Hubbard Brook watershed-ecosystem', *Ecology*, **40** (1970), 23–47

9. MACFADYEN, A. 'The contribution of the microfauna to total soil meta-
      bolism', in *Soil Organisms: Proc. of the colloquium on soil
      fauna, soil microflora and their relationships*, Oosterbeck, 1962,
      eds J. Doekson and J. van der Drift (1963)
10. MACFADYEN, A. 'The animal habitat of soil bacteria', in *The Ecology
      of Soil Bacteria*, eds T. R. G. Gray and D. Parkinson (1968)
11. HERING, T. F. 'Succession of fungi in the litter of a Lake District wood-
      land', *Trans. Br. mycol. Soc.*, **48** (1965), 391–408
12. HERING, T. F. 'Fungal decomposition of oak leaf litter', *Trans. Br.
      mycol. Soc.*, **50** (1957), 267–73
13. CARLISLE, A. 'Carbohydrates in the precipitation beneath sessile oak
      (*Quercus petraea* (Mattushka) Liebl.)', *Pl. Soil*, **22** (1965),
      399–400
14. CARLISLE, A. BROWN, A. H. F. and WHITE, E. J. 'The nutrient content of
      rainfall and its role in the forest nutrient cycle', *14th Congr. Int.
      Un. Forest Res. Org.*, **2** (1967), 145–58
15. CARLISLE, A., BROWN, A. H. F. and WHITE, E. J. 'Nutrient cycles in a semi-
      natural oak *Quercus petraea* woodland in a high rainfall area in
      north western Britain', *6th Wld For. Congr.*, **2** (1968),
      2457–61
16. ELLENBERG, H. 'Nitrogen content, mineralisation and cycling', in
      Productivity of Forestry Ecosystems, ed. P. Duvigneaud, UNESCO,
      Paris (1971)
17. DUVIGNEAUD, P. and DENAEYER-DE SMET, S. 'Biological cycling of
      minerals in temperate deciduous forests', in *Analysis of temperate
      forest ecosystems*, ed. D. E. Reichle (1970)
18. NEWNHAM, R. M. and CARLISLE, A. 'The nitrogen and phosphorus
      nutrition of seedlings of *Quercus robur* and *Q. petraea* (Mattuschka)
      Leibl.', *J. Ecol.*, **57** (1969), 272–84
19. RODIN, L. E. and BAZILEVICH, N. I. *Production and Mineral Cycling in
      Terrestrial Vegetation*, (translation of 1965 Russian publication)
      (1967)
20. ODUM, H. G. 'Rain forest structure and mineral-cycling homeostasis', in
      A Tropical Rain Forest Book 3, U S Atomic Energy Commission
      (1970)
21. SATCHELL, J. E. 'Resistance in oak (*Quercus* spp) to defoliation by
      Tortrix viridana L. in Roudsea Wood National Nature Reserve',
      Ann. appl. Biol., **50** (1962), 431–42
22. FELL, A. *The Early Iron Industry of Furness* (1908)
23. VARLEY, G. C. and GRADWELL, G. R. 'The effect of partial defoliation by
      caterpillars on the timber of oak trees in England', 11th Int.
      Congr. Ent., **2** (1962), 211–14
24. MACRAE, C. 'Some observations on *Tortrix* defoliation', *Q. Jl For.*, **51**
      (1957), 332–3
25. RAFES, P. M. 'Pests and the damage which they cause to forests', in
      Productivity of Forest Ecosystems, ed. P. Duvigneaud, UNESCO
      Paris (1971)
26. MARSHALL, J. D. and DAVIES-SHIEL, M. *The Industrial Archaeology of
      the Lake Counties*, Newton Abbot (1969)
27. MCCULLOUGH, D. R. 'Secondary production of birds and mammals',
      in *Analysis of Temperate Ecosystems*, ed. D. E. Reichle, Berlin
      (1970)

THE REPRODUCTIVE CHARACTERISTICS
OF OAK

M. W. SHAW

Merlewood Research Station, Grange-over-Sands

Introduction

It is widely assumed by ecologists and foresters alike, that natural regeneration of both our native oaks is either failing, or is severely deficient, in most British woodlands and that, in the absence of intervention by man, they will undergo a steady decline resulting in their gradual disappearance from woods. Such fears appear to be based mainly on the conditions observed in those woods in which oak is the dominant tree and which are, and usually for no more complex reason, called oak woods. The majority of such woods consist of large, mature, although not necessarily very old, trees with few saplings or young trees in evidence. Projection of this condition into the future leads most people to assume that, when the present trees die there will be little or nothing to replace them, or at least they will not be replaced by oak. The extreme view is that such woodlands may die out altogether, presumably being replaced by grassland. Amongst ecologists who regard oak forests as a climatic climax vegetation type, there is deep-rooted concern that oak woods tend to be even-aged and not all-aged as it is thought they should be. Since pollen records show that in the past, oak, without assistance from man, was the dominant tree over most of the land surface of Britain, it is generally concluded that changed conditions, and their effect on the reproductive processes of oak, have resulted in loss of the ability to be self-perpetuating.

It is argued later that some of the observations and many of the conclusions that have been drawn concerning the natural regeneration of oak in Britain are erroneous or based on false premises. It is, however, proposed to defer the detailed discussion of how such widely held opinions have arisen until after the main information regarding the reproductive processes of oak has been presented and, to some extent, interpreted. The basic philosophy that has been adopted is that of population dynamics; an approach more commonly found in the zoological field but employed with great success by Harper and others [1] in relation to arable weed species. The classic paper on oak regeneration by Watt [2] contained something of this approach, which I also adopted in previous papers [3] [4] and was particularly well used by Mellanby [5] in relation to the role of acorn predators. The basic argument is that, during a lifespan of up to 300 years (maybe more in exceptional cases), an individual oak tree is capable of producing several million acorns (small seeded species like birch produce more by several orders of magnitude). Biological success of the species is measured by the survival, on average, of just one of these acorns, to produce an adult tree which itself becomes capable of reproduction. Indeed, the failure of all but one of these propagules is a postive necessity if man himself is not be to eliminated by oak trees. It is a shortcoming of much of the previous work and related discussion that the major emphasis has been on the high losses that were observed and not on the low survival.

Only Watt[2] has previously attempted to discuss the reproductive cycle of oak as a complete entity and, although he paid more attention to the factors which affected the survival and germination of acorns, and less to what happened to seedlings, nearly all the major factors and basic field observations were covered by him.

Unless otherwise stated my own work refers to the Sessile oak in western Britain (North Wales or the Lake District).

Factors affecting seed production and germination

In all woods reported in the literature, and also in my experience, some acorn fall does occur at fairly regular intervals; usually more frequently and in larger amounts than casual observations would suggest. This acorn fall always results in the production of oak seedlings and their number in any given year is usually in excess of that of the parent trees. Complete replacement of the existing tree cover only requires their survival and satisfactory growth.

1. *Flowering*

Many details are given by Jones[6]. In Britain, maiden oak trees (trees of seed origin in which the shoot system has at no time been cut back) do not usually produce their first flowers until they are at least forty years old, although coppice shoots may commence earlier (20–25 years). There is some evidence that Pedunculate oak flowers at a younger age than Sessile oak. Separate male and female flowers are produced on the same tree but the relative amounts appear to vary quite widely. Most oak trees seem to produce some flowers every year but, as will be seen later, this does not necessarily lead to acorn production.

2. *Acorn production*

Table 1 shows the results of monitoring acorn production in four National Nature Reserves in North Wales using acorn traps[3]. The results are clear, and even Coed Camlyn, much of which consists of rather stunted, small-crowned trees (10m in c. 100 years) is shown to be capable of producing large crops of acorns. Observations of acorns on the ground grossly underestimate acorn fall, for even at peak density, which only lasts a few days and is easily missed, they have already suffered considerable depletion by predators. In measurements taken in North Wales, peak ground density was never greater than one third of total production and, of that third, only a still smaller proportion was immediately visible, most being already

TABLE 1
Seed trapping results for NNRs in North Wales
No. of acorns/m^2

Year	Coed Cymerau (75 traps)	Coedydd Maentwrog (25 traps)	Coed Camlyn (25 traps)	Coed Gorswen (25 traps)
1964	41.3	N.M.	N.M.	N.M.
1965	9.8	N.M.	N.M.	N.M.
1966	0.0	0.0	N.M.	N.M.
1967	0.0	0.0	N.M.	N.M.
1968	1.6	65.4	N.M.	N.M.
1969	8.3	4.1	2.5	3.4
1970	7.1	18.0	2.6	60.1
1971	65.5	5.2	43.8	2.8
1972	0.03	5.9	0.08	11.9

N.M.=No measurements taken

TABLE 2
Coed Cymerau seed trappings results 1964-72
No. of acorns/m^2

Year	Acorns (No./m^2)	Acorns cups (No./m^2)	Aborted peduncles No./m^2	Frass (g/m^2)
1964	41.3	N.M.	N.M.	N.M.
1965	9.8	11.5	28.9	N.M.
1966	0.0	0.0	8.2	N.M.
1967	0.0	0.0	0.2	20.5
1968	1.6	1.0	8.6	10.9
1969	8.3	8.4	49.6	10.2
1970	7.1	7.2	34.9	10.7
1971	65.5	55.3	106.5	6.8
1972	0.03	0.0	13.8	2.7

N.M.=No measurements taken

concealed in the vegetation and litter. The presence of acorn cups in the litter provides a much more reliable all-the-year-round guide to the fruiting performance of a wood.

Table 2 shows more detailed results from the seed traps in Coed Cymerau NNR. The main points to be noted here are (a) that in no year did numbers of acorn cups significantly exceed that of acorns, indicating minimal acorn predation prior to fall (cf Tanton[7]) and (b) that the number of aborted peduncles always exceeded that of acorns. Although there is by no means a constant relationship, they not surprisingly, show similar trends. It is probable that aborted penduncles are indicative of failure in later embryo development, but the causes of this are unknown[3]. The amount of frass collected is taken as giving an estimate of the caterpillar population, or more particularly of activity, and, as can be seen, there has been a steady decline in the population since 1967. The other trapping areas show a similar trend, which would appear to be

part of a long cycle (cf Varley[8]). There appears to be no
relationship between defoliation and acorn production and
Coedydd Maentwrog produced 18.0 acorns/m[2] in the sa
that a frass fall of 56.72 g/m[2] was recorded, nearly double the high
figure recorded by Carlisle et al[9].

3. *Acorn predation*

The literature contains a number of fascinating accounts of the
fate of acorns and the wide variety of animals and birds that are
responsible for their depletion[2 3 4 7 10 11]. All differ in the details of
what happens, but in no case was every single acorn consumed—
there were always survivors—and that is what is significant.
Mellanby[5] argues that removal of acorns by birds and animals is the
main means of dispersal for the heavy seeded oak. Bossema[12] takes
this argument even further in relation to the feeding habits of the
Jay (*Garrulus glandarius* L.), to which he claims acorns are specifically
adapted, but it seems probable that other corvids play a similar
role. Jones[6] quotes a number of striking examples of long-distance
dispersal of acorns by birds, and I have noted their efficiency in
promoting the up-hill spread of oak in the Lake District. Acorns
are an attractive food to a wide range of animals and presumably
this attraction has arisen quite simply as a result of natural selection,
good dispersion being of high selective advantage.

4. *Acorn germination*

In a good seed year, acorns tend to have a higher mean weight
and a higher viability which remains high over the winter[3]. In
western Britain acorns germinate freely in almost any situation; on
the soil surface, under litter or buried in the soil. The most common,
naturally-occurring position is under litter and not only is this the
most favourable position for germination, but it also confers some
protection from predation[4]. By contrast, in south-east England,
Watt[2] found that acorns exposed on the soil surface failed to
germinate as a result of water loss. In North Wales even acorns on
a mat of Wavy hair-grass, *Deschampsia flexusoa,* were found to
germinate reasonably well. Open bryophyte ground cover was also
highly conducive to good germination.

Factors affecting seedling growth and survival

From the arguments presented above, seedling growth and
survival may be regarded as the critical part of the reproductive
process and that part which determines success or failure of natural
regeneration in oak.

There are three main groups of factors involved:

1. Climatic—light in particular.
2. Edaphic—nutrients, water, and root competition for
   these with ground flora and adult trees.
3. Biotic—grazing, browsing, insect and fungal attack.

I propose to deal with these in order, with reference to the
literature: it should then be possible to define conditions under
which oak regeneration is likely to succeed.

1. *Climatic factors*

Since oak is a widespread native species in Britain it is unlikely that any of the major climatic factors are limiting to its progeny. Light as modified by larger trees, if present, or by the ground vegetation, has a profound effect on the performance of oak seedlings. Both drought (Jarvis[14]) and late frost may have local effects on regeneration.

(a) *Light:* Some preliminary work on the effects of light on the growth of oak seedlings was carried out by Ovington and MacRae[15], who concluded that this factor was more important than soil type (although only a fairly limited range of the latter was studied) in determining the growth of oak seedlings. They describe some of the basic responses of oak seedlings to light, ie increase in light results in an increase in total dry weight of seedlings but a decrease in height, at least in the early years. More extensive interpretation of their results is difficult because it can be shown[14] that the experimental method employed resulted in the development of water stress in the high light treatments. The definitive work on light is that of Jarvis[14], who determined the main characteristic responses of oak seedlings to this factor, eg relative growth rate, leaf area ratio, net assimilation rate, specific leaf area, total leaf area, dry weight increment, significant dry weight increment, root/shoot ratio and height. The main conclusions which are relevant in the present context can be summarised as follows:

    (i) Reduced light results in increased height, leaf area, leaf area ratio and chlorophyll content but in decreased root weight, root/stem ratio, net assimilation rate and relative growth rate. Stem weight was unaffected.

    (ii) Compensation point (carbon assimilation) for oak was estimated to be not more than 2% of full daylight but a more ecologically significant value of 5.9% was obtained by excluding leaf weight, which is inevitably lost at leaf fall.

    (iii) At low light intensities other factors, such as mildew, intervene and increase the effective compensation point to almost 8%.

    (iv) Oak seedlings were found to respond to changes in light intensity in a manner which was comparable to other shade plants (eg Wood avens, *Geum urbanum*) and also to be, to some extent, intolerant of high light intensities.

From what is known about more detailed studies of other species, Jarvis suggests that maximum growth of oak seedlings should occur at about 28% of full daylight (or at least in the range 20–40%), conditions which pertain in rather open canopied woodland or in small clearings.

It should be emphasised that all Jarvis's physiological experiments were conducted on first year seedlings and no comparable measurements were made on older seedlings. He did, however, carry out field experiments on the growth of seedlings for longer periods but consideration of these is deferred for the moment.

2. Edaphic factors

(a) *Nutrients:* Both Ovington and MacRae[15] and Jarvis[13] have grown oak seedlings in a range of soils and found few significant edaphic effects. In the former case, the range of soils was limited, and in the latter only one growing season was involved, so the subject cannot be regarded as closed. Jarvis[16] reported a positive response to addition of calcium and nitrogen to a low fertility soil in pot experiments. Newnham and Carlisle[17] have compared the nitrogen and phosphorus nutrition of the two species using nutrient solutions in sand culture and detected quite striking differences. Their results are, however, rather difficult to translate into field conditions because the experiments were carried out in a greenhouse where the growth response was rather different from the field; Pedunculate oak, in particular, flushed a whole succession of buds during the growth period, whereas the maximum number of flushes in the field is usually two. Plants grown in buckets of soil placed in the greenhouse showed similar foliar nitrogen concentrations to others placed in the wood but had only half the concentration of phosphorus. It was, however, concluded that in acid soils, it is phosphorus and not nitrogen that is likely to be deficient. I have treated experimental plantings of seedlings in woodlands with general fertiliser (N.P.K. 10:10:10) and, although there was a marked initial growth response, this rapidly disappeared and was replaced by a significant increase in mortality. The effect was most marked for seedlings growing in *Deschampsia flexuosa* and was attributed to increased competition from that species. The response to added nutrients under field conditions is clearly more complex than the same treatment in pot experiments.

It is clear, therefore, that comparatively little is known about the nutrient requirements of oak seedlings, although more information based on my own work will be presented later. There are, however, some grounds for supposing that oak seedlings are well adapted to a wide range of nutrient levels including quite low ones, in sharp contrast to other species such as ash, *Fraxinus excelsior* (Gordon[18]).

(b) *Water:* Comparatively little is known about this factor, although Jarvis[8] concluded that, in dry years water stress may well develop in seedlings growing under mature trees and in competition with their roots. He also reports increased water stress in the surface layers of the soil outside the wood as compared to within.

(c) *Root competition:* Both Jarvis[14] and I have found significant growth increases in response to reduced root competition, produced by severing roots entering a plot (in the former case stripping the ground vegetation as well). Whether the response is due to the effects of reduced root competition or to an increase in nutrients resulting from the decay of the severed roots, is not known. Jarvis[13] [19] has described and investigated the competition between oak seedlings and *Deschampsia flexuosa*. Root exudates from this species were shown to have an inhibiting effect on root growth of oak and other species. Continuous, unbroken swards of *Deschampsia* are, as Jarvis points out, the result of heavy grazing with consequent loss of tree litter resulting from the poor trapping potential of the ground vegetation. Reduced grazing results in increased litter retention and, being extremely sensitive to smothering, the *Deschampsia* becomes more tussocky and restricted to areas in which litter does not accumulate. In my experience, there is even more severe competition between oak seedlings and Creeping soft-grass, *Holcus mollis,* despite the improved nutrient conditions that might be expected to be associated with that species. The precise mechanism of this effect is not known, but may not be entirely root competition. Jarvis[14] found that Heather, *Calluna vulgaris* (except in the vicinity of birch), could restrict the growth of oak seedlings. The suggested mechanism here was toxic humus inhibiting the development of mycorrhiza. By contrast in one of my experiments, oak seedlings growing in *Deschampsia flexuosa* in the immediate vicinity of invading *Calluna* showed a marked increase in growth. Bracken, *Pteridium aquilinum,* is generally regarded as having an adverse effect on oak regeneration, both by the heavy shade it produces and by the lodging and smothering effect of dead fronds. I found that in dense bracken small mammal damage could be very severe whereas in the surrounding area it was virtually non-existent. In many areas of open bracken, conditions seem to be very favourable to oak regeneration, particularly at margins where the species is just beginning to be suppressed. In a wood in South Wales Gorse, *Ulex europaeus,* appeared to be a precursor of vigorous oak regeneration, there apparently being no question of protection against browsing sometimes produced by spiny species, eg Juniper and Hawthorn. Bilberry, *Vaccinium myrtillus,* seems to provide extremely favourable conditions for both the germination of acorns and the subsequent growth of oak seedlings[2]. Clearly the whole matter of inter-specific competition, whether above or below ground level, even through secondary effects, is extremely complex and far from understood. However, since oak is such a ubiquitous species it must be supposed that it is able to compete successfully with a wide range of other vegetation.

3. *Biotic factors*

In contrast to climatic and, to a lesser extent, edaphic factors, the activities of man have had a marked effect on many biotic factors, the most important being the introduction of domestic stock and the elimination of all large predators. Fortunately many of these effects are fairly easily rectified and the correct management of large herbivores provides the ecologist with a powerful tool.

(a) *Grazing and browsing:* Much has been written about the effects of grazing and browsing animals on woodland regeneration, and on oak in particular[2 7 10 11 20], and there can be no doubt that in all cases where there is overstocking of domestic animals, or for some reason the populations of various wild animals are grossly out of balance, this factor can virtually eliminate all woodland regeneration, and not just oak. Various workers have cited different agencies as being most important, but such conclusions would appear to be of local relevance only. Even the ubiquitous small mammals (Wood mouse, *Apodemus sylvaticus* and Bank vole, *Clethrionomys glareolus*), shown to be so destructive of regeneration by Ashby[10], I have found to be of little or no importance in North Wales. A certain amount of browsing is only 'natural' and, as will be shown later, oak is particularly well adapted, even as a small seedling, to survive this.

(b) *Insect and fungal attack:* Oak mildew, *Microsphaera alphitoides* Griff. & Maubl., can be a serious factor affecting oak seedlings growing under heavy shade, preventing the leaves from developing their full photosynthetic potential under already marginal conditions. Watt[2] noted that oak seedlings in his field experiments were partly or even totally defoliated by a leaf eating agency which he failed to identify. Similarly, Jarvis[14] noted the occurrence of such leaf damage by caterpillars but did not consider it to be of much significance. I would however argue that both the amount of defoliation that occurs and its effect on oak seedlings has been grossly underestimated and that this is a major factor, of the same magnitude as light, in determining the growth and survival of oak seedlings. Watt[2] and Jarvis[14] both record galls on oak seedlings: I can confirm this and add that seedlings under heavy shade are more severely attacked than those in the open.

Conclusion from the literature

It can be concluded from the literature that, providing they are not damaged by biotic agencies, oak seedlings growing in all but the most nutrient deficient soils should be able to achieve a significant growth rate at about 10% full daylight (conditions pertaining in a fairly dense oak wood) and should exhibit a maximum growth rate at about 30% full daylight (conditions pertaining in an open woodland or small clearings). This theoretical performance is however rarely supported by observation, which is the main cause for the view that oak is failing to regenerate and that something is wrong. It can be shown from field experiments[14] that considerably higher light is required for survival—c 30% of full daylight—and still higher values of this factor—50% or more—is required if reasonable growth rates are to be achieved. Table 3 shows the growth rate, in terms of height increment, and the survival of oak seedlings planted in 1965 (one year old pot grown seedlings planted in 1×1m plots in 5×5 configuration) in Coed Cymerau, in relation to light. Also included, are data on mean dry weight of seedlings harvested from this experiment at the end of the fifth year. It should be noted that height gives a comparatively poor indication of dry weight which, for many purposes, is the best measure of the seedling performance. This was, however, a long-term experiment (which is why destructive sampling was limited) and ultimately height and survival can be expected to differentiate between successful and unsuccessful seedlings.

TABLE 3

Coed Cymerau seedling planting experiments. Results 1965-72

Mean light		1965	1966	1967	1968	1969	1970	1971	1972	Max. ht 1972 (cm)	Mean wt 1969 (g)
85%	Height (cm)	6.28	10.75	14.37	16.69	20.39	23.79	32.95	35.35	150.0	7.04
	Survival (%)	100	94	92	82	74	72	72	72		
43%	Height (cm)	7.09	10.15	12.33	13.90	15.71	17.12	20.44	20.25	32.0	1.28
	Survival (%)	100	98	96	86	68	56	42	42		
31%	Height (cm)	6.79	9.63	11.50	13.55	18.09	21.37	22.46	25.95	41.0	1.02
	Survival (%)	100	92	84	76	32	24	18	16		
19%	Height (cm)	7.67	10.30	12.28	12.75	15.95	16.38	18.19	18.39	31.0	1.32
	Survival (%)	100	86	86	78	52	48	32	32		
15%	Height (cm)	6.91	8.83	11.12	12.20	14.20	15.40	16.46	17.71	22.5	0.97
	Survival (%)	100	100	86	78	48	40	18	18		

What, therefore, is the explanation for the discrepancy between the theoretical conditions for the satisfactory growth af oak seedlings and the conditions operative in the field? A dual explanation is offered, but should not be taken as precluding other possible mechanisms, about which less is known at the present time.

1. The effect of leaf damage by defoliating caterpillars.
2. That 'nutrient compensation point' is more critical, at least on the poorer soils, than photosynthetic compensation point.

Ovington and MacRae[15] suggest the latter possibility, saying that seedlings may have some difficulty in replacing the nutrients lost in autumnal leaf shedding.

Defoliation
Basic field observations
As soon as field experiments on the growth of oak seedlings were commenced in 1964 it was observed that many seedlings suffered severe defoliation in the early part of the growing season (May and June) and that the agency responsible for the damage was defoliating caterpillars falling from the tree canopy. Seedlings under trees with a high caterpillar population suffered more than those under trees with a lower population, and seedlings that were only a matter of a few metres away from any overhanging tree, excaped damage almost completely. In June, 1967 four blocks of seedling experiments (each block consisting of four plots of twentyfive seedlings) under different canopy densities in the wood were assessed for loss of foliage. Estimates were made for individual leaves of the proportion of their normal surface area which had been removed; a rather approximate method that does not allow for impaired expansion. The blocks were found to be 29, 36, 48 and 52% defoliated and a number of individual seedlings were 100% defoliated. By contrast, a fifth block outside the wood (about 10m from the nearest tree) was found to be only 3% defoliated. The same seedlings were re-assessed in early July when the blocks in the wood were 39–84% defoliated whilst those outside again showed only minimal effects. At the second assessment, many seedlings had commenced lammas growth which tended to mask the severity of the damage. In the same year, natural seedlings in another part of the wood were 55% defoliated in June. Similar effects were observed in the field in subsequent years with minor variations in severity. The phenomenon has since been observed in woods all over Britain, and one of the reasons why the widespread nature and severity of these attacks seems to have been overlooked, is that oak seedlings which have been defoliated cease to look like oak seedlings, and tend to merge with the ground flora. This also causes underestimation of the number of seedlings present. If subsequent lammas growth is produced the seedling can, to the casual observer, look quite normal again. Fig 1 shows a fairly typical case history taken from photographs.

FIGURE 1

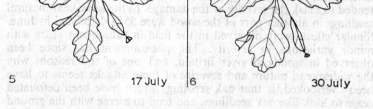

Progress of defoliation and subsequent recovery of a typical oak seedling.

Experiments to measure field defoliation

The approximate assessment of defoliation, by the method described above, was not considered satisfactory and more elaborate experiments were undertaken to determine the level of defoliation which occurred over a range of woodland conditions. Batches of randomised, pot grown seedlings were plunged into the soil, under various canopy conditions, in several woodlands in North Wales before they had flushed in the spring of 1969 and 1970. Leaf area was measured on the plant (using dot grid counts and a special leaf clamp) at intervals throughout the summer and the plants were harvested again in the autumn for dry weight and nutrient determination. Control seedlings were kept under defoliation-free conditions for comparison. On 2 July 1969 defoliation ranged from 25–96% loss (mean of ten seedlings) with an overall mean of 62%. Some recovery by re-flushing was evident at this date. By 12 September substantial recovery had taken place and defoliation ranged from 94% loss to excess foliation of 21%, ie a group of ten seedlings had produced more leaf area than the controls which were all in full daylight. Part of the excess can be accounted for by over-compensation and the rest by shading[14].

A repeat of the experiment in 1970, with fresh seedlings in exactly the same positions as in the previous year, produced less extreme results, with defoliation at the beginning of July ranging from a loss of 77% to an excess of 6%. Under conditions of reduced defoliation, re-flushing was less marked than in the previous year but odd leaves on nearly all plants were subject to some further defoliation before harvest in October. Additional control seedlings placed under 40% and 10% full daylight, produced excess leaf area of 9% and 35% respectively, which suggests that the defoliation levels have, if anything, been underestimated. The degree of re-flushing observed in this series of experiments was, of course, exaggerated by the use of two and three year old seedlings, whose previous growth had taken place in full daylight and whose reserves would be greatly in excess of similarly aged seedlings in a wood. In general, the denser the tree canopy, the heavier the defoliation, dense oak being worse than dense birch. Least defoliation occurred in gaps with no overhead canopy or under mixed birch and oak.

Most caterpillars feeding on seedlings apparently arrive in this situation by simply falling from the tree immediately overhead. Few if any eggs seem to be present on small seedlings and, although first instar caterpillars are widely dispersed by wind, these appear to do comparatively little damage before they disappear due to unknown causes.

Defoliation experiments

The hypothesis to be investigated was that loss of leaf due to defoliation had a much greater effect on the performance of oak seedlings than the straightforward loss of the relatively small amount of dry weight and nutrients involved because of:

1. The reduction in leaf area during the period of maximum

assimilation (it is normally mid-July before the leaf area can be effectively replaced by re-flushing).

2. The replacement leaves, produced at the expense of reserves in stem and root, can then only be used for about half the growing season before they are shed.

It was also postulated that seedlings under high light would be able to withstand the effects of defoliation better than those under low light although, in terms of field conditions, the overall inverse relationship between light and defoliation should not be forgotten.

A two treatment, three level, factorial experiment was therefore set up with light treatments of 80, 40 and 10% full daylight (a special shading material was developed) and defoliation treatments of 0, 50 and 100%. One year old, pot grown seedlings, produced from acorns of uniform weight were used in the experiment described here (ie had been grown for one year under their respective light treatment with no defoliation). Soil was taken from Coed Camlyn NNR (top 20cm mixed), being of brown-podsolic type with pH 4.0–4.2 and low exchangeable bases. Analysis suggests that the soil is probably slightly poorer than average for woods in the area. Artificial defoliation was effected using scissors, cutting-off all leaves for 100% defoliation and alternate sides of leaves for 50%. Early and late flushing seedlings were treated alike, surgery taking place over a matter of 1—2 days. This treatment was repeated on the same seedlings for up to three years, samples being removed for determination of dry weight and nutrient contents at the end of each growing season. Fig 2 shows the cumulative effect of these treatments for two years, on seedlings (minus their leaves), in terms of dry weight and total contents of the major nutrients K, Ca, Mg, P and N. The following conclusions may be drawn from the results:

(i) Defoliation has a comparable, but opposite effect to that of light on the dry weight content of oak seedlings.

(ii) The dry weight light relationship is similar to that found by Jarvis[14], with compensation point for three years growth being estimated as 2.5—4.5% of full daylight.

(iii) In terms of dry weight, calcium and magnesium, all treatments result in seedlings which are at, or over, compensation point (shown by the dotted line).

(iv) In terms of potassium and phosphorus, however, five out of the nine treatment combinations are below compensation point and several of them very seriously below. Even undefoliated seedlings at 10% light, are well below compensation point for both K and P, indicating that it is not dry weight *per se* that is limiting.

(v) The effect of nitrogen is intermediate between that of Ca and Mg on one hand and K and P on the other, defoliation having rather more effect than light.

It should be noted that, the mean for the most severe treatment combination of 10% light and 100% defoliation is probably somewhat elevated by mortality (ie only the more thrifty seedlings have

FIGURE 2

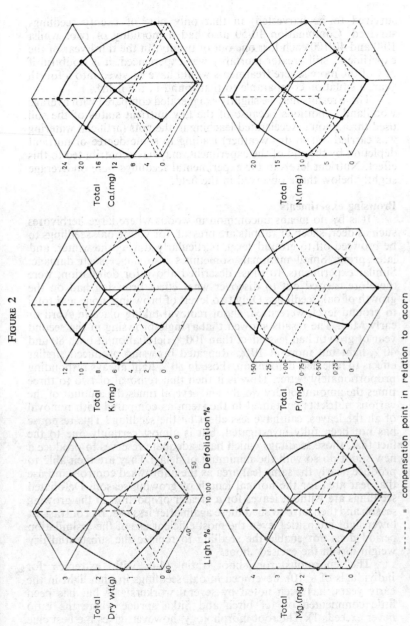

------ = compensation point in relation to acorn

The response surfaces for total dry weight, potassium, calcium, magnesium, phosphorus, and nitrogen in relation to light and defoliation (2 year cumulative effect).

survived to be harvested) in that only nine of twenty seedlings survived. Combination 10/50 also had a mortality of two, whilst 10/0 and 40/100 each lost one out of twenty. In the third year of the experiment, still greater mortality was experienced, it is doubtful if any of the more severe treatments would have survived into a fourth year, a situation comparable to that found in the field[3].

These results may be slightly exaggerated compared with average woodland conditions because of the low nutrient status of the soil used throughout. Accelerated leaching in the pots (artificial watering was carried out in dry weather) leading to some degree of nutrient depletion by the end of the experiment, may have contributed to this effect. Nutrient levels in the experimental seedlings were on average slightly below those observed in the field.

Browsing experiments
It is by no means uncommon in woods where large herbivores such as deer, sheep or rabbits are present, for young oak seedlings to be browsed off to ground level, particularly during the winter, and late spring. Small mammals sometimes also inflict such damage. Similar experiments, to those described above for defoliation, were therefore carried out to discover what effect browsing had on the growth of oak seedlings. Only two levels of browsing, none and total to ground level, were used, shoot removal taking place in April or early May. The results showed that a single browsing in the second year of growth had less effect than 100% defoliation at both 80 and 40% light but more at 10%. Repeated browsing produced similar effects to repeated defoliation, those in 80% light always responding proportionately better. How is it then that removal of two to three times the amount of dry weight and several times the amount of the various nutrients contained in the stem, as compared with removal of all the leaves, can have less effect on the seedling? This response has not been fully investigated, but is almost certainly due to the fact that, those seedlings which have adequate reserves to produce a new shoot do so with the minimum of delay. They are then able to produce nearly the same leaf area as the unbrowsed controls and use that leaf area for the normal length of growing season. Defoliated seedlings are without leaves for a greater proportion of the growing season and then have to shed these again after less use. By contrast, at lower light intensities, even the most efficient use of the assimilation period does not enable the seedling to replace the substantial dry weight lost in the excised shoot.

The enormous root/shoot ratio (4–6 with extremes for individuals of <10), developed in oak seedlings in high light in the early years, has been noted by several workers[14][15] but has been little commented on (cf birch and Sitka spruce where the ratio never exceeds 1). The root morphology, however, gives the best clue as to one of its functions, over 90% of the weight being located in a single (or sometimes multiple), swollen tap root. Such roots are obviously not required to anchor a plant with such modest aerial parts, and neither are they adapted to exploit a maximum volume of soil, which might be considered an advantage. One of the main functions is obviously storage, and this in turn can be interpreted as browsing resistance, the majority of the dry weight and nutrients being located in a position where they cannot be damaged by browsing animals. In heavily grazed woods I have found oak seedlings under 0.5m in height, on ageing by ring counts, to be more than 25 years old. Even temporary release from browsing, enables such seedlings to put on rapid growth, so that in two-three years they are out of danger.

Discussion and conclusions

The aim of this paper has been to investigate the widely held view that oak regeneration is failing, or is at least deficient, in British woodlands and that some sort of remedial action, in the form of woodland management, is required. Examination of the reproductive cycle of oak indicates that there is no apparent failure in the early stages of acorn production, fall, survival and germination. It is argued that high rates of acorn predation should not be regarded as a loss, but as an essential part of a highly effective means of dispersal. The fact remains that, in the spring following an acorn crop, substantial numbers of seedlings are produced, usually several times the number that would be required to replace the existing trees, but that under the tree canopy, at least, such seedlings rarely survive more than three-five years. In large clearings and outside the woodland, seedlings often do survive and grow to produce fully established saplings. A study of the literature on the growth characteristics of oak seedlings, and particularly the relationship with light, suggests that, providing they are not destroyed by browsing animals such as sheep, deer, rabbits or small mammals, they should be able to grow satisfactorily. Both field observations and more formal experiments refute this contention and some explanation is obviously required to account for this discrepancy. My work shows that the occurrence of widespread, and often severe, defoliation of oak seedlings, largely by caterpillars, can provide an adequate explanation for what is observed in the field. Experiments on defoliation have shown this factor to be as important as light in controlling the growth rate of oak seedlings. Non-defoliated controls in the same series of experiments also demonstrated that, at least in soils with low nutrient levels, it was the compensation point for certain nutrients and in particular potassium and phosphorus, that was limiting and not the compensation point for carbon assimilation, as is more normally asserted. Undefoliated seedlings in less than about 30% full daylight were simply unable to balance losses of potassium and phosphorus through leaf fall, and other minor causes such as root death, by sufficient uptake, a situation which inevitably results in death when the reserves contained in the acorn are exhausted.

It is not suggested that this is a complete explanation of what can be observed in the field. Very little is known concerning competition with the ground flora, both above and beneath soil level, and root competition with adult trees has been virtually ignored. In some of my experiments, severing all roots entering a plot still has a very significant effect on the growth of seedlings after eight years. Similarly, the mycorrhizal relationships of oak seedlings are completely unexplored but, in theory at least, the symbiotic nature of that relationship may be disturbed by low rates of assimilation on the part of the host plant.

Another matter that has received little or no attention, is variability in oak seedlings. In both field and more controlled pot experiments, there is a marked tendency for certain seedlings to do better or worse than the average. In many situations this could be ignored as merely random variation, and something that was a nuisance to the experimenter, but in the present case there is at least circumstantial evidence that such variation has ecological significance. For example, oak seedlings show a similar wide variation in flushing date to adult oak trees, the implications of which are discussed by Satchell[21]. In a field experiment, one particular seedling was noted as flushing at least two weeks before any other seedling, and that individual has continued to survive long after most of its companions have died. Similarly, certain oak seedlings seem to have a greater tendency to produce lammas growth which, depending on the situation, could be of either postive or negative selective advantage. Pot seedlings, grown under apparently uniform conditions of light and soil, produce quite a range of root/shoot ratios which, in terms of height increment or level of root reserves, could be of considerable selective advantage under the right conditions. Even if such variations in the responses of oak seedlings are only in part of genetic origin, it does suggest some fundamental differences between natural regeneration and planting as management techniques.

Finally, we must ask why so many people have apparently thought that oak should regenerate freely under oak and that, when this did not occur, it should be regarded as evidence of something wrong. Undoubtedly, part of this idea springs directly from forestry traditions, although it should be immediately emphasised that such conclusions are a misinterpretation. Many oakwoods on the continent are successfully managed by a system which utilises the acorns produced by the adult trees to produce oak seedlings which will grow up and ultimately replace them. Since this result is achieved by carefully planned, artificial manipulations of the tree canopy (and possibly some soil cultivation), the process cannot be called natural regeneration in the strictly biological sense of the word. What is also overlooked is that, once the seedlings are established on the ground, very rapid opening of the canopy is required if they are to survive, thereby creating conditions of high light (and presumably low defoliation) under which rapid growth has been shown to occur. No forester would attempt to manage an oak forest under the selection system, except by rather large groups. It is interesting to note that quite a different conclusion could have been drawn from forestry traditions, in which the statement that a particular species 'does not regenerate well under its own shade' is often encountered. Taken literally, this would appear to imply that light is the mechanism but, since some of the species cited are extreme shade-bearers, some other factor is obviously involved. There is a good example of this mechanism in many acid oak woods, where the much less shade tolerant birch can often be observed regenerating freely under an oak canopy. This apparent enhancement of intra-specific, as opposed to inter-specific, competition is a much more widespread phenomenon than is commonly supposed and, with some tropical species, actual chemical inhibition has been demonstrated. No such specialised mechanisms are, however, necessary to explain most examples of the phenomenon. Increased biotic pressure, due to so called 'pests' or 'disease organisms' in the immediate vicinity of other members of the same species, provide a quite adequate explanation, eg defoliating caterpillars on oak.

The other main source of misconception about oak and its reproductive processes appears to originate from the North American school of ecology, as exemplified by F. E. Clements, who, along with other workers, developed the ideas of succession and climatic climax vegetation, some of which were adopted by Tansley. In the absence of any good example of primeval woodland in Britain, descriptions of climax woodlands in North America were used as the model for the climax type here, namely oak. No allowance was made for the fact that oak had very different ecological characteristics from such North American climax species as Sugar maple, *Acer saccharum* Marshall, for neither as a seedling nor as an adult tree is oak really a shade-bearer. In Britain we have a very restricted tree flora, with no large, shade-bearing tree apart from beech. The characteristics of oak which result in its widespread climax role in Britain are three fold:

 (i) Longevity of the individual—once established it outlives most potential competitors.

 (ii) The two species between them are able to grow on an extremely wide range of soil types.

 (iii) Effective seed dispersal, which enables the oak to spread rapidly.

Oak has a considerable pioneer capacity in its own right, being able to invade many kinds of non-woodland vegetation and being in no way dependent on shade from other trees. This is quite the opposite of true climax species which are often unable to survive without shade.

The classical idea that climax woodland is intimately all-aged, with birth, life and death occurring simultaneously and as a continuous process in a very small area, is clearly quite out of the question in the case of species with ecological characteristics like oak. Indeed, many of the original ideas of climax forest have come to be modified by later workers who found that sub-climax species were able to maintain themselves in the climax condition and that, in any case, the whole system was not as continuous as formerly supposed and tended to change in a series of discrete steps precipitated by fairly major perturbations.

It is clear that, in comparison with other climax trees, our two native species of oak have characteristics which are more in keeping with sub-climax species, but they are, nevertheless, the most climax species we have in Britain. Our model of the climax must, therefore be suitably modified in the light of this knowledge, all the evidence pointing to some form of species alternation, but with a spatial and time scale that can only be speculated upon.

The case for the reproductive failure of oak is therefore rejected as totally unsupported by the available evidence, the main reason for bringing the case in the first place being largely the result of a misconception. The biotic pressures that prevent oak regenerating freely under its own shade, or rather in the close vicinity of other oak trees, is entirely natural. The only real threat to oak, in Britain, is over-grazing and over-browsing. Emphasis must, however, be placed on the 'over' part of these words, for some level of both factors must be regarded as natural and all tree species must be able to withstand this level; an apparent adaptation to browsing has been demonstrated for oak. Perhaps fortunately, the common practice of ring fencing woodlands that are to be maintained on conservation grounds is rarely effective in totally excluding all grazing and browsing, but tends merely to reduce the pressure. Total exclusion of large herbivores would undoubtedly lead to a reduction in diversity and might also, paradoxically, create regeneration problems of a different type, through a drastic reduction in the disturbance conditions that favour small-seeded species.

REFERENCES

1. CAVERS, P. B. and HARPER, J. L. 'Studies in the dynamics of plant populations. I. The fate of seed and transplants introduced into various habitats', *J. Ecol.*, **55** (1967), 59–71
2. WATT, A. S. 'On the causes of failure of natural regeneration in British oakwoods', *J. Ecol.*, **7** (1919), 173–203
3. SHAW, M. W. 'Factors affecting the natural regeneration of Sessile oak (*Quercus petraea*) in North Wales. I. A preliminary study of acorn production, viability and losses', *J. Ecol.*, **56** (1968), 565–83
4. SHAW, M. W. 'Factors affecting the natural regeneration of Sessile oak (*Quercus petraea*) in North Wales. II. Acorn losses and germination under field conditions', *J. Ecol.*, **56** (1968), 647–60
5. MELLANBY, K. 'The effects of some mammals and birds on regeneration of oak', *J. appl. Ecol.*, **5** (1968), 359–66
6. JONES, E. W. 'Biological Flora of the British Isles: *Quercus* L.', *J. Ecol.*, **47** (1959), 169–222
7. TANTON, M. T. 'Acorn destruction potential of small mammals in British woodlands', *Q. Jl For.*, **59** (1965), 1–5
8. VARLEY, G. C. and GRADWELL, G. R. 'Population models for winter moth', in *Insect Abundance*, ed. T. R. E. Southwood, Oxford (1968), 132–42

9. CARLISLE, A., BROWN, A. H. F., and WHITE, E. J. 'Litter fall, leaf production and the effects of defoliation by *Tortrix viridana* in a Sessile oak (*Quercus petraea*) woodland', *J. Ecol.*, **54** (1966), 65–85

10. ASHBY, K. R. 'Prevention of regeneration of woodland by field mice (*Apodemus sylvaticus* L.) and voles (*Clethrionomys glareolus* Schreber and *Microtus agrestis* L.)', *Q. Jl For.*, **53** (1959), 148–58

11. ASHBY, K. R. 'Studies on the ecology of field mice and voles (*Apodemus sylvaticus*, *Clethrionomys glareolus* and *Microtus agrestis*) in Hougall Wood, Durham', *J. Zool.*, **152** (1967), 389–513

12. BOSSEMA, I. 'Recovery of acorns in the European jay (*Garrulus G. glandarius* L.)', *Verh. K. ned. Akad. Wet.*, **71** (1968), 1–5

13. JARVIS, P. G. 'The effects of acorn size and provenance on the growth of seedlings of sessile oak', *Q. Jl For.*, **57** (1963), 1–9

14. JARVIS, P. G. 'The adaptability to light intensity of seedlings of *Quercus petraea* (Matt.) Liebl.', *J. Ecol.*, **52** (1964), 545–71

15. OVINGTON, J. D. and MACRAE, C. 'The growth of seedlings of *Quercus petraea*', *J. Ecol.*, **48** (1960), 549–55

16. JARVIS, P. G. 'Growth and regeneration of *Quercus petraea* in the Sheffield region', Ph.D. thesis, University of Sheffield

17. NEWNHAM, R. M. and CARLISLE, A. 'The nitrogen and phosphorus nutrition of seedlings of *Quercus robur* L. and *Q. petraea* (Matt.) Liebl.', *J. Ecol.*, **57** (1969), 271–84

18. GORDON, A. G. 'The nutrition and growth of ash, *Fraxinus excelsior*, in natural stands in the English Lake District as related to edaphic and site factors', *J. Ecol.*, **52** (1964), 169–87

19. JARVIS, P. G. 'Interference by *Deschampsia flexuosa* (L.) Trim.', *Oikos*, **15** (1964), 56–78

20. PETERKEN, G. F. and TUBBS, C. R. 'Woodland regeneration in the New Forest, Hampshire, since 1650', *J. appl. Ecol.*, **2** (1965), 159–70

21. SATCHELL, J. E. 'Resistance in oak (*Quercus* spp) to defoliation by *Tortrix viridana* L. in Roudsea Wood National Nature Reserve', *Ann. appl. Biol.*, **50** (1962), 431–42

THE EFFECT OF DEFOLIATORS ON TREE GROWTH

G. R. GRADWELL

Department of Forestry, University of Oxford

Introduction

In mature, pure oak woodland young trees can establish them-selves only when an older tree dies and makes way for them. In mixed woodlands the position is complicated by young seedlings having to compete both with members of their own and with other tree species. Also, for any one tree to be successful in having its genes represented in the next generation it is necessary only that one acorn, of the many thousands that a tree will produce in its lifetime, survives to produce a mature tree. Clearly, a detailed study of either the population dynamics or the population genetics of oak is not a practical proposition. It would take several of our generations to acquire the necessary information on only one generation of trees; so we cannot hope to know the precise role of defoliators in deter-mining the quantitative and qualitative changes in a population of oaks. However, there is information which can give us some insight both into the ways in which defoliating insects can affect the trees and into the ways in which, in return, the trees affect the populations of insects.

Young leaves of oak seedlings and saplings are eaten by her-bivorous mammals (rabbits, hares, deer etc). and in many places these are probably much more important defoliators of young trees than are insects. However, when the tree grows tall enough for its foliage to be out of the reach of these browsers, the main leaf-eating role is taken over by insects—and particularly by the Lepi-doptera.

In Great Britain caterpillars of over one hundred species of moth are recorded as feeding on oak leaves, but defoliation is almost invariably due mainly to either the Winter moth (*Operophtera brumata* (L.)) or the Green oak tortrix (*Tortrix viridana* (L.)). These species also defoliate oak in other parts of Europe, but here quite a number of other species which are also common in Britain, such as the Mottled umber (*Erannis defoliaria* (Clerck)), the Brown tail (*Euproctis chrysorrhoea* (L.)), the Buff tip (*Phalera bucephala* (L.)) and the Lackey (*Malacosoma neustria* (L.)) can build up to very high densities and cause defoliation. Even species which are somewhat less common in Britain such as the Great prominent (*Peridea* (=*Notodonta*) *anceps* (Goeze)), the Pale brindled beauty (*Apocheima* (= *Phigalia*) *pilosaria* (D. & S.)) and the Small brindled beauty (*Apocheima hispidaria* (D. & S.)) may also produce outbreaks in eastern Europe[1]. The Gypsy moth (*Lymantria dispar* (L.)) is a common defoliator of oak both in Europe and in the northeast of the United States into which it was introduced from Europe sometime about the middle of the 1800s.

The effect of defoliation on the tree

A simple experiment in Wytham Wood, Berkshire, in 1960 showed how such leaf-feeding caterpillars may effect the growth of young trees. Ten small oaks, between two and four feet (0.6–1.2m) in height, were paired for times of bud opening—both of a pair flushing at the same time in the year when the selection was made. One of each pair was defoliated soon after the buds had opened; the other of the pair was the control. One pair was untreated and kept to compare flushing times the following year. The reaction of the defoliated trees was remarkably quick; new buds were formed and opened so that within three weeks the trees were almost indistinguishable from the controls. They were therefore defoliated again. The first defoliation mimicked, in timing, the effects of late frosts. The second defoliation was made at about the time when feeding by caterpillars was completed. Measurements of twig length (previous year's growth) and bud number made at bud opening the following year showed that whereas twigs of the defoliated trees averaged 11cm and carried just under three open buds, the twigs of the control averaged 22.5cm and averaged over four open buds. The flushing times of the defoliated trees were also some two or three days later than the controls. The experiment was repeated in 1961; in two cases experimental trees were again defoliated and in the other two the roles of defoliated and control were reversed. There was only one defoliation at the time when it could have been due to caterpillar feeding. Measurements made in the spring of 1962 showed quite dramatic differences between the trees with the different treatments. There was not a lot of difference between the length of experimental and control twigs (11.5: 14.5), but the winter of 1961–62 was extremely cold and on the defoliated trees the secondary growth (lammas shoots), together with some of the primary growth, had withered and died. The live twig length was, again, less than half that of the control trees and the number of open buds on the defoliated and control was as 1.8: 4.3. Only one of the control trees produced secondary growth and neither this nor any primary growth was dead. In this year flushing times were not obviously related to treatment.

The small trees used in these experiments had regenerated naturally in a group and were within an area which could support, at the most, only two fully mature trees. If the experiments mimicked natural defoliation there can be no doubt that differences in susceptibility to attacks by caterpillars could greatly influence the outcome of competition between the trees for dominance within that area.

These effects on shoot growth and bud number seemed confined to the year of damage, but examination some three years later of a cross section of one of the trees which was defoliated two years in succession showed no sign of annual ring development after the second defoliation—although some slight increase in radial growth did occur. A tree defoliated in only one year showed a reduction in radial growth in the year of defoliation but subsequent growth appeared normal. This cumulative effect is in agreement with measurements of tree mortality made in the USSR[2] and the USA[3] [4]. Both show little or no mortality as a result of a single defoliation but increasing, and in the USA sometimes very high, mortality as heavy damage to leaves continues for two or more years. In Europe any large-scale dying of oak would seem only rarely to be due solely to defoliation, but occurs when the effects of defoliation are enhanced by the effects of drought[5] or frosts or pathogenic fungi[6]. If the tree can produce lammas shoots which are not then damaged by other insects or pathogens food reserves can be laid down and the trees can withstand repeated removal of the primary leaves. A good example of this can be seen at Wistman's Wood, Devon, where long continuing annual defoliation by Winter moth has produced a wood of stunted oaks and epiphytes which is almost unique in Britain.

A number of measurements has been made of the losses of current increment in tree growth which results from total defoliation. Semevskii[6] lists the results of some twenty-five such studies, mainly in the USSR, which show losses of increment varying from 16 to 77%; he suggests that an average figure for the reduction due to heavy (90%) defoliation is about 59%. However, in assessing how insects affect trees we are not only interested in what happens at defoliation. Data produced by Efremov (quoted in Semevskii) show a linear relationship between the percentage increment loss and the percentage of leaves removed by a defoliator such that at 90% loss of foliage the increment is reduced to 35% that of caterpillar-free trees. Measurements made over eight years on five oak trees at Wytham showed a similar linear relationship between the summer wood increment and the densities of caterpillars feeding on the trees[7]. Spring growth, which depends on food stores, was not related to defoliation; this again emphasises the importance to the trees of lammas shoots. The tree's ability to produce spring wood reduces the effect of defoliators on total wood production; it was estimated that over the eight years an absence of caterpillars would have increased the total production by some 40%. A later study on these same trees using 17 years' data[8] confirmed the linear relationship between summer wood production and caterpillar numbers, and showed that the relationship was strengthened when variations in wood density were also taken into account.

It must be emphasised, however, that whilst defoliators may be the main cause of year-to-year variations in the growth of trees, they are unlikely to be the main factor affecting growth *per se*. Of the five trees studied in detail at Wytham one tree has consistently carried much higher densities of caterpillars and suffered a greater damage to leaves than the others, yet the amount of summer growth has always been higher than on the other trees.

Experiments in the tops of mature trees have shown some further effects of defoliation. In 1961, and at the time when most caterpillar feeding had ended, twigs in the tops of trees were marked and half were defoliated. During the winter many of the marked twigs were recovered from the ground under the trees having undergone natural abscission; the proportion abscissing on the different trees was very different and not related to whether or not they had been defoliated. Counts in the spring of 1962 after leaf flush showed, again, that the control twigs had more open buds per twig than did those which had been defoliated; 5.3: 4.0. More surprising was that whereas the defoliated twigs had an average of 0.8 caterpillars per twig, those of the controls had 1.3 caterpillars. The experiment was repeated in 1962 and scored in 1963 using only one tree. Unfortunately natural abscission allowed us to recover only some 30 twigs and examine 280 buds so the results are not significant. Nevertheless, they agree with the previous experiment; the open buds on the experimental and control twigs were as 3.6: 7.9, and the caterpillars per twig as 1.6: 3.3. It was also observed in this year that only 13.6% of the buds on the experimental twigs bore male catkins compared with 58% of those of the controls; a similar effect has been seen in other experiments.

The effect of the tree on defoliators

So far the oak trees have been treated as if they were merely passive and unable to affect their defoliators. But the apparent reduction in the densities of caterpillars on defoliated twigs suggests that there is a more dynamic and interacting relationship between the eater and the eaten. A preliminary examination of a great amount of information on both changes in caterpillar numbers and the numbers of buds has failed to confirm the effects which appeared from the previous experiments though, for reasons which will be mentioned later, we feel that such effects may well occur. One difficulty in interpreting the data arises from not knowing whether buds have some function other than their obvious one of producing new growth. From a detailed examination of the data from one tree it is clear that whilst it has laid down a number of buds varying from as many as nine to as few as five buds per twig, the number of buds opened has been between three and four. It seems that, even in the defoliation experiments, the tree has always laid down more buds than it could open. Buds are attacked by gall wasps (Cynipidae), by gall midges (Cecidomyidae) and by weevils (Curculionidae), and some are effectively destroyed by having eggs laid into their bases by capsid bugs (Miridae), but the numbers destroyed in this way seem to be too small to warrant such an over-production, particularly when secondary growth is not produced from these buds. The excess buds are abscissed very rapidly; most can be shed from the tree within about ten days of bud opening and virtually all are lost within a month. In conifers it is known that at the time of shoot elongation food reserves, at least carbohydrates, are translocated from the old needles to take part in the new growth. Do deciduous trees use their excess buds in the same way? Such reserves could have little effect on the amount of twig growth, but it is possible that small reserves close to the site of growth affect the time at which growth could begin. We shall see below that the precise timing of this event can have very important consequences for the populations of defoliating caterpillars.

FIGURE 1

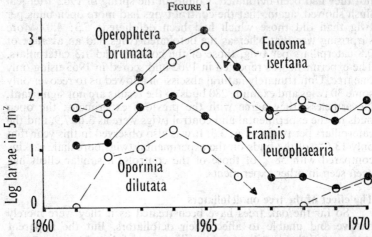

Changes in the total numbers of larvae falling into two 0.5 m traps under each of five oak trees

Fig 1 shows for four species that the year-to-year changes in the densities of oak-feeding caterpillars are often very similar both in direction and the amount of change. This can mean only that whatever causes the change acts in a similar way on each species. Of the examples in fig 1, *Operophtera brumata, Agriopis* (=*Erannis*) *leucophaearia* (D. & S.) and *Epirrita* (=*Oporinia*) *dilutata* (D. & S.) have very similar life-cycles. The eggs hatch at the time of bud opening (in Oxford usually in early April), the fully fed larvae spin down to the ground at the same time (usually in early June) and spend quite a long time as pupae in the soil. Adult *E. dilutata* emerge and lay eggs in October and November, *O. brumata* in November and December and *A. leucophaearia* usually in January and February. However, the life-cycle of *Zeiraphera* (=*Eucosma*) *isertana* (F.) is different in that the adult emerges in late June within three weeks of pupation and the eggs are laid on the tree at this time. Thus any factor which is to affect all four species in the same way must operate at some time between March, when all are in the egg stage, and late June when *Z. isertana* emerges. From a long-term, detailed study of the Winter moth (*O. brumata*)[9] we have been able to show that the factor which mainly determines the year-to-year changes in its density operates between the time when the eggs are laid on the tree and the time when the fully fed larvae fall to the ground to pupate. The experimental placing of eggs on the trees has shown that there is little mortality at this stage, and we have been able to detect no significant differences between the densities of young larvae feeding in the newly opened buds and the densities of fully fed larvae. So it would seem that the changes in density are mainly determined by how successful the newly hatched larvae are in finding a bud in which they can commence to feed; thus changes in the numbers of open buds and the distances between them must affect the chances of newly hatched larvae finding a suitable feeding site.

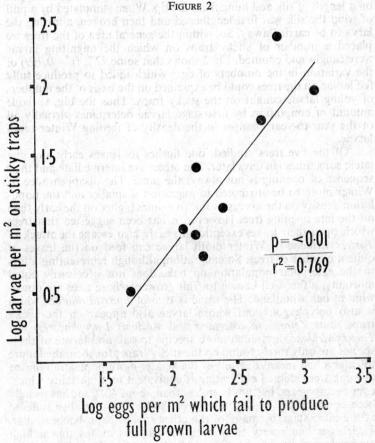

FIGURE 2

$p = < 0.01$

$r^2 = 0.769$

Log larvae per m² on sticky traps

Log eggs per m² which fail to produce full grown larvae

The relationship between winter moth disappearance from oak and appearance on sticky traps

There is further information which shows this to be a critical time for the young caterpillars. Female Winter moths are wingless and must climb the trees to lay their eggs in crevices high in the tree. Over a number of years we have intercepted and counted the females climbing up a known proportion of the circumference of each of five trees and from these figures estimated the total number of eggs taken up each tree by the untrapped females. Also, by collecting from a known proportion of the area beneath the canopy of each tree all the larvae which spin down to pupate, we have estimated the total number of larvae falling from each tree. Thus we have been able to measure how many eggs failed to produce fully fed larvae. Laboratory experiments showed that the newly hatched larva would climb up a twig seeking to enter a bud, but if it reached the tip without finding one it did not walk down again but dropped on a length of silk and hung from the tip. When stimulated by a puff of wind the silk was first lengthened and then broken, allowing the larva to be carried away. So, within the general area of the trees we placed a number of sticky traps on which the migrating larvae were caught and counted. Fig 2 shows that some 77% ($r^2=0.769$) of the variation in the numbers of eggs which failed to produce fully fed larvae on the trees could be explained on the basis of the numbers of young larvae caught on the sticky traps. Thus the big, variable amount of emigration by first stage larvae determines virtually all of the year-to-year changes in the density of feeding Winter moth larvae.

Of the five trees studied, one flushes its leaves early and one later; sometimes ten days later. The others are intermediate and their sequence of opening is not always the same. The disappearance of Winter moth to be attributed to migration is smaller and the population density on the average some five times higher on the early than on the late opening tree. However, it has been suggested that trees which open their leaves exceptionally early also escape the attack of *Tortrix viridana* [10]. Winter moth larvae can feed on the leaves of quite a number of trees. So emigration, although representing a loss to the caterpillar population on oak, does not necessarily equal mortality, a fact well known to fruit growers whose trees are down-wind of oak woodland. The same is true of *Epirrita dilutata* which is also polyphagous and whose larvae also appear on the sticky traps, but *Zeiraphera insertana* and *Agriopis leucophaearia,* like *Tortrix viridana,* are much more specific to oak and larvae of these species are only rarely found on the sticky traps; for them the failure to enter a bud means death. For the Winter moth population on the five oak trees studied emigration is equivalent to a mortality which, over twenty years, has not been less than about 40% and has usually been considerably higher, often over 90%. The mortality suffered at the same stage by many of the other species is probably similar. Their eggs hatch very early even though this means that a high proportion of the larvae fail to find an open bud. These high mortalities would be expected to exert a very strong selective pressure towards a later egg hatch when all the buds are open and there is a greater chance of finding food. That this has not happened must mean there is some greater mortality to be suffered through hatching late.

The partly open bud, in contrast to the fully open one, will provide a measure of protection for the young larvae; mainly against the risk of being washed off by rain or trapped in a film of water. But since the very few late feeding species can establish themselves on fully open leaves, the protection afforded by the bud is perhaps not a very important factor. In a study at Oxford, Feeny[11] showed that feeding on young or older leaves had an important effect on the weight of the fully grown larva and consequently on the weight of the pupa: some of his results are summarized in fig 3. Winter moth females, like those of most Lepidoptera, emerge from the pupa containing the eggs fully developed, and there are linear relationships between the weights of pupae and adults and between adult female weight and egg number, so a reduction in

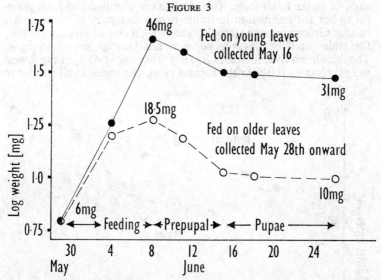

FIGURE 3

Proportional changes in the weight of winter moth larvae from 4th instar pupation (data from Feeny[11])

larval weight has the consequence of reducing the average egg production in the next generation. By the analysis of leaves throughout the summer Feeny was able to show an increase in the amount of condensed tannins in the leaves. These were absent from buds but contributed some 5% of the dry weight of September leaves. From experiments in which Winter moth larvae were fed on an artificial diet to which tannins were added, he was also able to show that the different mean weights of larvae fed on young and older leaves could be explained by the increased tannin content of the later leaves. Tannins form complexes with proteins, so the reduced growth of larvae may be either because in the chewed leaf the tannins combine with the leaf protein to make this indigestible, or because the tannin combines with the larva's digestive enzymes and inactivates them; probably both processes occur. There can be no doubt that the development of tannins is a defence mechanism of the tree against attack by insects and other herbivores; for maximum growth and reproduction most species of caterpillar must complete their feeding before any appreciable amount of condensed tannin is laid down in the leaves. The selective pressures exerted by the herbivores will ensure that only trees possessing this defence mechanism will survive to maturity.

A smaller egg production is not the only consequence of a reduction in larval weight. Dr. Lucyna Andrejewska has accumulated data on the effect of different food plants on the weight of Winter moth pupae as well as on the way pupal weight affects survival to the adult stage. This work is unpublished and I am grateful to her for permission to quote here a summary of some of her results. Grouping pupae into different weight classes gives, separately for males and females, the survival relationship shown in fig 4. The female survival increases linearly from about 65% in the lowest weight class to 100% in the highest class. No males at all survive in

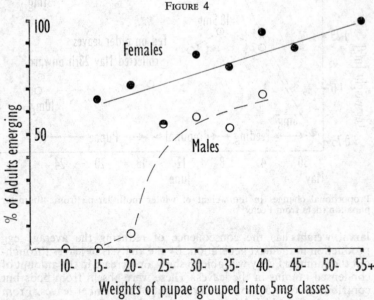

FIGURE 4

Relationships between pupal weight and adult emergence of winter moth (lines fitted by eye)

the lowest weight class, and the relationship between weight and survival is not linear. Also, for any given weight the survival of males is lower than that of the females. Most of the mortality observed was due not to the death of pupae but to the failure of fully formed adults to emerge from the pupal case; the reason for this is not known but is perhaps related to the amount of the energy reserves of the adult. The reason for the differential survival of males and females is known. Although fig 4 suggests otherwise, in most samples there has been no significant difference between the weights of male and female pupae, but at the time of emergence males are only about one quarter of the weight of the females. MacGregor[8] showed that during the later period of pupation the respiratory rate of the males was twice that of the females; weight was rapidly lost by males at this time. It would seem that even when male larvae pupate at low weight they still maintain the high respiratory rate even though this means that they reach too low a weight to successfully emerge; below a pupal weight of about 25mg virtually all males failed to emerge. It is not known why there is this difference in respiratory rate between the sexes.

There is yet another interesting observation on changes in the mean weight of Winter moth adults which seems to imply an interaction between the densities of feeding caterpillars and tree physiology. In fig 5, for a sequence of years, the mean weights of emerging females have been plotted against the population densities

FIGURE 5

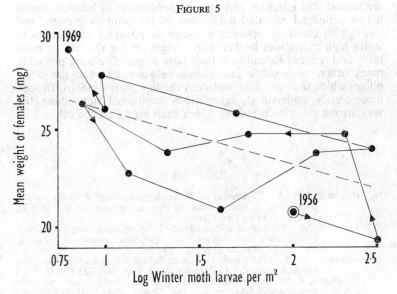

The effect of larval density of winter moth on adult weight (p < 0.02).

of the caterpillars from which they developed. The overall relationship (dotted line) shows the mean weight of females falling as the population density of caterpillars increases and, as was the case in the relationship between caterpillar density and growth increment of the trees, the relationship appears to be linear. More unexpected is the relationship which appears when the mean weights are joined in the sequence in which they occurred (solid line). During the period covered by the graph there has been one and a half cycles of Winter moth abundance and it would seem that at or near the peaks of the cycles the mean weight of females has quite sharply increased. Similarly there was one quite sharp fall in weight when caterpillar density was very low. Also, for a given density of caterpillars the weight of the females has usually been higher when the densities have been falling than when they were rising. Of course, many more observations are necessary before one can be sure that this is a correct interpretation of the relationship, but such a relationship might be expected. A number of studies, mainly on conifers, have shown that the soluble sugar content of leaves is increased in trees subject to water stress by drought and that this increases the weight and reproductive rate of insects feeding on those leaves[12]. Damage to leaves probably has effects similar to water stress, as tree increment measurements seem to suggest, the effects of stress are probably cumulative.

Conclusions

The established oak tree's adaptations to attack by herbivores are remarkably effective; through the production of lammas shoots it can withstand repeated defoliation of the primary growth, and through its chemical defences it forces its potential defoliators to suffer high mortalities in their early stages or run the risk of mortality and reduced fecundity in their later stages. There are probably many other, more subtle interactions between oaks and the caterpillars which feed on them, but even the few more obvious, though incompletely understood, interactions mentioned here show the very strong selective pressures which each exerts on the other.

REFERENCES

1. GOLOSOVA, M. A. 'Dynamics of *Biston hispidaria* and *Phigalia pedaria* population in oak-woods of the steppe zone of the USSR'. *12th, Int. Congr. Ent.* (1965), 702
2. RAFES, P. M. 'Estimation of the effects of phytophagous insects on forest production', in *Analysis of Temperate Forest Ecosystems,* ed. D. E. Reichle (1970), 100–96
3. STEPHENS, G. R. 'The relation of insect defoliation to mortality in Connecticut forests'. *Bull. Conn. Agric. Exp. Stn,* 723 (1971), 1–16
4. CAMPBELL, R. W. and VALENTINE, H. T. 'Tree condition and mortality following defoliation by the Gypsy Moth'. USDA Forest Service Research Paper NE–236, (1972), 331pp

5. YOUNG, C. W. T. 'Death of pendunculate oak and variations in annual radial increments related to climate'. *Forest Rec., Lond.*, **55** (1965), 1–15
6. SEMEVSKII, F. N. [Prediction in forest protection] (1971), 71pp. Izdatel'stvo 'Lesnaya Promyshlennost', Moscow. (In Russian)
7. VARLEY, G. C. and GRADWELL, G. R. 'The effect of partial defoliation by caterpillars on the timber production of oak trees in England'. *Int. Congr. Ent. 11th., Vienna*, **2** (1962), 211–14
8. MACGREGOR, K. A. *The Productivity Relations between Insects and Oak Trees.* D.Phil. Thesis, Oxford University (1968)
9. VARLEY, G. C. and GRADWELL, G. R. 'Population models for the Winter moth', in *Insect Abundance*, ed. T. R. E. Southwood, *Symp. R. entl. Soc., Lond.*, **4** (1968), 132–42
10. SATCHELL, J. E. *Rep. Nat. Conserv.*, 1959 (1960), 53
11. FEENY, P. 'Effect of oak leaf tannins on larval growth of the winter moth *Operophtera brumata*'. *J. Insect Physiol.*, **14** (1968), 805–17
11a. FEENY, P. 'Seasonal changes in oak leaf tannins and nutrients as a cause of spring feeding by winter moth caterpillars', *Ecology*, **51** (1970) 565–81
12. SCHWENKE, W. 'Neue Hinweise auf eine Abhaengigkeit der Vermehrung blatt- und nadelfressender Forstinsekten von Zuckergehalt ihrer Nahrung', *Z. angew. Ent.*, **61** (1968), 365–69

PHYSIOLOGY OF THE OAK TREE

K. A. LONGMAN

Institute of Tree Biology, Edinburgh

and

M. P. COUTTS

Forestry Commission, Northern Research Station, Roslin, Midlothian

Introduction

Special attention in this review of selected topics has been paid to precise measurements and experimental studies of features characteristic of *Quercus robur* and *Q. petraea*. The main areas considered are dormancy, growth and patterns of development in the life of the oak tree, the seasonal aspects of which are summarised diagrammatically in fig 1, and photosynthesis, water movement and stress physiology. Topics omitted include mineral nutrition, translocation, tropic responses and metabolism. Physiological knowledge of the two oaks is far from complete, and it has been supplemented by relevant information on other species.

Periodicity of shoot elongation

A remarkable feature of oaks is the brevity of the shoot elongation period, which can often be as short as 2–3 weeks[83] [121] [210]. Even in favourable growing conditions, the shoot becomes dormant and terminal buds form, though there may be another flush after a resting period of 4–6 weeks[22] [23] [44] [61] [62] [84] [89] [101] [120] [121] [210]. In various parts of Europe, *Q. robur* and *Q. petraea* make a first flush in April/May (fig 1), often a second around Midsummer's Day (*Johannistriebe*), sometimes a third in early August ('Lammas shoots' *sensu strictu*), and occasionally even a fourth around October[47] [76] [120] [121] [210]. Seedlings and coppice shoots under four years old reflush most frequently, whereas only two flushes occur in trees over 10 years, the second being confined to vigorous shoots. Longer, uninterrupted periods of growth under natural conditions have been recorded only in very young and vigorous coppice shoots, and here periods of slower growth sometimes coincide with the dormant period of older shoots[121]. It is interesting that a similar continuous growth habit is shown by young *Q.* × *hispanica* (*Q. lucombeana* Sw.)[73], though the probable parents of this evergreen hybrid, *Q. suber* L. and *Q. cerris* L., grow by flushes[128].

The precise timing of bud-break and cessation of elongation growth is influenced by season, site and provenance. Bud-break in *Q. robur* varied by only 24 days over a 20 year period at Giessen, Germany[23], whereas in Russia variation between provenances in a

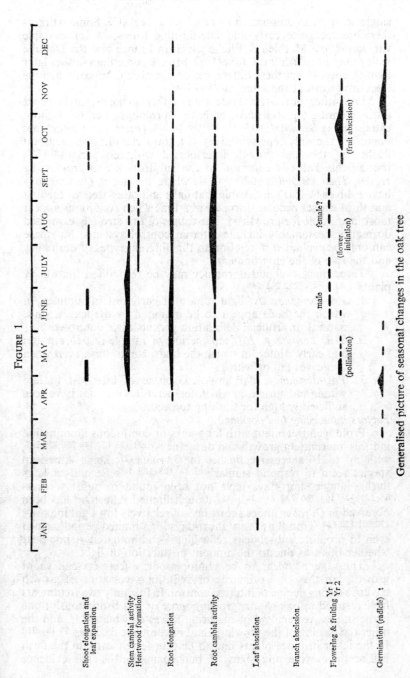

FIGURE 1

Generalised picture of seasonal changes in the oak tree

single season can amount to as much as 5 weeks[176]. Some workers therefore recognise early and late-flushing forms, as for example var. *tardissima* Mathieu & Fliche which in France and the Danube valley may not flush until June[24]. *Q. petraea* sometimes flushes later than *Q. robur*[24] but these differences do not always appear when the trees are grown at the same site[23 84 105].

Most other north-temperate trees either make a single short flush in spring (eg *Aesculus*), or have a prolonged period of shoot extension (eg *Betula*)[89 96 109 113 165 166 235 238]. *Quercus* and sometimes *Fagus* are the only representatives of a third class having recurrent flushes of terminal growth interspersed with rest periods[210 262], though this habit is common in the sub-tropics and tropics (eg *Hevea, Thea, Mangifera*)[120 133 262], where the genus *Quercus* may have evolved[30]. It is remarkable that oaks and other trees of the first and third classes become dormant at a time when conditions appear most favourable for growth[194]. The causes of this strongly expressed dormancy presumably include internal control systems, but these can only be evaluated in relation to the different types of dormancy and the role of the environment.

Three phases of bud dormancy may be recognised for woody plants[21 23 44 190 222 245 246]:

1. *Pre-dormancy*. A 'light' phase of early-rest in summer, in which the buds appear to be inhibited by the leaves, since natural or artificial defoliation permits their outgrowth.
2. *True dormancy*. A 'deep' period of middle-rest in autumn and early winter, in which the buds cannot flush even when the leaves fall or wither.
3. *Post-dormancy*. An 'imposed' phase of after-rest in late winter and spring, in which temperatures may not have been sufficiently high for flushing to occur.

Factors influencing bud dormancy

Prolonged treatment with long-days or continuous illumination induces intermittent growth and dormancy[89 121 128 129 140 238 239 247], with up to 16 successive flushes in *Q. robur*[121]; some American species seem to respond similarly[15 48 108 165 166]. Second or later flushes under short-days have not been found by most workers [65 127 128 165 166 238 239 245 246], though limited reflushing has been observed in *Q. robur* under short-days of relatively low light intensity [120 121 122 124]. Transfer to very short-days for a limited period seemed even to promote subsequent reflushing[206], although it is not clear whether this was due to the amount or duration of light.

Thus there appear to be photoperiodic effects on oak shoot growth, but these are primarily on reflushing, cessation of growth having a strong degree of internal control. In fact only two treatments have resulted in oak shoots growing more or less continuously: one is the successive removal of maturing leaves and buds[46 47], and the other the placing of the growing plant in complete darkness[89 124 210] In the latter instance plants had to be transferred early in the flush before there were any signs of bud formation[124]. The evidence suggests therefore that the onset of pre-dormancy under natural conditions may be due to inhibition by leaves in light, rather than to the exhaustion of internodes pre-formed in the bud[235] [238]. Indeed, vigorous flushes may consist partly of internodes produced after bud-break[121] [210].

Restarting of growth implies that conditions have changed within the plant, and these can apparently be influenced by a number of external factors. Earlier workers stressed the role of mineral nutrients[89] but Dostál[47] noted that small rooted cuttings of *Q. petraea* can make several flushes even when the roots are kept in water. The important factor appears to be the size of the root system: treatments which increase this relative to the shoots, such as coppicing and decapitation[121] [210], or application of fertilisers[47] tend to favour reflushing. On the other hand, complete darkness is inhibitory at this point[173] [238], while the prevention of bud-break generally found with short-days occurs whether the leaves or the buds are treated[238]. *Q. robur* makes successive flushes under intermediate day-lengths in the tropics[31] [41] [47] [200], suggesting modifying effects of temperature on photoperiodic responses.

In the autumn buds enter true dormancy, and it is no longer possible to induce outgrowth by extended day-length[63] [238] [239] [245] [247] or by defoliation and disbudding[1]. Apart from the application of chemicals (table 1), breaking of dormancy now requires a period of chilling at temperatures just above 0°C, followed by warmer conditions. Thus successive collections of oak twigs kept in water showed slight or no bud-break when collected in autumn, and progressively more rapid flushing from mid-winter onwards[121] [141]. The main factor in the post-dormant phase appears to be temperature [26] [111], photoperiodic treatments being ineffective in *Q. robur*[237] [261], though *Q. rubra* L. and *Fagus sylvatica* are responsive to long-days [108] [237]. Flushing was hastened in *Q. robur* and *Q. rubra* by the unusual method of growing the potted seedlings upside-down, and was delayed by ringing[154], so clearly the individual buds do not react independently from the rest of the plant (see also p. 201).

Hormones and bud dormancy

Applications of gibberellic acid stimulate bud-break of oaks but generally only in the pre- and post-dormant phases and not during true dormancy (table 1)[125] [126] [145]. Inhibition of pre-dormant buds by short-days can be overcome[165], and terminal buds seem to be more responsive than laterals, which may even be inhibited by a gibberellin or kinetin application to cut twigs[121] and decapitated plants[229]. Indole-3-acetic acid also inhibits lateral buds in decapitated plants[229] [231]. Many other chemicals have been reported to promote bud-break in oak (table 1) and other trees[44].

Endogenous growth substances have been detected by bioassay in detailed studies of oak by Lavarenne-Allary[2-5] [121] and Michalski and Krzysko[149]. Unlike other tree genera[245], only small quantities of gibberellin-like substances can be extracted from post-dormant[163] or breaking buds, but amounts increase markedly during rapid shoot

TABLE 1

Effects of applied Hormones and other chemicals on oak

Species	Age (yr)	Hormone, etc	Concentration (ppm)	Method of application	Bud-break			Rate of shoot growth	Annual height growth	Dry matter accumulation	Root growth	Germination %	Notes	Ref.
					Pre-dormant	True dormant	Post-dormant							
Q. robur	?	GA	100	dipping for 1 hr	+	O	+						Cut twigs in water	125, 126
Q. robur, Q. petraea, Q. frainetto Ten., Q. cerris L., Q. rubra L.	?	GA	{100, 20–100}	drops on term. bud, spray						+34 238%			Greatest effects in oaks compared with other trees	17
Q. robur	?	GA	100	1 or 2 sprays, 3 or 4 sprays	O +			O +	O +	O +30%			seedlings	64
Q. robur	1–2	GA	100–300		+	+			+		–			42
Q. robur	1–2	GA	100–400	spray				+ 200–500%	+ 200–500%	+ 80%				45
Q. robur	?	GA	50		O	O							Other trees were affected.	18
Q. robur?	0–1	GA	100–600	soaking acorns spraying seedlings					+				No significant effects on no. and size of leaves	152
Q. robur	0–1	GA, IAA, GA/IAA	200, 10, 200/10	8 × 2ml spraying of seedlings. Acorns soaked 2½ days					+ +		++	+		150
Q. robur?	?	IAA	?	Solution	O	+?	O +						Also Betula, Fagus	12, cited in 44
Q. robur, Q. petraea	?	IAA, GA, Kinetin, ferulic acid, ethylene, chlorhydrin	?, 50, 20, 20–50, 20 (0.1 ml)	apical injection	O O O O	+	+++						Lateral buds inhibited terminals promoted on cut from twigs coppice shoots	121

TABLE 1 (Continued)

Species	Age (yr)	Hormone, etc.	Concentration (ppm)	Method of application	Bud Break Pre-dormant	Bud Break True dormant	Bud Break Post-dormant	Rate of shoot growth	Annual height growth	Dry matter accumulation	Root growth	Germination %	Notes	Ref.
Q. petraea	?	thiamin / acetylene	1 / 10,000	injection of bud / gaseous			+ / +						Cut twigs in dim light	58
Q. rubra L.	0	GA	10–500	vacuum then aqueous				+		+34%	+ or –	+	Root growth inhibited in fully stratified acorns	230
Q. rubra L.	?	GA	(2 × 5 g/plant)	lanolin	+			+					Both under long- and short-days	165
Q. rubra L. / Q. macrocarpa Michx.	?	GA glycerol	2500 (100%)	lanolin		++		++					Seedlings	216
Q. rubra L. / Q. macrocarpa Michx.	1	GA glycerol	20,000 (100%)	lanolin drops			+		oo				Term. buds only / Lat. buds only	202
Q. palustris Muenchh.		GA / ethylene glycol	10,000 / 10,000 (100%)	glycerol in water drops			+++		ooo				Lat. buds only / Term. buds only / Lat. buds only	202
Q. rubra L.	?	GA	10,000	lanolin			O	O					Cut twigs (old trees and young coppice)	119
Q. phellos L.	1–3	GA	10,000	lanolin on stem			+	+ / 48–119%						142
Q. phellos L. / Q. falcata Michx.	1 / 1	GA	10,000	lanolin to term. bud				+ / 103–161%						160
Q. alba L. / Q. nigra L.	0 / 1							O						
Q. palustris Muenchh.	1	IAA	100–10,000	lanolin			–						Laterals on decapitated plants	231

GA = gibberellic acid
IAA = indole-3-acetic acid

+ = promotes (increases and/or hastens)
— = inhibits
O = no clear effects

Numerical data indicate % increase over control

elongation[149]. A promoter with Rf similar to indole-3-acetic acid increased at this time, and also before growth was resumed in first[149], second or third flushes; and when buds progressed from true to post-dormancy or when true dormancy was broken with ethylene chlorhydrin[121].

Conversely acid inhibitors, corresponding in Rf to the Bennett-Clark β inhibitor, remained steady in winter and diminished sharply just before flushing[121 149 244]. Their concentration also decreased with ethylene chlorhydrin treatment and with the midsummer and August flushes, a sequence not found in other tree genera. Thus changes in promoters and inhibitors in oak were correlated with bud-break, though not with the different types of dormancy[5 121] or age of tree[149]. Whether they are causative remains to be seen, but certainly there can be physiologically very active substances in buds, for homogenates from unfolding oak buds broke dormancy in ash[35], and extracts from dormant oak buds inhibited outgrowth of post-dormant oak buds[121].

Cambial activity

Re-activation of the vascular cambium in the spring has been detected by the swollen appearance of the meristem (March/April) or the presence of new vessels (April/May), namely about a week before the buds flush (fig 1)[70 116 260]. Cambial divisions may not resume immediately, and it is likely that the first-formed vessels originate from over-wintering xylem mother cells[190 260]. In *Q. robur* and other ring-porous trees, vessel production starts just below the buds and very rapidly reaches the base of the stem[67 116 175 178 180 213 236 240 262], in contrast to diffuse-porous trees including the mediterranean *Q. infectoria* Olivier[52] where 1–6 weeks elapse. It has been shown by disbudding and ringing experiments in oak and ash that vessels only form proximally to active buds or areas of bud regeneration, and their distribution leaves little doubt that resumption of cambial activity requires a stimulus from the buds[31 85 182 236 262]. The stimulus is operative even in darkness, and is probably auxin, since indole-3-acetic acid stimulates the dormant cambia of various tree species[39 155 209 263], and endogenous auxin-like substances in oak buds increase from February onwards[34 121 149]. Oak buds may be growing imperceptibly at this time[174], so a gradual basipetal translocation of the stimulus could proceed through sieve tubes, some of which can remain functional through the winter[6 57] while others differentiate very early in the spring from overwintering phloem mother cells[178].

Nevertheless, the almost simultaneous stages of vessel development found throughout a large oak tree[178 180 260] are baffling, in that a small signal from unopened buds is apparently able to stimulate many cells in remote parts of the tree to enlarge, sometimes to 500 times their previous cross-sectional area. It has been proposed therefore that the cambium itself is the source of some auxin, perhaps in the form of a precursor[85 156 209 236 260], and a 0.2–0.3 Rf promoter thought to be tryptophan has been detected in the cambial zone of oak in early spring[40]. There is also evidence that other growth substances are involved in resumption of cambial activity in trees, since the cambium is not always equally susceptible to auxin applications[182 262], gibberellins show interactions with auxins[39 248], while oak tissue cultures of cambial origin require cytokinins (other than kinetin) for continuous culture[79].

In the latter part of June, several weeks after the end of the first flush, there is an abrupt change to latewood formation, with much smaller vessels, and thick-walled fibres[31 116 179 256]. This change starts in the twigs before reaching the base of the main stem[116 179 260], and is delayed in shoots with multiple flushes, so that false rings are not normally formed[61 210 213 257], except by *Q. robur* in the tropics[31]. In other ring-porous trees, the correlation with the ending of shoot elongation is more precise, and latewood is associated with a decrease in auxin production[40]. Large vessels of the earlywood type can be induced by the application of high concentrations of indole-3-acetic acid; latewood vessels and tracheids by lower concentrations[39].

The time at which cambial divisions cease varies by a month from season to season[56 70], but is typically long before leaf senescence (fig 1)[37 67 78 116], though division may continue until this stage in *Q. robur* grown in the tropics[31]. The cause of cessation in oak is not understood, though in other ring-porous species it can be induced by short-days[251], especially at lower temperatures[234], which further reduce auxin levels[40].

Mature oakwood has several unusual features of physiological interest. Only *Castanea* and a few tropical trees and lianes have such large vessels (0.2–0.3mm diameter)[8 116], though they are smaller in seedlings and twigs of older trees[178 260]. The older stem wood also contains short uniseriate and very tall broad multiseriate rays (exceptionally 50×0.6mm)[8 97].

Further aspects of shoot physiology
Variations in growth rate

Contrary to experience with conifers[113 262], more shoot growth was made by day than by night in *Q. robur*[36] and *Q. rubra*[137], whereas many other broadleaved species grew at approximately the same rate throughout the 24 hours. These diurnal fluctuations in oak may reflect varying temperature conditions[36 137], and growth rates can clearly be affected by water stress, light intensity and many other external factors.

Applied hormones influence the rate of shoot growth of seedlings (table 1), and also leaf shape, which can become longer and narrower in *Q. robur*[145] or more like the leaf of the adult tree in several American species[160]. Leaf shape in certain varieties of *Q. robur* and *Q. petraea* differs markedly on first and second shoots, defoliation of the former inducing transitional forms[210] (Plate VI).

Patterns of branching

Terminal buds of *Quercus* spp show strong apical dominance

in the sense that all lateral buds on an expanding shoot are inhibited[19]. Simultaneous growth of laterals on an elongating terminal shoot (sylleptic or 'feather' shoots, *rameaux anticipés*) occurs only in very vigorous coppice, but both in the spring and later flushes laterals frequently grow out from wood of the preceding flush[121]. It is generally only the sub-apical lateral buds which do so, although the more proximal buds are potentially capable of outgrowth, since they flush if the elongating buds[121] or leaves[210] are removed. All the buds also grow in detached shoots in water, but the dominance of the terminal shoots is restored by apical injections of gibberellic acid, kinetin and also ferulic acid[121].

Conversely, oak may be described as having weak 'apical control', since branch growth often equals or exceeds that of the terminal[19] [262]. A 'decurrent' branching habit results, which is especially marked in *Q. robur,* with early loss of a single main stem [23] [24] [144] [203]. Branching patterns also depend on a wide range of other factors, a distinctive feature of oaks being the active abscission in autumn of leafy branchlets, often apparently healthy (fig 1)[84]. In *Q. petraea* portions up to 75cm long may be shed from lower, shaded branches, including even terminal shoots, affecting considerably the number and distribution of leaves the following year. Considerable quantities of starch remain in the shed twigs, and it has been claimed that the phenomenon is marked after stress conditions[23]. Clear-cut abscission zones, involving the partial dissolution of cell walls throughout the xylem, are formed at points where shoot growth had stopped (see Plate VI)[23] [24] [49] [113] [221]. Abscission has been enhanced in old but not in young *Q. alba* by 2-chloroethyl-phosphonic acid, which liberates ethylene in the tissues[27].

The regeneration of branches from long-dormant buds is also an important feature of oaks, especially *Q. robur*[24] and *Q. alba* L.[208]; in the latter species outgrowth of epicormic shoots was promoted in isolated sections taken from the trunk, and partly inhibited by applying auxins[16]. Considerable clusters of dormant buds can build up on the stems of old oaks, and undoubtedly contribute to the longevity of the tree, and to its coppicing power[60] [84] [113] [218]. It is also possible for adventitious buds to form *de novo* on sphaeroblasts, small rounded bodies which can be induced internodally by complete disbudding[255].

Leaf retention

An unusual feature of many oak trees is the retention during the winter of dead brown leaves, the abscission layer often not completing until spring (fig 1)[97] [115]. Common names for *Q. petraea, (Wintereiche, Chêne d'hiver)* indicate its special tendency in this respect[23] [24] [60] [139] [198] [224], although retention was more prevalent in the *Q. robur* in German provenance trials[105]. Although sizeable trees, especially of *Q. petraea,* can retain leaves right to the top, the habit is most pronounced in young trees, coppice and low epicormic branches [23] [97] [115] [198] [262], resembling the clear-cut juvenile stage of leafretention in *Fagus sylvatica*[197] [198] [199]. The tendency to retain or lose leaves is strongly inherited in oak, as has been shown in grafting experiments and by controlled breeding (fig 2)[198].

Although a relationship has been claimed between leaf-retention and greater growth rates[114] [115], the physiological significance of this habit remains unclear. It possibly represents a vestigial expression of the evergreen habit shown by most *Quercus* spp[139] [257]; during mild winters[24] [60] [84] and in the tropics[31] seedlings and coppice shoots of European oaks can retain green leaves until the new ones appear, showing what is strictly speaking a 'leaf-exchanging' habit[133].

FIGURE 2

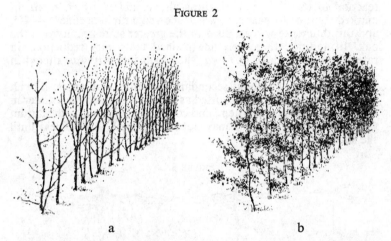

a   b

Winter leaf-retention as hereditary character in oak. Progeny after controlled crossing. a. *Quercus petraea* no. 1 ♀ × *Quercus robur* no. 2 ♂. Observe the paucity of foliage. b. *Quercus petraea* no. 1 ♀ × *Quercus robur* no. 3 ♂. Observe the copious foliage. Drawn March 1958 Noll. (From M. Schaffalitsky de Muckadell[198]).

Root growth
Periodicity of root growth
Roots appeared to elongate more by night than by day in *Q. robur*[88] and *Q. rubra*[137] unlike the shoots. Nor does the root system exhibit any clear-cut intermittent habit seasonally; for example pedunculate oak roots can be found growing at any time between April and November[71] or even later[87]. Rates and duration of elongation do fluctuate considerably however, but are not always clearly related to periodicity in the shoot (fig 1)[71] [123] [137] [181]. The patterns are doubtless influenced by environmental conditions, particularly temperature and stress, but little critical work has been done. At temperatures below 5°C roots but not shoots began to grow, while at 8–10°C the root growth was seven times greater than that of the shoots on a dry-matter basis, whereas at higher temperatures growth of the two was similar[177].

With shading to 20% of full day-light, shoot growth of 4-year-old *Q. robur* was relatively unaffected, but root growth was greatly reduced in amount and duration, and occurred mainly during periods of shoot elongation[71]. In younger plants under controlled environments, roots grew at a steady rate[123] [185] [253]. However, the direct influence of the acorn on growth may persist into the second year in *Q. petraea*[168] and *Q. rubra*[185], and even indirectly for 8–12 years in *Q. robur*[28] [50]; comparative studies of root growth using cuttings might be revealing. When light intensity was reduced from 5000 to 200 lux, root growth continued for a considerable time, but stopped up to 10 days sooner when acorns had been removed. A delayed reaction to low light intensity was also exhibited by *Q. rubra,* in marked contrast to *Acer* spp, which showed a rapid decline[97] [185] [253], and this difference was ascribed to the greater starch reserves in the oak. In addition there were unexplained temporary reductions in rate of root growth in *Q. rubra* when light intensity was altered in either direction.

Little is known about secondary growth of oak roots, though cambial activity has been reported as commencing 3–5 weeks later in surface roots than in the stem, and continuing longer into the autum (fig 1)[54] [116]. Deeper roots may not start growth in thickness until the summer[68].

FIGURE 3

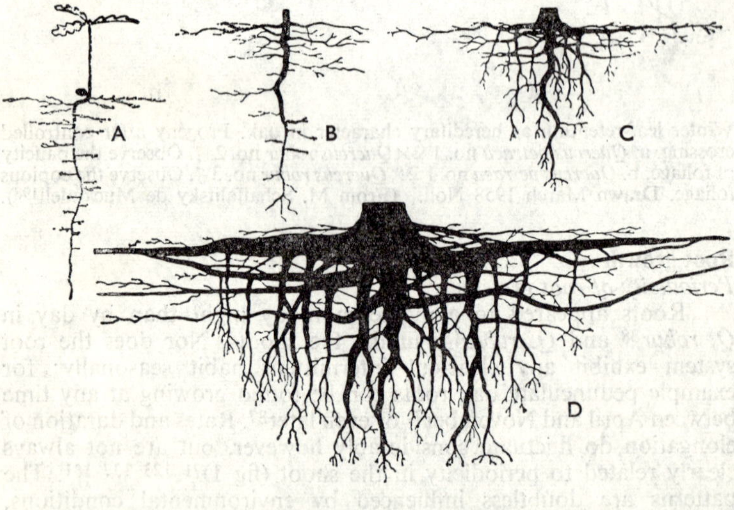

Development of oak root-systems with age in deep, loamy soil:
    (a) 1 year;
    (b) 10 years;
    (c) 25–30 years;
    (d) 70 years.

(From J. Jenik[81]).

Development of the root system

The strong seedling tap-root in *Q. robur* and *Q. petraea* has many very short laterals in the first year[135], and not until the 10th to 15th year are thick branch roots developed (fig 3)[81 84]. A well-defined tap-root may still be detectable after 20–30 years[204] but it is not necessarily an extention of the seedling radicle[25]. In time the laterals become relatively massive, with sinkers descending from them[204]. As with other species the development of the root system is greatly modified by soil conditions[81 92]; where circumstances permit oak is a deeply-rooting tree.

Physiological studies are scarce, but roots have been classified into two groups on the basis of end-root diameter[81 82], and into three classes: absorbing, conducting and intermediate[43]. In *Q. rubra* root-hairs are absent from the main roots, sparse and short on first-order laterals; while second-order laterals which have stopped growing are invested with root-hairs throughout their length, often including even the root tip[183]. As with other trees, the occurrence of mycorrhizae varies with soil conditions[25], and in *Q. robur* and *Q. petraea* they are of the ectotrophic type[81 97](see pps 223–229).

Patterns of rooting are indirectly influenced by light intensity, for in oaks as in other genera shading tends to reduce root development much more than that of the shoot[71 80 168]. In *Q. rubra* the root/shoot ratio decreased with every change from 68% to 1% of full light[138], while young *Q. robur* had nearly four times the rooting depth at 100% compared with 20% full day-light[71].

Root initiation

The formation of new laterals on root systems has received little attention, but in shoots adventitious root formation is possible with single nodes[13 47], and even detached leaves[14]. Most success with oak cuttings has been obtained when they are struck after the first flush when endogenous nutrient and hormone levels are presumably more favourable. Root initiation is stimulated in *Q. robur* by indole-3-acetic, indole-3-butyric and alpha napthaleneacetic acids [14 91 107 215]. As with other trees, rooting capacity declines with age [69 106 107], but this was not associated with reduced enzyme activity or respiration rate in *Q. suber*[91].

Reproduction

Flower initiation

Flowers are not generally formed until oaks are 20–30 years old[91 143 241], many reports of 40 years or more referring to the time of first substantial fruiting[60 86 113 164 211 219]. Shorter 'juvenile periods' were found in coppice shoots (10–20 years)[107 211], and in rapidly-growing *Q. robur* seedlings (3–5 years)[23 193]; the latter producing viable acorns after artificial pollination. Flowering has even been recorded in the first year but the trees died[86].

Axillary flower initials are formed within terminal and lateral buds, the female inflorescences at the more distal nodes, the male proximally, in the axils of basal leaves or bud scales. Both may occur on the same shoot, though exceptional trees occur bearing only male flowers[107]. Male flowers are initiated around July of the summer previous to flowering[22 24 93], and thus are unlikely to occur on shoots making a second flush (fig 1). Female flowers appear to be formed later in the summer, as is usual for temperate deciduous trees[131], and it has been reported that they form at the same time as future lateral vegetative buds[189]; the claim for their initiation in February/March of the flowering year[93] is unlikely to be correct.

Though there are generally intervals of 2–10 years between heavy acorn crops[107 143 188 219], initiation is more frequent, sometimes occurring in successive years in Q. robur[7 143] and many American species[167]. Since 5000 kg/ha of air-dry fruits can be produced[188], irregular bearing is not perhaps surprising but it has also been widely attributed to weather variations in the years of initiation and pollination.

Few attempts have been made to induce flowering of oak, or to shorten the juvenile period. Plants which had been continuously illuminated during the first 5 months after germination and then planted in the field subsequently flowered in their 8th year[164]. Quicker responses to rapid early growth have been reported in other genera[134 187 241], while it has been noted that flowering can occasionally occur in 'juvenile', leaf-retaining shoots of Q. petraea and Fagus sylvatica[198]. Male flowers have been induced in air-layers of 10–15 year old Q. suber[169], where the important factor was probably the complete 'ringing' of the bark, which is known to favour flower initiation in many woody plants[77 132 194]. Indole-3-acetic or alpha-napthaleneacetic acid was also applied in lanolin to the rings, but flowers did not form when concentration exceeded 0.25%[169].

Changes during fruit and seed development

Flowering and pollination occur during the first flush (fig 1) for no special dormancy appears to characterise flower buds, even when male buds contain no foliage leaves. The acorn of Q. robur and Q. petraea develops to maturity in one growing season, unlike several other species of oaks, the main period of abscission being October[84]. An important study of developing fruits by Michalski [146 147 148], shows the presence of two auxins, the more active of which was probably indole-3-acetic acid, both declining as the fruits enlarged, ripened and fell. Three chromatographic bands of gibberellins were also detected, two of which, probably corresponding with GA_{1+3} and GA_{4+7}, were most abundant during the period of rapid enlargement of the acorn.

Dormancy is often exhibited by freshly-fallen acorns, though this is never as profound as in ash[225 226 227 243]. Especially in Q. petraea and Q. alba some germination occurs at once under favourable conditions[24 29 167] or if they are harvested before being completely ripe[232], and occasionally even viviparously on the tree[84]. However, chilling is required by a proportion of the fruits, which is particularly high in *Q. robur*, the radicle then emerging in spring under natural conditions (fig 4). *Q. rubra* is similar, the acorns remaining dormant if stored at 20°C[20]. An interesting feature of unchilled acorns is that the radicle may emerge while the epicotyl remains dormant until chilled, such 'epicotyl dormancy' has also been reported for *Viburnum* spp [33 242 246 250]. Variation in promoters and inhibitors has been correlated with seed dormancy in other trees [55 225 226 227 242 246 248 252], but few studies have been done on oak. (See also table 1)[32].

Apart from dormancy, various other factors have been reported as affecting germination, including moisture content[11 113 161 167], and the short viable period of stored acorns[135]. An unusual effect reported for *Q. rubra* is the promotion of germination in acorns with the radicle horizontally placed and particularly when it lies uppermost[153].

Photosynthesis and storage
Detailed investigations by Jarvis[80] showed that *Q. petraea* reaches its maximum rate of photosynthesis at a relatively low light intensity, and this is also a feature of *Q. robur*[72], *Q. alba* and *Q. rubra*[112 130]. Thus rapid photosynthesis can even occur at 20% of full day-light, compared for example with *Pinus taeda* L., in which photosynthesis had dropped by a half at this light intensity[112]. Maximum photosynthetic rates achieved under the conditions used were also greater in *Q. lyrata* Walter than *P. taeda* on a leaf area, leaf dry weight and plant dry weight basis[95].

FIGURE 4

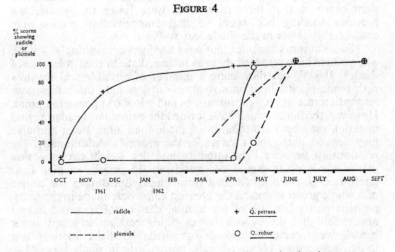

Dormancy of acorns under natural conditions in Rumania, showing a contrast between the usual appearance of the radicle in autumn in *Q. petraea* and spring in *Q. robur*. Note also the epicotyl dormancy.   (After G. Ciumac[29]).

Increasing atmospheric carbon dioxide to 0.3% enhanced rates of photosynthesis by 40–50% in *Q. robur*[233]; similar results are commonly found with other tree species[110]. Among other factors, leaf age affects the rate, with an increase to a maximum in leaves which have just completed expansion; though a temporary decrease in photosynthesis on a leaf area basis occurs when leaves of *Q. rubra* are expanding rapidly[186].

An interesting though somewhat speculative field is the possible influence of promoting and inhibiting volatiles from the leaves of other trees species upon photosynthesis in oak. For example it is claimed that volatile production is consistent with field observations that although *Gleditschia* and *Robinia* have similar growth habits and cast equivalant shade on oak when grown in mixtures, the oak thrives with the former but not the latter[90].

Shading prior to photosynthetic measurement also has marked effects, partly through modifications to leaf structure. Shade leaves are larger but thinner, have less cuticle and vascular supply, and fewer palisade cells and stomata than sun leaves[23 214 262]. Leaves of *Q. petraea* seedlings previously grown under 20% full daylight photosynthesised more at low light intensities than sun leaves[80], and the same was found for *Q. rubra* previously grown under 44% or 17% of full daylight; however when leaves had grown under 3% of full light, photosynthesis under low light intensity was equivalent to that of sun leaves[130].

Surprisingly, leaves developed under moderate shade also had higher *maximum* rates of photosynthesis than sun leaves in both species; this unusual feature may be partly attributable to the lower chlorophyll content of the latter[80 130 214]. A point of considerable significance is that respiration rates were lower the greater the previous shading had been, so that compensation points were considerably lower in the shade leaves[130].

Some authors consider that oaks are light-demanding[107 218 254], while others have regarded them as intermediate in their tolerance of shade[23 113 167], but they share a number of physiological features with shade plants: high photosynthesis at low light intensities; low respiration rate at all light intensities and a low compensation point. However, seedlings, which have formed the commonest experimental material, may be more tolerant of shade than adult trees, and also may depend partly on reserves in the acorn[168]. Additionally, the relationship between light intensity and dry weight accumulation of the whole plant should be considered. In periods of high light intensities, *Q. petraea* benefited from shade, but during the course of a whole growing season the greatest gains were made in the open, perhaps partly because of toe mutual shading of leaves[80]. Indeed absorption of light by oak leaves is higher than in many other broadleaved species[151], though sustained high light intensity can impair subsequent photosynthesis, particularly in shade leaves[80].

It is often overlooked that twigs and larger branches (and also fruits and even exposed roots) contain chlorophyll, and the authors have found that photosynthesis in leafless twigs of *Q. petraea* can exceed their respiration, the rates being greater on a surface area or dry weight basis than those for defoliated stems of *Picea sitchensis* (Bong.) Carrière[136]. Like leaf photosynthesis, rates in oak stems were still relatively high at lower light intensities; it is possible that stem photosynthesis may play an appreciable role in maintaining carbohydrate levels during the long leafless period.

As has been noted, the ray tissue in oaks is very extensive, occupying 15–40% of wood volume in various species[74 157]. This is considerably higher than that found in many other genera, and the quantities of food reserves can be correspondingly large[94 98]. Reserves consist mainly of starch, remaining in this form throughout the winter, unlike many other trees[23 195].

Water movement

Unlike diffuse-porous trees and gymnosperms, the main pathway of water movement in ring-porous trees is confined to the outer portion of the sapwood. In oaks 75% or more of the water has been shown with dyes to move in the outermost growth ring[100 116 171 262]. The most rapid rates are found in the very large springwood vessels; peak rates in *Q. robur* of 43.6m/h (c12 mm/sec) are amongst the highest recorded[75]. It has been estimated that 14.1 litres/h passed through a stem of 20cm diameter in summer[116], and that a tree 16.5m by 0.9m diam at the base transpired 154 litres during the day[170] while in the night the quantity was about 10% of this.

Water movement has been investigated in relation to oak wilt disease, caused by *Ceratocystis fagacearum* (Bretz) Hunt, because leaf symptoms apparently involve water stress. The normal diurnal fluctuations in stem diameter, due to changing water tensions in the xylem, ceased in inoculated trees a few days before they showed wilting, suggesting that vessels had become blocked[99]. Tyloses, which are regularly found in older growth rings, appear in the earlywood of the current year, and gummosis occurs in small vessels and tracheids[158 212]. Moreover, wilting is more pronounced by day, with recovery in the night, and further evidence of drastic reduction in amounts of water moving in the xylem has been provided by direct measurement[9]. The fungus does not appear to proceed by direct toxic action at the cambium, since this remains functional for several days after leaf symptoms appear[99]. It should not necessarily be assumed that tyloses are the primary cause of wilting, for gas embolism, induced by the host/pathogen interaction, may actually precede tylosis formation, thus merely hastening a process normal to the tree.

Physiological stress

Studies of drought resistance have ranged from field observation[10 201], growth and survival in dry soils[159 207], to growth of plants in polyethylene glycol solutions[118]. Oaks are undoubtedly mesophytic species, but the deep root system can be regarded as a drought-evading characteristic[205]. Indeed it has been suggested that the greater efficiency of photosynthesis shown by *Q. alba* in dry soil compared with *Pinus taeda* was attributable to the larger root system of the oak tree[94]. It has been calculated that reserves of water in the trunk of a sizeable oak tree could last for several weeks provided it was leafless[170 172].

Field observations suggest that *Quercus* spp are intolerant of flooding[53 59 217 258 259] or intermediate compared with other trees [66 191 228]. *Q. petraea* is apparently less tolerant than *Q. robur*[84], the seedlings of which were found to survive in laboratory experiments for at least 8 weeks. Although existing roots stopped growing 24 hours after submergence, new roots were formed[184].

Frost damage is commonest in spring, although oaks flush late, and young shoots can be killed by temperatures of $-3°C$[38]. *Q. petraea* has been claimed to be hardier than *Q. robur*[103 104], but the difference is not pronounced[84], and may in any event reflect differences in flushing and habitat. Seedlings appear to be more sensitive than older plants[51 104], and resistance in *Q. ilex* increases until trees reach the reproductive phase[117]. Oak seedlings are rarely damaged during winter in Britain, but are sometimes killed on the Continent by damage to the root collar and upper part of the tap-root[84]. These parts were damaged in *Q. robur* in Russia at $-21°$ and $-26°C$ respectively, terminal buds and late-flush material at $-31°C$, and older parts of the stem at $-36°C$[102]. Previous milder conditions reduced hardiness, even when temperatures remained below freezing point[220]. Acorns show variability of frost resistance depending on moisture content[162], and the duration and degree of cold[84]; they become much more sensitive as they germinate[223]. A great range of susceptibility has been observed even among acorns from a single tree[84].

Conclusion

Distinctive features of oak physiology include the intermittent type of shoot growth, with photoperiodic and hormonal control of bud-break rather than of terminal bud formation; and a precisely-timed, annual production of large new xylem vessels, capable of unusually rapid water conduction. The rather efficient photosynthetic and storage system, and the regenerative power of the tree from epicormic buds and coppice shoots may partly explain its extraordinary longevity, promoted also by the strong and durable heartwood and continued cambial activity in the trunk.

Tree physiology lags far behind other crop sciences, and in oak there are gaps even in the basic picture of life-cycle, structure and function. Information is scarce for example on root growth and flowering, and concerning factors affecting cambial activity and the role of hormones in seed dormancy. Investigations might usefully include comparative studies on seedlings with and without the acorn, and upon tissue of different ages, perhaps employing grafting techniques. For both scientific and practical reasons, more physiological knowledge would be valuable, particularly in Britain where the lack of research contrasts strangely with the unique position occupied by oaks in our language and traditions.

Acknowledgements

We would like to acknowledge the help given us in preparing this contribution by Mr I. G. White, Dr M. R. Bowen, Prof. F. T. Last and Mr G. M. Burnett.

REFERENCES

1. ALLARY, S. 'Remarques sur l'inhibition des bourgeons axillaires sur la pousse herbacée des végétaux ligneux', *C. r. hebd. Séanc. Acad. Sci., Paris*, **255** (1958), 1071–3
2. ALLARY, S. 'La liberation d'auxine diffusible par les organes aériens des végétaux ligneux', *C.r. hebd. Séanc. Acad. Sci., Paris*, **247** (1958), 2187–9
3. ALLARY, S. 'Substances de croissance et dormance des bourgeons de *Quercus pedunculata* Ehrh.', *C.r. hebd. Séanc. Acad. Sci., Paris*, **249** (1959), 1957–9
4. ALLARY, S. 'Evolution annuelle des substances inhibitrices acides des bourgeons de *Quercus pedunculata* Ehrh.', *C. r. hebd. Séanc. Acad. Sci., Paris*, **250** (1960), 911–13
5. ALLARY, S. 'Remarques sur le rôle du complexe inhibiteur dans la dormance des bourgeons de *Quercus pedunculata* Ehrh.', *C.r. hebd. Séanc. Acad. Sci., Paris*, **252** (1961), 930–2
6. ANDERSON, B. J. and EVERT, R. F. 'Some aspects of phloem development in *Quercus alba*', *Am. J. Bot.*, **52** (1965), 627
7. ANDERSON, M. L. *The selection of tree species*, Edinburgh (1950)
8. ANONYMOUS. 'Identification of hardwoods: a lens key', *Forest Prod. Res. Bull.*, **25** (1960), 126pp
9. BECKMAN, C. H., KUNTZ, J. E., RIKER, A. J. and BERBEE, J. G. 'Plugging of vessels associated with oak wilt development', *Phytopathology*, **42** (1952), 3
10. BOGGESS, W. R. 'Diameter growth of shortleaf pine and white oak following a mid-season drought', *Illinois agric. expl Stn Forest Note*, **65** (1955), 1p
11. BONNER, F. T. 'Water uptake and germination of red oak acorns', *Bot. Gaz.*, **129** (1968), 83–5
12. BORGSTRÖM, G. *The transverse reactions of plants*, Thesis, Lund (1939), 230pp (cited 44)
13. BORISENKO, T. T. 'On the feasibility of propagation of oak by single-node cuttings', *Dokl. Akad. Nauk SSSR*, **86** (1952), 1045–8
14. BORISENKO, T. T. 'The rooting capacity of oak leaves', *Priroda, Mosk.*, **42** (1953), 99–100
15. BORTHWICK, H. A. 'Light effects on tree growth and seed germination', *Ohio J. Sci.*, **57** (1957), 357–64
16. BOWERSOX, T. W. and WARD, W. W. 'Auxin inhibition of epicormic shoots in white oak', *Forest Sci.*, **14** (1968), 192–6
17. BOŽINOV, B. and ŠIPČANOV, I. 'Effect of gibberellic acid on some wood species', *Nauchni Trud. Vissh Lesotekh. Inst.*, **9** (1961), 37–45
18. BRIAN, P. W., PETTY, J. H. P. and RICHMOND, P. T. 'Effects of gibberellic acid on development of autumn colour and leaf-fall of deciduous woody plants', *Nature, Lond.*, **183** (1959), 58–9
19. BROWN, C. L., McALPINE, R. G. and KORMANIK, P. P. 'Apical dominance and form in woody plants: a reappraisal', *Am. J. Bot.*, **54** (1967), 153–62

20. BROWN, J. W. 'Respiration of acorns as related to temperature and after-ripening', *Pl. Physiol., Lancaster,* **14** (1939), 621–45
21. BÜNNING, E. 'Vorkommen und Arten des Activitätswechsels', *Handb. PflPhysiol.,* **2** (1956), 840–63
22. BÜSGEN, M. 'Blütenentwicklung und Zweigwachstum der Rotbuche', *Z. Forst- u. Jagdw.,* **48** (1916), 289–306
23. BÜSGEN, M. and MÜNCH, E. *'Structure and life of forest trees,* translated T. Thomson, London (1929)
24. CAMUS, A. *Les chênes: monographie du genre Quercus,* **1–3,** Paris (1936–54)
25. CARPENTER, L. W. and GUARD, A. T. 'Anatomy and morphology of the seedling roots of four species of the genus *Quercus', J. For.,* **52** (1954), 269–74
26. CHALUPA, V. 'The start, duration and end of growth activity in forest tree species', *Pr. vyzk. Ust. lesn. Hosp. Mysl.,* **37** (1969), 41–68
27. CHANEY, W. R. and LEOPOLD, A. C. 'Enhancement of twig abscission in white oak with ethepon', *Can. J. For. Res.,* **2** (1972), 492–5
28. CIESLAR, A. 'Untersuchungen über die wirtschaftliche Bedeutung der Herkunft des Saatgutes der Steileiche', *Zentbl. ges. Forstw.,* **49** (1923), 97–149
29. CIUMAC, G. 'Comparative development of *Quercus petraea* and *Q. robur* seedlings during their first two growing seasons', *Revta Padur.,* **81** (1966), 386–9
30. CORNER, E. J. H. *Wayside trees of Malaya,* **1** and **2,** Singapore (1940)
31. COSTER, C. 'Zur Anatomie und Physiologie der Zuwachszonen und Jahresringbildung in den Tropen', *Annls Jard. bot. Buitenz.,* **37** (1927), 49–160; **38** (1928), 1–114
32. COX, L. G. 'A physiological study of embryo dormancy in the seed of native hardwoods and Iris', *Abstr. Theses Cornell Univ.,* 1942, (1943), 354–7
33. CROCKER, W. and BARTON, L. V. *Physiology of seeds,* Waltham, Mass. (1953)
34. CZAJA, A. T. 'Der Nachweis des Wuchsstoffes bei Holzpflanzen', *Ber. dt. Bot. Ges.,* **52** (1934), 267–71
35. DANILOV, M. D. 'On the breaking of winter rest by buds of woody plants', *Dokl. Akad. Nauk SSSR,* **53** (1946), 267–9
36. DANILOV, M. D. 'Twenty-four hour cycle in the shoot growth of some tree and shrub species', *Dokl. Akad. Nauk SSSR,* **96** (1954), 205–8
37. DAUBENMIRE, R. F. and DETERS, M. E. 'Comparative studies of growth in deciduous and evergreen trees', *Bot. Gaz.,* **109** (1947), 1–12
38. DAY, W. R. and PEACE, T. R. 'The experimental production and the diagnosis of frost injury on forest trees', *Oxf. For. Mem.,* **16** (1934)
39. DIGBY, J. and WAREING, P. F. 'The effect of applied growth hormones on cambial division and the differentiation of the cambial derivatives', *Ann. Bot.,* **30** (1966), 539–48
40. DIGBY, J. and WAREING, P. F. 'The relationship between endogenous hormone levels in the plant and seasonal aspects of cambial activity', *Ann. Bot.,* **30** (1966) 607–22
41. DINGLER, H. 'Die Periodizität sommergrüner Bäume Mitteleuropas im Gebirgsklima Ceylons', *Sber. bayer. Akad. Wiss.,* **2** (1911), 217–47
42. DOBRESCU, Z. and CATRINA, I. 'The stimulating effect of gibberellin on some forest species', *Revta Padur.,* **78** (1963), 65–9
43. DOMANSKAJA, N. P. 'Formation of the root system of *Q. robur', Dokl. Akad. Nauk SSSR,* **119** (1958), 1233–5
44. DOORENBOS, J. 'Review of the literature on dormancy in buds of woody plants', *Meded. Lab. TuinbPlTeelt, Wageningen,* **53** (1953), 1–24
45. DOROHOVA, L. S. 'Nutrient uptake by seedlings under the influence of gibberellin', *Lesnoe Hozjajstvo, Moscow,* **18** (1965), 37–9

46. DOSTÁL, R. 'Über die Sommerperiodicität bei *Quercus* und *Fagus*', *Ber. dt. bot. Ges.*, **45** (1927), 436–47
47. DOSTÁL, R. in *On integration in plants*, ed. K. V. Thimann, Harvard (1967)
48. DOWNS, R. J. 'Photocontrol of growth and dormancy in woody plants', In *Tree growth*, ed. T. T. Kozlowski, New York (1962), 133–48
49. EAMES, A. J. and MACDANIELS, L. H. *An introduction to plant anatomy*, New York (1925)
50. EITINGEN, G. 'Der Wuchs der Eiche in Abhängigkeit von dem Gewicht der Eicheln', *Forstwiss. ZentBl.*, **48** (1926), 849–63
51. ESKIN, B. I. 'Anthocyanin and the frost resistance of plants', *Dokl. Akad. Nauk SSSR*, **130** (1960), 1158–60
52. FAHN, A. 'The development of the growth ring in wood of *Quercus infectoria* and *Pistachia lentiscus* in the hill region of Israel', *Trop. Woods*, **101** (1955), 52–9
53. FARSKY, O. 'The harmful results of the July 1954 floods in the marshy forests near Gabčikovo', *Lesn. Cas.*, **3** (1957), 100–57
54. FAYLE, D. C. F. 'Radial growth in tree roots: distribution; timing; anatomy', *Tech. Rep. Fac. For. Univ. Toronto*, **9** (1968), 183pp
55. FRANKLAND, B. and WAREING, P. F. 'Hormonal regulation of seed dormancy in Hazel (*Corylus avellana* L.) and Beech (*Fagus sylvatica* L.)', *J. exp. Bot.*, **17** (1966), 596–611
56. FRASER, D. A. 'Tree growth in relation to soil moisture', In *Tree growth*, ed. T. T. Kozlowski, New York (1962), 183–204
57. GILL, N. 'The phloem of ash (*Fraxinus excelsior* Linn.): its differentiation and seasonal variation', *Proc. Leeds phil. lit. Soc. (Sci.)*, **2** (1932), 347–55
58. GREBINSKII, S. O., LJUKOVA, L. A. and FRIŠKO, K. N. 'The influence of vitamins on the flushing of dormant buds', *Dokl. Akad. Nauk SSSR*, **105** (1955), 1361–3
59. GREEN, W. E. 'Effect of water improvement on tree mortality and growth', *J. For*, **45** (1947), 118–120
60. GROOM, P. *Trees and their life histories*, London (1907)
61. GRUDZINSKAJA, I. A. 'The influence of 'lammas' shoots on the formation of false annual rings in oak', *Dokl. Akad. Nauk SSSR*, **115** (1957), 392–5
62. GRUDZINSKAJA, I. A. 'Some results of study of shoot ontogeny in *Quercus robur*', *Bot. Zh. SSSR*, **49** (1964), 321–37
63. GULISASHVILI, V. Z. 'Breaking dormancy, periodicity and rhythm of growth in some tree species by cultivation in electric light', *Priroda, Mosk.*, **37** (1948), 63–6
64. GUZEEVA, M. A. 'Effect of gibberellin on seedlings of *Quercus robur*', *Byull. glavn. bot. Sada, Moskva*, **63** (1966), 89–91
65. GUZEEVA, M. A. 'Effect of photoperiod on *Quercus robur* seedlings treated with gibberellin', *Byull. glavn. bot. Sada, Moskva*, **64** (1967), 105–6
66. HALL, T. F. and SMITH, G. E. 'Effects of flooding on woody plants, West Sandy dewatering project, Kentucky reservoir', *J. For.*, **53** (1955), 281–5
67. HARTIG, R. 'Ueber neuere Untersuchungen zur Physiologie der Eiche', *Bot. Zbl.*, **56** (1893), 357–8
68. HARTIG, T. 'Über die Zeit des Zuwachses der Baumwurzeln', *Bot. Ztg.*, **21** (1863), 288–9
69. HARTMAN, H. and KESTER, D. *Plant propagation—Principles and Practice*, Englewood Cliffs, New Jersey (1968)
70. HENGST, E. 'Phenological studies in a hardwood stand', *Forstwiss. ZentBl.*, **84** (1965), 293–309
71. HOFFMANN, G. 'Wurzel-und Sprosswachstumsperiodik der Jungpflanzen von *Quercus robur* L. im Freiland und unter Schattenbelastung', *Arch. Forstw.*, **16** (1967), 745–9

72. HOLMGREN, P., JARVIS, P. G. and JARVIS, M. S. 'Resistances to carbon dioxide and water vapour transfer in leaves of different plant species', *Physiologia Pl.*, **18** (1965), 557–73
73. HOWARD, A. L. *Trees in Britain and their timbers*, London (1947)
74. HÜBER, B. and PRÜTZ, G. 'Über den Anteit von Fasern, Gefässen und Parenchym am Aufbau verschiedener Hölzer', *Holz Roh- u. Werkstoff*, **1** (1938) 377–381
75. HÜBER, B. and SCHMIDT, E. 'Weitere thermo-elektrische Untersuchungen über den Transpirationsstrom der Baüme', *Tharandt. forstl. Jb.*, **87** (1936), 369–412
76. ILLE, R. 'Zur Entwicklungsphysiologie der Knospenschuppen bei *Quercus pedunculata*', *Acta. Soc. Sci. nat. moravo-siles.*, **10** (1937), 1–19
77. JACKSON, D. I. and SWEET, G. B. 'Flower initiation in temperate woody plants', *Hort. Abstr.*, **42** (1972), 9–24
78. JACKSON, L. W. R. 'Radial growth of forest trees in the Georgia Piedmont', *Ecology*, **33** (1952), 336–41
79. JACQUIOT, C. 'The action of some adenine derivatives on the growth of cambial tissue of tree species grown in vitro', *C.r. hebd. Séanc. Acad. Sci., Paris*, **270** (1970), 493–5
80. JARVIS, P. G. 'The adaptability to light intensity of seedlings of *Quercus petraea* (Matt.) Liebl.', *J. Ecol.*, **52** (1964), 545–71
81. JENIK, J. 'Root system of *Quercus robur* L. and *Q. petraea* Liebl.', *Rozpravy čsl. Akad. Ved.*, **67** (1957), 1–85
82. JENIK, J. and SEN, D. N. 'Morphology of root systems in trees—a proposal for terminology', *Abstr. 10th Int. bot. Congr.*, (1964), 393–4
83. JOHNSON, J. P. 'Height growth periods of oak and pine reproduction in the Missouri Ozarks', *J. For.*, **39** (1941), 67–8
84. JONES, E. W. 'Biological flora of the British Isles: Quercus L.', *J. Ecol.*, **47** (1959), 169–222
85. JOST, L. Über Beziehungen zwischen der Blattentwickelung und der Gefässbildung in den Pflanze', *Bot. Ztg.*, **51** (1893) 89–138
86. JOST, L. *Vorlesungen über Pflanzenphysiologie*, Jena (1913)
87. KARANDINA, S. N. 'The duration of extension roots of *Q. robur* in the year', *Soobshch Lab. Lesov.*, (4) (1961), 54–69
88. KAZARJAN, V. O. and HURŠUDJAN, P. A. 'The seasonal and diurnal rhythm of stem and root growth of one-year seedlings of *Quercus robur* and *Elaeagnus angustifolia*', *Fiziologiya Rast.*, **13** (1966), 725–8
89. KLEBS, G. 'Über das Treiben der einheimischen Baüme, speziell der Buche', *Abh. heidelb. Akad. Wiss.*, **3** (1914), 1–116
90. KOLESNIČENKO, M. V. 'On the need to consider the biochemical influences of trees', *Lesnoe Hozjajstvo, Moscow*, **17** (1964), 15–19
91. KOMISSAROV, D. A. *Biological basis for the propagation of woody plants by cuttings*, translated Z. Shapiro, Jerusalem (1968)
92. KÖSTLER, J. N., BRÜCKNER, E. and BIBELRIETHER, H. *Die Wurzeln der Waldbaüme*, Hamburg (1968)
93. KOTOV, M. M. 'Flowering biology of *Quercus robur*', *Lesoved, Mosk.*, (4) (1969), 73–7
94. KOZLOWSKI, T. T. 'Light and water in relation to growth and competition of Piedmont forest tree species', *Ecol. Monogr.*, **19** (1949), 207–31
95. KOZLOWSKI, T. T. 'Effect of continuous high light intensity on photosynthesis of forest tree seedlings', *Forest Sci.*, **3** (1957), 220–4
96. KOZLOWSKI, T. T. 'Shoot growth in woody plants', *Bot. Rev.*, **30** (1964), 335–92
97. KOZLOWSKI, T. T. *Growth and development of trees*, **1** and **2**, New York (1971)
98. KOZLOWSKI, T. T. and KELLER, T. 'Food relations of woody plants', *Bot. Rev.*, **32** (1966), 293–382

99. KOZLOWSKI, T. T., KUNTZ, J. E. and WINGET, C. H. 'Effect of oak wilt on cambial activity', *J. For.*, **60** (1962), 558–61
100. KOZLOWSKI, T. T. and WINGET, C. H. 'Patterns of water movement in forest trees', *Bot. Gaz.*, **124** (1963), 301–11
101. KRAEVOJ, S. J. and ES'KIN, B. I. 'On the possible causes of successive shoot growth in *Quercus robur*', *Dokl. Akad. Nauk SSSR*, **117** (1957), 333–6 (243–6 in Engl. transl.)
102. KRAEVOJ, S. J., OKNINA, E. Z. and IPEKDZIJAN, V. M. 'The influence of low critical temperatures on *Quercus robur* seedlings', *Dokl. Akad. Nauk SSSR*, **96** (1954), 841–4
103. KRAHL-URBAN, J. 'Sessile and pedunculate oak in Sweden', *Forstwiss. ZentBl.*, **70** (1951), 319–36
104. KRAHL-URBAN, J. 'Frost damage in winter to *Quercus sessiliflora, Q. robur* and *Q. borealis*', *Forst-u. Holzwirt*, **10** (1955), 111–13
105. KRAHL-URBAN, J. 'Oak provenance trials—first report on the establishment of trial plots and some preliminary results', *Silvae Genet.*, **6** (1957), 15–31
106. KRAHL-URBAN, J. 'Versuche zur Bewurzelung von Eichen- und Buchenstecklingen', *Silvae Genet.*, **7** (1958), 58–65
107. KRAHL-URBAN, J. *Die Eichen*, Hamburg and Berlin (1959)
108. KRAMER, P. J. 'Effect of variation in length of day on growth and dormancy in trees', *Pl. Physiol., Lancaster*, **11** (1936), 127–37
109. KRAMER, P. J. 'Amount and duration of growth of various species of tree seedlings', *Pl. Physiol., Lancaster*, **18** (1943), 239–51
110. KRAMER, P. J. 'Photosynthesis of trees as affected by their environment', in *The physiology of forest trees*, ed. K. V. Thimann, New York (1958), 157–86
111. KRAMER, P. J. 'Thermoperiodism in trees', in *The Physiology of forest trees*, ed. K. V. Thimann, New York (1958), 573–80
112. KRAMER, P. J. and DECKER, J. P. 'Relation between light intensity and rate of photosynthesis of loblolly pine and certain hardwoods', *Pl. Physiol., Lancaster*, **19** (1944), 350–8
113. KRAMER, P. J. and KOZLOWSKI, T. T. *Physiology of trees*, New York (1960)
114. KRASNITSKIJ, A. M. 'Geographical, ecological and individual variability in leaf retention by oak in winter', *Lesoved, Mosk.*, (6) (1968), 42–9
115. KRASNITSKIJ, A. M. 'The forestry importance of winter leaf retention in *Quercus robur*', *Lesnoi Zhurnal, Arkhangel'sk*, **12** (1969), 161–3
116. LADEFOGED, K. 'The periodicity of wood formation', *Biol. Skr.*, **7** (1952), 1–98
117. LARCHER, W. 'The effect of environmental and physiological variables on the carbon dioxide gas exchange of trees', *Photosynthetica*, **3** (1969), 167–98
118. LARSON, M. M. and WHITMORE, F. W. 'Moisture stress affects root regeneration and early growth of red oak seedlings', *Forest Sci.*, **16** (1970), 495–8
119. LARSON, P. R. 'Gibberellic acid-induced growth of dormant hardwood cuttings', *Forest Sci.*, **6** (1960), 232–9
120. LAVARENNE-ALLARY, S. 'The characters and nature of dormancy of oak buds', *C.r. hebd. Séanc. Acad. Sci., Paris*, **256** (1963), 2217–9
121. LAVARENNE-ALLARY, S. 'Studies on the growth of buds on oak and on some other woody species', *Annls Sci. for., Nancy*, **22** (1965), 1–203
122. LAVARENNE, S. 'Croissance rythmique de quelques espèces de chênes cultivées en chambres climatisées', *C.r. hebd. Séanc. Acad. Sci., Paris*, **262** (1966), 358–61
123. LAVARENNE, S. 'Comparative growth of shoots and roots of young oaks grown in controlled conditions', *C.r. hebd. Séanc. Acad. Sci., Paris*, **266 D** (1968), 778–80

124. LAVARENNE, S. 'Déterminisme d'une croissance continue chez le chêne', *C.r. hebd. Séanc. Acad. Sci., Paris,* **269** D (1969), 2099–2102

125. LEIKE, H. 'Effect of gibberellic acid and kinetin on resting buds of various woody species', *Flora, Jena,* **158** A (1967), 351–62

126. LEIKE, H. 'Growth regulators in dormancy of tree buds', *Proc. 3rd Symp. Plant Growth Regulators,* Torun, Poland (1970), 33–42

127. LEMAN, V. M. 'Experiment on the practical utilisation of light culture of *Quercus pedunculata* Ehrh.', *Dokl. Akad. Nauk SSSR,* **59** (1948), 777–80

128. LEMAN, V. M. 'Behaviour of oak seedlings during continuous electrical illumination', *Dokl. Akad. Nauk SSSR,* **60** (1948), 1261–4

129. LEMAN, V. M. 'Forcing of woody seedlings with the aid of electric light', *Les. Khoz.,* **1** (1950), 60–3

130. LOACH, K. 'Shade tolerance in tree seedlings. 1. Leaf photosynthesis and respiration in plants raised under artificial shade', *New Phytol.,* **66** (1967), 607–21

131. LOHWAG, H. 'Beitrag zur Kenntnis der Zeit der ersten Blütenanlage bei Holzpflanzen', *Ost bot. Z.,* **60** (1910), 369–76

132. LONGMAN, K. A., HOWARTH, J. and BOWEN, M. R. 'Cone initiation in field-grown *Thuja plicata* D. Don. 1. Effects of bark-ringing', (in the press)

133. LONGMAN, K. A. and JENIK, J. *Tropical forest and its environment,* London., (1974)

134. LONGMAN, K. A. and WAREING, P. F. 'Early induction of flowering in birch seedlings', *Nature, Lond.,* **184** (1959), 2037–8

135. LOUDON, J. C. *Arboretum et Fruticetum Brittanicum; or the trees and shrubs of Britain,* **3,** London (1838)

136. LUDLOW, M. M. and JARVIS, P. G. 'Photosynthesis in sitka spruce (*Picea sitchensis* (Bong.) Carr. I. General characteristics', *J. appl. Ecol.,* **8** (1971), 925–53

137. LYR, H., ERDMANN, A., HOFFMANN, G. and KÖHLER, S. 'The diurnal growth rhythm of woody species', *Flora, Jena,* **157** B (1968), 615–24

138. LYR, H., HOFFMANN, G. and ENGEL, W. 'The influence of degrees of shading on dry-matter production in young plants of some forest species. Part 2', *Flora, Jena,* **155** (1964), 305–30

139. MAGNUS, W. 'Der physiologische Atavismus unserer Eichen und Buche', *Biol. Zbl.,* **33** (1913), 309–37

140. MAKSIMOV, N. A. and LEMAN, V. M. 'Culture of woody seedlings in electric light', *Dokl. Mosk. sel'.-khoz. Akad. K. A. Timiryazeva,* (3) (1946), 46–51

141. MÁNDY, G. and KÁRPÁTI, I. 'Experimental data on the rest period of trees and shrubs', *Kísérl. Közl.,* **54** C (1962), 69–97

142. MARTH, P. C., AUDIA, W. V. and MITCHELL, J. W. 'Effects of gibberellic acid on growth and development of plants of various genera and species', *Bot. Gaz.,* **118** (1956), 106–11

143. MATTHEWS, J. D. 'Production of seed by forest trees in Great Britain', *Rep. Forest. Res., Lond.,* 1953–4, (1955), 64–78

144. MAXWELL, H. *Trees: a woodland notebook,* Glasgow (1915)

145. MELCHIOR, G. H. and KNAPP, R. 'Gibberellin-wirkungen an Baümen', *Silvae Genet.,* **11** (1961), 29–39

146. MICHALSKI, L. 'Content of plant growth regulators in the developing seed of oak (*Qurcus robur* L.) 1. Gibberellin-like substances', *Acta Soc. Bot. Pol.,* **37** (1968), 541–6

147. MICHALSKI, L. 'Content of plant growth regulators in the developing seeds of oak (*Quercus robur* L.) 2. Auxin-like substances', *Acta Soc. Bot. Pol.,* **38** (1969), 157–63

148. MICHALSKI, L. 'Plant growth regulators in oak (*Quercus robur* L.) seeds during their development', in *Seed physiology of woody plants.,* ed. S. Bialobock and B. Suszka, Poznân (1970)

149. MICHALSKI, L. and KRZYSKO, K. 'Seasonal changes in the dynamics of auxins and gibberellin-like substances during the development of the terminal buds of oak', *Proc. 3rd Symp. Plant Growth Regulators*, Torun, Poland (1970), 147–52

150. MICHNIEWICZ, M. and SAMEK, T. 'Effect of auxin and gibberellin on growth of *Quercus robur* seedlings', *Sylwan*, **112** (1968), 55–61

151. MIEGROET, M. VAN, and VYNCKE, G. 'Transmission of light through tree leaves developed under different artificial illumination', *Sylva gandavensis*, **13** (1969), 1–37

152. MIŠNEV, V. G., MANCEVIČ, E. D. and SAVČENKO, V. K. 'The reaction of acorns and oak seedlings to gibberellin', *Dokl. Akad. Nauk belorussk. SSR*, **7** (1964), 410–13

153. MOLOTKOVSKII, G. H. 'The germinative energy and capacity of seeds of *Quercus rubra* and *Juglans regia* as related to their position in the soil', *Dokl. Akad. Nauk SSSR*, **102** (1955), 637–9

154. MOLOTKOVSKII, G. H. and MOLOTKOVSKII, J. G. 'New method of breaking dormancy in woody species', *Dokl. Akad. Nauk SSSR*, **90** (1953), 101–4

155. MOREL, G. 'Physiologie du cambium', In *Colloque de Xylologie*, 1959, *Mém. Soc. bot. Fr.*, (1960), 50–60

156. MUNCH, E. 'Untersuchungen über die Harmonie der Baumgestalt', *Jb. wiss. Bot.*, **86** (1938), 581–673

157. MYER, J. E. 'Ray volumes of the commercial woods', *J. For.*, **20** (1922), 337–51

158. NAIR, V. M. G., KUNTZ, J. E. and SACHS, I. B. 'Tyloses induced by *Ceratocystis fagacearum* in oak wilt development', *Phytopathology*, **57** (1967), 823–4

159. NAUMOV, Z. 'Soil moisture and afforestation', *Gorsko Stop.*, **14** (1958), 34–43

160. NELSON, T. C. 'Early responses of some southern tree species to gibberellic acid', *J. For.*, **55** (1957), 518–20

161. NEMKY, E. 'The principal problems in the germination ecology of acorns as bases for successful natural regeneration', *Erdö*, **13** (1964), 537–42

162. NEMKY, E. 'The influence of the water content of acorns on their frost sensitivity and the inception of germination', *Erdész., Faipari Egyetem tud. Közl., Sopron*, (1) (1964), 41–62

163. NETIEN, G. 'Presence of a gibberellin-like substance in the buds of woody species', *C.r. hebd. Séanc. Acad. Sci., Paris*, **256** (1963), 997–9

164. NIKITIN, I. N. —cited in 239

165. NITSCH, J. P. 'Growth response of woody plants to photoperiodic stimuli', *Proc. Am. Soc. hort. Sci.*, **70** (1957), 512–25

166. NITSCH, J. P. 'Photoperiodism in woody plants', *Proc. Am. Soc. hort. Sci.*, **70** (1957), 526–44

167. OLSON, D. F. (Jr) and BOYCE, S. G. 'Factors affecting acorn production and germination, and early growth of seedlings and seedling sprouts', *Proc. Oak Symposium, Morgantown, Upper Darby, Pennsylvania* (1971), 44–8

168. OVINGTON, J. D. and MACRAE, C. 'The growth of seedlings of *Quercus petraea*', *J. Ecol.*, **48** (1960), 549–55

169. PAIXÃO-CORREIA, C. A. DA, 'The formation of adventitious flower buds on cuttings of *Quercus suber* treated with 1-napthalene-acetic acid and 3-indole-acetic acid', *Port. Acta. biol.*, **4** A (1955), 249–63

170. PARKER, J. 'The cut-leaf method and estimations of diurnal trends in transpiration from different heights and sides of an oak and a pine', *Bot. Gaz.*, **119** (1957), 93–101

171. PARKER, J. 'Seasonal changes in water intake through bore holes in white oak trunks', *Can. J. Bot.*, **43** (1965), 1037–41

172. PARKER, J. 'Further studies of drought resistance in woody plants', *Bot. Rev.*, **35** (1969), 317–71

173. PAULEY, S. S. 'Influence of light on break of dormancy in various tree species', *Genetics*, **39** (1954), 987
174. PERRY, T. O. and SIMONS, R. W. 'Growth of bud scales and leaves during the winter', *Forest Sci.*, **13** (1967), 400–1
175. PHILIPSON, W. R., WARD, J. M. and BUTTERFIELD, B. G. *The vascular cambium: its development and activity*, London (1971)
176. PJATNICKII, S. S. ' 'Winter' and 'summer' oaks (ie late- and early-flushing forms of *Quercus robur*)', *Priroda, Mosk.*, **42** (1953), 97–102
177. POTAPOV, N. G. 'The influence of temperature on root growth in oak seedlings', *Agrokém. Talajt.*, **5** (1956), 69–74
178. PRIESTLEY, J. H. 'Radial growth and extension growth in the tree', *Forestry*, **9** (1935), 84–95
179. PRIESTLEY, J. H. and SCOTT, L. I. 'A note upon summerwood production in the tree', *Proc. Leeds phil. lit. Soc., (Sci.)*, **3** (1936), 235–48
180. PRIESTLEY, J. H. and MALINS, M. E. 'Vessel development in the angiosperm' *Proc. Leeds phil. lit. Soc., (Sci.)*, **3** (1935) 42–54
181. RAHTEENKO, I. N. 'The seasonal cycle of the growth of active roots of tree species', *Lesnoe Hozjajstvo, Moscow,* **12** (1960), 25–6
182. REINDERS-GOUWENTAK, C. A. 'Physiology of the cambium and other secondary meristems of the shoot', *Handb. PflPhysiol.*, **15** (1965), 1077–1105
183. RICHARDSON, S. D. 'A note on some differences in root-hair formation between seedlings of sycamore and American oak', *New Phytol.*, **52** (1953), 80–2
184. RICHARDSON, S. D. 'Effects of seawater flooding on tree growth in the Netherlands', *Q. Jl For.*, **49** (1955), 22–8
185. RICHARDSON, S. D. 'On the role of the acorn in the root growth of American oak seedlings', *Meded. Lab. TuinbPlTeelt, Wageningen,* **56** (1956), 1–18
186. RICHARDSON, S. D. 'The effect of leaf age on the rate of photosynthesis in detached leaves of tree seedlings', *Acta bot. neerl.*, **6** (1957), 445–57
187. ROBINSON, L. W. and WAREING, P. F. 'Experiments on the juvenile-adult phase change in some woody species', *New Phytol.*, **68** (1969), 67–78
188. ROHMEDER, E. 'The relationships between fruit or seed production and wood production of forest trees', *Allg. Forstz.*, **22** (1967), 33–9
189. ROMAŠOV, H. V. 'Laws governing the fruiting of oak', *Bot. Zh. SSSR,* **42** (1957), 41–56
190. ROMBERGER, J. A. 'Meristems, growth and development in woody plants', *Tech. Bull. U.S. Dep. Agric., no.* 1293 (1963), 214pp
191. RUBANOV, B. V. 'Features in establishing forest plantations in the Volga-Akhtuba flood-plain and the Volga delta', *Lesnoe Hozjajstvo, Moscow,* **12** (1959), 27–32
192. RUSSELL, T. E. 'Seeding and planting upland oaks', *Proc. Oak Symposium, Morgantown,* Upper Darby, Pennsylvania (1971), 49–54
193. RYBIN, V. A. and IL'INA, A. G. 'Early fruiting in *Quercus pedunculata',* *Priroda, Leningrad,* (4) (1956), 114–15
194. SACHS, J. VON, *Lectures on the physiology of plants* (Engl. transl.), Oxford (1887)
195. SAUTER, J. J. 'The influence of different temperatures on starch reserves in parenchyma tissues of tree stems', *Z. P. Physiol.*, **56** (1967), 340–52
196. SAX, K. 'Experimental control of tree growth and reproduction', in *The Physiology of forest trees*, ed. K. V. Thimann, New York (1958), 601–10
197. SCHAFFALITZKY DE MUCKADELL, M. 'Juvenile stages in woody plants', *Physiologia Pl.*, **7** (1954), 782–96
198. SCHAFFALITZKY DE MUCKADELL, M. 'Investigations on aging of apical meristems in woody plants and its importance in silviculture', *Forst. ForsVaes Danm.*, **25** (1959), 307–455

199. SCHAFFALITZKY DE MUCKADELL, M. 'Environmental factors in development stages of trees', in *Tree growth*, ed. T. T. Kozlowski, New York (1962), 289–97
200. SCHIMPER, A. F. W. *Plant geography on a physiological basis* (Engl. transl.), Oxford (1903)
201. SCHOBER, R. 'The influence of recent drought years on diameter increment', *Forstwiss. ZentBl.*, **70** (1951), 204–28
202. SCHOENEWEISS, D. F. 'Methods for breaking dormancy of oak seedlings in the greenhouse', *Proc. Am. Soc. hort. Sci.*, **83** (1963), 819–24
203. SCHWARTZ, O. 'Monographie der Eichen Europas und des Mittelmeergebietes', *Reprium Nov. Spec. veg.* Sonderb.D., **1** and **2** (1936–39)
204. SEEGER, M. 'Erfahrungen über die Eiche in der Rheinebene bei Emmendingen (Baden)', *Allg. Forst- u. Jagdztg*, **106** (1930), 201–19
205. SEIDEL, K. W. 'The drought resistance and internal water balance of oak seedlings', *Diss. Abstr.*, **30** B (1970), 3450
206. SHCHEPOT'EV, F. L. 'Influence of short-term treatment with short-days on the growth and development of common oak (*Quercus robur* L.)', *Dokl. Akad. Nauk SSSR*, **56** (1947), 429–31
207. ŠIPČANOV, I. 'Study of the drought resistance of local (Bulgarian) deciduous oaks and *Quercus borealis* var. *maxima*', *Gorsko Stop.*, **14** (1958), 24–30
208. SMITH, H. C. 'Epicormic branching on eight species of Appalachian hardwoods', *Forest Res. Notes.*, *NEast. Forest Exp. Stn.*, no. NE-53
209. SÖDING, H. 'Wuchsstoff und Kambiumtätigkeit der Baüme', *Jb wiss. Bot.*, **84** (1937), 639–70
210. SPATH, H. L. *Der Johannistrieb*, Berlin (1912)
211. ŠPIRANEC, M. 'More on the initial physiological maturity of forest trees', *Hrv. šum. List*, **75** (1951), 213–21
212. STRUCKMEYER, B. E., BECKMANN, C. H., KUNTZ, J. E. and RIKER, A. J. 'Plugging of vessels by tyloses and gums in wilting oaks', *Phytopathology*, **44** (1954), 148–53
213. STUDHALTER, R. A., GLOCK, W. S. and AGERTER, S. R. 'Tree growth: some historical chapters', *Bot. Rev.*, **29** (1963), 245–365
214. TAIRBEKOV, M. G. and STARZECKI, W. 'Dynamics of the processes of photosynthesis and respiration in leaves of *Quercus robur* in relation to light', *Fiziologiya Rast.*, **17** (1970), 686–92
215. THIMANN, K. V. and BEHNKE-ROGERS, J. *The use of auxins in the rooting of woody cuttings*, Harvard (1950)
216. TORTORELLI, R. L. and BOGGESS, W. R. 'Breaking dormancy of oak seedlings', *Rep. Univ. Ill. Forest Res.*, no. 70-4 (1970), 2pp
217. TREŠČEVSKIJ, I. V. 'Afforestation in the river flood-plains of droughty regions in the Volga-Don basin', *Lesnoe Hozjajstvo, Moscow*, **19** (1966), 40–5
218. TROUP, R. S. *Silvicultural systems*, edn. 2, ed. E. W. Jones, Oxford (1952)
219. TSCHERMAK, L. *Waldbau auf Pflanzengeographisch-ökologischer Grundlage*, Vienna (1950)
220. TUMANOV, I. I. and KRASAVČEV, O. A. 'The frost resistance of woody plants', *Fiziologiya Rast.*, **2** (1955), 320–33
221. VAN DER PIJL, L. 'Absciss-joints in the stems and leaves of tropical plants', *Proc. K. ned. Akad. Wet.*, **42** (1952), 574–86
222. VEGIS, A. 'Dormancy in higher plants', *A. Rev. Pl. Physiol.*, **15** (1964), 185–224
223. VELKOV, D. 'New data on the biological characteristics of acorns of (American) red oak', *Gorsko Stop.*, **15** (1959), 24–9
224. VICIOSO, C. 'Revision del Genero "*Quercus*" en Espana', *Boln Inst. For. Invest. Exp.*, no. 51 (1950)
225. VILLIERS, T. A. 'Dormancy in tree seeds', *Proc. int. Seed Test. Ass.*, **26** (1961), 516–36

226. VILLIERS, T. A. and WAREING, P. F. 'The possible role of low temperature in breaking the domancy of seeds of *Fraxinus excelsior* L.', *J. exp. Bot.*, **16** (1964), 519–31

227. VILLIERS, T. A. and WAREING, P. F. 'The growth substance content of dormant fruits of *Fraxinus excelsior* L.', *J. exp. Bot.*, **16** (1964), 533–44

228. VLAD, I. 'Flood-resistance of forest species in the lower Idlomita valley', *Revta Padur.*, **56** (1944), 85–93

229. VOGT, A. R. 'An investigation of physiological factors controlling initial sprouting of oak', *Diss. Abstr.*, **27** B (1967), 2563

230. VOGT, A. R. 'Effect of gibberellic acid on germination and initial seedling growth of northern red oak', *Forest Sci.*, **16** (1970), 453–9

231. VOGT, A. R. and COX, G. S. 'Evidence for the hormonal control of stump sprouting by oak', *Forest Sci.*, **16** (1970), 165–71

232. VOLKOV, F. I. 'Specific gravity of acorns as an index to their ripeness and their value for sowing', *Dokl. Akad. Nauk SSSR*, **85** (1952), 203–6

233. VORONKOVA, E. N. 'The effect of carbon dioxide on seedlings of woody plants', *Lesnoe Hozjajstvo, Moscow*, **18** (1965), 16–19

234. WAISEL, Y. and FAHN, A. 'The effects of environment on wood formation and cambial activity in *Robinia pseudacacia* L.', *New Phytol.*, **64** (1965), 436–42

235. WAREING, P. F. 'Photoperiodism in woody species', *Forestry*, **22** (1949), 211–22

236. WAREING, P. F. 'Growth studies in woody species. 4. The initiation of cambial activity in ring-porous species', *Physiologia Pl.*, **4** (1951), 546–62

237. WAREING, P. F. 'Growth studies in woody species. 5. Photoperiodism in dormant buds of *Fagus sylvatica* L.', *Physiologia Pl.*, **6** (1953), 692–706

238. WAREING, P. F. 'Growth studies in woody species. 6. The locus of photoperiodic perception in relation to dormancy', *Physiologia Pl.*, **7** (1954), 261–77

239. WAREING, P. F. 'Photoperiodism in woody plants', *A. Rev. Pl. Physiol.*, **7** (1956), 191–214

240. WAREING, P. F. 'The physiology of cambial activity', *J. Inst. Wood Sci.*, **1** (1958), 34–42

241. WAREING, P. F. 'Problems of juvenility and flowering in trees', *J. Linn. Soc. (Bot.)*, **56** (1959), 282–9

242. WAREING, P. F. 'The germination of seeds', In *Vistas in Botany*, **3**, ed. W. B. Turrill, London (1963), 195–227

243. WAREING, P. F. 'Endogenous inhibitors in seed germination and dormancy', *Handb. PflPhysiol.*, **15** (1965), 909–24

244. WAREING, P. F. 'Natural inhibitors as growth hormones', in *Trends in plant morphogenesis*, ed. E. G. Cutter, London (1966), 235–52

245. WAREING, P. F. 'Control of bud dormancy', *Symp. Soc. exp. Biol.*, **23** (1969), 241–62

246. WAREING, P. F. 'Germination and dormancy', in *The physiology of plant growth and development*, ed. M. B. Wilkins, London (1969), 605–43

247. WAREING, P. F. and BLACK, M. 'Photoperiodism in seeds and seedlings of woody species', in *The physiology of forest trees*, ed. K. V. Thimann, New York (1958), 539–56

248. WAREING, P. F., EAGLES, C. F. and ROBINSON, P. M. 'Natural inhibitors as dormancy agents', *Centre Nat. Rech. Sci., Paris*, ed. no. 123 (1964), 377–86

249. WAREING, P. F., HANNEY, C. E. A. and DIGBY, J. 'The role of endogenous hormones in cambial activity and xylem differentiation', in *Formation of wood in forest trees*, ed. M. H. Zimmermann, New York (1964), 323–44

250. WAREING, P. F. and PHILLIPS, I. D. J. *The control of growth and differentiation in plants*, Oxford (1970)

251. WAREING, P. F. and ROBERTS, D. L. 'Photoperiodic control of cambial activity in *Robinia pseudacacia*', *New Phytol.*, **55** (1956), 356–66

252. WAREING, P. F. and SAUNDERS, P. F. 'Hormones and dormancy', *A. Rev. Pl. Physiol.*, **22** (1971), 261–88

253. WASSINK, E. C. and RICHARDSON, S. D. 'Observations on the connection between root growth and shoot illumination in first-year seedlings of *Acer pseudoplatanus* L. and *Quercus borealis maxima* (Marsh) Ashe', *Proc. K. ned. Akad. Wet.*, **54** C (1951), 503–10

254. WATT, A. S. 'On the causes of failure of natural regeneration in British oakwoods', *J. Ecol.*, **7** (1919), 173–203

255. WELLENSIEK, S. J. 'Rejuvenation of woody plants by formation of sphaeroblasts', *Proc. K. ned. Akad. Wet.*, **55** C (1952), 567–73

256. WIELER, A. 'Über die jährliche Periodizität in Dickenwachstum des Holzkörpers der Bäume', *Thar. forstl. Jahrb.*, **48** (1898), 49–139

257. WIGHT, W. 'Secondary elongation growth in oaks. 1929', *Naturalist, Hull*, (1930), 65–70

258. WILLISTON, H. L. 'Inundation damage to upland hardwoods', *S. Forest Exp. Sta.*, *U.S.A., Notes*, no. 123 (1959)

259. YEAGER, L. E. 'Effect of permanent flooding in a river-bottom timber area', *Bull. Illinois nat. Hist. Surv.*, **25** (1949), 65pp

260. ZASADA, J. C. and ZAHNER, R. 'Vessel element development in the earlywood of red oak (*Quercus rubra*)', *Can. J. Bot.*, **47** (1969), 1965–71

261. ZELAWSKI, W. 'The heat and light factor in the flushing of trees', *Sylwan*, **98** (1954), 483–6

262. ZIMMERMANN, M. H. and BROWN, C. L. *Trees: structure and function*, New York (1971)

263. ZIMMERMANN, W. A. 'Untersuchungen über die räumliche und zeitliche Verteilung des Wuchsstoffes bei Bäumen', *Z. Bot.*, **30** (1936), 209–52

MACROFUNGI IN THE OAK WOODS OF BRITAIN

Roy Watling

Royal Botanic Garden, Edinburgh

Introduction

Very little work has been carried out specifically on the macrofungi to be found in British oak woods. Although a great number of isolated observations have been made and indeed even more can be sifted from the many popular accounts and lists of higher fungi, only two quantitative studies exist. This is in very marked contrast to continental Europe where several accounts are available, eg southern Finland, Poland and Czechoslovakia; indeed Kallio and co-workers[1][2] have indicated that boletes particularly can help to define the limits of the oak zone.

Wilkins, Ellis & Harley[3] studied twenty oak woods of *Quercus robur* in southern England on three different soil types: dry, well drained sandy soil (pH c 4.0–6.0); moist loam (pH c 5.0–7.0); and wet, heavy clay soil (pH c 5.0–7.0). Their observations indicated that a very rich flora is found in oak woods in contrast to the beech woods and conifer areas sampled during the same study. The number of species recorded is in marked contrast to the more recent work by Hering[4] who sampled three lakeland woods containing *Quercus petraea*, two on soil derived from slate and drift (pH 4.1–4.3) and a third on limestone (pH 6.1).

Wilkins et al record 391 species whereas Hering only recorded 45–50 species on acidic substrate and 52 on the limestone. Differences between the fungus flora of the individual quadrats analysed by Hering in his woodlands were no greater than expected, and in each woodland 15–20 of the species were common to all the three quadrats. Richardson[5] in sampling the higher fungi of pine woods indicates how some of the discrepancies between the figures of Hering and Wilkins probably occur. Richardson found that in his quadrats (ie equivalent to Hering's study) he recorded only 38% of the total number of species which were recorded from the entire wood on sporadic collecting visits (ie equivalent to Wilkins' study).

Hering found 94 species of larger fungi of which 70 accounted for less than 5% of the fresh weight or number in his woodlands; of this group he considered *Amanita rubescens*, *Paxillus involutus* and *Collybia peronata* as typical. He also considered three species as constituting a general element which could be found in any oakwood, six species as a 'slate' element, four species as a 'limestone' element (five if one includes the ashwood Hering studied) and four species which were specific elements to a particular wood, eg *Lactarius fuliginosus* in woods on limestone.

Wilkins et al found that the number of species collected at any one examination of a single station averaged 90 (40–164) and the number for oak woods was surprisingly much greater than that for beech woods. However, they also found that the constant species for oak woods represented one third of the total number of species and the constancy of a given species appeared to be slightly higher than those under beech. From qualitative observations it is suggested that the reverse is probably true in northern England and Scotland; indeed it seems that beech woods there have many more specific agarics than oak woods.

Wilkins et al also analysed figures for many individual species occurring in oak and beech woods including those of the genus *Lactarius* and these indicated that a higher number of species are found in the former and many species have a very high constancy. However, apart from specific parasites very few absolute exclusives were recorded and a large number of the species found in oak woods were found elsewhere in Europe and Britain not to be exclusive to oak woodland. Thus a very complex pattern of distribution emerges and it is certainly misleading to talk of fungi of an oak wood without taking into consideration the edaphic, climatic and biotic factors influencing the woodland under study.

Groups of fungi

The macrofungi of oak woods can be conveniently separated into five categories:

1. Parasites
2. Suspected mycorrhizals
3. Lignicolous saprophytes ie, on woody debris
4. Humicolous saprophytes ie, on leafy debris and humus
5. Associated elements

1. *Parasites* (see pps 235–249).

2. *Suspected mycorrhizals*

As in many types of broad-leaved and coniferous woodland, the more prominent of those higher fungi suspected as being mycorrhizal with oak belong to the families Boletaceae and Russulaceae. Several members of the genus *Cortinarius* (Cortinariaceae) may also be mycorrhizal with oak but the group is badly worked and the oak-dependent species relatively unknown. Orton recently[6] in a provisional key indicates that at least fifteen members of *Cortinarius* subgenus *Hydrocybe* are probably confined to oak woodland.

Over a dozen members of the Boletaceae typify oak woods perhaps the best known being *Boletus rubinus, Gyroporus castaneus* and *Leccinum crocipodium* (table 1, a & b) though all three are much more common in southern England and the first was, for a long time, thought to be endemic to the British Isles. There does not appear, however, to be a single genus or group of species which is

TABLE 1

Oak Boletes

a. **Suspected mycorrhizal boletes (excluding the genus Boletus) with habitat data**
(Green & Watling unpublished data).
Aureboletus cramesinus (Secr.) Watling—in woodland clearings and at sites
of bonfires in southern oak woods.
Gyroporus castaneus (Fr.) Quél.—exclusively with *Quercus*.
Leccinum spp—generally associated with Betulaceae.
L. carpini (R. Schulz.) Moser ex Reid—with *Corylus* or *Carpinus*, less
frequently with *Quercus;* southern
and western distribution.
L. crocipodium (Let.) Watling—exclusively (?) with *Quercus;* probably
widespread in southern England.
L. quercinum (Pilát) Green & Watling—possibly also associated with *Tilia*
and less frequently with *Fagus;*
widespread.
Porphyrellus pseudoscaber (Secr.) Singer—with *Quercus, Fagus* etc, in broad-
leaved or mixed woodland; not
infrequent under *Q. petraea* in
northern areas.
Tylopilus felleus (Fr.) Karst.—with *Fagus* and in mixed or broad-leaved
woodland with *Quercus;* widespread.

b. **Suspected mycorrhizal boletes of the genus Boletus with habitat data**
(Green & Watling unpublished data).
B. aereus Fr.—with *Quercus* and *Fagus;* rare although occurring regularly
in south-east England.
B. aestivalis Fr.—with *Quercus* and *Fagus;* particularly in England, although
widespread.
B. albidus Roq.—generally with broad-leaved trees especially with *Quercus*
and *Fagus* on calcareous soils; typically southern in Britain.
B. appendiculatus (Fr.) Secr.—with broad-leaved trees; more frequent in
southern England and then usually with
Quercus.
B. calopus Fr.—in mixed woodland with *Quercus* or *Fagus* on siliceous soils.
B. edulis Fr.—a complex species aggregate; var *quercicola* Vassilkov occurs
with *Quercus* and *Fagus*.
B. fechnteri Vel.—in broad-leaved woods with *Quercus* and *Fagus*.
B. impolitus Fr.—typical of oak woods on clayey soils.
B. junquilleus (Quél.) Boudier—rare, under *Quercus*.
B. leonis Reid—in parkland with *Quercus*.
B. luridus Fr.—in broad-leaved woods usually with *Quercus* and *Fagus* on
calcareous soils.
B. porosporus (Imler) Watling—in mixed broad-leaved woodland with
Quercus.
B. pruinatus Fr. & Hök—in mixed broad-leaved woodland possibly always
with *Quercus*.
B. pseudosulphureus Kallenbach—with broad-leaved trees particularly
Quercus; also with *Fagus* and *Tilia*.
B. pulverulentus Opat.—with broad-leaved trees or exotic conifers; frequently
with *Quercus*.
B. queletii Schulzer—with broad-leaved trees; locally common with *Quercus,
Fagus* and *Tilia*.
B. regius Krombh.—probably with *Quercus*.
B. rubinus W. G. Smith—exclusively with *Quercus;* in southern England.
B. satanoides Smotlacha—rare, with *Quercus*.
B. satanus Lenz—with broad-leaved trees, particularly *Quercus* and *Fagus;*
characteristic of calcareous soil.
B. versicolor Rostk.—in grass with broad-leaved trees; characteristic of
oak woods and parklands in southern England

entirely restricted to oak woodland; field observations by Green[7] show that several species including *Boletus pseudosulphureus* appear to be just as frequent within the tree root area of *Fagus* and *Tilia* as they are with *Quercus,* whilst *Leccinum quercinum* is as frequent with *Castanea.*

It is evident from field observations and cultural work that a host tree may associate with other less frequent fungus species probably when the more characteristic ones are absent or, if the fungus is present, for some reason it is not available to take part in the association. Equally evidence is available which suggests that a single agaric (or bolete) species may be either mycorrhizal or humicolous—ie a gradation of mycorrhizal ability is present. Cultural experiments have shown without doubt that different, although morphologically indistinguishable, strains are present in a single species, eg *Boletus subtomentosus*[8] and *Paxillus involutus*[9], both species which are known to grow with oak.

As already indicated, although a particular agaric may be associated with oak in southern areas this might not be so in the north; equally the reverse may be true. Thus although there is no clear association of *Boletus subtomentosus* with southern oak woods, in the cool, wetter, more acidic woodlands of north England and Scotland it is very common, often accompanied by the related *B. chrysenteron.* Two questions arise: (1) has temperature an effect on the initial formation of the relationship in the field? (2) does temperature control the fruiting of mycorrhizal agarics? We know that in culture temperature controls two separate but intimately connected processes, vegetative growth and primordial initiation. Perhaps this is reflected in field observations also. For instance after hot summers in Scotland boletes and agaric species more frequent in the south of England, eg *B. pseudosulphureus,* have been found. It would appear that the mycelium was there already and that the higher temperatures simply favoured fruiting or triggered off a process which promoted fruiting.

The European mapping scheme has indicated that *Boletus parasiticus* which grows on earth balls (*Scleroderma citrinum*—a mycorrhizal with oak) and is locally common, eg in Windsor Great Park, is less frequent as one travels northwards, its distribution just reaching south-west Scotland. *Scleroderma citrinum* is, on the other hand, common throughout the British Isles. *B. parasiticus* is also apparently less frequent even in areas where it was formerly (70 years ago) considered not infrequent although there has not been a similar disappearance of the earth ball from the same areas[11]. *Amanita phalloides* and *Boletus pulverulentus* in the British Isles are even more basically southern and western in distribution, both occurring in western Scotland; the latter fungus is typically associated with oak.

Although the present account is concerned specifically with British oak woods it is important to point out the apparent anomalies when one applies the data to woodlands on the continent of Europe and elsewhere. Thus *Rozites caperata* is found under oak in both mid-west America and in central Europe; in Greenland it has been recorded with *Betula tortuosa*. In Great Britain *Rozites* is frequent only in Scotland—and there under *Pinus sylvestris*!

During the preparation of the data for this review an analysis was made of European records of those higher fungi which we normally associate in this country with oak. Thus of 145 species analysed 23% are found with oak alone, 28% occur in mixed assemblages of trees including oak and other deciduous trees, 10% occur with some other member of the Fagaceae (*Fagus* and *Castanea*) and, of particular interest, 14% of these occur with some member of the Coniferae (16% with some other member of the Fagaceae and Coniferae). Although some relationship between certain groups of fairly closely related plants and certain fungi is often emphasised, *Quercus* and Coniferae are not related. Of the remainder, 5% have little or no pattern, occurring in a wide range of plant assemblages; 6% occur with some member of the Fagaceae and some other family of deciduous trees, eg Ulmaceae, Corylaceae and Betulaceae. Even in Britain no host pattern can at the moment be demonstrated for some species, eg *Boletus luridus* is found under oak but it is also not infrequent with *Corylus* and is a very important member of the *Salix repens*—*Dryas* communities in Sutherland. Perhaps in these examples one should examine the importance of soil condition, for a base rich soil is common to all the communities supporting *B. luridus* irrespective of the hosts present.

Trappe[11] has reviewed the mycorrhizals for a whole range of tree-species including several species of oak. His results for oak are based on observational data only, except for two species, ie *Hebeloma crustuliniforme* and *Tuber magnatum* which have been shown to form mycorrhiza under laboratory conditions. Hence my preference to speak of suspected mycorrhizals and not mycorrhizals. Trappe lists 156 species which are recorded for specific oaks or for 'oak' in general. A large number of these refer to North America and although some are found in Europe they are not found in Britain, eg *Amanita caesarea*, 'Caesar's mushroom', a much prized edible fungus. One wonders why this fungus is not found in the British Isles.

The species names listed by Trappe and those in Wilkins' analysis must be put into perspective as, over the last twenty-five years, many nomenclatural and taxonomic changes have been made and a narrower species concept adopted. If this concept is applied greater correlation between host and species can be demonstrated, eg Trappe's *Leccinum aurantiacum* undoubtedly includes *L. quercinum* and it seems probable that all records of *L. aurantiacum* under oak refer to this species. In Europe *L. aurantiacum* in the original sense is found with *Populus tremula* and in North America with *P. tremuloides*. *Boletus porosporus* is frequent under oak but its true distribution is not known. It has only been recently recorded in Britain, not apparently because it is uncommon but beacuse it had not been recognised. These examples illustrate a very important objection to the use of older field information: in higher fungi, particularly the agarics, the species concept has only recently been stabilised. It is only now that an attempt can be made to understand the distribution of species in relation to climate, soil and temperature.

TABLE 2

Suspected myocrrhizal Russulas and Lactarii of oak woods
(Watling unpublished data)

Russula brunneoviolacea Crawshay—leafy woods especially with *Quercus*.
R. emeticella (Singer) Hora—leafy woods especially with *Quercus*.
R. laurocerasi Melzer—particularly common with *Quercus* in parkland.
R. pectinata (Bull.) Fr.—with *Quercus* or conifers.
R. pseudointegra Arn. & Goris—with *Quercus* and *Betula;* characteristic of oak
                                                                                                    woods on clayey soils.
R. smaragdina Quél.—rare; with *Quercus*.
R. sororia Fr.—almost exclusively with *Quercus*.
R. subfoetens W. G. Smith—infrequent; with *Quercus* (including *R. grata* Britz.)
R. vesca Fr.—leafy woods especially with *Quercus;* often on siliceous soils.
R. xerampelina (Schaeff. ex Secr.) Fr.–a very variable species or species complex;
                                                                in broad-leaved woodland especially with *Quercus*
                                                                and *Fagus*.

Lactarius chrysorheus Fr.—fairly common with *Quercus*.
L. fuliginosus (Fr.) Fr.—in broad-leaved woods with *Quercus*.
L. glaucescens Crossl.—in broad-leaved woods frequently with *Quercus*.
L. quietus Fr.—very common in oak woods, particularly on siliceous soils.
L. volemus (Fr.) Fr.—in broad-leaved woods often with *Quercus*.

TABLE 3

Other suspected mycorrhizal oak wood agarics
(Watling unpublished data)

Hygrophoraceae
Hygrophorus chrysodon (Batsch ex Fr.) Fr.

Tricholomataceae
Collybia dryophila (Bull. ex Fr.) Kummer—common in mixed woodland but
                                                                            particularly so in oak woods.
C. peronata (Bolt. ex Fr.) Kummer
Tricholoma acerbum (Bull. ex Fr.) Quél.
T. sulphureum (Bull. ex Fr.) Kummer

Amanitaceae
Amanita phalloides (Vaill. ex Fr.)—rare in northern England and Scotland.

Rhodophyllaceae
Entoloma porphyrophaeum (Fr.) Karst.—in parkland under *Quercus*.

Coprinaceae
Psathyrella obtusata (Fr.) A. H. Smith—on twigs and under *Quercus*.

Cortinariaceae
Inocybe asterospora Quél.—broad-leaved woods especially with *Quercus*.
I. flocculosa (Berk.) Sacc.—broad-leaved woods specially with *Quercus*.
I. grammata Quél.—in parkland, with *Quercus* and *Betula*.
I. pusio Karst.—damp oak woods.

Probably the Boletaceae is the family with the largest number of species preferring to fruit in association with oak; some are restricted to oak woods (table 1) whereas others are more frequent in mixed oak communities. The genus *Boletus* (table 1b), in its strict sense particularly, has many such members.

TABLE 4

Lignicolous saprophytes on trunks and stumps of oak
(Watling unpublished data)

Agaricales
    Coprinus silvaticus Peck—on stumps.
    Mycena inclinata (Fr.) Quél.—on stumps and fallen trunks.
    Omphalotus olearius (DC. ex Fr.) Fayod.—a single British record.
    Xerula fusipes (Bull. ex Fr.) Quél.

Aphyllophorales

    Fistulinaceae
    Fistulina hepatica Schaeff. ex Fr.—also recorded on *Castanea*.

    Polyporaceae
    Daedalea quercina Linn. ex Fr.—on stumps.
    Grifola frondosa (Dicks. ex Fr.) S. F. Gray (including f. *intybacea* (Fries) Pilát)—on trunks.
    Buglossoporus quercinus (Schrad. ex Fr.) Kotl. & Pouz.—on shanks and standing trees; single British record.
    Laetiporus sulphureus (Fr.) Murrill—on shanks and standing trees; host range wide but common on *Quercus* in south.
    Pseudotrametes gibbosa (Pers.) Bond. & Singer—on stumps, more common on *Fagus*.
    Xylodon versiporus (Pers.) Bond. (=*Schizopora paradoxa*)—on branches.

    Hymenochaetaceae
    Hymenochaete rubiginosa (Dicks.) Lév.—on branches and trunks.
    Inonotus dryadeus (Pers. ex Fr.) Murrill—on standing trees.
    Phellinus ferreus (Pers.) Bourd. & Galz.—on larger branches.
    P. robustus (Karst.) Bourd. & Galz.—on trunks.

    Stereaceae
    Stereum (Xylobolus) frustulosum (Pers. ex Fr.) Fr.
    S. gausapatum Fr.—on branches and standing trunks causing a white rot.

    Corticiaceae
    Hyphodontia quercina (Fr.) J. Erikss.—on small and large branches.
    Peniophora quercina (Pers. ex Fr.) Cooke—on small and large branches often when still attached to the tree.
    Hymenomycetous Heterobasidiae
    Femsjonia pezizaeformis (Lév.) Karst.—on old wood especially of *Quercus*.

In the large family Russulaceae the genus *Russula* is represented in oak woods by many species: *Lactarius,* the only other genus in the same family, has a smaller but nevertheless characteristic number of species (table 2). *Hygrophorus chrysodon* (Hygrophoraceae) is said to be characteristic of oak woods but is infrequent in Britain; in continental Europe several other species of *Hygrophorus* (true Hygrophori) are found under oak. It is very probable that *Tricholoma sulphureum* and *T. acerbum* are also mycorrhizal with oak; both belong to a genus which, certainly in its former delimitation, contained mycorrhizal and non-mycorrhizal members. Members of the genus *Cortinarius* have already been mentioned and it would be folly to connect with oak many of the 85 British members of the related genus *Inocybe* which, like species of *Cortinarius*, are notoriously difficult to identify. However, this would be a valuable field of future study (table 3).

3. *Lignicolous saprophytes*

Some species of higher fungi growing on wood are widespread and grow on various hosts, eg *Coriolus versicolor* and *Armillaria mellea*, but there are more fungi characteristic of particular species in this category than amongst the suspected mycorrhizals (see table 4).

Daedalea quercina is almost confined to oak whilst *Mycena inclinata, Coprinus silvaticus* and *Xerula* (*Collybia*) *fusipes* are all preferentially found on oak stumps fruiting in huge tufts. *Hypholoma fasciculare,* 'Sulphur Tuft', in contrast, has the same habit of growth and also favours stumps although not specifically those of oak; it can be found on many deciduous tree-species, and even conifers.

Just as some species only fruit upon stumps there is evidence available that the wood-inhabiting fungi preferentially colonise wood debris of a particular range of size. Some attack shanks and trunks, some branches and others twigs. Branches and twigs are commonly covered by the flattened fruit-bodies of *Peniophora quercina Hymenochaete rubiginosa, Hyphodontia quercina* and *Stereum gausapatum*. Although the first three are typically resupinate, the last species forms crusts with a hairy upper surface when a cap is formed; it is known to form a white pocket rot of oak and related trees.

Two large polypores are found on oak butts and both may act as weak parasites, ie *Fistulina hepatica,* 'Beef Steak fungus' and *Inonotus dryadeus*. The former is very much rarer in Scotland than even in the north of England; it may also grow on *Castanea*. *Grifola frondosa* and its form *intybacea* are probably two of the largest non-parasitic polypores on oak, and *Phellinus ferreus* is a feature of oak woods particularly in the south.

Not only is size of wood debris important but the degree of decay probably also plays a part; thus on old, partially decayed, oak branches *Xylodon versiporus* is very common and a feature of oak woods although the frequency of the records might be equally attributed to the conspicuous colour, compared with that of many other resupinate fungi.

Recently *Omphalotus olearius,* 'Jack o' Lantern', has been recorded for the first time in the British Isles. This fungus is frequent throughout north temperate countries on oak stumps, though it is not confined to oak. It forms large tufts which, in the dark, give off a phosphorescent glow—hence its common name. Thus fungi typically associated with oak in other countries are still being discovered in the British Isles.

Each type of woodland has a distinctive list of lignicolous fungi and, although there is some overlapping in the species of agarics which appear in different woods, there seems little overlapping between an oak wood and a beech wood and less with a pine or birch wood.

4. *Humicolous saprophytes*

This is a mixed group of fungi, some of which may be loosely related to the tree's root-system, eg *Laccaria laccata*, whilst others decompose cellulose and the lignin of plant-litter, such as that of small twigs, petioles and leaf veins. Thus this group is an overlapping one growing on soft and partially decomposed herbaceous and leafy debris, ie intermediate between groups 2 and 3. This group is also fairly widespread and reflects the status of the community more than it characterises one particular type of woodland. *Mycena galopus* and *Collybia peronata* are two such species and both are discussed at length by Hering[12]. *M. mucor,* although common on oak debris, will also grow on that of other higher plants. In contrast *M. polyadelpha,* growing on dead leaves, is characteristic of oak woods.

It may of course be the small humicolous species that ultimately provide the key to an understanding of the specificity of a particular group of agarics. This is certainly true of the more conspicuous inoperculate discomycetes, eg *Sclerotinia candolleana* causing brown spots on oak leaves, *Ciboria batschiana* on fallen acorns, *Rutstroemia firma* on twigs or petioles, *Phialina puberula* on leaves, *Hymenoscyphus phyllogenus* on leaves and *Dasyscyphus niveus* which characterises old wood[12]. The smaller fungi, particularly the agarics, are often difficult to identify or, more correctly, they require examination of microscopic details for accurate determination and, as they only make up at the most 5% of the major haul of fruit-bodies by dry weight in a collection from oak woods, they are often disregarded and rarely appear in species lists. Thus the distribution of species of *Leptonia, Nolanea* and *Lepiota,* for example, in woods on limestone soils may deserve greater attention than has been previously afforded.

There is no doubt that the humicolous members of the flora are important organisms of decay. *Mycena galopus* has been shown by Hering[12] to decompose leaves very rapidly under favourable conditions to the order of 17% of the dry matter in six months. *Thelephora anthocephala* and *Collybia peronata* similarly grow on leaves and are equally active in their decomposition. In fact *C. peronata* attacks lignin more vigorously than *M. galopus.*

Some of the larger hydnaceous fungi may also be strictly humicolous, or in some more obscure way be connected to the host tree. *Hydnum repandum* and *Hydnellum scrobiculatum* are two such fungi and both occur in Britain under oak. However, *Sarcodon imbricatum* demonstrates again the phenomenon described earlier where a typical fungus of oak woodland in one part of the northern hemisphere is found growing under pine in another, in this case, Michigan, USA and Scotland, respectively. Perhaps we are today looking at the result of the advantages taken by the limited number of species which recolonised Britain after the Pleistocene, advantages not available to the same species on the continent of Europe because of competition from members of a much larger fungal flora.

5. *Associated elements*
   Epiphytic fungi include several species of *Galerina*, eg *G. hypnorum*, and *Mycena*, eg *M. hiemalis*, which grow on moss-covered trunks. The moist climate of the western oak woods favour such a series of small fungi but some of these areas (eg Killarney) have been very inadequately worked. Loss of bryophyte cover because of drought or pollution greatly affects the occurrence of these rather delicate agarics.

   Bonfires within the oak wood have their characteristic fungi also but none of the species is apparently specific to oak wood 'charcoal'; what is very apparent is that oak provides a very much more favourable substrate after burning than pine or other coniferous species. However, *Aureoboletus cramesinus* appears to favour burnt areas in oak woods and their margins more than any other oak bolete.

   Dung fungi are also part of the oak wood ecosystem and reflect the comparative richness of the vegetation. Thus sheep-grazed oak woods on the millstone grit escarpments of Yorkshire and Derbyshire provide comparatively acidic dung dominated by *Stropharia semiglobata*, whereas dung in limestone plateau woodlands in the same counties are characterised by a vast array of agarics often dominated by *Conocybe* spp, *Panaeolus semiovatus* and *Coprinus radiatus*.

Discussion
   Our knowledge of most higher fungi is so very meagre at the moment because our results are dependent entirely on observing fruit-bodies and these are only a small part of the actual fungus. They are erratic in fruiting so that it is difficult to ascertain their distribution, except after very lengthy study.

   Recent field observations, in conjunction with information from the literature, suggest that few fungi are restricted to oak woodland and there are many fewer characteristic taxa than in, say, birch or beech woods: many of the higher fungi in British oak woods are common to many other kinds of woodland. The community displayed at any one time may reflect the stage of a given woodland's evolution, eg *Laccaria laccata*, a pioneer agaric growing in regenerating areas of woodland and rough pastures invaded by *Q. petraea*, or the particular stage in the annual cycle of a woodland, eg *Amanita rubescens* and *Russula ochroleuca* becoming abundant after late summer rains.

   The field mycologist is fully aware of the habitat preferences of particular species, eg *Lactarius vietus* and *Russula claroflava* in wet ditches and hollows in birch woods, whereas others, eg *L. glyciosmus,* fruit on drier well-drained soils. Is this a problem of field capacity of the soil, or is it that we are examining differences between different tree taxa, *Betula pubescens* in wet areas and *B. verrucosa* in drier areas? The differences between *Q. robur* and *Q. petraea* communities are yet to be analysed but *Inocybe pusio* prefers wetter oak woods or wet areas within an oak wood. In open woodlands *Laccaria laccata* is a common component (Wilkins et al[3] record it with 80–100% constancy) whereas under deeper shade, as in beech woods, it is apparently more frequently replaced by the closely related *L. amethystea*. Apparently within oak woods there are similar differences in distribution.

Hering[4] indicates that soil acidity may play an important role in fungal distribution but examination of lists given for the lakeland woodlands he studied shows that there were also slight differences in the vascular plants. Could the differences in fungal distribution be related more directly to the associated vascular plant than to the soil type? One mechanism might be the production by the plants of substrates favourable or unfavourable to components in the soil microflora which themselves favour or discourage the development of a given fungal mycelium. There is copious evidence to show that the soil microflora is in a very delicate balance with the mycorrhizal fungi.

Hora's experimental work in a conifer plantation[14] [15], may give some indication of the complexity of the problem although the community he analysed is not strictly comparable with an oak wood. He studied an extremely base-poor community and artificial assemblage where an increase in base status might be expected to have rather large effects. He found that fruiting of higher fungi was greatly influenced by the addition of a range of fertilisers and soil conditioners. Species rarely or never recorded before in the plantation appeared, indicating the previous presence of the fungi in a vegetative phase.

As is true of all woods no oak wood is homogeneous although it may be a classic and 'uniform' community in the ecologist's sense. Thus temperature, moisture and light vary from one place in the wood to another; the variation however small will be sufficient to effect the colonization by fungi. When different woods are compared mycologically the nature of the soil (and subsoil) and consequently the co-dominant, sub-dominant and ground flora must all be taken into consideration.

It is usual to consider the fungi of different woodlands separately and compare the lists produced but one must be cautious of using this method in isolation as it can only show the major difference noted above.

It is difficult to compare the saprophytic constituents with the mycorrhizals as the latter really are a union with another equally dynamic unit, the tree, to make a 'dual-organism'; this increases the factors affecting the fungus including, for example, increase in photosynthesis of the tree and the physiological processes coupled with it. However, as indicated before, it is very difficult to draw the line between the two extremes of saprophytes and mycorrhizals which pass gradually from one to the other.

How do these ecologically orientated studies fit in with the taxonomy of the higher fungi concerned? Within a single genus the species which appear to be associated with oak are not necessarily similar enough in morphology to warrant being classified in the same group. Related species of fungi are frequently associated with different trees and thus in the past some selection has enabled certain variants from a supposedly original stock to establish themselves independently on a separate and quite different host. Conversely the same species may not be confined to a single tree-species and, whilst the fruit-bodies of a species found under oak may be similar morphologically in all respects to those found under beech, pine etc, in culture they differ markedly in physiological characteristics.

The study of oak wood fungi is at an intensely analytical stage; the future looks promising with the imminent introduction of a British recording system for the higher fungi following closely on the European Mapping Scheme for Macromycetes, which began in 1962.

Acknowledgements

I am indebted to Dr T. J. Hering, University of Nottingham, for making available his field data covering oakwoods other than those mentioned in his scientific papers, and particularly to E. E. Green, Ascot, Berkshire who has, by his unselfish attention, made it possible for me to see fresh material of many oak boletes typical of the south-east of Britain. He has also allowed me to freely use his field notes and paintings and call on his experience of many years collecting in the south of England; this survey would have been impossible without his help.

APPENDIX

Check-list of fungi mentioned in text but not listed in tables 1–4

Amanita caesarea Fr.
A. rubescens ([Pers.] Fr.) S. F. Gray
Armillaria mellea (Vahl. ex Fr.) Kummer
Boletus chrysenteron Bull. ex St Amans
B. parasiticus Bull. ex Fr.
B. subtomentosus Linn. ex Fr.
Ciboria batschiana (Zopf) Buchwald
Coprinus radiatus (Bolt. ex Fr.) S. F. Gray
Coriolus versicolor (Linn.) Quél.
Dasyscyphus niveus (Hedwig ex Fr.) Sacc.
Galerina hypnorum (Schrank ex Fr.) Kühn.
Hebeloma crustuliniforme (Bull. ex St Amans) Quél.
Hydnellum scrobiculatum (Fr. ex Secr.) Karst.
Hydnum repandum Fr.
Hygrophorus chrysodon (Batsch ex Fr.) Fr.
Hymenoscyphus phyllogenus (Rehm) O. Kuntze
Hypholoma fasciculare (Huds. ex Fr.) Kummer
Laccaria amethystea (Bull. ex Mérat) Murrill

L. laccata (Scop. ex Fr.) Cooke
Lactarius glyciosmus (Fr. ex Fr.) Fr.
L. vietus (Fr.) Fr.
Leccinum aurantiacum (Bull. ex Fr.) S. F. Gray
Mycena galopus (Pers. ex Fr.) Kummer
M. hiemalis (Osbeck ex Fr.) Quél.
M. mucor (Batsch ex Fr.) Gill.
M. polyadelpha (Lasch.) Kühn.
Panaeolus semiovatus (Sow. ex Fr.) Lundell
Paxillus involutus (Batsch ex Fr.) Fr.
Phialina puberula (Lasch.) von Höhnel
Rozites caperata (Pers. ex Fr.) Karst.
Russula claroflava Grove
R. ochroleuca (Pers. ex Secr.) Fr.
Rutstroemia firma (Pers.) Karst.
Sarcodon imbricatum (Fr.) Quél.
Scleroderma citrinum Pers.
Sclerotinia candolleana (Lév.) Fuckel
Stropharia semiglobata (Batsch ex Fr.) Quél.
Thelephora anthocephala Fr.
Tuber magnatum Pico

REFERENCES

1. KALLIO, P. 'Zur Verbreitung einiger in Finnland sudlichen Pilze, besonders in der Sudwestlichen Eichenzone', *Karstenia*, **6** (1963), 35–76
2. KALLIO, P. and KANKAINEN, E. 'Contributions to the macromycetes in the oak zone', *Karstenia*, **8** (1967), 9–13
3. WILKINS, W. H., ELLIS, E. M. and HARLEY, J. L. 'The ecology of the larger fungi. I. Constancy and frequency of fungal species in relation to certain vegetation communities especially oak and beech', *Ann. appl. Biol.*, **24** (1937), 703–32
4. HERING, T. F. 'The terricolous higher fungi of four Lake District woodlands', *Trans. Br. mycol. Soc.*, **49** (1966), 369–83
5. RICHARDSON, M. J. 'Studies on *Russula emetica* and other agarics in a Scots pine plantation', *Trans. Br. mycol. Soc.*, **55** (1970), 217–29
6. ORTON, P. D. (1971) Personal communication
7. GREEN, E. E. (1970–72), Personal communications
8. PERSSON, O. (1972), Personal communication
9. LAITHO, O. '*Paxillus involutus* as a mycorrhizal symbiont of forest trees', *Acta for. fenn.*, **106** (1970), 1–72
10. WATLING, R. 'Records of Boleti and notes on their taxonomic position', *Notes R. bot. Gdn, Edinb.*, **28** (1968), 301–16
11. TRAPPE, J. M. 'Fungus associates of ecototrophic mycorrhiza,' *Bot. Rev.*, **28** (1967), 538–606
12. HERING, T. F. 'Fungal associations in broad-leaved woodlands in northeast England', *Mycopath. Mycol. appl.*, **48** (1972), 15–21
13. McGARVIE, Q. D. 'Ascomycetes of Oak Park', *Scient. Proc. R. Dubl. Soc.*, Series A, **4** (1972), 218–29
14. HORA, F. B. 'Quantitative experiments on toadstool production in woods', *Trans. Br. mycol. Soc.*, **42** (1959), 1–14
15. HORA, F. B. Productivity of toadstools in coniferous plantations—natural and experimental', *Mycopath. Mycol. appl.*, **48** (1972), 35–42

THE FUNGAL PATHOGENS OF OAK

J. S. MURRAY

Department of Forestry, University of Aberdeen

Introduction

An account of the pathology of oak in Britain encounters the difficulty that little detailed study has been made of certain aspects of it in Britain. Thus, for completeness, reference must be made to work abroad. This recourse is favoured by the widespread distribution of our native oaks in Europe and their importance in various European countries. Many of our oak pathogens, besides being generally distributed in Europe are found on oak species in America and Asia, and material has been used from these sources also, especially with regard to the white oak group.

Certain textbooks have been used as basic works of reference. They include: *Pathology of Trees and Shrubs* by T. R. Peace, *Pests and Diseases of Forest Plantation Trees* by F. G. Browne, *Diseases of Forest and Shade Trees of the United States* by G. H. Hepting and *Decay of Timber and its Prevention* by K. St. G. Cartwright and W. P. K. Findlay. There seemed little point in duplicating lists and descriptions in these books and an attempt was made rather to integrate material from them and from individual papers.

A list of organisms mentioned in the text with authorities is given in table 1 (see p. 247).

Diseases of acorns

Little work has been done in Britain on diseases of oak inflorescences or acorns. No pathogens have apparently been recorded on the flowers, staminate or pistillate.

Acorns would furnish a good substrate for various organisms because of their good carbohydrate reserves and high moisture content. Agencies allowing ingress to the acorn are therefore important as is borne out by Hepting's statement that in America most acorn decay by fungi is associated with weevil injury[15].

Jones writing about English conditions states that in a good seed year as many as 25% of the acorns may be damaged by insects, principally by weevils and a tortricid[18]. Thus in Britain, it is likely that some of the pathogens of acorns are also associated with insect attack. Jones also emphasises the susceptibility of acorns to injury by dehydration and frost. He quotes $-6°C$ as a killing temperature, a relatively high one for temperate forest tree fruit generally. How far such damage predisposes acorns to subsequent infection has not, however, been studied.

Acorns may be infected on the ground or during storage. They may also be infected by organisms in the soil and seed beds. Some of these organisms may also attack the emerging part of the seedling and thus be implicated in damping off.

Ciboria batschiana may infect acorns either lying on the surface of the ground or in storage. The whole fruit becomes blackened and the brown, stalked apothecia arise from the cotyledons in the autumn. Jones suggested that infection probably occurred following injury by desiccation or frost but this has not been studied. The disease occurs in Britain and is common in Europe. It may be controlled by fungicides[5].

A number of *Phomopsis* spp have been described as pathogens of acorns in different countries, especially in eastern Europe. *P. glandicola* has been recorded causing a dry rot of acorns in America though proof of pathogenicity is lacking[15]. In eastern Europe *P. quercella* has been recorded on a number of occasions attacking acorns in storage[33] [35]. It causes a blackening of the fruit, especially of the cotyledons on which the pycnidia are produced. Urosevic also recorded *Fusarium oxysporum* as a cause of decay of acorns in storage.

A notable feature of several organisms attacking acorns is their apparent ability to attack the developing seedling. In collaboration with Jancarik, Urosevic isolated *Coniothyrium quercinum* from acorns and showed that it was responsible for wilt and dieback of red oak plants over a considerable area. Similarly, *Phomopsis quercella, Fusarium oxysporum,* a *Ceratocystis* sp and a *Pestalotia* sp have been recorded both on acorns and as a cause of seedling disease[35]

Gloeosporium quercinum, better known as a cause of leaf spots, has also been recorded infecting acorns[25].

A feature of the above organisms is their general non-specificity. They show little host specialisation, either to particular oak species or to the genus itself. Practically all of them have been recorded on the fruit of other broadleaved trees, especially *Castanea* and *Fagus*. They are apparently not particularly specific to the fruit as a substrate. They are also very widespread, so that the fact that some of them have not been recorded on acorns in Britain probably reflects the lack of work here on this aspect of oak pathology. It is perhaps significant that *Ciboria batschiana,* one of the most conspicuous in the group, has been well recorded in Britain.

Diseases of oak foliage

Pathogens of *Quercus* foliage fall into two main categories. Firstly, there is a group of strongly, or obligately, parasitic organisms associated with attack on the young leaves. The only one which is really damaging in Britain is oak mildew, the others being either unimportant, eg *Uredo quercus,* or only sporadically damaging. Secondly, there is a group, the members of which are associated with attack on the leaves relatively late in the season, a characteristic which by itself tends to limit their pathogenic importance even though they cause spots and blotches on living leaves. The latter organisms tend to grade off into saprophytic forms colonising senescing foliage and it is difficult in some cases to say whether the damage an organism does, merits its being treated in a section on tree diseases.

One of the important features of oak pathology in Britain, and indeed in most of Europe, is the absence of rust species alternating between oaks and pines. In America and Asia such relationships are an important source of damage to pine species.

Oak mildew, *Microsphaera alphitoides* is the only foliage disease regarded as serious on oaks in Britain (see Plate VII). Most species can be affected, but susceptibilities differ widely. *Quercus robur* is regarded as susceptible, *Q. petraea* less so and *Q. cerris* even less. Successful inoculations have been made on *Fagus* and *Castanea*[20].

In Britain conidia are responsible for the greater part of the infection. Until ascocarps were first recorded in Britain in 1945[28], the known methods of perennation were by chlamydospores on the surfaces of old leaves and mycelium in buds. Since 1945, the perfect stage has been sporadically recorded, often in hot dry summers such as 1955 and 1959, but also in wet summers such as 1950. The perfect stage has been most common in southern England and, following a survey in 1959, was not recorded north of Fife[3] (see Plate VII).

Damage is reflected in reduced growth, reduced acorn crops, imperfect ripening off of shoots and increased liability to attack by secondary parasites. Damage occurs mainly in three situations—on nursery and young natural regeneration material, on the second flush of leaves after initial defoliation and on coppice material. In the nursery oak mildew can be controlled with chemicals. It has probably attracted most attention, as a component of one type of oak dieback common in Europe, including Britain, and much has been written about its importance in the dieback syndrome. Mildew is also very common on oak coppice, especially in the few years after cutting, and in the early years of this century silviculturalists in western France recommended conversion of coppice to high forest as a control. However, with the decline in importance of simple coppice and coppice-with-standards as silvicultural systems in western Europe, this aspect of its damage has also declined in importance.

No other mildew species have been recorded on oak in Britain though they have elsewhere in Europe. Roll-Hansen in 1961 described *Microsphaera hypophylla* as a mildew new to Norway. Later, in 1966 he recorded it in Switzerland, Norway, Sweden and Austria, these being new records in the interval[29]. Unlike *M. alphitoides*, *M. hypophylla* attacks the spring leaves of *Q. robur* and produces ascocarps in abundance in the Atlantic climate of north western Europe and thus would be an unwelcome addition to the microflora of British oaks.

The obligate parasite, *Taphrina caerulescens,* causes rounded blisters on oak leaves, the asci forming as a layer under the cuticle. Although the blisters and associated leaf distortion are conspicuous, the disease is of little importance in Britain. In America, however, it is important on the red oaks where they are used as shade trees and control by spraying has been applied[15].

Sclerotinia candolleana is very common on both *Q. robur* and *Q. petraea* in Britain. Infection by ascospores leads to yellow spots on leaves from July onwards, the greater part of the leaf often being infected. The parasite over-winters as sclerotia among fallen leaves, producing its brown, stalked apothecia in the spring. In some years oaks may be epidemically infected but the parasite is not regarded as important in Britain.

Gloeosporium quercinum is also fairly common on oak leaves, causing irregular brown patches, often adjoining veins, and of a papery texture. The acervuli appear in late summer mainly on the veins. This parasite has often been confused with the conidial state of *Gnomonia veneta* but work both in Europe and America has shown differences between the two conidial states, for instance in spore size. A complication is that *Gnomonia veneta* from *Platanus* has been successfully inoculated on the oak and infects *Quercus* species in the field in America.

Uredo quercus, the only rust on oak in Britain, has been recorded rarely in southern and eastern England on *Q. robur* and *Q. ilex.* No alternate host, or aecial stage has been recorded in Europe although the telial stage has been recorded once[36]. There is some doubt whether this form is related to *Cronartium quercuum* which causes galls on pine in Japan. Damage in Britain is unimportant.

Various *Septoria* species attack oak leaves abroad. Hering mentioned a *Septoria* on his collections from the Lake District but the genus does not seem to be important on *Quercus* in Britain[16].

Other leaf spots on oak

Several fungal species attack oak leaves late or towards the end of the growing season and have been studied mainly as early colonists in the process of litter breakdown.

One of the first such studies in Britain was by Hering in a mixed broadleaf wood in the Lake District supplemented by some observations in Sussex[16]. The oak component in the Lake District was *Q. petraea.* Hering examined living leaves from midsummer onwards both by culture and incubation. He concluded that with some exceptions, species dominant on the fallen litter in winter were not present to any great extent before leaf fall in October and November. He concluded, however, that *Cryptocline cinerescens* and to a lesser extent *Aureobasidium pullulans,* were inhabitants of living oak leaves. Hering recorded perithecia of *Mycosphaerella punctiformis* and *M. maculiformis* on leaves within six months of leaf fall. The imperfect state of the latter, *Phyllosticta maculiformis,* has previously been associated with leaf spots on oak in Britain in late summer.

Hering's comments on *Aureobasidium* are of interest in view of Hudson's work demonstrating the presence of a *Guignardia* species,

G. fagi on leaves of various broadleaved species, including oak, shortly after leaf fall and showing that it had an *Aureobasidium pullulans* conidial state[17]. Hering had mentioned two strains of *A. pullulans* in his isolations. It seems that *A. pullulans* is able to colonise some part of the oak leaf while it is still living and its role as a parasite needs investigation.

'Decline' or 'Dieback' of oak

A feature of oak pathology is the frequency of reports from various regions, of 'decline' or 'dieback' in oak stands. Both natural and planted stands and oak species on both sides of the Atlantic have been involved.

Such dieback was well known in England earlier this century. Robinson in 1927 described 'excessive mortality' of oaks in southern England and said that the trouble began with defoliation caused by the oak leaf roller, *Tortrix viridana,* followed by oak mildew, *Microsphaera alphitoides,* on the second flush of leaves of the season[27]. *Armillaria mellea* was a very noticeable feature of the dead trees and Robinson thought in many cases the trees had been 'weakened' by mining and pumping operations or the removal of cover. In the same note, Robinson refers to apparently similar damage in Slovakia quoting that over 125,000 acres (50,000ha) of *Q. robur* had been decimated during 15 years and that the volume of timber in the dead trees was upwards of one million cubic metres. Osmaston described the damage in England at the same time and while agreeing with Robinson about the biotic factors mentioned the 1921 drought as a 'debilitating' cause in one or two cases[21]. A point of interest made by Osmaston was that Turkey oak (*Q. cerris*) in the Forest of Dean was not attacked by caterpillar and did not suffer deaths.

Day, also in 1927, referred to various accounts of dying of Pedunculate and Sessile oak from western Europe and agreed with Falck[12] that the general history of decline began with caterpillar attack on the leaves[9]. This was followed by defoliation by oak mildew and attack by various secondary organisms such as bark fungi, root fungi, notably *Armillaria mellea,* and stem borers. Drought was implicated in the early stages of the process. This early account serves curiously well as a model for several later studies, the actual organisms, both insect and fungal, varying according to locality.

Since the twenties, various papers on oak dieback have been published. Marcu has reviewed the subject generally and in a comprehensive list of papers his co-authors have fully described the situation for eastern Europe[19]. Great attention was paid in these papers to insects and fungi as primary defoliators and also to moisture relationships and soil properties. As well as *Q. robur* and *Q. petraea, Q. cerris* and *Q. frainetto* Ten. were affected.

Not all explanations have followed the same course however. Padula investigating dieback in mixed *Pinus pinea* and *Q. robur* woodlands where both species were affected, ascribed the onset of

symptoms to increasing salinity of ground water and a rise in the
water table plus increasing pollution damage from Ravenna[22].

Young in 1965 described dieback of *Q. robur* in Norfolk,
England[33] (see Plate VIII). *Q. petraea* was not, or scarcely, injured
in this case although stands of it were present. Young suggested
that over a number of years the stands had been affected by various
adverse factors. The most important of these, according to Young,
was drought, but a most interesting part of the study was the way in
which the drought explanation was refined to associate the damage
with a combination of drought and persistent drying northerly
winds. The crops were attacked by *Tortrix viridana* and mildew and
attacks by these agencies declined as the surviving trees later
recovered.

Staley reviewed past cases of oak dieback in the United States
and made an intensive study of dying of red oaks *Q. rubra* L. and
Q. coccinia Muenchh. in Pennsylvania[32]. He concluded that the
primary cause of the decline was the oak leaf rollers *Argyrotoxa
semipurpurana* and *A. albicomana* influenced by climatic and edaphic
factors. A mildew species was not present in this complex, as in
practically all the European cases, but *Armillaria mellea* was important in a secondary capacity as were certain bark fungi and stem
insects.

Staley made a notable attempt to relate the early facets of dieback to the production and maintenance of carbohydrate reserves in
the tree. He emphasised that the moisture stresses which he demonstrated in the areas would reduce photosynthesis as would the
primary defoliators. With declining vigour of the tree, shoots and
especially rootlets would be attacked by weak parasites (including
A. mellea) reducing still further the carbohydrate reserves and tree
vigour. With sustained attack by secondary parasites moisture
stresses would finally cause mortality.

Thus since the 1920s workers have in the main produced
remarkably consistent accounts of oak dieback and have been
concerned with the interrelationships of various factors. Perhaps
the most hazy point is the precise significance of drought in the
complex. Young for instance, seems to attach more weight to drought
than does Staley, though he does not actually say that drought
caused the first symptoms in the case he investigated. Usually the
difficulty is because study often commences considerably later than
the syndrome. Thus a primary defoliating agency may have waned
or disappeared by the time an investigation starts. Most investigators
have been forced to use radial increments to postulate the history
of an outbreak. Generally the date of a significantly narrow ring is
taken to coincide with the start of the syndrome and this is an
important assumption when particular years of climatic stress are
invoked as initiating agencies.

Diseases of bark and shoots

Bark pathogens of oak belong to a number of categories.

Some are restricted to bark and cambium, a few are associated with foliage as well as shoots and some attack both bark and timber. Most of them require wounds for entry, or require the bark to be predisposed to infection in some way.

Several serious bark diseases of oak abroad are associated with climatic injury. Thus, from circumstantial evidence, *Strumella coryneoidea* and *Nectria galligena* which cause serious cankers on oak in America are thought to be associated with axillary cracks following ice or snow damage to tree crowns. Young reported dead patches of bark on oak stems in association with suspected drought damage[38]. Isolations from the patches did not yield known pathogens in this case, but in Britain, *Hercospora taleola* and *Diaporthe leiphaemia* have been associated with similar patches and drought. It is not known whether such infections are predisposed by an actual small wound or by some physiological change in the bark. One of the most common bark fungi on oak in Britain is *Colpoma quercinum* commonly recorded on trees suffering from 'dieback'. Both in Europe and in America it is described as a secondary pathogen implicated in the latter stages of the dieback but, again, the way in which the bark is predisposed to infection has not been investigated.

'Peckholes' caused by birds on the bark of oak may form another type of entry for bark pathogens. Damage of this type, consisting of lines of holes pecked transversely across the stem have been recorded on oak in the south west of England, and agree with that described as woodpecker damage to sycamore[6], and lime[37] in Britain. Similar damage to oak has been described in Germany and ascribed to woodpeckers[39]. Most of the indentations heal up without further complication but in the English examples extended death of bark and canker formation took place around some of them though the organisms involved were not identified.

Certain fungi can enter wounded bark and attack both bark tissues and timber. They are presumably relatively strong parasites, at least with reference to decay fungi. Banerjee investigated a stem canker of oak in Scotland and found it caused by *Stereum rugosum*[1]. Inoculation work showed the fungus capable of killing bark and of invading the sapwood behind the point of inoculation and causing a white rot.

There is, however, no record of a fungus on oak acting as a 'canker rot' as described by Toole for *Polyporus hispidus* on some oak species in eastern America[34]. In this case, the rot fungus gains entry to the tree and produces a column of heart rot from which it can grow out across the sapwood and kill the cambium, forming elongated cankers several feet from the point of entry. *P. hispidus* is common on ash in Britain and has been recorded on some other genera here, but not, apparently, on oak.

A notable omission from the flora of bark parasites on oak in Britain is the genus *Nectria*. In Europe, Asia and America damage to oak by *N. ditissima*, *N. galligena* and *N. coccinea* has been reported though, due to confused nomenclature, the species identification is

not always reliable. However *N. galligena* is well known as the cause
of an important target canker of oaks in America and is also known
as a serious canker causing agent of various genera in Britain. Yet
Booth in his monograph of *Nectria* cited only two species collected
on oak, *N. coccinea* and *N. mammoidea* var. *rugulosa,* with no
implication that either was parasitic[4].

Root diseases

Organisms causing root disease on oak may attack the plant
from the earliest stages. Some of them, indeed, are numbered among
diseases of the acorn since they may attack the emerging radicle.

Probably due to economic reasons and the emphasis on conifers
in British forestry, little work has been done in Britain on damping
off and nursery diseases of hardwoods such as oaks. The scattered
records for Britain have to be supplemented by consideration of
records from abroad.

Among the earliest stages of root attack on oak, *Phytophthora*
is well represented both in Britain and abroad. *P. cactorum* has
been reported from Britain on oak seedlings and *P. cinnamomi*
has been frequently cited elsewhere[31]. *P. cambivora* has been recorded
killing cambium and bark tissues of older stages of oak up to
maturity. Since recent work has shown *Phytophthora* species to be
relatively widespread in Britain, it is likely that further work here
would confirm the liability of oak to be attacked at various ages by
members of this genus especially where high soil moisture content
and relatively high soil temperatures would favour the parasites.

Other common nursery and seedling root rots have been
reported on oak: *Rhizoctonia solani,* the mycelial state of *Thanatephorus cucumeris* has been recorded on oak in Britain, as has violet root
rot, *R. crocorum,* the mycelial state of *Helicobasidium purpureum*[31].
These two species have also been recorded elsewhere in Europe and
in America on various oak species as well as on a variety of other
genera both broadleaved and coniferous. *Cylindrocarpon radicicola*
(*C. destructans*), both in America and Europe, has been recorded
causing root death and below ground lesions in various oak species[14].
The general pathogenicity of this species to forest trees was long in
question but such work as Hart's and also that of Evans et al who
showed its ability to produce the toxin 'nectrolide' have confirmed
its pathogenicity under certain circumstances[11]. The fungus has
never been reported damaging oak in Britain though extremely
common here.

Three *Rosellinia* species are often mentioned with regard to
root attack on oak. They are *R. quercina, R. thelena* and *R. necatrix*
All three are characterised by their ability to exist on decaying
material in the soil and to form a parasitic web of mycelium over
root systems, especially the upper roots, sclerotia and perithecia
forming directly on the mycelial network and on the decaying
bark. The former two species have been especially associated with
young stages but *R. necatrix* especially with older ones. The species

are not easily distinguished in the field. *R. thelena* has a wide host range but *R. quercina* is usually recorded on oak and may be confined to it. All three species occur in Britain but attacks tend to be local and sporadic.

Armillaria mellea, honey fungus, is a characteristic member of the mycoflora of oak woodlands in Europe. The suitability of oak stumps as a substrate for it has been shown by various workers including Rishbeth, who demonstrated its ability to colonise oak stumps for long periods and to sustain rhizomorph production from them[26]. Yet oaks in Britain and elsewhere are obviously able to develop on sites with large reservoirs of *A. mellea* apparently without being seriously damaged. Reports of *A. mellea* attack on oak are nearly always concerned with some form of oak dieback or decline. In these, the fungus is almost always regarded as a secondary agent on a weakened crop, but an agent which is very important in possibly assuring the death of trees which otherwise might recover. A view that *A. mellea* could act in a primary capacity on unweakened oak trees would require to explain the long continued good health of oak on typical sites.

On the other hand, the ability of *A. mellea* to attack various conifers planted on ex-hardwood sites, especially former oak woodland, is well known and constitutes a grave difficulty in the conversion of such sites. Barrett has also brought forward evidence suggesting that conifers planted on an old hardwood site, such as felled oak woodland, are rendered susceptible to attack by the root and stem decay fungus *Phaeolus schweinitzii* which enters through wounds caused by *A. mellea* infection[2].

Unlike *A. mellea*, *Heterobasidion annosum* (*Fomes annosus*) is not typical of the microflora of oak woods, but is common in coniferous associations especially where management has provided stumps. Where oak has been introduced to such sites killing of the oak has occurred. In all such cases conifer stumps were present from a previous crop, or thinning of conifers had been carried out in a mixture of oak and conifers. Deaths in oak up to 50 years of age have been reported and red oak seems particularly susceptible.

Several decay fungi are associated with the lower stem and upper roots of oak and are in a sense root fungi. British examples include *Inonotus dryadeus* which has a very wide host range including conifers. One American worker considered it more important as a low grade root fungus than as a decay organism[13]. *Ganoderma lucidum*, though generally regarded as a decay agent of the stem is widely regarded abroad as a root parasite of many genera. Both these species typically produce their large fructifications at the base of the stem.

A feature of the root attacking fungi discussed above is their wide host range. Only *Rosellinia quercina* can be doubtfully regarded as exclusive to oak. Many of the others attack conifers as well as broadleaved trees. Practically all the species discussed occur in Britain although not necessarily recorded on oak here. It is likely, however, that if further interest were taken in the pathology of oak in Britain, new records would be made to match those abroad.

Decay of the standing tree

In some respects perhaps the organisms causing decay in oak are the best investigated aspect of oak pathology in Britain. This is partly because oak for long dominated large areas of broadleaved forest, both natural and planted, affording ample and pleasant opportunities for mycological collection and recording. The larger size of the fruit bodies tended to focus attention on them compared to the microfungi often responsible for other classes of disease. Thus an early corpus of knowledge was built up. Then the great economic importance which oak has traditionally had in the supply of a variety of products encouraged investigations of the kind embodied in the text book by Cartwright and Findlay[8].

Both as individual trees and as a crop, oak has certain characteristics favouring the entry of decay fungi. With few exceptions, infection requires a wound, in some cases exposure of the heart wood, or a substantial volume of dead tissue such as a branch or a root. Past silvicultural treatment of oak in Britain has often involved coppicing or pollarding and these provided large entry wounds for decay fungi. Shoots then arising from the infected stump are liable to be infected from it after they have formed heartwood. A study of such decay in America showed that *Stereum gausapatum* was an important agent, as was *Fistulina hepatica* to a lesser degree[30].

Oak is relatively intolerant of shade. When grown with beech large branches may be overshadowed and killed by the beech growing up from the under canopy. An extensive number of lignicolous fungi can colonise these dead branches and some can enter the stem from the branch stub. Much the same result can follow from faulty tending of oak stands. In 1933 Pearson described a heart rot in oak due to *Stereum spadiceum* (*S. gausapatum*). The evidence from an examination of nearly 2,000 trees pointed to the decay being primarily a result of excessive thinning in the early youth of the oak stands, followed by the death of the large lateral branches when canopy was again allowed to form[24]. Oak has also been grown as a long-lived parkland tree in conditions of free growth under which it tends to produce large, spreading branches. These are vulnerable to breakage by agencies such as glazed frost and snow, again yielding opportunities for the entry of decay organisms such as *Laetiporus sulphureus*.

Crown dieback in oak may follow sudden exposure and isolation of the tree, as may occur in some silvicultural systems. It has been recorded also following both drought and elevation in water table. Where the dieback involves branches which have produced heartwood there is the opportunity for entry by the various 'top rot' fungi such as *Stereum gausapatum* and *S. hirsutum*.

The thick bark of oak is not easily damaged and gives good protection against fungal entry. Occasionally, however, oak suffers splits in the lower stem, expecially due to frost crack, and such splits have been associated with slime fluxes and decays[18].

Although the heartwood of oak when converted is regarded as relatively durable in service a large number of decay fungi have been reported in the standing tree. These are fully discussed by Cartwright and Findlay and there seems little point in repeating the information here. Hepting has pointed out the risks involved in estimating the relative importance of different species by numbers of sporophores[15]. Some species abroad such as *Poria andersonii* do not fruit on living trees and may thus be missing from lists despite the decay they cause. Other species may fruit very readily although colonising only a small part of the stem. However, based partly on sporophore appearance and partly on cultures, it seems that only a few decay fungi cause serious damage to oak in Britain. Of these *Laetiporus sulphureus* is probably the most important on mature oak causing a typical cuboidal brown rot of the heart wood. *Stereum gausapatum* causes typical 'pipe rot' of the stem, in Britain usually emanating from broken branches. *Fistulina hepatica,* the beef-steak fungus, is one of the best known of decay fungi on oak, partly because of its edible fruit body and evocative name and partly because of the brown colour assumed by oak timber in an early stage of the decay it causes. It may however be important, along with the other fungi such as *Ganoderma lucidum,* in attacking the butt and contributing to the collapse and windthrow of old trees.

Although certain decay fungi have been recorded from various heights of the stem, others seem to be associated with particular parts of the tree. Thus writers have employed categories such as 'top rots', 'butt rots' or 'trunk rots'. *Hymenochaete rubiginosa* is typically found on dead branches but can invade the stem and attack the heartwood. *Phellinus robustus,* judged by its sporophores, tends to occur fairly high up the tree while *Inonotus dryadeus, Fistulina hepatica* and *Ganoderma lucidum* fruit generally on the bottom part of the stem. The reasons for such positional preferences have not been investigated for oak and are no doubt complex. Etheridge showed that in subalpine spruce, temperature and moisture gradients existed in the stem heartwood and that the positions of various heartwood fungi reflected their growth reactions to temperature and wood moisture content in laboratory tests[10]. In general, he found that in sub-alpine spruce, typical butt rots were favoured by wetter, cooler conditions and he speculated on this as a possible adaptation to a particular environment in the stem.

As in some of the other disease categories discussed, there are examples of fungi causing damage to oak abroad which apparently cause little or no damage in Britain, although they are present here. *Inonotus hispidus* is perhaps the commonest species causing decay of standing ash in Britain. Apparently it has not been recorded on oak here. Yet in America it is recorded as a serious cause of loss in oak species[15].

In general the decay fungi of standing oak display little host specificity. Some, eg *L. sulphureus,* are found on a range of conifers and hardwoods. The majority, eg *Ganoderma applanatum,* occur on a wide range of broadleaved trees. As host specificity narrows the range tends to narrow to oak and related genera especially *Castanea.* Thus *F. hepatica* is almost confined to oak but occurs also on *Castanea.* Similarly *Grifola frondosa* is almost confined to oak but again has been recorded on *Castanea* in America[7]. It is always too risky to ascribe host specificity to a particular pathogen but possibly the only decay species in Britain which has been recorded only on oak is *Stereum frustulatum.* This is in spite of its being widely distributed in the north temperate zone.

Conclusion

Many parasitic fungi have been recorded on oak in Britain. In few cases, however, have the diseases they cause been worked on from a pathological point of view. This may be mainly because oak, during this century when the bulk of research in tree pathology has been carried out, has declined in importance as an industrial, timber producing species. Indeed some of the most critical data are derived from research not particularly oriented towards pathology. An example is the leaf infecting fungi which have attracted the attention of workers interested primarily in the breakdown of litter. Another reason may be that in Britain few pathogenic fungi on oak are both widespread and serious.

The general situation in Britain, indeed, presents certain important features. The damaging diseases tend to occur at extreme ends of the age range, for example root rots of young oaks and decays, especially heart rots, of the older stages. A wealth of evidence suggests that most pathogens on oak have become serious only after the trees have been predisposed to infection following environmental upset or insect attack. Such a situation has much in common with one where a tree species through long association has reached some stage of equilibrium with its associated pathogenic flora. Whether this is the case with oak in Britain or not, it may be noteworthy that oak mildew, usually regarded as one of the more serious pathogens of oak, had not apparently been reported in Europe before 1902 though various European countries reported it after that date[9].

Study of oak pathology abroad discloses the existence of several important oak parasites both on our native oak species and also on related species within the white oak group. They are responsible for important diseases of the acorns, of roots, of bark and cambium and of foliage. Their introduction into Britain could conceivably alter the whole picture of our oak pathology partly as a result of direct damage but also by their effect on our present pathogenic spectrum.

Finally, the tendency in Britain has been for forest pathology to be concentrated on the few trees species of commercial importance.

Thus a general neglect of hardwood pathology has resulted. But amenity and recreational forestry, which are now being more strongly emphasised, will inevitably entail new criteria of species choice, tending measures and rotation length. The importance of oak in the future may thus increase since it possesses so many qualities desirable in an amenity species. There is need therefore for further research in oak pathology in Britain to advance it from its present category of a collection of records into a thorough etiological study leading to measures for avoidance and control.

TABLE 1

Fungal species mentioned in the text

On acorns

Ceratocystis sp
Ciboria batschiana (Zopf) Buchwald
Coniothyrium quercinum (Bon.) Sacc.
Fusarium oxysporum Schlecht.
Gloeosporium quercinum Westd.
Pestalotia sp
Phomopsis glandicola (Lév.) Grove
P. quercella Died.

On leaves

Aureobasidium pullulans (de Bary) Arn.
Cronartium quercuum Miyabe
Cryptocline cinerescens (Bub.) Von Arx
Gloeosporium quercinum Westd.
Gnomonia veneta (Sacc. & Speg.) Kleb.
Guignardia fagi Huds.
Microsphaera alphitoides Griff. & Maubl.
M. hypophylla Nevod.
Mycosphaerella maculiformis (Pers. ex Fr.) Schroet.
M. punctiformis (Pers. ex Fr.) Starbäck
Phyllosticta maculiformis Sacc.
Sclerotinia candolleana (Lév.) Fuck.
Septoria sp
Taphrina caerulescens (Mont. & Desm.) Tul.

On bark and shoots

Colpoma quercinum (Pers.) Wallr.
Diaporthe leiphaemia (Fr.) Sacc.
Hercospora taleola (Fr.) E. Muller (=*Caudospora*)
Inonotus hispidus (Bull. ex Fr.) Karst.
Nectria coccinea Pers. ex Fr.
N. ditissima Tul.
N. galligena Bres.
N. mammoidea var. *rugulosa* Weese
Polyporus hispidus Fr.
Stereum rugosum (Pers.) Fr.
Strumella coryneoidea Sacc. & Wint.

On roots

Armillaria mellea (Vahl. ex Fr.) Kummer
Cylindrocarpon destructans (Zins.) Scholten
Ganoderma lucidum (Leyss. ex Fr.) Karst.

Helicobasidium purpureum Pat.
Heterobasidion annosum (Fr.) Bref.
Inonotus dryadeus (Pers. ex Fr.) Murr.
Phaeolus schweinitzii (Fr.) Pat.
Phytophthora cactorum (Leb. & Cohn) Schroet.
P. cambivora (Petri) Buism.
P. cinnamomi Rands
Rhizoctonia crocorum Fr.
R. solani Kuehn
Rosellinia thelena (Fr.) Rabenh.
R. necatrix Prill.
R. quercina Hartig
Thanatephorus cucumeris (Frank) Donk

On timber

Fistulina hepatica Fr.
Ganoderma applanatum (Pers. ex Wallr.) Pat.
Grifola frondosa (Dicks ex Fr.) S. F. Gray
Hymenochaete rubiginosa (Fr.) Lév.
Laetiporus sulphureus (Bull. ex Fr.) Murr.
Phellinus robustus (Karst.) Bourd. & Galz.
Poria andersonii (Ellis & Everhart) Neuman
Stereum frustulatum (Pers. ex Fr.) Fuck.
S. hirsutum (Willd. ex Fr.) S. F. Gray
S. gausapatum (Fr.) Fr.

REFERENCES

1. BANERJEE, S. 'An oak (*Quercus robur* L.) canker caused by *Stereum rugosum* (Pers.) Fr.', *Trans. Br. mycol. Soc.*, **39** (1956), 267–77
2. BARRETT, D. K. '*Armillaria mellea* as a possible factor predisposing roots to infection by *Polyporus schweinitzii*', *Trans. Br. mycol. Soc.*, **55** (1970), 459–62
3. BATKO, S. 'Perithecia of oak mildew in Britain', *Pl. Path.*, **11** (1962), 184
4. BOOTH, C. 'Studies of Pyrenomycetes: IV. *Nectria* (Part 1)', *Mycol. Pap.*, **73** (1959), 45, 68
5. BORNEBUSCH, C. H. 'Meddelelser fra Frøudvalget. Agern og bog fra Holland og Belgien. Afsvampningsforsøg med agern', *Dansk Skovforen. Tidsskr.*, **26** (1941), 371–3
6. BROADHEAD, G. R. J. 'Unusual damage to young sycamores caused by the Greater Spotted Woodpecker', *Q. Jl For.*, **57** (1963), 368
7. BROWNE, F. G. *Pests and Diseases of Forest Plantation Trees,* Oxford (1968)
8. CARTWRIGHT, K. St. G. and FINDLAY, W. P. K. *Decay of timber and its prevention,* HMSO, London, (1958)
9. DAY, W. R. 'The oak Mildew *Microsphaera quercina* (Schw.) Burrill and *Armillaria mellea* (Vahl.) Quel. in relation to the dying back of oak', *Forestry,* **1** (1927), 108–12
10. ETHERIDGE, D. E. 'Moisture and temperature relations of heartwood fungi in subalpine spruce', *Can. J. Bot.*, **35** (1957), 935–44
11. EVANS, G., CARTWRIGHT, J. B. and WHITE, N. H. 'The production of phytotoxin, 'nectrolide', by some root surface isolates of *Cylindrocarpon radicicola* Wr.', *Pl. Soil*, **26** (1967), 253–60
12. FALCK, R. 'Über das Eichensterben im Regierungbezirk Stralsund, nebst Beitragen zur Biologie des Hallimaschs und Eichenmehltaus', *Forst- u. Jagdw.*, **55** (1923), 298–317
13. FERGUS, C. L. 'Some observations about *Polyporus dryadeus* on oak', *Pl. Dis. Rept.*, **40** (1956), 827–9
14. HART, A. C. 'Root rot of oak associated with *Cylindrocarpon radicicola*', *Phytopathology*, **55** (1965), 1154–5

15. HEPTING, G. H. *Diseases of forest and shade trees of the United States*, U.S. Dep. Ag. For. Serv. Handbook No. 386 (1971), 658
16. HERING, T. F. 'Succession of fungi in the litter of a Lake District oakwood', *Trans. Br. mycol. Soc.*, **48** (1965), 391–408
17. HUDSON, H. J. 'An ascomycete with *Aureobasidium pullulans*-type conidia', *Nova Hedwigia*, **10** (1966), 319–28
18. JONES, E. W. 'Biological Flora of the British Isles, *Quercus* L.', *J. Ecol.*, **47** (1959), 169–222
19. MARCU, G. 'Causes, prevention and control of the dieback of oak', *Centrul de Documentare Technica pentru Economia Forestiera, Bucharest*, (1966), 582pp. [*For. Ab.*, (1957), 6085]
20. NEGER, F. W. 'Der Eichenmehltau (*Microsphaera alni* (Wallr.) var. *quercina*)', *Naturw. Z. Land-u. Forstw.*, **13** (1915),1–30
21. OSMASTON, L. S. 'Mortality among oak', *Q. Jl For.*, **21** (1927), 28–30
22. PADULA, M. 'Studies on the ecological condition of the woodlands of San Vitale and of Classe (Ravenna) with a view to their silvicultural improvement with an examination of the root systems of *Pinus* and *Quercus*', *Annali Accad. ital. Sci. for.*, **17** (1968), 173–246
23. PEACE, T. R. *Pathology of Trees and Shrubs*, Oxford (1962)
24. PEARSON, R. S. Address to the Society. *Forestry*, **7** (1933), 1–3
25. POTLAYCHUK, V. I.,'Vrednaja mikroflora zeludei i ee razvitie v zavisimosti ot uslovii proizrastanija i khranenija', *Bot. Ztg*, **38** (1953), 135–42
26. RISHBETH, J. 'The production of rhizomorphs by *Armillaria mellea* from stumps', *Eur. J. For. Pathol.*, **2** (1972), 193–205
27. ROBINSON, R. L. 'Mortality among oak', *Q. Jl For.*, **21** (1927), 25–7
28. ROBERTSON, N. and MACFARLANE, I. 'The occurrence of perithecia of the oak mildew in Britain', *Trans. Br. mycol. Soc.*, **29** (1946), 219–20
29. ROLL-HANSEN, F. 'Some notes on *Microsphaera hypophylla* Nevodovskij', *Meddr norske SkogsforsVes.*, **78** (1966), 19–22
30. ROTH, E. R. and SLEETH, B. 'Butt rot in unburned sprout oak stands', *Tech. Bull. U.S. Dep. Agric.*, no. **684** (1939), 1–43
31. SPAULDING, P. 'Foreign diseases of forest trees of the world', *Handbk U.S. Dep. Agric.*, no. **197** (1961), 1–361
32. STALEY, J. M. 'Decline and mortality of Red and Scarlet oaks', *Forest Sci.*, **11** (1965), 9–17
33. STRAUCH-VALEVA, S. A. 'O biologii nekotorykh gribov, vyzyvajuscikh zabolevanija zeludei', *Trudý Inst. Lesa, Mosk.*, **16** (1954), 269–80
34. TOOLE, E. R. 'Canker rots in southern hardwoods', *Forest Pest Leaft U.S. Dep. Agric.*, no. **33** (1959), 1–4
35. UROSEVIC, B. *More important seed-borne diseases of Czechoslovak forest trees, F.A.O./Int. Un. Forest Res. Org.* Symposium on Internationally Dangerous Forest Diseases and Pests, Oxford (1964)
36. VIENNOT-BOURGIN, G. 'Mildous, oldiums, caries, charbons, rouilles des plantes de France', *Encycl. mycol.*, **26** (1956), 1–317
37. WYNNE-EDWARDS, V. C. 'A lime tree ringed by woodpeckers', *Br. Birds*, **27** (1933–4), 261
38. YOUNG, C. W. T. 'Death of pedunculate oak and variations in annual radial increments related to climate', *Forest Rec., Lond.*, (1965), 1–55
39. ZYCHA, H. 'Spechtschaden an Roteichen', *Forstwiss. ZentBl.*, **89** (1970), 349–55

THE EPIPHYTES OF OAK

FRANCIS ROSE

Department of Geography, King's College, London

Vascular epiphytes

The two native British oaks, *Quercus robur* and *Q. petraea,* are very rich in epiphytes. This is not surprising when one considers the status of oak as the principal dominant tree of deciduous mixed oak forests of the Atlantic period, and also of much of the modern rural landscape.

Angiosperm epiphytes occur from time to time on *Quercus,* but these are all cases of facultative or even chance epiphytism, and there are no British angiosperms which are exclusively epiphytic. It is normally a case of a hollow trunk, or a forked crown, forming a 'flower pot' in which humus and moisture can collect. *Oxalis acetosella* and *Vaccinium myrtillus,* for example, are occasionally to be found in such situations on old trees in damp woodlands. Among the ferns, *Polypodium vulgare* (mostly it seems *sensu stricto*) is however a very characteristic true epiphyte of oak, well adapted to grow on sloping or horizontal boughs with its rhizomes running in humus-filled fissures in the rugged bark. It is far commoner in such situations in the more humid climate of south and west Britain than it is in the Midlands or East Anglia; air pollution may also have some importance in this connection. *Dryopteris filix-mas* and *D. dilatata* are also ferns commonly found as epiphytes on old oaks, but in this case usually of the 'flower pot' type. (See also p. 134).

Non-vascular epiphytes

It is among the non-vascular cryptogams, however, that epiphytism on oak reaches the maximum development. It is perhaps simpler to deal with the two great epiphytic groups, the Bryophytes and the Lichens, separately.

a. *The bryophytes epiphytic on oak*

I have been able to trace records, from my own and other workers' field surveys, of 65 bryophytes that occur, or have occurred, on living oak bark in Britain. Certainly there are more. Many of these, however, are only 'incidental' epiphytes, species normally found on woodland floors that creep on occasion to a greater or lesser degree on to the roots and up the trunks of oaks. It is not easy to draw a clear line here, but I have tried to do so, and it seems that of these 65 taxa, some 43 are normally found as epiphytes on trees in this country. Many of these, however, which occasionally occur on oaks are much more frequent on other trees, for example

Leptodon smithii on elms and on Field maple, *Acer campestre* (see table 1).

If we take the total bryophyte flora of the British Isles at 974 taxa[1][2][3], we find that only about 6.7% of our bryophytes occur on oak, and if we confine our figure to those that are regular epiphytes, only 4.5% occur on oak.

b. *The lichens epiphytic on oak*

If however we turn to the lichens, epiphytism is here much more marked, both in numbers of taxa and in the degree of restriction of these taxa to corticolous (or lignicolous) habitats.

TABLE 1

Bryophytes recorded as epiphytes on Quercus in the British Isles

Amblystegium serpens (Hedw.) B., S. & G.
Antitrichia curtipendula (Hedw.) Brid. E
Aulacomnium androgynum (Hedw.) Schwaegr. E
Brachythecium rutabulum (Hedw.) B., S. & G. E
B. populeum (Hedw.) B., S. & G.
B. velutinum (Hedw.) B., S. & G.
Bryum capillare Hedw. E
Camptothecium sericeum (Hedw.) Kindb. E
Campylopus flexuosus (Hedw.) Brid.
Dicranoweissia cirrata (Hedw.) Lindb. E
Dicranum fuscescens Sm. E
D. montanum Hedw. E
D. scoparium Hedw. E
D. strictum Schleich. ex Schwaegr. E
Eurhychium confertum (Dicks.) Milde
E. praelongum (Hedw.) Hobk.
Fissidens taxifolius Hedw.
Hypnum cupressiforme Hedw.
  var *cupressiforme* E
  var *filiforme* Brid. E
  var *resupinatum* (Wils.) Schimp. E
Isothecium myosuroides Brid. E
I. myurum Brid. E
Leptodon smithii (Hedw.) Mohr E, R
Leucobryum glaucum (Hedw.) Schp.
Leucodon sciuroides (Hedw.) Schwaegr. E
Mnium hornum Hedw.
Neckera complanata (Hedw.) Hüben. E
N. crispa Hedw. E
N. pumila Hedw. E
Omalia trichomanoides (Hedw.) B., S. & G.
Orthodontium lineare Schwaegr. E
Orthotrichum affine Brid. E

O. lyellii Hook. & Tayl. E
O. stramineum Hornsch. ex Brid. E, R
O. tenellum Bruch ex Brid. E, R
Plagiothecium latebricola B., S. & G.
P. silvaticum (Brid.) B., S. &. G.
Pterogonium gracile (Hedw.) Sm. E
Scleropodium caespitosum (Wils.) B., S. & G.
Tetraphis pellucida Hedw. E
Thamnium alopecurum (Hedw.) B., S. & G.
Thuidium tamariscinum (Hedw.) B., S. & G.
Tortula laevipila (Brid.) Schwaegr. E
T. latifolia Hartm.
Ulota bruchii Hornsch. ex Brid. E
U. crispa (Hedw.) Brid. E
U. phyllantha Brid. E
Zygodon viridissimus (Dicks.) R. Br. var *vulgaris* Malta E

Bazzania trilobata (L.) Gray O
Cololejeunea minutissima (Sm.) Schiffn. E
Frullania dilatata (L.) Dum. E
F. fragillifolia (Tayl.) Tayl. E
F. tamarisci (L.) Dum. E
Jamesoniella autumnalis (DC.) Steph. O
Lejeunea ulicina (Tayl.) Tayl. E
Lepidozia reptans (L.)Dum. E
Lophocolea bidentata (L.) Dum.
L. heterophylla (Schrad.) Dum. E
Metzgeria fruticulosa (Dicks.) Evans E
M. furcata (L.) Dum. E
Plagiochila punctata Tayl. O
P. spinulosa (Dicks.) Dum. O
Ptilidium pulcherrimum (Weber.) Hampe E
Radula complanata (L.) Dum. E
Scapania gracilis (Lindb.) Kaal. O

NOTES E—normally epiphytic (43 spp)
  O—Confined to areas of highly oceanic climate
  R—rare

TOTAL—65 taxa

I have traced records of over 300 lichens (and this is probably an understatement) occurring as epiphytes on our two native species of *Quercus* in the British Isles (see table 2). The lichen flora of the British Isles comprised 1368 taxa accepted by February 1973 (plus 4 undescribed taxa in table 2)[4,5], so that the lichen taxa found as epiphytes on oak comprise c 22% of the known British lichen flora.

TABLE 2

Lichens recorded as epiphytes on *Quercus* in the British Isles

Alectoria bicolor (Ehrh.) Nyl. U
A. capillaris (Ach.) Cromb U
A. fuscescens Gyeln.
A. smithii Du Rietz U
A. subcana (Nyl. & Stiz.) Gyeln.
A. vrangiana Gyeln. U
Anaptychia ciliaris (L.) Körb. Eu
A. fusca (Huds.) Vain. M
Arthonia cinereopruinosa Schaer.
A. didyma Körb.
A. impolita (Hoffm.) Borr.
A. leucopellaea (Ach.) Almqu.
A. lurida Ach.
A. punctiformis Ach. T
A. radiata (Pers.) Ach. T
A. spadicea Leight.
A. stellaris Kremp.
A. tumidula (Ach.) Ach.
Arthopyrenia antecellans (Nyl.) Arnold T
A. biformis (Borr.)Massal.
A. cinereopruinosa (Schaer.) Körb.
A. faginea (Schaer.) Swinsc.
A. fallax (Nyl.) Arnold T
A. gemmata (Ach.) Massal.
A. punctiformis (Pers.) Massal. T
Arthothelium ilicinum (T. Tayl.) P. James T
Bacidia affinis (Stiz.) Vain.
B. beckhausii Körb.
B. chlorococca (Stiz.) Lett. T
B. endoleuca (Nyl.) Kickx.
B. phacodes Körb. Eu
B. pruinosa P. James
B. quercicola (Nyl.) Vain. R
B. rubella (Hoffm.) Massal. Eu
B. sphaeroides (Dicks.) Zahlbr.
B. umbrina (Ach.) Bausch T
Biatorella microhaema Norm. ex Th. Fr.
B. moriformis (Ach.) Th. Fr.
B. ochrophora (Nyl.) Arnold
Bombyliospora pachycarpa (Del. ex Duby) Massal.
Buellia alboatra (Hoffm.) Deichm. Br. d. Rostr. Eu
B. canescens (Dicks.) DNot. Eu
B. disciformis (Fr.) Mudd
B. erubescens Arnold

B. griseovirens (Turn. & Borr. ex Sm.) Almb.
B. punctata (Hoffm.) Massal. Eu
B. schaereri DNot.

Calicium abietinum Pers. L.
C. lenticulare (Hoffm.) Ach. *L
C. quercinum Pers.*
C. salicinum Pers.
C. subtile Pers. *
C. viride Pers.
Caloplaca citrina (Hoffm.) Th. Fr. Eu
C. ferruginea (Huds.) Th. Fr.
C. herbidella (Nyl. ex Arnold) Magnusson
C. sarcopisioides (Körb.) Zahlbr. Eu
Candelariella reflexa (Nyl.) Lett. Eu
C. vitellina (Hoffm.) Mull. Arg. Eu
C. xanthostigma (Ach.) Lett. Eu
Catillaria atropurpurea (Schaer.) Th. Fr.
C. griffithii (Sm.) Malme
C. lightfootii (Sm.) Oliv.
C. pulverea (Borr.) Lett.
C. sphaeroides (Massal.) Schul.
Cetraria chlorophylla (Willd.) Vain.
C. glauca (L.) Ach.
Cetrelia cetrarioides (Del. ex Duby) Culb. & Culb.
Chaenotheca aeruginosa (Turn. ex Sm.) A. L. Sm.
C. brunneola (Ach.) Mull. Arg.
C. chlorella (Ach.) Mull. Arg. *
C. chrysocephala (Ach.) Th. Fr.
C. ferruginea (Turn. ex Sm.) Mig.
Cladonia caespiticia (Pers.) Flörke
C. chlorophaea (Flörke ex Sommerf.) Spreng.
C. coniocraea (Flörke) Spreng.
C. digitata (L.) Hoffm.
C. fimbriata (L.) Fr.
C. floerkiana (Fr.) Sommerf.
C. impexa Harm. R
C. macilenta Hoffm.
C. ochrochlora Flörke
C. parasitica (Hoffm.) Hoffm.
C. polydactyla (Flörke) Spreng.

C. squamosa (Scop.) Hoffm.
  var *squamosa*
  var *allosquamosa* Hennipm.
Collema fasciculare (L.) Web. **Eu, R**
C. furfuraceum (Arnold) Du Rietz **Eu**
Coniocybe furfuracea (L.) Ach. **Rt**
C. sulphurea (Retz.) Nyl. **Rt**
Cyphelium inquinans (Sm.) Trevis. **R**
C. sessile (Pers.) Trevis.
Cystocoleus niger (Huds.) Hariot

Dermatina quercus (Massal.) Zahlbr.**T**
Dimerella diluta (Pers.) Trevis.
D. lutea (Dicks.) Trevis.

Enterographa crassa (DC.) Fée
Evernia prunastri (L.) Ach.

Graphina ruiziana (Fée) Mull. Arg.
Graphis elegans (Borr. ex Sm.) Ach.
                                    T, Y
G. scripta (L.) Ach. **T**
Gyalecta flotowii Körb.
G. truncigena (Ach.) Hepp.
Gyalidiopsis anastomosans P. James
                          & Vĕzdar **Y**

Haematomma elatinum (Ach.) Massal.
H. ochroleucum (Neck.) Laund.
  var *porphyrium* (Pers.) Laund.
Hypogymnia physodes (L.) Ach.
H. tubulosa (Schaer.) Bitt.

Lecanactis abietina (Ach.) Körb.
L. amylacea (Ehrh. ex Pers.) Arnold *
L. corticola (Ach.) Lett. **R**
L. premnea (Ach.) Arnold
Lecania cyrtella (Ach.) Th. Fr. **Eu**
Lecanora chlarona (Ach.) Nyl.
L. chlarotera Nyl.
L. confusa Almb.
L. conizaeoides Nyl. ex Cromb.
L. dispersa (Pers.) Sommerf.
L. expallens Ach.
L. intumescens (Rebent.) Rabenh.
L. jamesii Laund.
L. pallida (Schreb.) Rabenh.
L. piniperda Körb.
L. varia (Hoffm.) Ach. **L, R**
Lecidea berengeriana (Massal.)
                          Th. Fr. **R**
L. cinnabarina Sommerf.
L. granulosa (Hoffm.) Ach. **L**
L. quernea (Dicks.) Ach.
L. scalaris (Ach.) Ach.
L. sublivescens (Nyl.) P. James **R**
L. symmicta (Ach.) Ach.
L. templetonii T. Tayl.
L. tenebricosa (Ach.) Nyl.
L. uliginosa (Schrad.) Ach.
L. cf vernalis (L.) Ach.
Lecidiella elaeochroma (Ach.) Hosz.
Lepraria candelaris (L.) Fr.

L. incana (L.) Ach. .
L. membranacea (Dicks.) Vain.
Leprocaulon microscopicum (Vill.)
                                    Gams **R**
Leptogium burgessii (L.) Mont. **R**
L. lichenoides (L.) Zahlbr.
L. teretiusculum (Wallr.) Arnold
Lithographa dendrographa Nyl.
Lobaria amplissima (Scop.) Forss.
L. laetevirens (Lightf.) Zahlbr.
L. pulmonaria (L.) Hoffm.
L. scrobiculata (Scop.) DC.
Lopadium pezizoideum (Ach.) Körb.
Lopidia sp (undescribed)

Melaspilea ochrothalamia Nyl.
Menegazzia terebrata (Hoffm.)
                                    Massal.
Micarea chrysopthalma P. James
M. cinerea (Schaer.) Hedl.
M. denigrata (Fr.) Hedl. **L**
M. melaena (Nyl.) Hedl. **R**
M. nitschkeana (Lahm ex Rabenh.)
                                    Harm. **Y**
M. prasina Fr.
M. violacea (Crovan ex Nyl.) Hedl.
M. sp (undescribed, pycnidiate)
Microthelia micula Körb. **T, Y**
Mycoblastus sanguinarius (L.) Norm.

Nephroma laevigatum Ach.
N. parile (Ach.) Ach.
Normandina pulchella (Borr.) Nyl.

Ochrolechia androgyna (Hoffm.)
                                    Arnold
O. inversa (Nyl.) Laund.
O. parella (L.) Massal.
O. tartarea (L.) Massal. **U**
O. turneri (Sm.) Hasselr.
O. yasudae Vain.
Opegrapha atra Pers.
O. gyrocarpa Flot.
O. herbarum Mont.
O. lyncea (Sm.) Borr. ex Hook.
O. ochrocheila Nyl.
O. prosodea Ach.
O. rufescens Pers.
O. sorediifera P. James
O. varia Pers.
O. vermicellifera (Kunze) Laund.
O. vulgata (Ach.) Ach.

Pachyphiale cornea (With.) Poetsch
Pannaria mediterranea Tavares
P. pityrea (DC.) Degel.
P. rubiginosa (Thunb. ex Ach.) Del.
P. sampaiana Tavares
Parmelia acetabulum (Neck.) Duby
P. arnoldii Du Rietz

P. borreri (Sm.) Turn.
P. caperata (L.) Ach.
P. crinita Ach.
P. elegantula (Zahlbr.) Szat.
P. endochlora Leight. U
P. exasperata (Ach.) DNot.
P. exasperatula Nyl.
ssp *glabratula*
ssp *fuliginosa* (Fr. ex Duby) Laund.
P. horrescens T. Tayl.
P. laciniatula (Flag. ex Oliv.) Zahlbr.
P. laevigata (Sm.) Ach. U
P. omphalodes (L.) Ach.
P. perlata (Huds.) Ach.
P. reddenda Stirt.
P. reticulata T. Tayl.
P. revoluta Flörke
P. saxatilis (L.) Ach.
P. soredians Nyl.
P. subaurifera Nyl. Y
P. subrudecta Nyl.
P. sulcata T. Tayl.
P. taylorensis Mitch.
P. tiliacea (Hoffm.) Ach.
Parmeliella atlantica Degel.
P. corallinoides (Hoffm.) Zahlbr.
P. plumbea (Lightf.) Vain.
Parmeliopsis aleurites (Ach.) Nyl. L
P. ambigua (Wulf.) Nyl.
P. hyperopta (Ach.) Arnold
Peltigera canina (L.) Willd. RT
P. collina (Ach.) Schrad.
P. horizontalis (Huds.) Baumg.
P. praetextata (Flörke ex Sommerf.)
Zopf

Pertusaria albescens (Huds.)
Choisy & Wern var *albescens*
var *corallina* (Zahlbr.) Laund.
P. amara (Ach.) Nyl.
P. coccodes (Ach.) Nyl.
P. coronata (Ach.) Th. Fr.
P. flavida (DC.) Laund.
P. hemisphaerica (Flörke) Erichs.
P. hymenea (Ach.) Schaer.
P. leioplaca (Ach.) DC. Y
P. multipuncta (Turn.) Nyl.
P. pertusa (L.) Tuck.
P. velata (Turn.) Nyl.
Phaeographis dendritica (Ach.) Mull.
Arg. Y, T
P. lyellii (Sm.) Zahlbr. Y
Phlyctis agelaea (Ach.) Flot.
P. argena (Ach.) Flot.
Phyllopsora sp (undescribed)
Physcia adscendens (Th. Fr.) Oliv. em.
Bitt.
P. aipolia (Ehrh. ex Humb.) Hampe
P. labrata Mereschk.
P. leptalea (Ach.) DC.

P. tenella (Scop.) DC. em. Bitt.
P. tribacia (Ach.) Nyl.
Physciopsis adglutinata (Flörke)
Choisy R
Physconia enteroxantha (Nyl.) Poelt
P. farrea (Ach.) Poelt
P. grisea (Lamarck) Poelt
P. pulverulenta (Schreb.) Poelt
Platysmatia glauca (L.) Culb. & Culb.
Polyblastia allobata (Stiz.) Zsch.
Porina chlorotica (Ach.) Müll. Arg.
var *carpinea* (Pers.) Keissl. T
P. coralloidea P. James
P. hibernica P. James & Swinsc.
P. leptalea (Dur. & Mont.) A. L. Sm.
P. olivacea (Pers.) A. L. Sm.
Pseudevernia furfuracea (L.) Zopf
Pseudocyphellaria aurata (Ach.)
Vain.*
P. crocata (L.) Vain.
P. thouarsii (Del.) Degel.
Psoroma hypnorum (Vahl.) Gray Rt
Pyrenula nitida (Weig.) Ach. Y
P. nitidella (Flörke) Mull. Arg. Y

Ramalina calicaris (L.) Fr. T
R. farinacea (L.) Ach.
R. fastigiata (Pers.) Ach. T
R. fraxinea (L.) Ach.
var *calicariformis* (Nyl.) B.de Lesd.
R. obtusata (Arnold) Bitt.
R. pollinaria (Westr.) Ach.
Rinodina exigua (Ach.) Gray
R. isidioides (Borr.) Oliv.
R. roboris (Duf. ex Nyl.) Arnold

Schismatomma decolorans (Turn. &
Borr. ex Sm.) Clauz. & Vězda
S. niveum D. Hawksw. & P. James
S. sp (undescribed)
Sphaerophorus globosus (Huds.) Vain.
S. melanocarpus (Sw.) DC.
Sticta dufourii Del.
S. fuliginosa (Dicks.) Ach.
S. limbata (Sm.) Ach.
S. sylvatica (Huds.) Ach.

Teloschistes flavicans (Sw.) Norm. T
Thelopsis rubella Nyl.
Thelotrema lepadinum (Ach.) Ach.
Tomasellia ischnobela (Nyl.) Keissl.
Y, R
Toninia caradocensis (Leight. ex Nyl.)
Lahm

Usnea articulata (L.) Hoffm.
U. ceratina Ach.
U. extensa Vain.
U. filipendula Stirt. T
U. flammea Stirt. R
U. florida (L.) Web. T

U. fragilescens Hav. ex Lynge
U. fulvoreagens (Räs) Räs
U. intexta Stirt.
  var *intexta*
  var *constrictula* (Stirt.) D.
  Hawksw. & Chapman.

U. rubiginea (Michaux) Massal.
U. subfloridana Stirt.

Xanthoria candelaria (L.) Th. Fr.
X. parietina (L.) Th. Fr.
X. polycarpa (Hoffm.) Oliv. T

TOTAL—303 taxa

NOTES
*—probably extinct on *Quercus* in Britain. I have personally seen nearly all the others on *Quercus.*
Eu—on eutrophicated bark of *Quercus*
L—on decorticate wood
M—in maritime situations only
R—rare
Rt—on roots only
T—on twigs only
U—upland species
Y—on young *Quercus* only

Numerical comparison of epiphyte floras of different species of host trees

a. Bryophytes

If we attempt a numerical comparison of the total recorded cryptogamic epiphyte floras of different tree species in Britain, we run into difficulties with the bryophytes, because in many cases the species or genus of tree on which a particular bryophyte occurs or does not occur, is not fully documented in the literature, and because of the difficulty above mentioned of deciding what is, or is not, an epiphyte. There are a number of bryophytes which occur on decaying logs and stumps, and others associated with both tree roots and woodwork below flood level of rivers. It is impossible to make a definitive list of epiphytic bryophytes without encountering grave problems of definitions. It is possible to say however, that more bryophytes appear to occur on *Quercus* collectively than on most other trees. I have attempted a list of *Ulmus* epiphytes on a similar basis to that for *Quercus,* and have arrived at a figure of 40 taxa. *Fraxinus* has a very similar recorded flora, but it should be emphasised that no bryophyte epiphytes appear to be strictly host-specific.

b. Lichens

With the lichens, such a comparison has proved rather easier, because in most cases it is clearer which taxa should be regarded as epiphytes, and the distinction between terricolous species that creep on to roots, and actual epiphytes of bark or decorticate wood, is clearer, and because the epiphytic lichens have received much more attention in field surveys in recent years than have the bryophytes[6].

I have attempted a numerical comparison of those lichen taxa that have been recorded on a number of native British, and one introduced, tree taxa, and the results are given in table 3. It was

TABLE 3

Comparison of numbers of lichen taxa recorded as epiphytes
on 13 tree genera or species in the British Isles

Tree species	number of lichen taxa	Notes
Quercus (Q. robur and Q. petraea)	303	
Fraxinus excelsior	230	Bark fissured and rather similar to Quercus, but often of higher pH, lacks certain species of old Quercus
Fagus sylvatica	194	In spite of smooth bark, carries a flora very like Quercus in the New Forest, but has few epiphytes in chalk woodlands. Bark of low pH
Ulmus spp	171	High water retentivity and pH, has a specialised flora
Acer pseudoplatanus	170	Carries a flora remarkably like elm (pH high)
Salix (S. cinerea and S. caprea)	128 ⎱	Quite rich especially in humid western areas
Corylus avellana	124 ⎰	
Betula (B. pubescens and B. pendula)	93	Very acid bark
Acer campestre	88	Very favourable bark of high pH, but of limited occurrence as a large tree
Alnus glutinosa	72	Has a very acid bark of low water retentive capacity
Ilex aquifolium	68	Has a limited but specialised flora
Tilia spp	66	Bark lacks water-retentive character
Carpinus betulus	42	Limited by its smooth bark and its occurrence only in the driest part of England

found more convenient in several cases to take genera, rather than species, of trees except in the case of the two *Acer* species, as there was found to be no marked difference in the epiphyte floras on the species within most genera.

It is clear that the native *Quercus* species have a considerably greater number of lichen epiphytes recorded on them than any other tree species, or genera, occurring in Britain. However, this analysis revealed one important fact that is not obvious from the figures themselves. No species of epiphytic lichen is specific to oak in this country. *Arthonia didyma* is very nearly confined to oak, but it has been found on Sweet Chestnut, *Castanea* and Sycamore, *Acer pseudoplatanus* by Mr P. W. James, (pers. comm.). *Opegrapha lyncea,* similarly nearly confined to oak, occurs rarely on beech, *Fagus*, in the New Forest and in Windsor Forest. *Dermatina quercus* may however be specific to *Quercus* twigs.

It seems that the bark of *Quercus* is of a very favourable texture for the growth of the greater number of lichen (and bryophyte) epiphytes, as compared with other trees. Also, having a relatively high porosity and absorptive capacity, it is capable of becoming enriched with nutrients in situations where animals are grazing, as in pasture land. In these circumstances, salts in dust and splash derived from animal excreta and urine may so enrich the bark of old *Quercus* that it is able to support lichen associations more like those normally found on *Ulmus,* which has bark of relatively high pH and normally high nutrient content. Thus most of the lichens regarded as characteristic of *Ulmus* bark can at times be found upon *Quercus*. Also, young *Quercus* trees, and the smaller branches and twigs of mature trees, have relatively smooth bark resembling in surface texture that of mature *Fagus* so that the lichens characteristic of smooth bark may also be found in particular sites on *Quercus*. There may also be significance in the fact that deciduous species of *Quercus* have been apparently the major dominants of our primeval forests in north-west Europe, both in the post-glacial and in several interglacial periods. Such dominance over long periods would be likely to lead to the gradual development of an assemblage of lichen species particularly adapted to growth on the dominant species of trees.

Pinus and other evergreen conifers have poor epiphyte floras in southern Britain, though richer ones in Scotland. The acidity of the bark of conifers and the shade they cast on their own trunks must be important factors in this poverty as compared to *Quercus*.

Epiphytes and light
It is interesting that the great majority of epiphytic lichens, and of bryophytes to a rather lesser but still significant extent, found on *Quercus,* as well as on other trees, are light-demanding species. This raises an interesting point. If the primeval oak forests were uniformly dense, where did all these species grow? The same point incidentally arises with regard to many other groups of plants and animals associated with oak woodland. A great number of them occur today mainly at or near the edges of woodlands, in woodland that is regularly coppiced, or along rides or glades. These facts suggest that the primeval oak forests were not uniformly dense and that numerous glades were a feature, perhaps maintained by large herbivores present.

The epiphyte flora of primeval oak forests

a. *The number of lichen species present*
Survey of a large number of sites known to be very old woodland in this country in areas free from marked air pollution reveals some interesting facts. While sites subjected to coppice management, or known to have been replanted, have in general limited floras numerically of the order of 30–50 taxa per square kilometre, old uneven-aged high forest of oak with glades may have as many as 110, or even in a few cases of up to 180, lichen taxa per square kilometre, of which as many as 150 may be epiphytic on oak itself.

TABLE 4

Numbers of lichen taxa recorded per square km for a number of examples of British oak woodlands, and figures for the Index of Ecological Continuity (IEC)

Site	No of taxa in 1 sq km or less	Index of Ecological Continuity
a. Ancient mixed oak forests, in high canopy, with glades, either medieval parklands or old Royal hunting forests, *known to have been forested at least in part in medieval times		
*Boconnoc Park, Cornwall	180	100
The Dizzard, Cornwall	114	45
Arlington Park, Devon	120	60
Walkham Valley, Devon	116	60
*Holne Chase, Devon	70†	70
*Horner Coombe, Somerset	114	70
Mells Park, Somerset	115	50
*Longleat Park, Wiltshire	117	70
*Savernake Forest, Wiltshire	112 (in c. 8 sq km)	55
Great Ridge Wood, Wiltshire	98	50
*Cranborne Chase, Dorset/Wiltshire	133	50
*Melbury Park, Dorset	140	85
*New Forest, Hampshire (whole)	259 (in 36 sq km)	100
New Forest, individual woodlands ⎰ Mark Ash Wood	160	95
Vinney Ridge	116	80
Busketts Wood	159	90
Shave Wood	120	90
Wood Crates	135	70
Rushpole Wood	123	80
Bramshaw Wood	118	85
Bignell Wood	116	95
Lucas Castle Wood	132	95
*Up Park, Sussex	98	45
*Parham Park, Sussex	138	50
*Eridge Park, Sussex	163	85
*Ashburnham Park, Sussex	155	60
*Heathfield Park, Sussex	73	35
*Wychwood Forest, Oxfordshire	86†	30
*Staverton Park, Suffolk	65	30
*Sotterley Park, Suffolk	92	15
Moccas Park, Herefordshire	96	20
Downton Castle Park, Herefordshire	67	35
Brampton Bryan Park, Herefordshire	106	50
Coed Crafnant, Merioneth	100	60
Coedmore Woods, Cardigan	110	45
Shipley Wood, Durham	103 now 109 in 1800[16]	50 now 60 in 1800[16]
*Naddle Low Forest, Westmorland	73	25
Witherslack Woods, Westmorland	52†	40
Great Wood, Derwentwater, Cumberland	101	65
*Low Stile Wood, Borrowdale, Cumberland	103	55
*Gowbarrow, Cumberland	72†	45
*Camasine Woods, Loch Sunart, Argyllshire	174	70

(Table 4 contd)

Site	No of taxa in 1 sq km or less	Index of Ecological Continuity
b. *Old naturally developed mixed oak forests on former common grazing land: now similar in structure to many sites in* a.		
Ebernoe Common, Sussex	70	35
The Mens, Sussex	70	25
c. *Mature oak forest, known to have been clear-felled and replanted with oak in late 18th century or early 19th century*		
Pitts Wood Inclosure, New Forest, Hampshire	53	30
Pondhead Inclosure, New Forest, Hampshire ..	31	20
Brockishill Inclosure, New Forest, Hampshire ..	80	35
Nagshead Inclosure, Forest of Dean, Gloucestershire	16	0
Dalegarth Woods, Eskdale, Cumberland ..	68	15
d. *Old coppice woodlands with oak standards*		
Combwell Wood, Kent	62	25
Brenchley Wood, Kent	44	5
Ham Street Woods, Kent	43	5
East Dean Park Wood, Sussex	70	40
East of Loxwood, Sussex	33	0
Nap Wood, Frant, Sussex	45	5
Marline Wood, Sussex	54	15
Maplehurst Wood, Sussex	54	5
Hintlesham Great Wood, Suffolk	10	0
Foxley Wood, Norfolk	15	5
Hayley Wood, Cambridgeshire	34	5
e. *Former ancient deer forest, now much modified by replanting and clearing, but with detailed records available from early 19th century*		
St. Leonard's Forest, Sussex (1973)	107	55
St. Leonard's Forest, Sussex (19th century)[16] ..	143	95

† Survey incomplete

Table 4 gives a list of examples of different types of oak forest, mixed oak forest, and other types of woodlands containing oak. Except where stated, the sites are all of the order of 1 sq km in area or rather less. The first column of figures gives the number of lichen epiphytes recorded, nearly all on oak, but in some cases on other acid-barked trees such as *Fagus* and *Fraxinus,* of the mixed oak forest. Nutrient enriched bark communities have been excluded to make the data comparable. Reference to the first section a) of this table suggests that the total epiphytic lichen flora per sq km of the primeval mixed oak forests may well have been at least of the order of 120–150 taxa, if the evidence from this large sample of the most ancient and least-modified relics of our old mixed oak forests has any value. Allowing for the changes that have occurred everywhere in Britain, it may have been even greater. Sites in northern England and in Scotland lack in any case certain more southern species, presumably for climatic reasons, and yet there is a remarkable consistency in the figures within certain limits. Sites where there is significant air pollution have been excluded from the table to eliminate that variable. It should be noted that certain sites marked †️ have probably not been exhaustively surveyed. Comparisons of the totals in section a) with those in sections b) c) and d), which represent increasingly managed or modified oakwoods, are very significant. Coppice-woodlands in particular have very reduced lichen floras.

I have attempted a similar exercise with the bryophyte epiphytes, but the numbers of these are so much fewer, and they show in general such little *numerical* correlation with the continuity of the environment or otherwise, that I have not included the data here.

b. *The particular species present*

Purely numerical comparisons of total lichen epiphyte floras do not tell us everything. A wide range of ecological types of lichens may occur in a wood; and different species may be there for different reasons. The question is, can we detect any group, or groups, of indicator species particularly sensitive to change in the forest environment with time, whose presence, or absence, may indicate continuity, or otherwise, of the forest environment, and hence give us some evidence as to whether a woodland that *looks* old really *is* old and has been relatively little altered with time?

Study of a very large number of oakwood sites in Britain and also in France in areas where air pollution is low has revealed:

> i. that certain species of lichen and bryophyte epiphytes occur in all, or nearly all, woodlands containing standard oaks or ash trees, whether these are old high forest, coppice-with-standards, or areas of mature oak plantations. Table 5 lists a number of examples of such species, which are also, in many cases, found equally commonly on oaks (or ash trees) in open parkland, pasture, of minor-road verge situations.
>
> ii. that a number of other lichen and bryophyte species are only normally found in mature, or old, stands of oak or mixed oak high forest.

In many cases, it is very difficult to establish the past history of such sites in any detail, but whenever it *has* been possible to do so, it has become clear that they are very old, probably primary, woodlands, with strong evidence of some continuity of a high tree canopy (as opposed to coppice) since at least medieval times.

Such sites are found in the following types of terrain:

> a. in the 'ancient and ornamental woodlands' of the New Forest, the only old Royal hunting forest that has remained, in part, open and free from active silvicultural management (see[7]).

TABLE 5

Some lichen and bryophyte epiphytes common and general on Quercus (and on Fraxinus) in both woodland and in more open situations in unpolluted areas of lowland Britain.

Lichens

Calicium viride	P. glabratula ssp glabratula
Catillaria griffithii	P. perlata
Cetraria chlorophylla	P. revoluta *
Evernia prunastri	P. saxatilis
Graphis elegans	P. subrudecta *
G. scripta	P. sulcata
Lecanora chlarotera	Pertusaria amara
L. expallens	P. hymenea
Lecidea quernea	P. pertusa
L. scalaris	Phlyctis argena
Lepraria incana	Platysmatia glauca
Ochrolechia androgyna	Ramalina farinacea
O. yasudae	Schismatomma decolorans *
Parmelia caperata *	Usnea subfloridana

Bryophytes

Bryum capillare	Orthotrichum affine
Camptothecium sericeum	O. lyellii
Dicranoweissia cirrata *	Tortula laevipila
Hypnum cupressiforme	Ulota bruchii (usually in shade or
var cupressiforme	shelter)
var resupinatum	Frullania dilatata
Isothecium myosuroides	Lophocolea heterophylla *
I. myurum	Metzgeria furcata
Leucodon sciuroides	Radula complanata
Neckera complanata	

* Taxa becoming rarer or absent in north and east Scotland

    b. in more fragmentary form in the relics of other old Royal, or subject, deer forests, such as Savernake Forest, Wychwood Forest, and Cranborne Chase, and until last century in St Leonard's Forest, Sussex,

    c. in the wooded parts of deer parks set up in medieval times or earlier.

    d. in more remote parts of Devon, western Wales, the Pennines, Lakeland, and west Scotland, in steep-sided ravines and on scarps where active forestry has been at a minimum for reasons of remoteness or of topography.

Such sites are not found in parks first created in the 18th century landscape-gardening phase or later. There is good evidence[8] that many medieval deer parks were formed from relic areas of the primeval wilderness, still existing at that time, and probably containing fragments at least of primary oak forest.

Table 6 lists many of the species of lichens and bryophytes that are found more or less frequently in such sites as those listed above but not in other woodlands, that are 'faithful' to these types of woodlands. Some of these species however show some degree of

TABLE 6

Lichen and bryophyte epiphytes that are 'faithful' to old oak, or mixed deciduous relic forest in lowland Britain (see text for further details)

Lichens

Arthonia didyma	Pachyphiale cornea
A. stellaris	Pannaria mediterranea
Arthopyrenia cinereopruinosa	P. pityrea
Biatorella ochrophora	P. rubiginosa
Bombyliospora pachycarpa	P. sampaiana
Caloplaca herbidella	Parmelia arnoldii
Catillaria atropurpurea	P. crinita
C. pulverea	P. horrescens
C. sphaeroides	P. reddenda
Chaenotheca brunneola	Parmeliella corallinoides
Dimerella lutea	P. plumbea
Haematomma elatinum	Peltigera collina
Lecanactis premnea	P. horizontalis
Lecidea cinnabarina	Pertusaria velata
Leptogium burgessii	Porina coralloidea
L. teretiusculum	P. hibernica
Lobaria amplissima	Pseudocyphellaria crocata
L. laetevirens	P. thouarsii
L. pulmonaria	Rinodina isidioides
L. scrobiculata	Schismatomma niveum
Lopadium pezizoideum	Sticta limbata
Nephroma laevigatum	S. sylvatica
N. parile	Thelopsis rubella
Ochrolechia inversa	Thelotrema lepadinum
Opegrapha lyncea	

Bryophytes (only faithful as epiphytes)

Antitrichia curtipendula	Zygodon viridissimus var vulgaris
Neckera crispa	Frullania fragillifolia
N. pumila	F. tamarisci
Pterogonium gracile	Jamesoniella autumnalis

TABLE 7

A short list of twenty 'old forest' lichen epiphytes still widespread, at least in southern Britain
(These are used in table 4 to calculate the Index of Ecological Continuity)

Arthonia didyma*	Ochrolechia inversa*
Catillaria atropurpurea*	Opegrapha lyncea†
C. sphaeroides*	Pachyphiale cornea*
Dimerella lutea*	Pannaria pityrea*
Enterographa crassa‡	Parmelia crinita*
Haematomma elatinum	P. reddenda*
Lecanactis premnea†	Peltigera horizontalis*
Lecidea cinnabarina	Sticta limbata*
Lobaria laetevirens*	Thelopsis rubella*
L. pulmonaria*	Thelotrema lepadinum

* Not now in the Midlands and East Anglia where there has probably been too much environmental modification and pollution.
† Not now extending north of the Humber-Mersey line.
‡ Present in N. England and Scotland but less common there.

restriction geographically within Great Britain, presumably due to climatic factors, so a short list of twenty lichens among these species have been selected (table 7) that are still widespread in lowland southern Britain in old high forests of oak though even here some become rarer northwards, and some do not reach Scotland: all of them occur in the old unenclosed woodlands of the New Forest, taken as a whole.

It would appear that such species may in fact be relics of the ancient forest epiphyte flora—similar phenomena can be seen among the Coleoptera and Hemiptera in the forest fauna—and it is suggested that the presence of a sufficient number of them in a site could be taken as evidence of continuity of the ancient forest canopy at that site. They could therefore be regarded as indicator species in two senses:

a. as ecological indicators of the existence of a particular type of forest environment at the present time; and

b. as historical indicators of lack of environmental change, within certain critical limits, over a long period of time.

Within the more or less continuous blanket of primeval forest cover that existed in many parts of Britain even into early medieval times, the conditions for the dispersal and colonisation of epiphytic lichens, and bryophytes, were probably such that they were more or less ubiquitous in their appropriate ecological niches. From early medieval times to the present day, however, the old oak woodlands became more and more fragmented, and most of those that remained became modified by various forms of management. The isolated scattered fragments that remained least modified in such sites as those discussed above would have provided habitats where many forest epiphytes could have survived, but as they were now surrounded by unfavourable terrain for colonisation, re-establishment of such species in new plantations, or in felled woodlands showing regeneration, would have become increasingly difficult. The general drying-out of the landscape, due to agricultural practice in the last few hundred years, must have played a part in this. It is noteworthy in this connection that some epiphytic lichens[18] and bryophytes that were known to produce fructifications freely up to the early or mid-19th century in many parts of lowland Britain—there is abundant evidence of this fact from both written data and old herbarium specimens—are now rarely found fertile, even in relatively unaltered old woodlands in lowland Britain, though some still fruit freely in areas such as the humid west of Scotland.

Thus we have the concept of many of the forest epiphytes today being not only indicator species but also relic species.

c. *The Index of Ecological Continuity*

Let us now return to the list of twenty lichens faithful to apparently ancient woodlands in table 7. I have used these in an attempt to calculate an 'Index of Ecological Continuity' (IEC) of the forest environment, by calculating the percentage of the species in this list that occur in many oak, or mixed oak, woodlands, to see if any meaningful data ensue.

The results of this analysis for the list of woodland sites in table 4 is given in the second column of figures.

The great majority, 28, of the 41 sites in category a) prove to have an IEC of over 50 while none of the sites in categories b), c) and d) reach this figure.

The sites in category a) that fall below 50% may seem to create a discrepancy but prove, on inspection, to have good reasons for this in most cases. I shall discuss four examples of these.

   i. The Dizzard in Cornwall is a very unusual site. Though apparently an oak wood of completely natural origin, it occurs on a north facing slope down to the sea and is clearly periodically subject to mass movement of the rather soft terrain. It contains no large or well-grown oaks. On the other hand, there are many indicator species of lichens here besides those in my basic list. If one substituted alternative species in the basic list such as *Pannaria rubiginosa, Parmeliella plumbea, Lobaria scrobiculata, Nephroma laevigatum* and *Pseudocyphellaria crocata* for species missing at the Dizzard, such as *Lecanactis premnea, Opegrapha lyncea, Arthonia didyma, Thelopsis rubella,* and *Thelotrema lepadinum* (all characteristic of *old* oaks) one could obtain easily an index of 70% or more.

This underlines a possible weakness of trying to keep such an index too simple. One might improve it by taking a list of, say, 30 indicator species, and then assessing the percentage index figure on the occurrence of *any* 20 of these species.

   ii. Up Park, Sussex is a very old, well-documented early medieval parkland with old forest relics present, but it has deteriorated as a habitat through felling in the last 70 years or so. *Pannaria pityrea* occurred there last century and probably other 'old forest' species. The data really prove the point, that although Up Park is an ancient site, recent environmental modification has affected it, and the Index indicates this well.

   iii. Staverton Park, Suffolk is a site which has been studied by Peterken[9] who has given strong historical evidence of continuity of naturally regenerating uneven-aged forest there until recent times. Today however the site has become in part much more open, due to lack of regeneration, and in this low-rainfall part of East Anglia this opening-up may well have caused drying-out of the former forest environment. The larger foliose 'old forest' species such as *Lobaria pulmonaria* are not there now (though this species was certainly present not far away in the early 19th century[10]), while species such as *Lecanactis premnea* and *Opegrapha lyncea* (which though old woodland species characteristic of ancient oaks, can survive in drier more open parkland-type situations) survive well there today. The low index indicates the realities of the situation ecologically quite well.

   iv. Sites in northern England and Scotland (particularly Shipley Wood, Great Wood, and Low Stile Wood) are affected by the absence of some species of more southerly geographical range.

There is clearly a risk of circular argument in an exercise of this kind, but I have tried to overcome this by testing the Index against sites where there is good historical documentation either of continuity or of change.

In categories c) and d) of table 4 the low figures for the IEC are striking. In the case of Dalegarth Woods in Cumberland, there is an oak forest which at first sight looks like a category a) site, but the owner informed me that most of it was clear-felled and replanted in 1770. Hence the low IEC is what one would expect; as Eskdale was already largely disforested by then, this would have made recolonisation very difficult.

Planted Inclosures in the New Forest may give higher IEC values than one would expect but in this forest many Inclosures are adjacent or close to ancient woodlands, so that recolonisation would have been much easier than with more isolated plantations.

Most of the old coppice woodlands in category d) have very low IEC values. Although most of them are primary woodlands in the sense that they have probably always been woodland sites from primeval times, clear felling and subsequent coppice management (with the drastic alternations of high and low light intensity, and low and high humidity that this produces in the bark environment of standard oaks) seems to have eliminated much of the lichen flora and nearly all of the old forest species. One coppice-with-standards site in this list, however (East Dean Park Wood, West Sussex) is rather different. It carries old oak and ash trees in the rides and has been woodland since at least medieval times: it appears to have been a former deer park, and is intermediate in structure between the sites of categories a) and d). These facts may account for its very different IEC.

St. Leonard's Forest, included in a separate category e), is of interest, as it is well-documented as regards its lichen flora over 170 years[16]. In the 19th century it must have resembled the New Forest old woodlands closely in ecological structure and epiphyte vegetation: today, much cut up and modified, it has greatly altered in its epiphyte flora and its IEC.

It is worth adding that Degelius[17] recorded 127 epiphytic lichen taxa, 118 of them on *Quercus* itself, in an old oak forest, Hald Egeskov, of some two square kilometres, near Viborg in Jutland, Denmark. The IEC for this site is 20, though the more continental character of the lichen flora there makes a strict comparison difficult.

To summarise the discussion, one can say that the method of calculating the Index of Ecological Continuity could probably be improved upon, but that the principle seems to work well, and offers us a technique for assessment of continuity of *forest* environment, as opposed to continuity of *some* sort of woodland, in sites of unknown history that may be studied in the future.

d. *The number of epiphytes per individual tree*

This varies enormously. The number is normally greater on older trees than younger ones, and greater on well-lit than on very shaded trees. Old, but not senescent, oaks in parkland or in forest glades tend to have the highest numbers. The record at present seems to be held by an oak in Fairoak Park, Rogate, Sussex, which has 52 lichen epiphyte taxa and 2 bryophytes growing on it. Figures of 30 species per tree are not however unusual.

The distribution in space of epiphytes on oak trees

The epiphyte communities† on oak follow a definite spatial pattern. Normally, in more open situations, the bulk of foliose, fruticose and crustose species of lichens occur on the south to south-west side of the tree which receives most sunshine (mornings tend to be misty in fine weather hence perhaps the south-east side is less favoured). The bulk of the rain actually striking the trunk will tend to fall on the south-west side of the tree also, because of the prevailing wind direction in this country. The north side of the tree tends to carry more limited numbers of species, usually with a lower percentage cover, and the communities consist largely of crustose species. Rain-tracks tend to modify the pattern where they exist down the trunk, being usually dominated by bryophytes near the centre, but with foliose lichens coming in at the edges. Non-vertical (leaning) trunks show a modification of the pattern, most epiphytes occurring on the upper side.

The roots tend to be occupied by bryophytes together with some foliose lichens, especially in concavities where there is protection from cattle or horses which tend to rub against trees in open pastures.

In forest situations, lichens similarly dominate the south and south-west sides of the trunks, but bryophytes take over dominance on the north and north-east sides and, to a varying degree, on the roots. In very shady situations bryophytes may dominate the lower trunk completely, and lichens only come in higher up on the upper trunk and main boughs. This is especially true in very humid sheltered forest areas such as those in south-west Ireland around Killarney and in parts of west Scotland where the bryophytes may be completely dominant up to a considerable height.

The boughs often show an interesting distribution of epiphytes. There most of the lichens and bryophytes tend to occupy the upper sides of horizontal boughs, with the bryophytes in the central most horizontal part, and the lichens often more to the edges. This effect appears to be related to the accumulation of water. Twigs tend to have their own characteristic flora of such fruticose lichens as *Usnea* and *Ramalina* species, and foliose species such as *Parmelia physodes* and *P. aspera,* while slightly further back larger twigs bear crustose lichen species of *Graphis, Phaeographis* and *Opegrapha*.

The bryophyte flora of the twigs is limited but often includes *Ulota* spp, *Orthotrichum* spp and small Lejeuneaceae, especially in oceanic districts.

---

† The use of names to describe plant communities in this paper is in no way to be taken as evidence of their valid publication or of any such intention.

The vertical distribution of lichens on trees has been studied by Kershaw[11] and by Harris[12] [13]. The first author found in North Wales that *Parmelia caperata* and *P. sulcata* dominated oak trunks up to 12 feet; *P. sulcata, P. physodes,* and *Cetraria glauca* up to 24 feet; and up to 36 feet, *P. sulcata, P. glabratula* and *P. subaurifera* were dominant. Harris working in South Devon found a similar vertical zonation on *Quercus petraea,* with *Parmelia caperata, P. physodes* and *P. sulcata* dominating the basal, middle and tree-top zones respectively.

Air pollution and epiphytes

The situation so far described may all be altered by air pollution. Until the first Industrial Revolution at the end of the 18th century all trees everywhere, except in the few small towns that existed, bore, it is now clear, a more or less complete epiphyte cover on their trunks and major branches unless very shaded. The situation is now very different over much of Britain and indeed of north-western Europe. Over about one-third of England and Wales in a belt from the London region up to Lancashire, Yorkshire and on to Tyneside, most of the epiphyte communities have been destroyed by SO_2 pollution. Most trees in this zone now bear a cover of the SO_2-tolerant crustose lichen *Lecanora conizaeoides* and little else[14]. Since lichen and bryophyte epiphytes show differential and specific sensitivity to SO_2 pollution, it has been possible to construct a 'pollution scale' for the recognition of a continuum of zones of pollution by means of the lichen (and bryophyte) epiphyte communities present on free standing mature oaks (and ash trees, which have similar bark from the ecological standpoint). These zones have been correlated with definite limits of mean winter levels of SO_2 in the atmosphere[14].

Eutrophication of bark

Eutrophication* of the bark of oaks can lead to the development of lichen and bryophyte communities different from those on normal acid bark. If this eutrophication is due to the presence of grazing animals (wind-blown dust from faeces and urine) etc, then the communities of the Xanthorion alliance of Barkman[15] may develop,

---

* The usage of the term 'eutrophication' originally referred to essentially aquatic habitats, and is therefore to be considered as misapplied here and in other recent papers on this aspect. In future it is suggested that those concerned with studies on epiphyte ecology adopt the following, etymologically more correct, terminology; nutrient enriched substrates (ie above the natural norm of the phorophyte) should be termed *hypertrophic;* leached substrates, (ie below the natural norm) *hypotrophic;* and those within the natural range, *mesotrophic.*

The terms 'natural hypertrophication' and 'artificial hypertrophication' are recommended to distinguish hypertrophication from organic sources such as animal excreta in pastures and on birds' perching stones and boughs, on the one hand, from hypertrophication due to heavy applications of artificial inorganic fertilisers, on the other hand.

F. ROSE and P. W. JAMES

even on *Quercus,* if old, though more characteristically on *Ulmus. Acer* and *Fraxinus.* Stronger eutrophication by artificial fertilisers, however, tends to destroy epiphytic lichens and bryophytes; *Buellia canescens* and *B. punctata* become dominant at intermediate levels, and at very heavy levels of fertiliser application to the pasture or nearby arable land, all epiphytes other than algae disappear.

The distribution of epiphytes and epiphyte associations on oaks with time and space

Harris[12] found a relationship between lichen cover and tree age on *Q. petraea* in a South Devon wood. He found *Parmelia sulcata* reached maximum cover on trunks or branches from 10–15 years old, *P. physodes* on 20 year old stems, and *P. caperata* at 35 years. He found also a group of pioneer species, including crustose species such as *Arthopyrenia fallax* and *Lecidea limitata,* to be characteristic of the smooth bark of twigs in the very dry environment of tree tops. He also found[13] that the optimal water content for net carbon assimilation varied both a) between a tree top species, *Parmelia sulcata,* with 40% of saturation, and a basal species, *P. caperata,* with 75% saturation, and b) that *P. caperata* material had a lower optimum water content when collected for experimental study from the top of a tree than from the basal region, suggesting some adaptation to habitat. Indeed, plants of *P. caperata* from tree tops showed a much higher algal cell count than plants of the same species collected lower down.

Study of a very large number of oak trees of all ages and in a wide variety of situations has enabled me to draw up the following sequence of epiphyte communities on *Quercus* in both space and time which are represented diagrammatically in Figs 1 and 2.

Barkman[15] has assembled much phytosociological data on epiphytic communities of lichens and bryophytes.

It is difficult at present to fit our British communities into his scheme which in any case covers many parts of Europe, some with much more continental climates than ours. I have not therefore attempted to use his names, but have merely used the dominant species to indicate the communities that occur on British oaks. Much more work is needed to produce a satisfactory comprehensive phytosociological scheme to cover Britain, let alone the rest of Europe.

Bark pH

The measurement of bark pH is clearly of great importance as an environmental indication for epiphytes, but different workers (see Barkman[15]) have employed such different techniques for measuring it that one hesitates to compare their data. However, some figures obtained in our laboratory by Mr B. J. Coppins (pers. comm.) by glass electrode measurement on ground samples of the top 1 mm

FIGURE 1

Senescence

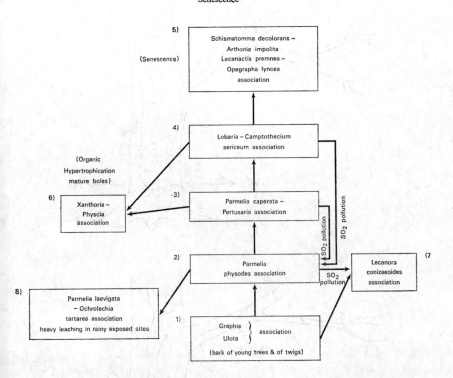

The pH of the bark decreases with time from 1 to 2, then
increases up to 5. It increases further to 6, but falls to 7
and to 8.

Change in associations on *Quercus* with time.

FIGURE 2

A.

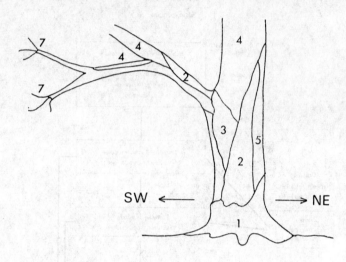

B.

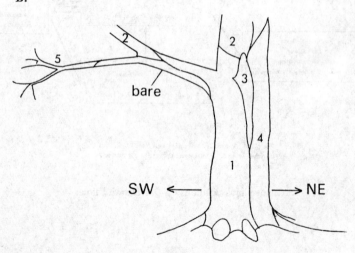

Patterns of epiphyte communities in space on mature oaks:
A.   In closed forest
B.   In open situations

of the surface of barks of *Quercus* from different sites mixed with de-ionised water are interesting. They are as follows:

i. Bark from trunks with *Lobaria* communities, sheltered sites near sea level, Loch Sunart, Scotland: pH 5.45–5.60

ii. Bark of twigs bearing *Parmelia physodes* and *Lecanora conizaeoides,* New Forest: pH 4.40

iii. Bark from trunks in exposed upland woodland, at 350ft (107 m), Ariundle Wood, Loch Sunart, Scotland, bearing *Ochrolechia androgyna* and *Parmelia laevigata*: pH 4.34

Upland epiphyte communities on oak

The epiphyte communities developed on mature *Quercus* boles in sheltered, or low rainfall, lowland situations tend to differ considerably from the communities developed on *Quercus* of similar size in exposed upland woodlands in high rainfall areas in highland Britain. One can even see this difference within single woodlands in such places as Borrowdale, Lakeland; the Maentwrog Valley, North Wales; and on the north shores of Loch Sunart, Argyllshire. In these areas the oaks at the lowest, most sheltered, levels of the woodlands bear typical lowland bryophyte and lichen communities, in which such bryophytes as *Isothecium myosuroides, Hypnum cupressiforme* var. *filiforme,* and *Orthotrichum lyellii* are prominent, and the lichen communities consist of the *Parmelia caperata-Evernia-Pertusaria* association and the Lobarion (*Lobaria pulmonaria, L. laetevirens, Sticta* spp and *Parmeliella plumbea,* with *Camptothecium sericeum*). The oaks in the upper parts of these woodlands either bear dense 'stockings' of hepatics, such as *Plagiochila spinulosa,* etc, in more sheltered places, or carry a community composed of such lichens as *Parmelia laevigata, P. taylorensis, Hypogymnia physodes, Ochrolechia androgyna, O. tartarea, Mycoblastus sanguinarius, Sphaerophorus globosus,* and *Cladonia* spp. In part this phenomenon is apparently due to the steep rainfall gradient up hillsides in such districts, certainly as far as the bryophyte-rich communities of more sheltered sites are concerned; but in more exposed sites, I suspect that the difference is due to much greater leaching effect on the bark due to direct rain-beat in the exposed sites, producing an effect akin to podsolisation in soils. In this connection it is interesting to compare the pH data from oak bark at the two sites near Loch Sunart in Scotland given above, (i) close to sea level, and (ii) in an exposed site at about 350 ft (Ariundle Wood).

Just as enrichment of bark by nutrients from an external source can alter epiphyte communities on oak profoundly in one direction, so leaching from an external source (ie heavy beating of rain) can alter them profoundly in another.

Conclusions

Many epiphytes of oak take a long time to develop, and are only to be seen well-developed, or even at all, on mature or ancient trees. Many require, as we have seen, the shelter of an unbroken, but not too densely shady, forest environment. Hence there is a great need for the preservation of old trees, for the planting of new oaks to replace them when the time comes, and for the active conservation and regeneration of what is left of our ancient forests.

Most epiphytes, whether bryophytes or lichens, are very sensitive, often extremely so, to air pollution, Over wide areas of Britain there are now almost no epiphytic lichens or bryophytes of any interest left, and even outside these areas, many epiphytes in the (at present) only slightly polluted areas are confined to relic communities on older trees. These communities, though often apparently healthy, are frequently not fertile and are probably of relic nature at the present time. Unless we can hold SO_2 concentrations in our atmosphere at the present level, or even perhaps reduce them, we shall lose a lot more of our epiphytes at least over the greater part of lowland Britain.

Acknowledgements

I would like to thank particularly Mr Brian Coppins, Mr Peter James and Mr E. C. Wallace, who have not only assisted me considerably in developing my knowledge of epiphytes in various ways, but who have also accompanied me on numerous survey excursions in the field. Mr James has also kindly criticised my manuscript.

I would also like to thank the Nature Conservancy and the University of London for financial assistance over travel costs, and all the land owners, far too numerous to mention, who have so willingly allowed me to work on their properties.

REFERENCES

1. WARBURG, E. F. *Census Catalogue of British Mosses* (ed. 3), British Bryological Society, London (1963)
2. PATON, J. A. *Census Catalogue of British Hepatics* (ed. 4), British Bryological Society, London (1965)
3. see *Transactions of the British Bryological Society,* 1963–1971, for later additions to our bryophyte flora
4a. JAMES, P. W. 'A new check-list of British Lichens', *Lichenologist,* 3 (1965), 95–153
  b. JAMES, P. W. 'Corrections to a new check-list of British Lichens. 1', *Lichenologist,* 3 (1966), 242–7
5. see *The Lichenologist,* 1967–72 for later additions and nomenclatural changes: also Culberson, W. and Culberson, C. *Contr. U.S. natn. Herb.,* 34 (1968), 419–558
6. ROSE, F. and JAMES, P. W. 'Regional studies on the lichen flora of Britain. I. The corticolous and lignicolous lichen flora of the New Forest, Hampshire', *Lichenologist,* 8 (1974), 1–72
7. TUBBS, C. R. 'Early encoppicement in the New Forest', *Forestry,* 37 (1964), 95–105
8. BRANDON, P. F. *The common lands and wastes of Sussex,* Ph.D. Thesis, University of London (1963)
9. PETERKEN, G. F. 'Development of vegetation in Staverton Park, Suffolk', *Fld Stud.,* 3 (1969), 1–39
10. HENSLOW, J. S. and SKEPPER, E. *Flora of Suffolk,* London & Bury St. Edmunds (1860)

11. KERSHAW, K. A. 'Preliminary investigations on the distribution and ecology of epiphytic lichens in Wales,' *Lichenologist*, **2** (1964), 263–76
12. HARRIS, G. P. 'The ecology of corticolous lichens. I. The zonation on oak and birch in South Devon', *J. Ecol.*, **59** (1971), 431–9
13. HARRIS, G. P. 'The ecology of corticolous lichens. II. The relationship between physiology and the environment', *J. Ecol.*, **59** (1971), 441–52
14. HAWKSWORTH, D. L. and ROSE, F. 'Qualitative scale for estimating sulphur dioxide air pollution in England and Wales using epiphytic lichens', *Nature, Lond.*, **227** no 5254 (1970), 145–8
15. BARKMAN, J. J. *Phytosociology and ecology of cryptogamic epiphytes*, Assen, Netherlands (1958)
16. TURNER, D. and DILLWYN, L. W. *The Botanists' Guide through England and Wales*, London (1805)
17. DEGELIUS, G. 'Lavfloran i Hald Egeskov Jylland Ett bidrag till de danska ekskogsresternas naturhistoria', *Bot. Tidsskr.*, **61** (1965), 1–21
18. HAWKSWORTH, D. L., ROSE, F. and COPPINS, B. J. 'Changes in the lichen flora of England and Wales attributable to pollution of the air by sulphur dioxide', in Ferry, B. W., Baddeley, M. S. and Hawksworth, D. L. (eds) *Air Pollution and Lichens*, Athlone Press, London (1973)

OAK AS A HABITAT FOR INSECT LIFE

M. G. MORRIS

Monks Wood Experimental Station, Abbots Ripton, Huntingdon

Introduction

All naturalists know that in Britain more species of insects are associated with oak than with any other tree, or indeed with any other plant. The meaning of the term 'associated' will be examined in the course of this paper, but can be taken to refer to any relationship which is not purely casual or accidental. As pointed out by Southwood[1], the two basic requirements of insects which are provided by plants are food and shelter, although the former is often emphasised at the expense of the latter. Southwood draws attention to the fact that insects of only a few orders feed on plants, although of course as regards numbers of species phytophagous insects are very abundant. In evolutionary terms Southwood distinguishes four 'hurdles' which an insect must overcome in order to feed on plants, the nutritional, attachment, desiccation and host-finding hurdles. A considerable amount of recent work, particularly on the nutritional 'hurdle' and the chemical defences of plants, is discussed by him. In an earlier and now classic paper Southwood[2] suggested that in general the number of phytophagous insect species associated with any particular tree reflected the abundance of that tree in recent time and particularly since the last glaciation. As Godwin & Deacon[3] have shown, after a period of recolonisation following the Weichselian glaciation, oak had a long period of dominance in Britain until the clearances of the last few thousand years. The much smaller quantity of entomological work on fossil faunas [4] [5] of course supports this. Southwood[6] further developed his hypothesis by suggesting that the abundance of any tree species would be directly related to the chances any particular insect species would have of overcoming its natural defences. Actual instances of changes of host-plant which have been recorded, e.g. the Heteroptera *Plesiocoris rugicollis* (Fallen) and *Orthotylus marginalis* Reuter moving from *Salix* to *Malus*[1], the weevil *Caenorhinus aequatus* (L.) feeding on fruits of *Malus* instead of those of *Crataegus*[7] and the probably unsuccessful change of the weevil *Attelabus nitens* (Scopoli) from *Quercus* to *Castanea*[8], may be attributed to changes in the relative abundance of the hosts. However, these changes involve only local populations, not each species as a whole. Many examples are known of insects which have different food plants in different parts of their range.

At least some of the constituents of the oak fauna are of considerable antiquity. Shotton & Osborne[9] record abundant fossil remains of the stenophagous oak-feeding weevil *Rhynchaenus quercus* (L.) in the Nechells deposits which are of Hoxnian age (about 350,000 years B.P.). Remains of *R. avellanae* (Donovan), which feeds on *Quercus* and *Corylus,* were also present. Coope[10] points out that the characteristic feature of quaternary insect fossils, of which beetles (Coleoptera) form by far the greatest part, is their constancy of form throughout the whole of the Pleistocene period. If the Coleoptera are typical of insects as a whole, and there is no reason to suppose that they are not, the fauna of oak may have been established by the beginning of the Pleistocene. The great morphological stability of Coleoptera occurred at a time when environmental conditions fluctuated widely, though of course on a geological scale of time. The fauna responded to these fluctuations of climate by migrating with its habitat. Large geographical displacements of species are characteristic of the Pleistocene period. It is, of course, perfectly possible for an insect species to change its host plant without evolving morphologically. On the other hand the evolution of the fauna of oak has probably not been considered sufficiently fully in the light of the evidence from quaternary palaeontology.

Whatever the history of its evolution and origins the richness of the insect fauna of oak is well-established[2] [11]. In this account a very liberal interpretation is given to the term 'insect', as is ecologically justifiable. Other arthropods, especially spiders and mites are important constituents of the fauna of oak and it would be unreasonable to exclude them on purely taxonomic grounds. Insect nomenclature follows the appropriate part or edition of Kloet & Hincks[12] [13] [14] and names of spiders are those in Locket & Millidge[15].

Oak in its habitat

Except perhaps in a few cases the oak tree is not the total environment, or habitat, of any insect species. The tree cannot exist, of course, without the soil in which it grows or the air which surrounds it. But the soil is also essential to a wide range of species which either pupate or overwinter in it, even though they actually feed on oak foliage, while the air is obviously the medium by which colonisation of new trees by flying insects is effected. Many species which either feed on quite different plants, or are general predators not specifically preying on oak-feeders, may make use of the oak tree in many different ways. Some of these are quite casual, nonspecific and unimportant but others, apparently of a minor nature, are actually essential for the maintenance of populations of particular species.

It is relevant, therefore, to consider the oak tree in its woodland, forest, park or hedgerow habitat and to recognise the potential importance of factors such as differences in climate, latitude and soil and the proximity of ponds or streams in modifying a part of the fauna. The individual tree is also often part of a much larger entity—woodland or forest—and this may be an important factor for some insect species, though not for others. Oak as the ecologically dominant, or co-dominant, species in many woodlands may have a considerable influence on other plant species which themselves have their own associated insect faunas.

By considering oak at different levels of complexity a comprehensive and complicated picture of the ecology of woodlands can be built up, such as that given in outline by Elton[16]. Here, the oak-insect relationship is considered chiefly in terms of the different habitat components which the tree provides.

Structural diversity of the oak tree

In this paper the word 'habitat' is used to denote what might be called the 'total habitat' of a species. Thus, if an insect species feeds on oak leaves, pupates in the soil and overwinters among leaf litter its habitat is conceived as consisting of oak foliage+soil+litter. In this sense, foliage or soil or litter may be considered as components of the habitat; an alternative term might be 'biotope'. Some authors, particularly in America, use the term niche in the sense of total habitat, eg Pielou[17]. The obviously different structures which constitute an oak tree provide many of the habitat components of a very varied number of insect species. Phytophagous species are emphasised in this paper at the expense of predatory and parasitic ones, not only because the feeding relationship between insect and tree is direct, rather than indirect, but also because the relationship has been more thoroughly studied. Fig 1 gives a simple division of oak into its obvious constituent structures and compares these with the overall classification of woodland 'habitat types' of Elton & Miller[18].

The whole tree

An entire single tree can form an important ecological component of a species' habitat in a behavioural sense. Perhaps the best-known example is the 'master oak' which serves as an important, indeed essential, landmark for the assembling of the sexes of the Purple emperor butterfly (*Apatura iris* (L.))[19]. The phenomenon appears to be similar to that of 'hill topping' which is known to occur in some tropical species of butterfly. Unfortunately the literature on the 'master trees' of the Purple emperor is fragmentary and tantalisingly scanty. A fairly wide range of tree species may serve as 'master trees', but oaks are by far the most popular. Some information has been acquired when a master tree has been felled; this often results in the extinction of a colony, or its reduction in numbers. It appears that species which have populations with small numbers of adults, which are relatively well scattered, derive an important benefit by assembling together at a fixed point for courtship and mating flights. This may be a more important feature of the behaviour of some butterflies than has been realised. The mechanism whereby it is achieved is not known.

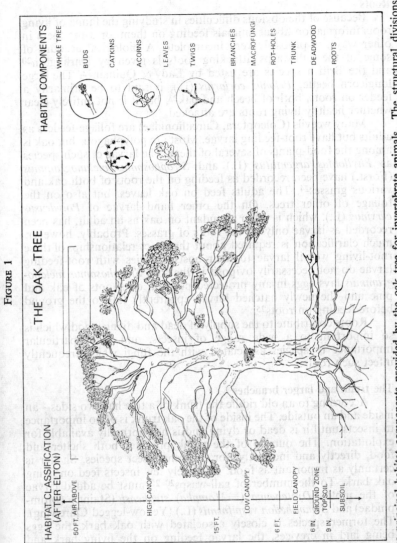

FIGURE 1

THE OAK TREE

HABITAT COMPONENTS

WHOLE TREE
BUDS
CATKINS
ACORNS
LEAVES
TWIGS
BRANCHES
MACROFUNGI
ROT-HOLES
TRUNK
DEADWOOD
ROOTS

HABITAT CLASSIFICATION
(AFTER ELTON)

50 FT. AIR ABOVE
HIGH CANOPY
15 FT.
LOW CANOPY
6 FT.
FIELD CANOPY
6 IN. GROUND ZONE
TOPSOIL
9 IN.
SUBSOIL

The principal habitat components provided by the oak tree for invertebrate animals. The structural divisions of the habitat classification of Elton are included for comparison.

Roots

Because of the obvious difficulties in studying the fauna of living roots information about animals feeding on them, or using them in other ways, is probably very incomplete. A biological account of some of the gall-wasps attacking roots is given by Darlington[20] and the British species are listed by Eady & Quinlan[22]. The large longicorn beetle, *Prionus coriarius* (L.), is said to be primarily a feeder on roots, both of beech and oak[23], but it is not entirely clear whether healthy living roots are attacked.

Many weevils (Coleoptera, Curculionidae) are foliage-feeders as adults but have root-feeding larvae. Most are polyphagous but oak is among the food-plants of several of them. The larvae of such species as *Phyllobius argentatus* (L.) and *Strophosomus melanogrammus* (Forst.) have been recorded as feeding on the roots of both oak and various grasses[24]. The adults feed on oak leaves, but also on the foliage of other trees. On the other hand larvae of *Polydrusus cervinus* (L.), which is often abundant on oak as an adult, has been recorded as larvae only on the roots of grasses. Probably, however, much clarification is required about the exact relationships of these root-living weevil larvae to their hosts. Species with root-feeding larvae do not necessarily oviposit in the soil. *Strophosomus melanogrammus* lays eggs in any protected position on shoots of oak and pine and the newly hatched larvae apparently fall to the ground before feeding on roots[25].

Roots contribute to the supply of dead and dying wood which is so important to a wide range of insects, and is of particular importance to species associated with the fungi which frequently infect such roots.

The trunk and larger branches

According to an old riddle the trunk of a tree has two sides—an inside and an outside. The inside of the oak trunk is of no importance to insects until it is dead or dying and is not normally available for exploitation. The outside of the trunk provides both shelter and food, directly and indirectly, for different insect species. Shelter is certainly as important as food. Relatively few insects feed on living oak bark. To the number of gall-wasps[20] [22] must be added larvae of the moths *Dystebenna* (=*Mompha*) *stephensi* (Staint.) (Momphidae) and *Synanthedon vespiformis* (L.) (Yellow-legged Clearwing). The former species is closely associated with oak bark, the eggs being laid in crevices, the larvae feeding on the living bark and pupating there, and the adults resting on the trunk[54]. *S. vespiformis* does not seem to be so clearly associated with living bark, since it also attacks stumps[28]. Of the five species of Coccidae (Homoptera) which attack oak *Kermes quercus* (L.) is specifically associated with crevices in the bark, *K. roboris* (Fourc.) occurs on terminal branches, whilst *Eulecanium ciliatum* (Dougl.) is chiefly found on branches three to five years old[55]. Two species of *Stomaphis* (Aphidae) also feed on oak bark[11].

The trunk and large branches of an oak tree are normally the habitat of many algae and lichens and sometimes mosses which live epiphytically on the tree. Gilbert[29] distinguished seven basic components of the external tree-trunk ecosystem on the bark of ash (*Fraxinus excelsior* L.) , of which six were animal groups. It is likely that the fauna of oak bark consists of the same ecological components but that these are richer in species. The herbivores which graze the autotrophic plants, algae and lichens, include such animals as bark-lice (Psocoptera), lepidopterous larvae, expecially Psychidae and Arctiidae-Lithosiinae, and beetle-mites (Acari-Cryptostigmata). Preferences of the animal species for epiphytes on particular tree species have not been frequently recorded, but Scorer[30] lists the species of Macrolepidoptera associated with lichens growing on different trees. Oak has seven species, beech five, and Scots pine three but no other tree species more than two. Although some of the bark-inhabiting Psocoptera show preferences between the bark of coniferous and deciduous trees[31] most occur on both types of tree and no great differences are known between the fauna of oak bark and the bark of other broad-leaved trees.

Many of the predators inhabiting bark also occur just as commonly on twigs and foliage and few if any predators are specific to the bark of oak. The cryptic coloration of the adults and larvae of the arboreal species of the mirid bug genus *Phytocoris* (subgenus *Phytocoris sensu stricto*) indicates that they rest on bark and Gilbert[29] found *P. populi* (L.) common on ash bark. All the species in this subgenus are found on oak[32] but also on other trees; the predatory biology of some species which are also found on apple was studied by Collyer[33]. Other predatory bugs found especially on the trunk and branches of oak include the Reduviid *Empicoris vagabundus* (L.)[34] and the Micryophysid *Loricula elegantula* (Baerens.)[35] [36] which numbers barklice among its prey[37]. Predacious Diptera of the families Empidae (Tachydrominae)[38] and Dolichopodidae (species of *Medeterus*)[39] are also particularly associated with tree-trunks. Species of both groups tend to run over the trunk surface rather than to take flight[40]. The spiders of tree trunks include representatives of several families, both web-spinners and others[41]; all are, of course, predacious.

The shelter provided by the oak trunk can be considered as three-dimensional or two-dimensional. The bark is deeply fissured and cracked compared, for instance, with the bark of beech. A recent study shows that more spiders are associated with oak bark than with that of birch or Scots pine[41], presumably because of its more deeply fissured structure. Some spiders are well known to over-winter in the cracks of oak bark, for example *Clubiona brevipes* Blackwall, which moves from oak foliage in autumn to sites either on trunks or on the ground[42]. The larva of the Merville du Jour moth (*Dichonia aprilina* (L.)) is both cryptic and behaviourally adapted for concealment, as it wedges itself tightly into a crevice of oak bark by day[26]; at night it feeds on the foliage. Few species of Lepidoptera pupate on the trunks of trees but among them are such examples as the Brussels lace moth (*Cleorodes lichenaria* (Hufn.)) and some of the Lymantriidae (Tussock moths etc)[43]. The fissured bark of oak is particularly suitable for the spinning of cocoons. The trunk is also suitable as a place for oviposition sites in some species. The Oak bush-cricket lays eggs in crevices in the bark of oak and other trees[53].

Tree trunks are regarded as being the natural resting sites of most cryptically coloured moths[44]. The principles of concealment in animals have been discussed in detail by Cott[45]; except that a richer growth of epiphytes may be favoured on rough bark compared with smooth, cracks and fissures are not advantageous to cryptic animals and the concealment achieved may be considered to be two-dimensional. Although there are many species of cryptic moths only two groups are mentioned here, the Geometridae-Ennominae and the Pyralidae-Scopariinae, In the latter group two genera, *Scoparia* and *Eudonia* are now recognised, but formerly all the species were classified as *Scoparia*. The group has mosses as its predominant larval food and most species rest by day on tree-trunks, from which they are often readily disturbed. A few species, such as *E. murana* (Curt.), rarely settle on tree-trunks, but others, particularly *S. ambigualis* (Treits.) and *S. basistrigalis* Knaggs prefer the trunks of oak to those of other trees[46]. Attention has been drawn to the ecology and genetics of crypsis in Lepidoptera through the phenomenon of industrial melanism[47], about which there is now a considerable literature. It is established that this crypsis is primarily a defence against predation by birds[48], and the ecological role of the tree-trunk and its epiphytes is well known. It is of interest that many of the cryptic geometrid moths, and indeed those of other groups, feed as larvae on oak foliage. A few, such as the Great oak beauty (*Boarmia roboraria* (Denis & Schiff.)), are more or less restricted to oak, but most, like the Peppered moth (*Biston betularia* (L.)), on which so much work on melanism has been done, are rather polyphagous. The importance of bird predation in the ecology of these moths is further indicated by the fact that most pupate underground. The exceptions usually pupate in cocoons among the foliage. The Lymantriids mentioned above as pupating on the trunk are frequently protected by urticating hairs.

Twigs

In one sense twigs may be regarded as intermediate between the larger branches and the leaves. When young they are still soft enough to provide the food of some species and healthy twigs, unlike the healthy branches, have a number, although a small number, of internal feeders. In one important aspect they resemble branches, and to some extent buds, but differ from the leaves: they are present throughout the year.

The sawfly, *Janus femoratus* Curt., has larvae which bore in twigs of oak[49] producing slight swellings[50]. Although the Twig-cutting weevil, *Rhynchites caeruleus* (Deg.), usually oviposits in twigs of rosaceous shrubs and trees it has been recorded locally in numbers on oak[27]. The twigs are severed by the female weevil after the eggs are laid and the larvae feed in the dying tissue. The eggs of *Lasiorhynchites cavifrons* (Gyll.) are laid in the thickening of one year old twigs at the insertion of a bud[24] and the larva bores in the twig. Eggs of *L. olivaceus* (Gyll.) (=*ophthalmicus* auct) are also laid in oak twigs[24].

Twigs and leaves are contiguous on a tree and many species of invertebrates, especially of course the predators, are found on both twigs and foliage. Twigs are particularly important to animals on a deciduous tree in a temperate climate, in which a long period must be spent between one growing season and the next. Many insect species over-winter away from, but near, the oak tree as adults amongst litter or mosses or as pupae in the soil. Such species re-invade the tree in spring or summer in the adult stage, often by flight. Other species over-winter as eggs or larvae, and for these animals twigs are especially important. Eggs may be laid either in the wood or on its surface. Twenty-seven species of mirid bugs are associated with oak in Britain[32] and all but one (*Deraeocoris lutescens* (Schill.)) over-winter in the egg stage. The eggs are deeply inserted into the twigs, but the species vary in preferring the plain wood (several species) or leaf scars (*Megacoelum infusum* (H.-S.)) or cracks and lenticels (*Psallus perrisi* (Muls. & Rey), *Cyllecoris histrionicus* (L.))[32 33 51]. Most insects which lay over-wintering eggs lay them on, rather than in, the bark, but crevices and cracks are often preferred. Winter moth (*Operophtera brumata* (L.)) eggs are laid in such places[52 63].

Those insect larvae which over-winter usually do so on the twigs, or amongst the buds. Many small lepidopterous larvae spin stout silken hibernacula in which to over-winter but the oak-feeding *Coleophora lutipennella* (Zett.) has been observed to attach its larval case to twigs and to remain in it during the winter in Monks Wood, Huntingdon. Four other species of *Coleophora* also feed on oak.

Before twigs become woody they may be described as shoots. The growing points of plants, besides their obvious indirect relationships to insects, provide food for Heteroptera, which suck the sap of such structures in preference to less nutritious ones. This is discussed more fully under the fauna of buds. The scale-insect *Asterodiapsis* (= *Asterolecanium*) *variolosa* (Ratz.) develops on twigs[55]; Darlington classifies it as forming the simplest of galls on oak[20]. Most insect predators of the oak canopy cannot be associated particularly with either twigs or leaves; they will be considered together as an ecological component of the foliage.

Buds

The buds of trees are a specialised habitat component for insects because of their relatively small size and the fact that they are well protected by bud scales for long periods of their existence. Both reproductive and vegetative buds may be attacked, but the former tend to be both larger and more nutritious in that they contain more protein. When the buds break and then burst in spring the winter protection afforded by the bud scales is largely lost. There is thus a clear distinction between the fauna of the buds in their protected phase and that found after the buds are more vulnerable to attack. In the protected phase buds are attacked by the larvae of several species of gall-wasp[20] [21] [22] [66], by gall-midges (Cecidomyiidae)[67], and also by the larvae of weevils. *Caenorhinus aeneovirens* (Marsh.) appears as an adult beetle for a very short time on oak trees in spring as the leaves expand, the larvae feeding in the buds[24]. It is probable that some species of the weevil genus *Coeliodes* also feed as larvae in buds, particularly *C. dryados* (Gmel.) but the biology of these species is very imperfectly known. Unlike some other trees and shrubs *Q. robur* and *Q. petraea* do not appear to be the hosts of bud-inhabiting gall mites (Eriophyidae) [56] [57], but this may very well be because such mites have not been looked for.

Many foliage-feeding insects over-winter in sites in or near the buds, enabling them to reach their source of food as soon as the buds burst. The eggs of the Purple hairstreak butterfly (*Quercusia quercus* (L.)) are often found among the terminal buds of an oak twig. The eggs hatch about mid-May and the larvae feed in the buds and later on the expanded leaves. The larva is cryptically coloured and patterned, bearing a close resemblence to the bud scales which are discarded from the tree after expansion of the foliage. Other Lepidoptera also frequently lay their eggs close to the buds. Some mirid bugs oviposit directly into the buds instead of laying eggs in the wood of twigs. *Calocoris quadripunctatus* (Vill.) is particularly known to do this, the buds very often being killed[51].

Although many insects feed on the tissue of buds before the leaves expand this type of feeding is less opportunistic in some groups than in others. Heteroptera, particularly the Miridae, differ from other Hemiptera in being selective feeders on tissues with high protein content[1]. Many also take animal food, an obvious alternative source of protein, though in varying degrees. Pollen may also be taken as a protein source. In a study of a phytoseid mite on apple, pollen was found to be effective in permitting the development of the first generation of mites in the absence of animal prey[58].

Catkins

Pollen appears to be a relatively unimportant source of food to the insect fauna of oak. Indeed, the fauna of the catkins is small in *Quercus* and dominated by the gall-causing Cynipidae[20] [21] [22] [50]. However, the larvae of at least one gall-midge inhabit oak catkins; it has been given the name *Contarinia amenti* Kieffer. The catkins of all trees are very short-lived but those of Salicaceae, for instance, appear to support a much larger fauna than those of oak. Several factors seem to be responsible for this, but the more important ones seem to be the dryness and attenuated structure of the oak catkin and its appearance relatively late in the year, when drying and shrivelling occur rapidly. Also, the oak catkin appears to shrivel in situ on the tree more often than the catkins of *Salix* and *Populus*. These genera have catkins which support the early larvae of Lepidoptera; these caterpillars feed on plants in the ground flora after the aments fall to the ground. In a rather similar way the larvae of the moth *Adela reamurella* (L.) (=*viridella* (Scop.)) feed first on oak flowers (and those of other trees) and then fall to the ground where they form a case of vegetable fragments and feed on dead leaves[59]. An alternative way of life is for the insect larva to feed up rapidly in the catkin so that it is mature and ready to pupate in the soil when the catkins fall, or very shortly afterwards. This occurs in the weevil genus *Dorytomus,* species of which have larvae which feed in the catkins of *Salix* and *Populus.*

The pollen of many plants is gathered by bees, and that of oak is certainly collected by honeybees (*Apis mellifera* L.)[60], and possibly by other species. This is despite the fact that oak is anemophilous.

Acorns

Considering their importance to vertebrate animals acorns are attacked by relatively few insects. Two of the commonest species which infest living, healthy acorns are the weevils *Curculio venosus* (Grav.) and *C. glandium* Marsh., whose larvae, like those of most weevils, feed internally. The comparative ecology of the two species is not known. Larvae of two tortricid moths, *Cydia* (=*Laspeyresia*) *splendana* (Hübn.) and *Pammene fasciana* (L.) (=*juliana* (Steph.)) are also internal feeders in acorns. Information about the larvae of gall-midges which inhabit acorns was summarised by Barnes[61]. Four species have been reared from acorns. One, a *Dasyneura* species perhaps referable to *D. (Perrisia) squamosa* Tavares, appears to feed actually within the acorn, in contrast to *Contarinia* sp which apparently lives between the acorn proper and its cup. *Clinodiplosis* sp is probably an inquiline of the galls caused by *Dasyneura* while *Lestodiplosis* is likely to be a predator of the *Contarinia* larvae. The gall-wasp *Synergus clandestinus* Eady lives as a larva in stunted acorns, either forming gall-tissue or being free-living; this is unusual, since all other *Synergus* species are inquilines in the galls of other Cynipidae[22]. *Andricus quercuscalicis* (Burgs.), a gall wasp forming conspicuous galls on the surface acorns, is mentioned by Darlington[20] (see pps 309-310), while two species of *Callirhytis* form galls in acorns of *Q. cerris*[22].

The organisms associated with the acorns of *Q. rubra* were studied in Illinois by Winston[62]. The acorn microsere he describes starts with the living fruit, which, like the acorns of *Q. robur* and *Q. petraea,* is initially attacked by a species of *Curculio*. Essentially, however, the microsere described is a series of stages in the decay of the acorn and has affinities with the successions observed in dead wood.

Leaves

Oak foliage is the most important source of food which the tree provides, both in terms of biomass consumed and the number of species directly and indirectly dependant on it. Certain aspects of the biology of phytophagous insects on oak foliage have been intensively studied and some are described by Gradwell[63]. (see pps 182-192). A characteristic of oak leaves, besides the very large number of insects which feed on them, is their increasing tannin content as summer succeeds spring[64]. This certainly affects the growth of some species of Lepidoptera[65] and may well account, at least in part, for the fact that fewer insects are found feeding on oak foliage in late summer than in spring.

Insects feeding on leaves are particularly vulnerable to predation. The problem of visual exposure has been solved by the adoption of cryptic colouration and in other ways. Notwithstanding the thin, lamina-like structure of the leaves many insects feed internally in them. The gall-causing species have specialised structures in which to live and feed, and many species of Cynipidae[20] [21] [22] [50] [60] and Cecidomyiidae[67] gall leaves, variously preferring the leaf-blade, the veins, or the petiole and midrib. The larval habitat of the moth *Heliozela stanneella* (F.R.) has been described as a gall[50] but the feeding habit may perhaps best be described as intermediate between mining and gall-causing as the species is not mentioned by Mani[68]. *H. sericiella* (Haw.) also feeds in petioles and midribs of oak leaves[50] [54], but is perhaps not specifically distinct[69].

Leaf mining is a very common phenomenon among insects and has evolved in several orders, notably the Lepidoptera, Coleoptera, Hymenoptera and Diptera. The structure of the mine has received considerable attention and a specialised terminology[70], and there are comprehensive catalogues and descriptions of European mines and miners[71] [72]. Although the mining larva is not protected against browsing animals, the mine is often a visual protection against predation and, unless the whole leaf is removed, the larva is also safeguarded against detachment from its host. Larvae of the different orders which mine leaves show remarkable convergence of morphology, with loss of legs and the adoption of a depressed body-form. Many different kinds of mine have been described and named but here it is perhaps only necessary to distinguish *blotch* and *serpentine* (or gallery) miners and to note that the leaf parenchyma may be removed from the upper or lower sides of the leaf, or both together, in which case the mine is particularly visible. Lepidopterous larvae greatly predominate among the leaf-miners of oak, there being about thirty species of Microlepidoptera known from Britain, although many more occur in Europe[71]. Some species have larvae which are miners in the early instars. For instance, *Bucculatrix ulmella* Zell. later feeds externally on the undersides of the leaves, whilst

Lampronia oehlmanniella (Treits.) constructs a case and feeds on dead leaves[54]. The oak-feeding *Coleophora* species are included among the miners because they eat out the parenchyma and leave the epidermis; the larval case forms, in a sense, an extension of the mine. Two large groups of leaf-mining Lepidoptera which both have several species feeding on oak are the Nepticulidae (*Stigmella* and *Ectoedemia* spp) and Gracillariidae-Lithocolletinae (*Phyllonorycter* (=*Lithocolletis*) spp). All the species in these two groups can be identified not only from the adult insects but also from the mines in most cases[71] [72] [74]. The Nepticulidae variously make blotch or serpentine mines and although no species of oak-feeding *Phyllonorycter* mines the upperside of the leaf, as do some species associated with other trees, the mines can be distinguished by other characteristics. Miller[74] has very recently published results of studies on the distribution and parasites of two species of *Phyllonorycter* feeding on oak, *P. quercifoliella* (Zell.) and *P. harrisella* (L.). Larval mines (both species combined) had an aggregated distribution on trees and also on leaves. Second generation mines were $4\frac{1}{2}$ times more abundant than those of the first generation. There was no difference between density of mines on leaves at 6m and those on lower leaves, but at 18m the density of mines was significantly smaller. 15 species of Hymenoptera, mostly Chalcidoidea, were recorded as parasites of the two species.

Three species of the weevil genus *Rhynchaenus* (Coleoptera) commonly form blotch mines, *R. pilosus* (F.) and *R. quercus* (L.) which are restricted to oak and *R. avellanae* (Donovan) which also feeds on *Corylus*[24]. The sawfly *Profenusa pygmaea* (Klug) mines as a larva in the upper side of the leaf and is apparently parthenogenetic[73].

The insects which feed externally on leaf-tissue may be basically divided into two types, those with sucking mouthparts which feed on the sap and those with biting mouthparts which ingest whole particles of green leaves; both groups contain numerous representatives which are associated with oak. The group with suctional mouthparts contains only the Hemiptera and some Thysanoptera. The species of Hemiptera may be classified into an ecological series in which activity is by degrees reduced. The Hemiptera-Heteroptera consist of entirely active species which can exploit the more nutritious soft parts of the foliage and shoots and are also able to take animal food to an extent which varies from species to species and according to the availability of other proteinaceous food. Large, particularly active forms, such as species of *Phytocoris*, consume much animal food[33] and even more delicate bugs, such as the many species of *Psallus,* probably need animal food, or at least an amount of protein, to complete development[51] [52].

The Leafhoppers (Auchenorhyncha) are also fairly active Hemiptera on oak, although they are not known to take animal food. About thirty species are associated with *Quercus* in Britain, but only a few are particularly restricted to it. The Typhlocybids *Eurhadina concinna* (Germ.), *E. kirschbaumi* (Wagner)[76] and *E. pulchella*

(Fall.) are specific to oak[77] [78] [79]. Other species of Typhlocybidae are mostly associated with several species of tree and not exclusively with oak[80]. The Cicadellidae which feed on oak, but also on other trees or field layer vegetation, include *Ledra aurita* (L.)[81], *Thamnotettix dilutior* (Kirschb.) and *Speudotettix fusculus* (Fall.)[82]; *Iassus lanio* (L.) is perhaps more consistently found on *Quercus*[81]. On the other hand several Auchenorhyncha which occur commonly as adults on oak can only feed on the foliage in the adult state. The larvae of *Cercopis vulnerata* Illig.[83] and species of *Cixius*[84] (two unrelated groups) are subterranean and probably feed on grasses. Auchenorhyncha are subject to parasitism by a particularly interesting range of parasitoid insects, including Strepsiptera, Dryinidae (Hymenoptera) and Pipunculidae (Diptera). *Ledra aurita* is the likely host of the largest British pipunculid, *Nephrocerus flavicornis* Zett.[85].

Among the Sternorhyncha (Hemiptera) only a single psyllid, *Trioza remota* Först., feeds on oak foliage; it is said to over-winter on conifers[77]—another example of oak forming only a part of an insect species' habitat. Six species of aphids, other than the bark-inhabiting *Stomaphis*, are recorded from oak in Britain by Jones[11], but Dr H. L. G. Stroyan tells me that this number has recently been increased. The aphids on oak are members of the more primitive groups. These Hemiptera are not as active as Heteroptera or Auchenorhyncha but are less sedentary than Coccoidea (scales) or Aleyrodidae (white flies) among the sternorhynchous Hemiptera. In the former group males of *Quadraspidoitus zonatus* (Frauenfeldt) are fixed on the undersides of leaves but the females occur invariably on branches[55]. The aleyrodid *Pealius quercus* (Signoret) is found on foliage of oak[86], where the larvae have been found to have aggregated populations[87]. Psyllids, aleyrodids and coccids are all to some extent protected in their early stages by secretions of wax.

A few Thysanoptera feed on oak leaves by sucking sap from the cells. Morrison[88] mentions *Oxythrips quercicola* Bagnall, and *Thrips minutissimus* L. also occurs on oak.

The biting insects which feed externally on oak leaves are taxonomically more diverse than the species with suctorial mouth-parts but exhibit a similarly large range of adaptations to reduce predation. A very large number of lepidopterous caterpillars feed on oak. Scorer lists 110 Macrolepidoptera[30], but includes some doubtful or unusual records, whilst 43 species of Microlepidoptera, other than miners and casebearers, feed on oak leaves[54]; a few other species are added by Jones[11] from Professor Varley's records. Leaf-rolls are commonly formed by some species, particularly Tortricidae, whilst many species spin leaves together to give protection. The leaves may be spun together loosely or a fold may be made in a single leaf or, again, two leaves may be joined tightly together. Several species have larvae which live communally in a silken web; examples are the Lackey moth, *Malacosoma neustria* (L.), the Blossom underwing, *Orthosia miniosa* (Denis & Schiff.) and the pyralid, *Acrobasis consociella* (Hübn.) Leaf-rolls are also formed by insects of other orders. The characteristic rolls of the weevil *Attelabus nitens* (L.) contain the larvae but are constructed, not by them, but by the adult female weevils after the eggs are laid; in Europe, at least, another attelabid is an inquiline as a larva in the *A. nitens* leaf-rolls[24].

Benson[89] discusses the protective devices of sawfly larvae, which superficially are very similar to lepidopterous caterpillars, and often have very similar defence mechanisms. Only about twelve sawfly species, in fact, feed externally on oak leaves[49 73 90], but these exhibit several of the methods of protection which Benson lists. Thus the larvae of three species of *Caliroa* (only one of which is specific to oak) are covered with slime, whilst the rare *Neurotomus mandibularis* (Zadd.) forms leaf-rolls which are inhabited, unusually, by pairs of larvae; *Pamphilius sylvarum* (Steph.) probably forms a specialised larval abode on oak leaves as do other species of *Pamphilius* on other trees[91].

Many Coleoptera feed on oak leaves in the adult stage, expecially the 'short-nosed' weevils which are root-feeders as larvae. Several of the *Phyllobius* and *Polydrusus* species are metallic green in colour and may be protectively adapted to inhabit oak foliage. Weevils with specialised larvae feeding in oak galls, leaf-mines, buds and acorns all eat oak leaves in the adult stage.

The gall midges of oak leaves are described by Barnes[19] and some of the species are mentioned by Darlington[20], who also gives accounts of some of the cynipid galls on leaves. These are also fully described and figured by Eady & Quinlan[22]. Askew[21] has studied the food-webs based on several of these cynipid galls, particularly that of *Cynips divisa* Hartig on oak leaves.

Not all phytophagous insects which inhabit oak foliage actually feed on the leaves. Like aphids on most trees, especially *Tilia,* those species associated with *Quercus* occasionally produce honeydew in copious amounts. This is a source of food to many species of invertebrate animals, particularly ants[92]. The Purple emperor butterfly feeds very largely from oak foliage on 'moisture'[19]. Feeding trees are distinct from the master trees discussed earlier. Honeydew is a favourable substrate for the growth of fungi and other forms of microflora which develop on the surfaces of the leaves of plants[93]. New has described the abundance of foliage-frequenting Psocoptera, which feed indiscriminantly on different plant constituents of such microfloras, on different species of trees[94]. Oak and hawthorn (*Crataegus monogyna* Jacq.) are particularly favoured hosts among the deciduous trees. Oak leaves usually support large populations of *Ectopsocus briggsi* McLachlan and *Caecilius flavidus* (Steph.), and smaller numbers of other species. Both of the species occurring abundantly on oak have three generations a year and over-winter in various developmental stages[95]. Dead foliage on the tree is the commonest over-wintering site for *E. briggsi*.

Associated with the diverse and abundant phytophagous fauna of oak foliage are an immense number of predacious, parasitic and, particularly, parasitoid animals. In the last group are the parasitic flies (Diptera, Tachinidae) and parasitic Hymenoptera. Tachinids parasitize beetles, sawfly larvae and many other animals, but particularly lepidopterous larvae. Most of these parasitoids have a range of hosts, though they tend to keep to one type, for instance butterfly and moth larvae occurring in a particular biotope. The abundant oak-feeding larvae are, of course, hosts for many species. Records of hosts are given by Audcent[96] and Day[97] and summarised information by Emden[89]. The parasitic Hymenoptera consist of several groups and families and the range of hosts is much wider than in the Tachinidae; a very useful summary is given by Richards[99]. Askew's study of the food-webs based on various cynipid gall-wasps[21] has already been mentioned. He records 44 species of Chalcidoidea of which these galls are the hosts. It is evident that no more can be done here than to indicate briefly the enormous numbers of parasitoid insects indirectly associated with oak, and the great complexity of their relationships with their hosts and the hosts' foodplant. Of course, hyperparasitism is an additional complexity in this web of inter-relationships.

With such a rich source of potential prey the foliage of oak is well endowed with a wide range of predacious species. Many of these are more or less adventitious on the tree, such as some of the common ladybirds (Coleoptera, Coccinellidae), which also occur on many other plants. Many predators, however, are more closely associated with *Quercus*. Thus the Oak bush-cricket (*Meconema thalassinum* (Deg.)), despite being almost entirely carnivorous, is particularly found on oak trees where it feeds nocturnally on any suitable prey[53]. *Calasoma inquisitor* (L.) is a large 'ground' beetle associated particularly with oak[100], where it feeds at night, mainly on caterpillars, like other species in the genus[101]. Although the British Neuroptera (lacewings) are all predacious both as adults and larvae many species prefer either deciduous or coniferous trees. Among the former *Hemerobius humulinus* L., *H. lutescens* F., *Sympherobius elegans* (Steph.), *S. pygmaeus* (Rambur), *Chrysopa flava* (Scop.) and *Nathanica fulviceps* (Steph.) are particularly found on oak[102]. Jones[11] lists other predators which inhabit oak foliage, among them species of Phytoseid mites, which feed mainly on phytophagous mites. Such general predators as the flower bugs, species of *Anthocoris* (Heteropera), are very characteristic of oak foliage in summer both as adults and larvae; the eggs are often laid in the leaf blade[32]. As a final example of a group of general predators the spiders (Araneae) may be mentioned. *Theridion pallens* Blackwall is often extremely abundant on oak foliage, while *Anyphaena accentuata* (Walck.), *Evarcha falcata* (Clerck) and *Diaea dorsata* (F.) (a green species) are examples of other species which are frequently found on oak, though also on other trees.

Occasionally phytophagous insects which are restricted to other plants are found in numbers on oak (and also on other trees). The reasons for this behaviour are not known but are possibly to be sought in the microclimatological characteristics of oak foliage. An example is the aggregation of species of *Apion,* particularly those feeding on legumes, on oak[103]; this appears to occur particularly in the autumn.

Macrofungi

Elton[16] uses the useful term MFB (Macrofungi fruiting body) as shorthand to denote those structures which are important as habitats for many different arthropods—mites, beetles and flies in particular—and are formed by various species of fungi, mostly Basidiomycetes. Although not as well studied as some other fungi, especially *Polyporus betulinus* (Bull.) Fr. on birch[104] [105], some fungi associated with oak and their fauna are discussed by Elton[16]. Hingley has studied the fauna of the MFB of the Ascomycete, *Daldinia concentrica* (Bolton ex Fries) Cesati & Notaris, which has been recorded on oak though its usual host is ash, and has reviewed the literature on the animals associated with this group of fungi[106]. The coleopteran associations of MFBs have been particularly studied; Elton lists five species of MFB specifically attached to oak and 16 species of several families found in varying degrees of dependence in them by Dr K. Paviour-Smith (Southern). Most of the beetles feed on the MFB itself and some are restricted to particular species of fungi. For instance the small rove-beetle *Gyrophaena strictula* Erichs. feeds particularly in the fungus *Daedalea quercina* L. ex Fr.

Dead and dying wood

The substrate on which macrofungi grow is dead wood, but this is only a minor facet of its importance to a very large number of animals. Elton described dying and dead wood as 'one of the two or three greatest resources for animal species in a natural forest'[16]. To this resource oak makes a very sizeable contribution, but it is probably true to say that in general there is a lower degree of specificity of animal species associated with dead wood of a particular tree species than is the case with the living habitat components of the tree. For instance, Duffy[107] gave it as his experience that the physical condition of the dead wood was more important than the species of tree to which it belonged to the larvae of the longhorn beetles (Cerambycidae).

Although succession is an important ecological phenomenon in all the habitat components of insects which are provided by oak it is particularly relevant to the fauna of dead wood. It is unusual for insects to actually kill an oak tree. Much more frequently a part of the tree, or the whole plant, dies or is killed and this initiates a succession of animal species which exploit the wood in various stages of decay. Even the bark beetles (Scolytidae), which are often the first colonists of dead wood, attack only after the tree has been killed[108]. Fourteen species attack oak in Britain, but many of them also occur on wood of other trees. The initial colonists of dead wood usually consist of species which either themselves possess a cellulase or are able to use symbiotic fungi to break down the resistant wood (eg the Ambrosia beetles). These are followed by mycetophagous species, there being a close relationship between dead wood, fungal infection and the fauna. In this phase of succession subcortical species may be important. The bugs *Aradus depressus* (F.) and *Aneurus* spp feed on fungal mycelia beneath bark of boughs and stumps of oak and other trees[32], where many other insects, such as species of *Rhizophagus* (Coleoptera) are found. Predators and parasites follow many of these species. The exclusively sub-cortical bug *Xylocoris cursitans* (Fall.) preys on beetle larvae and springtails (Collembola) among other animals[32]. Later colonists may use dead wood for nesting, for example species of Crabronidae (Hymenoptera) [109]. In the later stages of decay wood-mould may be formed, an important habitat for beetles such as the rare *Gnorimus variabilis* (L.)[23][110]. Often, however, the fauna becomes more generalised until it becomes similar to that of the soil to which the end-products of decay of the wood contribute.

Once living wood becomes dead its role in providing habitat components for species of invertebrate animals is determined by several factors. It may remain attached to the tree for a while, or fall to the ground. It may be exposed totally or in part to the heating and drying power of the sun or remain in shaded and moist conditions. And its physical and chemical state may be conditioned by the animals attacking it. The fauna of dead wood has long attracted the attention of ecologists in Britain and the U.S.A. Much of the early work was done on felled logs[111][112] (see also Fager[113]). Elton's masterly account of the animals which inhabit dead wood[16] reflects his long-standing interest in this particular subject, an interest which Dr K. Southern and Mr C. A. Elbourn are developing. The mite fauna of dead wood proves to be of particular importance and interest but taxonomic problems tend to hold up the ecological work.

Information on the specific fauna of dead oak may be obtained from more general accounts and from the more anecdotal records of collectors, particularly of Coleoptera. Many rare beetles, such as species of Cerambycidae, Elateridae, Pselaphidae and many other families, are associated with old dead trees, often oaks, and these perhaps have been overemphasised in the literature at the expense of the commoner species. Fisher gave[114] an account of the insects attacking oak timber, from a forester's point of view. Larkin and Elbourn[115] investigated the fauna of dead wood on live trees and concluded, in general, that the fauna was less rich than that of dead wood on the ground, probably because the wood was drier.

Rot-holes

Cavities in the trunk and larger branches are characteristic of mature trees. When the cavities are dry they may contribute to the supply of dead wood in the tree but when they are rain-filled they provide a distinct habitat component of their own for aquatic animals. However, the animal species which rot-holes support are rarely, if ever, specific to the tree species in which the rot-holes are. The so-called 'arboreal' species of mosquitos are among the best known animals of rot-holes. *Anopheles plumbeus* Steph. and *Aedes geniculatus* (Oliv.) have been recorded from rot-holes in oaks, but also more commonly from holes in other tree species[116]. Other Diptera and the beetle *Prionocyphon serricornis* (Müll.) also breed in rot-holes[16] [110].

Nests

Animal products such as carrion and dung may be occasionally associated with oak, but animal artefacts[16] [18] are frequently present in the form of nests, not only of birds and squirrels but also of social insects such as ants, bees, wasps and hornets. Nests of any one species are never specific to oak though they may be characteristic of it. In the absence of such specificity it is sufficient merely to mention the very large literature on the occurrence of insects and mites in nests. References to the fauna of birds' nests have been compiled by Hicks[117]. Woodroffe[118] has examined some of the ecological relationships of insects in birds' nests. Besides the species associated with the nests themselves, ectoparasites of birds occur in nests; probably the nest and tree together are a habitat component for such species, in that transfer from one host to another takes place within them.

Distribution in time and space

Succession of animal species has been briefly described with reference to dead wood, but is a phenomenon also on the living tree in terms both of the seasons, in a temperate region such as Britain, and the life of an individual tree. In addition succession may be considered in relation to the whole plant community, perhaps in relation to changing climate, and as an evolutionary phenomenon. These different types of succession are on completely different scales of time but each affects the oak tree as a habitat for insect life.

Seasonal succession is readily observable in the insects of oak and certain aspects such as the influence of the changing tannin content of foliage have been mentioned. Two conflicting trends can be seen in the fauna, a tendency to exploit as soon as possible the breaking leaf and reproductive buds in the spring (either directly or indirectly) and a proclivity towards an apparent sharing out of a particular resource. The oak Miridae (Heteroptera) feed on the same kinds of food in the main, but there is a well-marked seasonal succession of species from *Harpocera thoracica* (Fall.), which becomes adult in May and may live up to 11 months in the year as an egg, to *Megacoelum infusum* (H.-S.) which is not adult until late July at the earliest.

Animal succession within the lifetime of a tree has also been documented. Several gall-wasps prefer young trees, even saplings and seedlings, to older ones[20] [22] and the same is true of some Lepidoptera. The tree as a habitat may be changed by man, not always for the worse. Haggett[119] states that caterpillars of the rare Lunar double-stripe moth (*Minucia lunaris* (D. & S.)) feed only on the coppiced shoots of stool oak, never on trees, and coppice oaks are also said to be preferred by the weevil *Attelabus nitens* (Scop.). Very old trees are the habitat of many of the rarer wood-inhabiting Coleoptera and the importance of ancient woodland sites for these species is well established.

Much less is naturally known about animal succession in the long term, but some interesting ideas have been put forward recently by Janzen on the evolution of tropical forest trees and their seed predators[120] [121]. Put very briefly, Janzen supposes that the predation of seeds by animals such as Bruchidae (Coleoptera) determines the evolutionary life of each tree species and ensures that a continual supply of such species is present in the ecosystem. How far these ideas are relevant to oak and its fauna is questionable but it seems probable that in temperate regions the seasons effectively interrupt, or at least delay, such evolutionary trends.

In Britain most insect species are found in the South of England and far fewer in the North of Scotland (or western Ireland). The fauna of oak is thus richer in the South of Britain than in the North, but is impoverished in comparison with continental Europe. Certain species of insect are very localised and their localities often coincide and are well known. Thus the New Forest is important for rare Lepidoptera and Coleoptera of oak, while such places as Windsor Forest, Sherwood Forest, Moccas Park (Herefordshire) and others are known particularly for their uncommon beetles. Much still remains to be learnt about the reasons for the existence of these favoured areas, but the presence of old, over-mature trees is known to be of great importance. Many of these areas are managed for amenity rather than timber production. Felling oak at maturity cuts short the full succession of animal species which is present in natural forest.

Postscript

The bewildering variety of form, food, habits and behaviour of the insect species, numbering several thousands, of oak in Britain suggests that a synthesis of the ecology of oak insects is not easy to produce—a conclusion which as well as being trite is also an obvious understatement of the facts. Studies of species diversity have multiplied in recent years and major advances are being made which in ecological theory may modify the ideas of Margalef [122] and Hutchinson[123]. It may be that the fauna of oak, as well as providing material for other important ecological studies, will be studied to elucidate problems of richness and diversity in the natural world. Elton's conclusion[16] was that the complexity of ecological relationships points irresistably to the need for conservation of habitats and habitat diversity. Whether this is so or not, and the signs are that the basis for such a belief will be critically examined in the coming years, the ecological complexity of natural ecosystems is an observable phenomenon and well illustrated by oak as a habitat for insect life.

Acknowledgements

Dr E. Duffey & Dr H. L. G. Stroyan gave me information about the spiders and aphids associated with oak, respectively. I have benefitted from discussions with very many ecologists and entomologists, particularly with Dr Duffey and Dr K. Southern. The figure was drawn by Mr Brian Buck.

REFERENCES

1. SOUTHWOOD, T. R. E. 'The insect/plant relationship—an evolutionary perspective', *in* van Emden, H. F. (edit.) *Insect/Plant relationships*, Oxford (1973)
2. SOUTHWOOD, T. R. E. 'The number of species of insect associated with various trees'. *J. Anim. Ecol.*, **30** (1961), 1–8
3. GODWIN, H. and DEACON, J. 'Post-glacial history of oak in the British Isles', *in* Morris, M. G. and Perring, F. H. (edit.) *The British oak: its history and natural history*, Faringdon (1974)
4. KELLY, M. and OSBORNE, P. J. 'Two faunas and floras from the alluvium at Shustoke, Warwickshire'. *Proc. Linn. Soc., Lond.*, **176** (1964), 37–65
5. BUCKLAND, P. C. and KENWARD, H. K. 'Thorne Moor: a palaeo-ecological study of a Bronze Age site'. *Nature, Lond.*, **241** (1973), 405–6
6. SOUTHWOOD, T. R. E. 'The evolution of the insect-host tree relationship—a new approach'. *Int. Congr. Ent. 11th, Vienna 1960*, **1** (1961), 651–4
7. MASSEE, A. M. 'The apple fruit Rhynchites (*Rhynchites aequatus* L.)'. *Rep. E. Malling Res. Sta. for 1931*, (1932), 53
8. SHARPE, D. '*Attelabus curculionoides* L. attacking Chestnut'. *Entomologist's mon. Mag.*, **37** (1901), 280–1
9. SHOTTON, F. W. and OSBORNE, P. J. 'The fauna of the Hoxnian Interglacial desposits of Nechells, Birmingham'. *Phil. Trans. Roy. Soc., Lond.*, B **248** (1965), 353–78
10. COOPE, G. R. 'Interpretations of quaternary insect fossils'. *A. Rev. Ent.*, **15** (1970), 97–120
11. JONES, E. W. 'Biological Flora of the British Isles. *Quercus* L.'. *J. Ecol.*, **47** (1959), 169–222
12. KLOET, G. S. and HINCKS, W. D. *A check list of British insects*, Southport (1945)
13. KLOET, G. S. and HINCKS, W. D. *A check list of British insects* (second edition) Part 1. Small orders and Hemiptera, London (1964)
14. KLOET, G. S. and HINCKS, W. D. *A check list of British insects* (second edition) Part 2. Lepidoptera, London (1972)
15. LOCKET, G. H. and MILLIDGE, A. F. *British spiders*, London, **1** (1951); **2** (1953)
16. ELTON, C. S. *The pattern of animal communities*, London (1966)
17. PIELOU, E. C. 'Niche width and niche overlap: a method for measuring them', *Ecology*, **53** (1972), 687–92
18. ELTON, C. S. and MILLER, R. S. 'The ecological survey of animal communities with a practical system of classifying habitats by structural characters'. *J. Ecol.*, **42** (1954), 460–96

19. HESLOP, I. R. P., HYDE, G. E. and STOCKLEY, R. E. *Notes and views of the Purple emperor*, Brighton (1964)
20. DARLINGTON, A. *The pocket encyclopedia of plant galls in colour*, London (1968)
20a. DARLINGTON, A. 'The galls on oak', *in* Morris, M. G. and Perring, F. H. (edit.) *The British oak: its history and natural history*, Faringdon (1974)
21. ASKEW, R. R. 'On the biology of the inhabitants of oak galls of Cynipidae (Hymenoptera) in Britain'. *Trans. Soc. Brit. Ent.*, **14** (1961), 237–68
22. EADY, R. D. and QUINLAN, J. 'Hymenoptera Cynipoidea. Key to families and subfamilies and Cynipinae (including galls)'. *Handbk Ident. Br. Insects*, **8** (1a) (1963), 1–81
23. FOWLER, W. W. *The Coleoptera of the British Islands*, **4**, London (1890)
24. SCHERF, H. 'Die Entwicklungsstadien der Mitteleuropäischen Curculioniden (Morphologie, Bionomie, Ökologie)'. *Abh. senckenb. naturforsch. Ges.*, **506** (1964), 1–335
25. BREESE, M. H. 'Notes on the oviposition site and method of reproduction of the weevil *Strophosomus melanogrammus* (Forster) (Col.)'. *Proc. R. ent. Soc. Lond.* (A), **23** (1948), 62–5
26. SOUTH, R. *The moths of the British Isles*, London (new ed. 1961)
27. MASSEE, A. M. *The pests of fruits and hops*, London (3rd ed. 1954)
28. MEYRICK, E. *A revised handbook of British Lepidoptera*, Hampton (reprinted 1970)
29. GILBERT, O. L. 'Some indirect effects of air pollution on bark-living invertebrates'. *J. appl. Ecol.*, **8** (1971), 77–84
30. SCORER, A. G. *The entomologist's log book*, London (1913)
31. NEW, T. R. 'An introduction to the natural history of the British Psocoptera'. *Entomologist*, **104** (1971), 59–97
32. SOUTHWOOD, T. R. E. and LESTON, D. *Land and water bugs of the British Isles*, London (1959)
33. COLLYER, E. 'Biology of some predatory insects and mites associated with the Fruit Tree Red Spider Mite (*Metatetranychus ulmi* (Koch)) in South-eastern England. II. Some important predators of the mite. III. Further predators of the mite'. *J. hort. Sci.*, **28** (1953), 85–97, 98–113
34. DICKER, G. H. L. 'Notes on some Hemiptera-Heteroptera taken in the Reading district during 1940'. *Entomologist's mon. Mag.*, **77** (1941), 101–4
35. SCUDDER, G. G. E. 'A contribution to a survey of the distribution of the Hemiptera-Heteroptera of Wales'. *Entomologist's mon. Mag.*, **92** (1956), 54–64
36. MASSEE, A. M. 'The Hemiptera-Heteroptera of Kent'. *Trans. Soc. Br. Ent.*, **11** (1954), 245–80
37. CARAYON, J. 'Observations sur la biologie des Hémiptères Microphysidés'. *Bull. Mus. Hist. nat., Paris*, **21** (1949), 710–16
38. COLLIN, J. E. *British flies*, **6**, Cambridge (1961)
39. OLDROYD, H. *The natural history of flies*, London (1964)
40. COLYER, C. N. and HAMMOND, C. O. *Flies of the British Isles*, London (1951)
41. CURTIS, D. J. and MORTON, E. 'Notes on the spiders from tree trunks of different bark textures; with indices of diversity and overlap'. *Bull. Br. arach. Soc.* (in press)
42. DUFFEY, E. 'The seasonal movements of *Clubiona brevipes* Blackwall and *Clubiona compta* C. L. Koch on oak trees in Monks Wood, Huntingdonshire'. *Bull. Br. arach. Soc.*, **1** (1969), 29–32
43. STOKOE, W. J. and STOVIN, G. H. T. *The caterpillars of British moths*, London (1948)
44. ASKEW, R. R., COOK, L. M. and BISHOP, J. A. 'Atmospheric pollution and melanic moths in Manchester and its environs'. *J. appl. Ecol.*, **8** (1971), 247–56

45. COTT, H. B. *Adaptive colouration in animals*, London (1940)
46. BEIRNE, B. P. *British pyralid and plume moths*, London (1952)
47. KETTLEWELL, H. B. D. 'The phenomenon of industrial melanism in Lepidoptera'. *A. Rev. Ent.*, **6** (1961), 245–62
47a. KETTLEWELL, H. B. D. *The evolution of melanism*, Oxford (1973)
48. FORD, E. B. *Ecological genetics*, London (1964)
49. BENSON, R. B. 'Hymenoptera Symphyta'. *Handbk Ident. Br. Insects*, **6** (2a) (1951), 1–49
50. BUHR, H. *Bestimungstabellen der Gallen (Zoo- und Phytocecidien) an Pflanzen Mittel- und Nordeuropas*, **2**, Jena (1965), 763–1572
51. KULLENBERG, B. 'Studien über die Biologie der Capsiden'. *Zool. Bidr. Upps.*, **23** (1944), 1–522
52. BRIGGS, J. B. 'Some features of the biology of the winter moth (*Operophtera brumata* (L.) on top fruits'. *J. hort. Sci.*, **32** (1957), 108–25
53. RAGGE, D. R. *Grasshoppers, crickets and cockroaches of the British Isles*, London (1965)
54. FORD, L. T. *A guide to the smaller British Lepidoptera*, London (1949)
55. NEWSTEAD, R. *Monograph of the Coccidae of the British Isles*, London **1** (1901); **2** (1903)
56. FARKAS, H. 'Spinnentiere: Eriophyidae (Gallmilben)', *Die Tierwelt Mitteleuropas*, **3** (Neubearbeitung Liefg. 3) (1965), 1–155
57. MASSEE, A. M. 'The gall mites (Arachnida: Acarina: Eriophyidae) of Kent'. *Trans. Kent Fld Cl.*, **1** (3) (1961), 110–18
58. DOSSE, G. 'Über die Bedeutung der Pollennahrung für *Typhlodromus* (*T.*) *pyri* Scheuten (=*tiliae* Oud.) (Acari, Phytoseidae)', *Ent. exp. appl.*, **4** (1961), 191–5
59. JACOBS, S. N. A. The 'British Lamproniidae and Adelidae'. *Proc. Trans. S. Lond. ent. nat. Hist. Soc.*, 1947–48 (1949), 209–19
60. WEDMORE, E. B. *A manual of bee-keeping for English speaking bee-keepers*, London (2nd ed. 1945)
61. BARNES, H. F. 'Gall midges reared from acorns and acorn-cups'. *Entomologist's mon. Mag.*, **91** (1955), 86–7
62. WINSTON, P. W 'The acorn microsere with special reference to arthropods'. *Ecology*, **37** (1956), 120–32
63. GRADWELL, G. R. 'The effect of defoliators on tree growth', *in* Morris, M. G. and Perring, F. H. (edit.). *The British oak: its history and natural history*, Faringdon (1974)
64. FEENY, P. P. and BOSTOCK, H. 'Seasonal changes in the tannin content of oak leaves'. *Biochemistry*, **7** (1968), 871–80
65. FEENY, P. P. 'Effect of oak leaf tannins on larval growth of the Winter Moth, *Operophtera brumata*'. *J. Ins. Physiol.*, **14** (1968), 805–17
65a. FEENY, P. P. 'Seasonal changes in oak leaf tannins and nutrients as a cause of spring feeding by winter moth caterpillars'. *Ecology*, **51** (1970), 564–81
66. ASKEW, R. R. 'The distribution of galls of *Neuroterus* (Hym.: Cynipidae) on oak'. *J. Anim. Ecol.*, **31** (1962), 439–55
67. BARNES, H. F. *Gall midges of economic importance*, **5** Trees, London (1951)
68. MANI, M. S. *Ecology of plant galls*, The Hague (1964)
69. FORD, L. T. 'The Glyphipterygidae and allied families'. *Proc. Trans. S. Lond. ent. nat. Hist. Soc.*, 1952–53 (1954), 90–9
70. HERING, E. M. *Biology of the leaf miners*, The Hague (1951)
71. HERING, E. M. *Die Blattminen Mittel- und Nord-Europas einschliesslich Englands*, Neubrandenburg (1937)
72. HERING, E. M. *Bestimmungstabellen der Blattminen von Europa, einschliesslich des Mittelmeerbeckens und der Kanarischen Inseln*, The Hague (1957)
73. BENSON, R. B. 'Hymenoptera Symphyta'. *Handbk Ident. Br. Insects*, **6** (2b) (1952), 51–137

74. JACOBS, S. N. A. 'On the British species of the genus *Lithocolletis* Hb.'.
Proc. Trans. S. Lond. ent. nat. Hist. Soc., 1944–45 (1945), 32–59

74a. MILLER, P. F. 'The biology of some *Phyllonorycter* species (Lepidoptera:
Gracillariidae) mining leaves of oak and beech'. *J. nat. Hist.*,
7 (1973), 391–409

75. MORRIS, M. G. 'Some aspects of the biology of *Psallus ambiguus* (Fall.)
(Heteroptera: Miridae) on apple trees in Kent'. *Entomologist*,
98 (1965), 14–31

76. WOODROFFE, G. E. 'The first British record of *Eurhadina kirschbaumi*
(Wagner) (Hem., Typhlocybidae)'. *Entomologist's mon. Mag*,
107 (1971), 44

77. EDWARDS, J. *The Hemiptera-Homoptera (Cicadina and Psyllina) of the
British Islands,* London (1896)

78. RIBAUT, H. *Homopteres Auchenorhynques. I. (Typhlocybidae). Faune de
France,* **31** Paris, (1936)

79. RIBAUT, H. *Homopteres Auchenorhynques. II. (Jassidae). Faune de
France,* **57,** Paris (1952)

80. CHINA, W. E. 'New and little-known species of British Typhlocybidae
(Homoptera) with keys to the genera *Typhlocyba, Erythroneura,
Dikraneura, Notus, Empoasca* and *Alebra*'. *Trans. Soc. Br.
Ent.*, **8** (1943), 111–53

81. LE QUESNE, W. J. 'Hemiptera Cicadomorpha (excluding Deltocephalinae
and Typhlocybinae)'. *Handbk Ident. Br. Insects*, **2** (2a)
(1965), 1–64

82. LE QUESNE, W. J. 'Hemiptera Cicadomorph Deltocephalinae'. *Handbk
Ident. Br. Insects*, **2** (2b) (1969), 65–148

83. CHINA, W. E. 'Notes on the life-history of *Triecphora vulnerata* Illiger
(Homoptera, Cercopidae)'. *Entomologist's mon. Mag.*, **61**
(1925), 133–4

84. CHINA, W. E. 'A revision of the British species of *Cixius* Latr.
(Homoptera), including the description of a new species from
Scotland'. *Trans. Soc. Br. Ent.*, **8** (1942), 79–110

85. COE, R. L. 'Diptera Pipunculidae'. *Handbk Ident. Br. Insects*, **10**
(2c) (1966), 1–83

86. MOUND, L. A. 'A revision of the British Aleyrodidae (Hemiptera:
Homoptera)'. *Bull. Br. Mus. (nat. Hist.)*, **17** (1966), 399–428

87. WILLIAMS, C. B. *Patterns in the balance of nature,* London (1964)

88. MORISON, G. D. 'Thysanoptera of the London area'. *London Nat.*,
26 (1947), 1–36; **27** (1948), 37–75; **28** (1949), 76–131

89. BENSON, R. B. 'An introduction to the natural history of British sawflies
(Hymenoptera Symphyta)'. *Trans. Soc. Br. Ent.*, **10** (1950),
45–142

90. BENSON, R. B. 'Hymenoptera Symphyta'. *Handbk Ident. Br. Insects*,
6 (2c) (1958), 139–252

91. CHAMBERS, V. H. 'The natural history of some *Pamphilius* species (Hym.,
Pamphiliidae)'. *Trans. Soc. Br. Ent.*, **11** (1952), 125–40

92. NIXON, G. E. J. *The association of ants with aphids and coccids,* London
(1951)

93. LAST, F. T. and DEIGHTON, F. C. 'The non-parasitic microflora on the
surface of living leaves'. *Trans. Br. mycol. Soc.*, **48** (1965), 83–99

94. NEW, T. R. 'The relative abundance of some British Psocoptera on
different species of trees'. *J. Anim. Ecol.*, **39** (1970), 521–40

95. NEW, T. R. 'The early stages and life histories of some British foliage-
frequenting Psocoptera, with notes on the overwintering stages
of British arboreal Psocoptera'. *Trans. R. ent. Soc. Lond.*,
121 (1969), 59–77

96. AUDCENT, H. 'A preliminary list of the hosts of some British Tachinidae'.
Trans. Soc. Br. Ent., **8** (1942), 1–42

97. DAY, C. D. *British Tachinid flies,* Arbroath (1948)

98. EMDEN, F. I. VAN. 'Diptera Cyclorrhapha Calyptrata (I) Tachinidae and
Calliphoridae'. *Handbk Ident. Br. Insects*, **10** (4a) (1954), 1–133

99. RICHARDS, O. W. 'Hymenoptera. Introduction and keys to families'. *Handbk Ident. Br. Insects*, **6** (1) (1956), 1–94
100. FOWLER, W. W. *The Coleoptera of the British Islands*, **1**, London (1887)
101. BALDULF, W. V. *The bionomics of entomophagous Coleoptera*, New York (1935) (reprint Hampton (1969))
102. KILLINGTON, F. J. *A monograph of the British Neuroptera*, London **1** (1936); **2** (1937)
103. FOWLER, W. W. *The Coleoptera of the British Islands*, **5**, London (1891)
104. PAVIOUR-SMITH, K. 'The fruiting-bodies of macrofungi as habitats for beetles of the family Ciidae'. *Oikos*, **11** (1960), 43–71
105. PAVIOUR-SMITH, K. 'Insect succession in the 'birch bracket fungus', *Polyporus betulinus*'. *Int. Congr. Ent.* 11th, *Vienna* 1960, **1** (1961), 792–96
106. HINGLEY, M. R. 'The ascomycete fungus, *Daldinia concentrica*, as a habitat for animals'. *J. Anim. Ecol.*, **40** (1971), 17–32
107. DUFFY, E. A. J. 'Coleoptera Cerambycidae'. *Handbk Ident. Br. Insects*, **5** (12) (1952), 1–18
108. MUNRO, J. W. 'British bark-beetles'. *Bull. For. Commn, Lond.*, **18** (1926), 1–77
109. HAMM, A. H. and RICHARDS, O. W. 'The biology of the British Crabronidae'. *Trans. R. ent. Soc., Lond.*, **74** (1926), 297–331
110. STUBBS, A. E. 'Wildlife conservation and dead wood'. *Jnl Devon Trust Nature Cons.*, suppl., (1972), 1–18
111. GRAHAM, S. A. 'The felled tree trunk as an ecological unit'. *Ecology*, **9** (1925), 397–411
112. SAVELY, H. E. 'Ecological relations of certain animals in dead pine and oak logs'. *Ecol. Monogr.*, **9** (1939), 321–85
113. FAGER, E. W. *A study of invertebrate populations in decaying wood*, D. Phil. thesis, Univ. Oxford (1955)
114. FISHER, R. C. 'Insects attacking the timber of English oak'. *Forestry*, **10** (1936), 47–57
115. LARKIN, P. A. and ELBOURN, C. A. 'Some observations on the fauna of dead wood in live oak trees'. *Oikos*, **15** (1964), 79–92
116. MARSHALL, J. F. *The British mosquitoes*, London (1938)
117. HICKS, E. A. *Check-list and bibliography on the occurrence of insects in birds' nests*, Iowa (1958)
117a. HICKS, E. A. 'Check-list and bibliography on the occurrence of insects in birds' nests'. Supplement 1. *Iowa St. Coll. J. Sci.*, **36** (1962), 233–348
118. WOODROFFE, G. E. 'An ecological study of the insects and mites in the nests of certain birds in Britain'. *Bull. ent. Res.*, **44** (1953), 739–72
119. HAGGETT, G. 'Larvae of the British Lepidoptera not figured by Bucker. V'. *Proc. Trans. S. Lond. ent. nat. Hist. Soc.*, 1960 (1961), 130–7
120. JANZEN, D. H. 'Host plants as islands in evolutionary and contemporary time'. *Amer. Nat.*, **102** (1968), 592–5
121. JANZEN, D. H. 'Herbivores and the number of tree species in tropical forests'. *Amer. Nat.*, **104** (1970), 501–28
122. MARGALEF, R. *Perspectives in ecological theory*, Chicago (1968)
123. HUTCHINSON, G. E. 'Homage to Santa Rosalia or why are there so many kinds of animals?' *Amer. Nat.*, **93** (1959), 145–59

THE GALLS ON OAK

ARNOLD DARLINGTON

5 *Firs Close, Malvern, Worcestershire*

Introduction

Plant galls (cecidia) are so numerous, varied in form and widespread among infested hosts that most observers are probably familiar with examples even if they sometimes confuse them with very different objects which, on occasions, appear on plants. A gall invariably develops as a result of a parasitic attack. It represents the growth reaction of the host (a plant, usually holophytic but, in some circumstances, saprophytic or itself parasitic) to the attack of some kind of parasite—a bacterium, fungus, nematode, mite or insect—and it is formed either by an increase in the number of the host's cells or by these cells becoming abnormally enlarged. This definition is sufficiently precise to exclude numerous deformities brought about by living organisms during the course of their attacks on food plants. A fundamental characteristic of a gall is that it is constituted wholly from the tissues of the host, so that the parasite is the gall-*causer* but, in no sense, the gall-*maker*.

In view of the fact that at least some 500 different species of insect are believed to derive sustenance in some way from our native British oaks, it is not surprising to find that the commonest parasites inducing oak galls are insects[1]. Oak-feeding insects which bring about deformities other than galls, but whose activities are sometimes held to result in gall development, belong to three main groups.

Liquid-feeders. These organisms have mouthparts shaped in a manner reminiscent of hypodermic needles: they pierce the leaf lamina and suck the plant juices. *Hemiptera-Homoptera* (bugs such as aphids and leaf hoppers) are of paramount faunistic importance. One of the commonest on oak leaves is *Phylloxera quercus* Fonsc., whose stabs cause small yellow patches to form and the lamina to arch upwards. Mirid bugs (*Hemiptera-Heteroptera*), larger than aphids, include species which feed on the sap in oak leaves and flowers: they may also take the body juices of small insects and mites and thus, at times, become predators. *Dryophilocoris flaviquadrimaculatus* (Deg.) and *Phylus melanocephalus* (L.) are examples.

Defoliators. The damage effected by such browsers as goats is far less significant than that of insects, which may remove any part of a leaf except, perhaps, the petiole and the sclerenchymatous veins. Beetles and moth caterpillars are among the most important defoliators of oak. Thus weevils of the genus *Phyllobius* eat out holes in the lamina and the cockchafer *Melolontha melolontha* (L.) apparently shows a preference for oak foliage over that of other forest trees. Should the cockchafer population reach plague proportions a single oak can be stripped of its entire foliage in a day or so; and much the same is true of trees attacked by the caterpillar of the oak-leaf roller moth (*Tortrix viridana* (L.)) which rolls up the leaf into a scroll secured by silk and shelters inside.

Leaf-miners. Leaf-miners on oak commonly include weevils, microlepidoptera and sawflies: these tunnel between the two epidermids of the leaf and set up either *blister* (blotch) *mines* or *serpentine mines.* A blister mine is produced by such a larva as that of the weevil *Rhynchaenus quercus* (L.) or the sawfly *Profenusa pygmaea* (Klug), which starts to feed in a small cavity and subsequently enlarges this in all directions as it grows. The larvae of several of the Nepticulidae (Lepidoptera) make serpentine mines, each of which generally runs for a time along the leaf margin before turning inwards towards the midrib.

All the insects mentioned cause a measure of deformity without inducing true galls, as there is no localized increase in the biomass of the host. Leaf-miners are perhaps the most deceptive in that their activities frequently result in a certain amount of bulging of the epidermis. No leaf-miner on oak seems to bring about gall formation, although the larvae of certain Diptera which mine into the foliage of holly (*Ilex aquifolium*) and goosefoot (*Chenopodium* spp.) and devour the mesophyll have the capacity for inducing the host to replace the destroyed tissues by more and larger cells of the same kind so that here the bulging is due, partly at least, to the development of a simple type of gall. No equivalent reaction has been detected in oak leaves.

Evidently a gall benefits both host and parasite: it supplies the latter with shelter and a concentration of food, and it illustrates the classical reaction of a host to the presence of a parasite whereby the attacker becomes encapsulated and its effects more or less localized. In terms both of the structure of the galls themselves, and the behaviour of their causers, those infesting oaks show a considerable range. All the cecidozoa examined here are insects and it is useful to consider them in order of complexity of the galls they bring about.

Hemiptera-Homoptera: Coccoidea (Scale Insects)
A gall-causing coccid which attacks the green twig in the early stages of secondary thickening is *Asterodiapsis* (=*Asterolecanium*) *variolosa* (Ratz.). It sets up the simplest gall known on oak (fig 1). As with coccids generally, the female is sessile: she remains fixed for life in one place on the stem and sucks juices through stylets inserted in the cortex. This action arrests much of the tissue differentiation; but on the side where she is feeding the outer layers undergo such localized development that she becomes surrounded by a wall of young bark 1 mm high. An oval pit about 3×2 mm is

enclosed by the wall, and such pits generally contain feeding insects from May to October. The males are winged and fly about in search of the females.

A. variolosa is one of the most exposed of all gall-causing insects, as she remains permanently on the host's surface without becoming enclosed within its tissues. The aphid *Eriosoma lanigerum* (Hausmann), the agent in American blight disease on apple trees, is another external gall-causer.

Diptera: Cecidomyiidae (Gall Midges)

Galls folded along the margins of leaves, and liable to be confused only with such leaf-scrolls as those caused by caterpillars like *Tortrix viridana* from which they are separable by the absence of binding silk and the presence of thickening at the fold, are of common occurrence and are induced by the larvae of Diptera belonging to the genus *Macrodiplosis*. There are two species. Marginal folds induced by *M. dryobia* (Loew) lie at the distal end of a leaf vein and bend towards the lower surface: those caused by *M. volvens* Kieffer lie between two veins and bend towards the upper surface (fig 2). Although the pocket of the larvae of the *M. volvens* fold tends to be more crescentic than that of *M. dryobia,* and somewhat longer, the

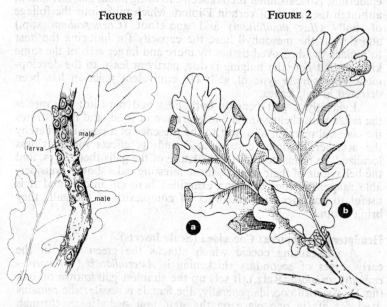

FIGURE 1   FIGURE 2

The most exposed gall-causer on oak: the coccid *Asterodiapsis variolosa* in its cecidia. The sessile females are *in situ* within the pits. Length of leaf, 100 mm.

Fold galls of midges, *Macrodiplosis* spp: (a) *M. dryobia,*; (b) *M. volvens*. Length of leaf, 100 mm.

actual overlap in both is about 4 mm. About four larvae occur together in a single fold, which is glabrous. Initially the fold is tightly adpressed against the lamina, but after the larvae have ceased feeding it gapes and allows the insects to fall into the soil where they pupate. Galls are normally plentiful from June until September. Another gall midge, *Monodiplosis liebeli* (Kieffer), frequently occurs in both as an inquiline ('lodger').

Hymenoptera: Cynipidae (Gall Wasps)

More species of these small wasps occur on oaks than on any other host. Some 30–35 frequent the British mainland, and although some are rare, 20–25 may be expected to occur in any sizeable region south of the Trent. Gall wasps are noteworthy on two counts at least: histologically the growths they induce are the most highly specialized of the galls on oak; and many of them pass through a well-defined alternation of generations in the course of their life cycle.

Alternation of generations

Three groups of gall-causing organisms—gall wasps, aphids and fungi—exhibit alternation of generations. Its most clearly defined form is seen in gall wasps on oak, when it involves two generations in the course of the life-cycle (sometimes within the span of a single year), one consisting exclusively of females— the agamic generation—and the other of both males and females— the sexual generation. During such a cycle a gall wasp typically brings about the formation of galls of two distinct kinds, very different in appearance and considered by some early observers to represent the work of separate species. Females of the agamic generation normally emerge from stout galls which have over-wintered and have been protected in some way. Such protected galls may be established underground on the roots, developed at the bases of twigs springing up from the bottom of scrub oaks in hedgerows where they had been covered by drifting leaf litter, or detached from the foliage before this fell so that eventually the autumn leaves had blanketed them. Agamic females arise as a result of sexual fusion. They exemplify the ecological principle that, should an organism undergo two methods of reproduction, asexual and sexual, the sexual phase follows a period of plenty and precedes one of scarcity. Females of both generations are invariably diploid and the males invariably haploid. Every agamic female receives her diploid condition from the union of her parents' haploid gametes. Such females appear to be of two types. One lays eggs which have not undergone meiosis, are consequently diploid, and inevitably yield females. The other produces eggs which have undergone reduction division, are therefore haploid and, since no fertilization takes place, give rise to males. These are the individuals of the sexual generation which develop rapidly in galls derived from catkins, buds or leaves and which, on mating, become the parents of the agamic generation.

Several examples of gall wasps which alternate their generations are now considered. Where two galls occur in alternation, each is named after the generation which develops in it and not the generation which lays the egg leading to its formation. Larvae of gall wasps always pupate inside their galls.

FIGURE 3

A simple method of rearing occupants of the 'apples' induced by offspring developing from the parthenogenetic ova of the gall-wasp *Biorhiza pallida*.

Oak-apple gall wasps (*Biorhiza pallida* (Oliv.))

Development of the 'apple' follows the insertion by an apterous female of the agamic generation of numerous eggs in the base of a leaf bud which is almost severed from the twig in the process, and most of which is lifted off by the rapidly swelling gall in early May. When mature, about midsummer, this bud gall is pale pink, somewhat spongy in texture, and 2.0–4.0 cm in diameter. The males and females of the sexual generation, all of them fully winged, emerge from the bud galls in June and July (fig 3). Mating is in July, after which the females penetrate the soil and insert their eggs in the tissues of oak rootlets. Oviposition results in the development of the root galls, each a rounded brown structure about 0.75 cm across, which may occur singly or in groups which frequently coalesce (fig 4). The galls become mature after 16 months and the adult wasps, which normally leave at the end of the second winter, are the wingless females of the agamic generation.

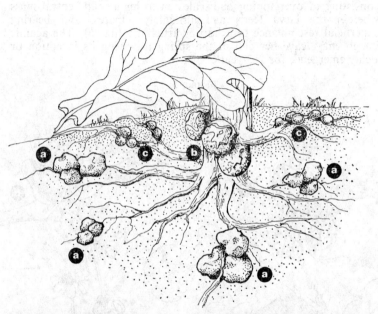

Gal's of the agamic generation of three gall-wasps which gain protection by developing at the soil surface or below it: (a) *Biorhiza pallida;* (b) *Andricus quei cusradicis·* (c) *A. rhizomae.* Length of leaf, 100 mm.

Complex communities frequently develop in the bud galls and, to some extent, in the root galls, the members including parasites and inquilines. *Biorhiza pallida* affords a good example of a cynipid whose agamic females are protected from climatic adversities by developing underground.

Oak Apple Day, May 29, at a season when the bud galls are expanding and becoming colourful and attractive, commemorates the Restoration of the Monarchy, Charles II having returned to this country on May 26, 1660. It has nothing to do with the Boscobel incident, when he hid from his enemies in the branches of an oak during his wanderings as a fugitive after the Battle of Worcester. This was fought on September 3, at a time when the galls had withered and turned black.

Oak-artichoke gall wasp (*Andricus fecundator* Hartig)

The life history is of the basic type, but in contrast to *Biorhiza pallida* the agamic female of *Andricus fecundator* develops in a gall exposed on a high twig and gains protection from the thick wall and core of the swollen structure. There are two galls. The more familiar is that of the agamic generation—the so-called 'hop strobile' or 'artichoke gall'. This forms as a result of oviposition of a fertilized egg in a bud and becomes a body 2.0 cm long, russet-green in colour, consisting of overlapping bud scales enclosing a solid central mass wherein the larva feeds and ultimately pupates, and bearing superficial resemblance to a hop or artichoke (fig. 5). The agamic imago may leave her gall in the spring following its inception or delay emergence for 2–3 years.

FIGURE 5

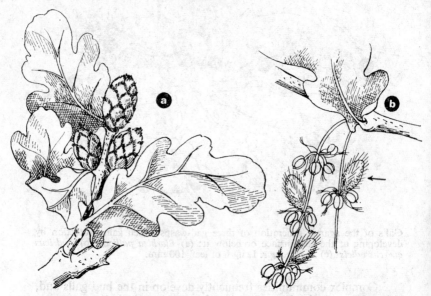

Regular alternation of generations in the gall wasp *Andricus fecundator*: (a) 'oak artichoke' gall of agamic generation; (b) 'hairy catkin' gall of sexual generation. Length of leaf, 100 mm.

Her parthenogenetic ova are inserted into the buds of the male catkins. She tends to select catkins of *Quercus robur* which come into flower a fortnight or so before those of *Q. petraea*, a fact seemingly correlated with the differential distribution of the wasp, which is more plentiful south-east of the Trent than to the north-west, *Q. robur* being the predominant oak of clay soils in the south. As a result 'hairy catkin galls' develop as solitary, oval, pointed bodies within the catkins; they are 0.3 cm long and covered with whitish hairs. On maturing in spring they give rise to the sexual generation whose mated females initiate the agamic galls when they oviposit in unopened leaf buds.

Complex communities may again develop in both galls. Another cynipid, *Andricus curvator* Hartig, shows a preference for depositing her own eggs on buds already colonized by *A. fecundator*, and may represent an early phase in evolution of the inquiline mode of life.

Red-barnacle gall wasp (*Andricus testaceipes* Hartig)

Protection of the agamic females is promoted by the siting of their galls which, although not actually buried in soil, develop so near the surface of the ground that they are concealed more or less permanently by litter or rank herbaceous growth. Mated females of the sexual generation commonly select young twigs arising from the

FIGURE 6

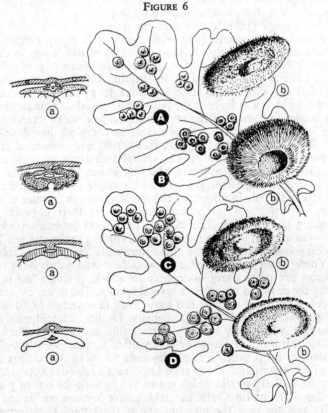

Small agamic galls (spangles) of *Neuroterus* spp. (gall wasps) which gain protection by falling from leaves and becoming buried under litter: (a) in section, enlarged; (b) in perspective, natural size and enlarged; A. *N. quercusbaccarum;* B. *N. numismalis;* C. *N. tricolor;* D. *N. albipes.* Length of leaf, 100 mm.

bottom of a hedgerow oak before these have hardened sufficiently to impede insertion of the ovipositor. Initially the fluted 'red-barnacle galls' induced by larvae from fertilized eggs develop deep in the cortex and then break through the surface as pyriform swellings which push up the outer tissues like a cap. Each is 0.6 cm high, at first red and soft and later brown and hard, and encloses a single insect. Barnacle galls mature in April of the third year when they fall from the stem and become intermingled with debris from dead leaves, broken twigs and fallen bark fragments accumulated along the hedgerow base by wind.

Galls of the sexual generation, relatively inconspicuous, are merely green, oval swellings in the leaf midrib or veins. They mature in August-September. A record from Devon of barnacle galls developing at the base of a sapling ash tree has been brought to the writer's attention. As is generally the case when a parasite reaches the wrong host, the causers failed to mature.

Oak-leaf spangle gall wasps (*Neuroterus* spp)

Probably the agamic galls most familiar to many people are the hard disc-like spangles on the undersides of oak leaves in early autumn induced by wasps of the genus *Neuroterus* (fig 6). Four species have a wide distribution in Britain. A feature common to all is that the short stalk attaching them to a leaf vein fractures before the abscission layer at the base of the petiole. Consequently the spangles fall first and become covered a few weeks later by the dying foliage. Here on the ground the larvae complete their development. They are protected in part from frost and concealed from predators such as game birds. The spangles continue to swell, even after their separation from the host, by absorption of water. In spring a single female emerges from each spangle and lays parthenogenetic ova, usually in unopened oak buds, although females of one species, *N. tricolor* (Hartig) commonly insert their eggs in the expanding leaf laminae. The galls of the sexual generation which develop as a result differ in appearance according to the species. The main diagnostic features of the alternating galls are given in table 1.

Young trees near the edge of woodland and scrub oaks in a hedgerow are particularly susceptible to attack, a single leaf often bearing the crowded spangles of several species. The writer estimates that colonization of a single leaf may result in coverage of 80–90% of the lower surface. Such a density implies competition for *lebensraum,* which may be both intraspecific and interspecific.

One feature of intraspecific competition appears shortly before the spangles drop, when a small dry area forms in the leaf around each of the older galls. Water is so important to the development of the spangles that any die which are so young as to be out of phase with the more mature galls but which have become positioned on the dry patches near the attachments of the latter. Therefore the earlier a female of the sexual generation can lay the better.

Despite differences from year to year and from one situation to another, the same general trends persist. At one extreme is *N. albipes,*

TABLE 1

The galls of species of Neuroterus

Species	Agamic (Autumn-Winter)	Sexual (Spring-Summer)
N. quercusbaccarum (L.)	*Common spangle gall*	*Currant gall*
	Flat, reddish green disc, 6 mm diameter, with stellate hairs.	Resembles a red currant, 4 mm diameter in male catkins.
N. numismalis (Geoff.)	*Silk-button spangle gall*	*Blister gall*
	Thick, golden brown disc, 3 mm diameter, with depression in centre, densely covered with glossy hairs.	Appears as a blister, 3 mm diameter in lamina.
N. tricolor (Hartig)	*Cupped spangle gall*	*Hairy pea gall*
	Greenish-yellow disc, 3 mm diameter, with raised margin, bearing scattered hairs.	Sphere, 6 mm diameter, more or less hairy, on underside of leaf vein.
N. albipes (Schenck)	*Smooth spangle gall*	*Schenck's gall*
	Cream-coloured saucer, 4 mm diameter, glabrous.	Oval green body, length 2 mm, in recess on margin of lamina.

whose sexual galls develop by the end of March. The females which emerge from these begin ovipositing immediately the leaf laminae have fully expanded. At the opposite extreme is *N. tricolor,* whose sexual galls only appear while the leaves are expanding and whose spangles first show at least a month after those of *N. numismalis* and six weeks after the agamic galls of *N. albipes* and *N. quercusbaccarum.* This points to interspecific competition for the same host and to a diversity of ecological niches and suggests the hypothesis that pressures from competition are reduced by one or more of three adaptations:—1, an individual host (tree) is colonized exclusively by one particular species; 2, different areas of a single leaf are utilized by different species; and 3, different regions of an entire host (tree) become colonized by different species. Simple observations show the first to be untenable.

Investigations of the second possible adaptation by random sampling indicate that, irrespective of pre-colonization, spangles of *N. numismalis* are scattered almost to the lateral margins of a leaf, with *N. albipes* (the earliest arrival) predominating near the midrib and *N. quercusbaccarum* occurring most plentifully near the apex. The pattern of colonization by *N. tricolor* (the latest of the four to initiate its spangles) is the least clearly defined: although there is a tendency for the middle regions, between the midrib and lateral margins and between the apex and base, to be utilized, this is a more general distribution than the others and suggests the importance of initial colonization by competitors in determining what happens to this species, which seems merely to occupy any spaces they leave. A noteworthy feature is that *N. tricolor* is the rarest of the four over much of the country: the other three retain their pattern of spatial selectivity irrespective of whether or not they come to share the same leaf. These results differ from those obtained by Askew[2], but the pattern of distribution of galls of *N. quercusbaccarum* is similar to that found by Hough[3].

The third possible adaptation was also investigated by counts made at random. These showed *N. numismalis* to predominate at the top and periphery of a given oak, *N. quercusbaccarum* in the middle, *N. albipes* towards the bottom, and *N. tricolor* to be an 'opportunist' which fills gaps indiscriminately. These findings are in broad agreement with those of Askew[2].

Certain hymenopteran cecidozoa have undergone partial or full elimination of males from the life cycle with consequent disturbance of alternation. Although some of these are associated with oak, a better-known example is the gall wasp *Diplolepis rosae* (L.) which induces the bedeguar gall (moss gall) on wild rose. Whenever large numbers of bedeguars have been reared, less than 1% of the emergent causers have been males. Reproduction is normally by parthenogenesis and regular alternation of generations is unknown.

Oak-marble gall wasp (*Andricus kollari* (Hartig))

The causer of the oak-marble gall (Devonshire gall)—the hard, woody, brown sphere, better known to many than the oak apple —is another example of a gall wasp in which alternation of generations has been modified (fig 7). There is little in common between the 'marble' and the 'apple', as the former is a gall of an agamic female and the 'apple' that of a sexual generation. Although now widespread throughout Britain on scrub oaks in coppices and young trees in hedges, *A. kollari* is an introduced species which reached this country about 1830 when galls were deliberately imported from the Levant into Devon. They were used for dyeing cloth and for ink-manufacture, the galls containing up to 17% of tannic acid. The galls became the subject of controversy in the mid-19th century when fears were expressed in the press that the acorn crop would be ruined by its rapid spread and farmers thereby deprived of valuable pannage for pigs.

Only females leave the 'marbles', and these insects evidently represent an agamic generation surviving the winter in exposed situations protected by the stoutness of the enclosing structures. For a long time, it was generally believed that the sexual generation of *A. kollari* did not exist. M. W. Beyerinck, in 1882, was the first to draw attention to its presence in softer, smaller galls resembling ant

FIGURE 7

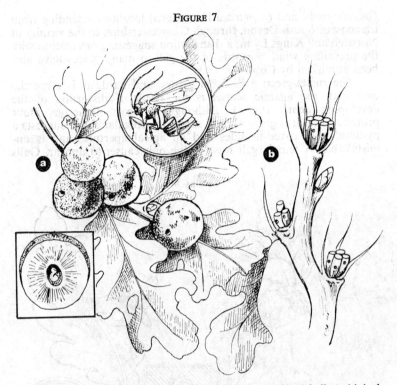

Irregular alternation of generations in the gall-wasp *Andricus kollari:* (a) 'oak marble' gall of agamic generation on *Q. petraea* or *Q. robur;* (b) gall of sexual generation on *Q. cerris.* Length of leaf, 100 mm.

pupae and forming in the axillary buds of Turkey oak (*Quercus cerris*). These sexual galls appear to be scarce; typically reproduction is by unfertilized eggs, and the extent to which periodic fertilization is necessary to maintain the species is uncertain. The agamic galls are often abundant in stations far distant from those of the nearest *Q. cerris.*

Andricus quercuscalicis (Burgsdorff)

The galls caused by this wasp have no English name. *A. quercuscalicis,* the latest addition to the list of British gall wasps, was first taken as agamic material by Dr M. F. Claridge in the early 1960s[4], since when something of a population explosion has occurred. Evidently there was an invasion from the Continent via the Channel Islands and it is noteworthy that, as with *A. kollari,* Devonshire became the region where early establishment in mainland Britain took place. However, the first arrivals of *A. quercuscalicis* were probably unassisted by human agency and seem to have been airborne. Since 1971 the writer has been notified of agamic galls on

Quercus robur and *Q. petraea* in scattered localities extending from the coast of South Devon, through Gloucestershire, to the vicinity of Norwich and Kings Lynn, a distribution suggesting orientation with the prevailing wind. Records of the gall in many places have also been published by Cobb[5].

The russet-green gall, 2 cm across, and hard, as is often the case with the agamic phase, is the result of distortion of the developing acorn (fig 8). Although it bears numerous blunt protuberances it is glabrous and shiny. Its irregular shape suggests a pyramid with caved-in sides and an apical aperture, and is unmistakable. A female gall wasp is the only causer to appear. Galls

FIGURE 8

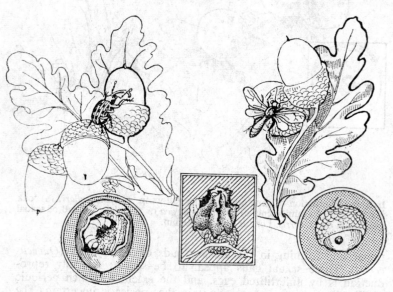

Distortions in acorns: *left*, the weevil *Curculio* sp.; *centre*, the gall wasp *Andricus quercuscalicis*, on the increase in Britain; *right*, the gall wasp *Synergus* sp. The last two distortions are true galls. Length of leaf, 100 mm.

of the sexual generation are known on the Continent but there are no British records so far and the writer has seen no material. They are said to develop on catkins of *Q. cerris* in spring. It is certainly curious that, as with *A. kollari* where alternation is irregular, the sexual stage appears on Turkey oak. The life cycle in Britain of this new arrival needs further study.

Opportunties were lost in the last century for investigating the pattern of spread of oak-marble galls, and the writer would be grateful for additional records of galls of *A. quercuscalicis*.

Acknowledgement

All the figures are taken from my recent book[6] and were drawn by Mary Wilhelmina Guymer.

REFERENCES

1. DARLINGTON, A. *The pocket encyclopaedia of plant galls in colour*, London (1968)
2. ASKEW, R. R. 'The distribution of galls of *Neuroterus* (Hym.: Cynipidae) on oak', *J. Anim. Ecol.*, **31** (1962), 439–55
3. HOUGH, J. S. 'Studies on the common spangle gall of oak. III. The importance of the stage in laminar extension of the host leaf', *New Phyt.*, **52** (1953), 229–37
4. CLARIDGE, M. F. '*Andricus quercus-calicis* (Burgsdorff) in Britain (Hym.: Cynipidae)', *Entomologist*, **95** (1962), 60–1
5. COBB, P. R. 'The gall-wasp *Andricus quercuscalicis*—further news', *Proc. Heacham W. Norfolk nat. Hist. Soc.*, **5** (1) (1971), 8
5a. COBB, P. R. 'More galls *(Andricus quercuscalicis)*', *Proc. Heacham W. Norfolk nat. Hist. Soc.*, **5** (2) (1972), 27–8
6. DARLINGTON, A. *The world of a tree*, London (1972)

THE IMPORTANCE OF OAK TO MAMMALS

GORDON B. CORBET

*Department of Zoology, British Museum (Natural History),
London S.W.7*

Introduction

It is common knowledge that a great variety of mammals feed upon oak—for example that squirrels eat acorns on the trees, that pigs grow fat on them in autumn, that voles and mice eat and in some cases store fallen acorns and that deer browse on oak leaves. But when it comes to quantifying this information or finding precise accounts of qualitative observations the situation is very different. Although the food eaten by large mammals has for long been of economic importance, and although small mammals played a dominant role in the growth of quantitative ecology, the quantitative study of food has lagged far behind other aspects such as population dynamics. It is only in very recent years that any systematic attention has been paid to the feeding ecology of most of our native species and for many the data remain fragmentary and almost anecdotal.

It can safely be said, however, that no species of mammal is wholly dependent upon oak. It is also true that all our woodland species that are not wholly insectivorous or carnivorous make extensive and direct use of oak when it is present. The most widespread of these, probably present in every deciduous wood on the British mainland, are the wood mouse, *Apodemus sylvaticus* (L.), and the bank vole, *Clethrionomys glareolus* Schr., whilst the badger, *Meles meles* (L.), must be very nearly as ubiquitous. Equally widespread, but found mainly on the margins and in clearings, is the rabbit, *Oryctolagus cuniculus* (L.). Squirrels are present in virtually all lowland woods, but are absent from many highland oak woods. These are the introduced grey squirrel, *Sciurus carolinensis* Gm., over most of England and parts of the central lowlands of Scotland, and the red squirrel, *S. vulgaris* L., in most of Scotland, northern England and parts of Wales, Cornwall and Norfolk. Two additional rodents occur in southern England and Wales: the yellow necked mouse, *Apodemus flavicollis* (Melchior), present in most woods in south-eastern England and the Severn basin, and the common dormouse, *Muscardinus avellanarius* (L.), which is rather more restricted by its dependence upon a dense shrub layer. An even more localised rodent is the introduced fat dormouse, *Glis glis* (L.), confined to the Chiltern Hills. Two further species that are widespread but very marginally relevant, being primarily herbivores of open country, are the brown hare, *Lepus capensis* L., and the field vole, *Microtus agrestis* (L.).

Deer are more erratic in their distribution, but one or more species is present in most deciduous woodland throughout the country. In the lowlands the fallow deer, *Dama dama* (L.), is the most widespread and in the highlands (but not Wales) the roe, *Capreolus capreolus* (L.). The introduced sika, *Cervus nippon* Temminck, and muntjac, *Muntiacus reevesi* (Ogilby), are more local, while in the highland areas red deer, *Cervus elaphus* L., penetrate woodland, especially in winter.

The situation in Ireland is similar except that some species are totally absent, namely the dormice, yellow-necked mouse, field vole, roe deer and muntjac, whilst the bank vole is confined to the south-west. Provisional distribution maps of all these species in Britain and Ireland have been published by Corbet[7].

On the continent of Europe several additional species are present. Amongst the rodents there are two further species of dormice but of greater relevance are three larger species that formerly occurred in Britain, the beaver, *Castor fiber* L., the wild boar, *Sus scrofa* L., and the brown bear, *Ursus arctos* L.. The bison, *Bison bonasus* (L.), is also a species of deciduous forest as was the extinct urus, *Bos primigenius* Bojanus. Although not relevant to the importance of oak for the present mammalian fauna of Britain, these species must not be overlooked in any consideration of the role of mammals in the evolution of the oaks themselves. In addition, the domesticated descendants of the wild boar and of the urus have continued, at least until very recently, to play a role in the ecology of oak in Britain.

Systematic survey of mammalian groups

Squirrels

Western Europe is peculiarly deficient in squirrels, with only a single native species, the red squirrel, *Sciurus vulgaris*. This has a wide range throughout the forested parts of the Palaearctic Region but it must be considered as primarily a species of the boreal coniferous forests. Further south in Europe it occurs especially in montane coniferous forest but also to a lesser extent in mixed and deciduous lowland forest. By contrast the grey squirrel, *Sciurus carolinensis,* is, in its native range, a species primarily of deciduous forest and it is therefore not surprising that the introduced populations in Britain have expanded in deciduous woodland at the expense of the native red squirrel.

The red squirrel has had an erratic history of expansion and contraction of range in Britain even before introduction of the grey[29] and it is significant that in the Scottish highlands, where greys have not yet penetrated, the red squirrel is not commonly found in oak woods[9]. Likewise, in those mixed lowland woods occupied only by red squirrels they tend to favour conifers and beech rather than oak.

It can be concluded that although the red squirrel will exploit oak in the same ways as described below for grey squirrel, it is on a much smaller scale and oak does not hold for it the importance that it does for the grey squirrel.

Grey squirrels show a strong preference for deciduous woodlands where they feed on a wide variety of tree species, including oak. In spring they feed predominantly on buds; in summer on a great variety of foods but including cambium stripped from young trees or from the smaller branches of older trees; in autumn and winter on nuts and seeds, including acorns both before and after they fall. There is no indication of a strong preference for oak although it is extensively used when it is present. Beech and sycamore are more vulnerable than oak to bark-stripping[29] and nuts of sweet chestnut and beech tend to be used before the squirrels turn to acorns[18]. However in experiments in which a variety of food was offered to grey squirrels (in Georgia, U.S.A.) it was found that no use was made of buds, cambium or leaves if acorns were available[10]. In Britain acorns of *Quercus petraea* have been reported to be generally preferred to those of *Q. robur*, with a considerable degree of selection by the squirrels for acorns of high sugar and low tannin content, both of which vary considerably in both species[29]. Grey squirrels avidly bury acorns in autumn, but they are dispersed and buried singly and it is rare for a cache of any size to be found in one place.

Although acorns, when they are plentiful, make up a very large proportion of the diet in autumn and winter, many other kinds of food are eaten, including fungi, grain, other nuts and bark. No measurements appear to have been made of the effect on winter survival of large and small acorn crops but it seems very probable that it could be considerable.

Wood mice and bank vole

Both species of *Apodemus*, the wood mouse, *A. sylvaticus*, and the yellow-necked mouse, *A. flavicollis*, along with the bank vole, are major users of oak. Their ecology in woodland containing oak has been extensively studied and it is convenient to treat them together. Little can be said, however, of differences between the two species of *Apodemus*. Most studies in England have concerned *A. sylvaticus* whilst on the continent *A. flavicollis* has been investigated in some of the most significant studies. There is evidence, especially from Poland, that *A. flavicollis* habitually forages in the canopy, probably to a greater extent than does *A. sylvaticus*.

Comparison of the food of wood mice and bank voles has shown an overall similarity in the annual sequence but with a difference in emphasis between the two species[13] [22] [36]. Buds and insects are important in spring and summer, nuts and seeds in winter. But the mice eat relatively more insects and seeds whilst the voles take considerably more soft fruit (in autumn), fresh leaves (eg of *Rubus* spp) and, in winter, twigs and bark.

As in the case of the squirrels, there is no evidence of any preference for oak except as determined by the size of the acorn crop. In spring both species feed on buds, the mice climbing higher into the trees than the voles, which are more restricted to young growth and the shrub layer. In oak woodland in Czechoslovakia Holisova found that the animal component in the diet of bank voles reached a peak in May, coinciding with a mass occurrence of geometrid moth larvae[15].

In autumn and winter the mast crop, of both oak and beech, is of major importance and it has been shown that the size of the crop has a major influence on winter survival, length of the reproductive season, range and density; and that these effects may persist even into the following autumn[14] [37]. Both mice and voles store acorns, forming caches in cavities under logs and in burrows[3]. Many measurements have been made of the rate of disappearance of fallen acorns during the winter[2] [27] [28] [30] [35]. Although it has been demonstrated that the experimental exclusion of small mammals results in a great increase in germination of acorns, opinion has been divided on the extent to which mice and voles are responsible for removal of the acorn crop. From work done at Monks Wood, Huntingdonshire, Tanton concluded that when the fall of acorns is heavy (eg up to 645 kg dry weight per hectare), only a small proportion are removed by wood mice and bank voles[30]. He estimated that a population of 60 rodents per hectare would eat about 0.16 to 0.32 kg dry weight of acorns per hectare per day. From the point of view of the small rodents the fall of acorns is affected not only by the size of the crop but also by the extent to which the crop is consumed by other species before it falls. Tanton recorded extremes of 92% and 8% of the acorn crop removed from the trees by wood pigeons (*Columba palumbus* L.)[30].

Turcek has also calculated, in terms of energy flow, the extent to which these species, along with the red squirrel and jay, *Garrulus glandarius* (L.), utilize the primary production of acorns, beech mast and spruce seeds[33]. His figures for oak are given in table 1. He concluded that in a year of maximum productivity of acorns only about 10% of the energy in acorns was utilized by mice, bank voles and jays together.

TABLE 1

Estimates of consumption of acorns by small rodents in a year of heavy crop, from Turcek[33]

	Apodemus	Clethrionomys
No. of rodents/hectare	50	20
Duration of feeding on acorns ..	180 days	120 days
Total energy intake during this period	135×10^3 kcal	28.8×10^3 kcal
Mass of acorns consumed	45 kg	9.6 kg

Dormice

Both dormice found in Britain, the native common dormouse, *Muscardinus avellanarius,* and the introduced fat dormouse, *Glis glis,* feed predominantly on fruit and nuts, including acorns. Since they both hibernate more completely than any other British species of mammal, the supply of food in autumn is of critical importance for adequate fattening and winter survival. The common dormouse, however, is very much a species of the shrub layer and it is likely that it derives most of its food from here, rarely climbing into the canopy or descending to feed on the open ground. Although acorns are undoubtedly eaten, it is likely that hazel nuts are more important. In contrast the fat dormouse is more at home in the canopy, frequently nesting in the middle of the crown of mature trees. Leaves of many species, including oak, are eaten in summer[34] and bark is stripped from the smaller branches, although this has been reported mainly for conifers, eg spruce and larch[31] [34]. In autumn acorns are eaten and because of the animal's habitat are likely to be more important to the fat dormouse than to the common dormouse, although many other foods are eaten in autumn including especially cherries and apples.

When the mast crop is poor it is likely that bark, twigs, buds, seeds of herbs and shrubs, and pupating insects are more heavily exploited during the winter, and Turcek has shown that in oak-hornbeam forest in Czechoslovakia both bank voles and yellow-necked mice feed on the larvae and pupae extracted from galls[32]. He found that almost all fallen galls were opened during the winter and 54% of galls destroyed *in situ* on the trees. Several species of gall were attacked but the preference was for those of *Andricus lucidus* (Hartig) (Hym., Cynipidae), a non-British species, although the closely related marble gall caused by, *A. kollari* (Hartig) was also used.

Beaver

The beaver became extinct in Britain probably in medieval times, but is likely at one time to have been widespread wherever there were slow-flowing rivers or lakes with wooded banks. Beavers eat a great variety of vegetation during the summer but their principal specialization is the felling of small trees, usually with trunks up to 150 mm diameter, to obtain bark and twigs. This is not only for immediate consumption, but logs and branches from felled trees are transported for storage under water and constitute the principal food during the winter. A study in Louisiana, U.S.A., at a site where only a small proportion of the available trees were oak (*Quercus falcata* Michaux) showed that they were used to a moderate extent, about 50% of trees in the appropriate size range being cut or barked each year[6]. Throughout the beaver's range, however, it is probable that oak plays a relatively minor part in its diet, the emphasis being on poplar, aspen, maple and birch and more specifically river-side species such as willow and alder.

Rabbit and brown hare

Both of these species feed predominantly in open ground, on grass and herbs. Rabbits however frequently make their burrows in woodland and either forage in adjacent grassland and crops or within the wood if it is open enough for a rich ground layer to be present. Although rabbits do eat acorns it is unlikely that they are as important a food as they are for squirrels, mice and the bank vole. Rabbits are notorious for their prevention of regeneration by browsing seedlings and young trees. All hardwoods suffer this attention. Several studies have indicated however that the rabbits are usually forestalled by mice and voles which rarely allow many seedlings to survive[24][25].

In parkland conditions Mellanby found that rabbits usually browsed off only the new growth of oak seedlings whereas cattle and sheep tended to graze them to the ground[20]. He also pointed out that oak seedlings were common on grassland adjacent to oak woods (presumably derived from acorns buried by squirrels or jays) but rare under the oak trees themselves. Since it is these peripheral areas of open ground that are the chief feeding areas of rabbits it is probably there that they have the greatest effect on oak, preventing colonization of new ground. Experimental sowing of acorns on heathland has also shown that under these conditions rabbits were responsible for consumption of almost the entire sowing before germination[21]. During hard weather in winter rabbits will feed on bark of a variety of young hardwoods, including oak, and may cause considerable damage.

All that has been said about the rabbit is probably applicable, but to a lesser degree, to the brown hare. Hares shelter in the margins of woods but are rarely found in dense woodland and it is in parkland that they are most likely to interact with oak. An exception has been described in Russia where in one area brown hares have adapted to a woodland existence and in winter feed mainly on sprouts of maple (*Acer platanoides* L.), oak (*Quercus robur*) and elm (*Ulmus* sp.)[26]. In Poland winter browse is cut to encourage hares for sporting purposes and it has been found that oak is utilized to a moderate extent, less so than apple, hawthorn, poplar and willow, but comparably with ash, pine and lime[19].

Deer

Only two species of deer are indigenous in Britain, the red deer *Cervus elaphus,* and the roe, *Capreolus capreolus.* The red deer is a species of deciduous forest and montane coniferous forest throughout the Holarctic Region. The roe has a similar range in the Palaearctic but also extends further north into the boreal forest although it is associated with birch and other broad-leaved trees rather than with the conifers. In addition we have one long-established introduction, the fallow deer, *Dama dama,* probably introduced by the Romans from southern Europe, and three more recent introductions, the sika, *Cervus nippon,* the muntjac, *Muntiacus reevesi* and the Chinese water deer, *Hydropotes inermis,* all from eastern Asia.

All of these occur in deciduous forest and utilize oak to some extent in the form of summer browsing, winter browsing or consumption of acorns. Most red deer in Britain occupy open hill country and only enter woodland to any extent in winter. Detailed studies of food in woodland on the continent, in Denmark[17] and Poland[12] have shown that browsing of deciduous foliage in summer is relatively unimportant compared with grazing but that oak was prominent amongst species that were browsed. In winter heathers were important and tree browsing was mainly confined to conifers.

Roe are more permanently woodland animals but they feed mainly on grass and herbs with heather and bramble playing an important part in winter. Again, browsing on trees is relatively unimportant in the summer when grazing is abundant and in winter is mainly on conifers.

Of the introduced deer, fallow is very closely associated with deciduous woodland but it is even more of a grazer than the native deer. Some browsing is done in summer, including oak, and acorns are eaten avidly in autumn. The rutting season, during which males eat little, takes place in October and November. The acorn crop therefore becomes available at a very opportune time and it has been maintained that quick recovery of condition after the rut and ability to withstand hard weather are to a considerable extent dependent upon the acorn crop[5]. This assessment is supported by experimental work on white-tailed deer, *Odocoileus virginianus* (Zimmerman), in Michigan, U.S.A.—penned deer on a starvation ration of browse were given a supplement of 1.5 lb of acorns/day/cwt (13.5 gm/day/Kg) and this was found to be critical for survival[11].

Sika likewise are predominantly grazers and where they do take a significant amount of browse, as in the New Forest, this consists mainly of conifers[16]. Acorns are eaten, however, and since the rutting behaviour is similar to that of the fallow it is likely that they could play a significant nutritional role in early winter.

Muntjac are now fairly widespread in south-eastern England. Being considerably smaller than roe their range of browse is more restricted. They feed mainly on ivy, bramble and grasses but will browse on hardwood seedlings. Dansie has recorded that they are 'adept at shucking out acorns and chestnuts but will also swallow them whole and grind them later'[8]. The Chinese water deer has an even more restricted distribution and little has been recorded of its ecology. It is however likely to be even more a grazer than our other species of deer.

All deer will eat bark in hard weather but as with squirrels oak tends to come off lightly in comparison with other species, elm and ash being especially vulnerable[38]. In deer parks browse wood used to be cut extensively to feed the deer in winter.

Wild boar

The wild boar became extinct in Britain during the 17th century, but it remains common in some parts of the continent and demands attention here as a major consumer of acorns. Oak and beech mast are the dominant components of the diet in autumn and winter[23] and the remarkable fattening ability of the domestic pig can be accounted for in no small degree in terms of an ancestral adaptation to making use of the autumnal glut of mast. Squirrels also put on fat in autumn but it is likely that their need to maintain agility in the face of predation imposes a limit at a much lower level than in the case of the large and well protected boar. Squirrels are therefore obliged to store most of their acorn harvest externally, rather than internally as do the boars.

Wild boars feed voraciously on mast—up to 5 kg have been found in one stomach. Fat production is reputed to be better after feeding on acorns than it is after feeding on beech mast, in spite of the lower fat content of acorns, and the fat itself is different, being more granular, lighter in colour and firmer[23].

Badger

The badger is the only carnivore in Britain that takes any significant amount of vegetable food, amongst which acorns are prominent. During most of the year badgers feed predominantly upon invertebrates and especially earthworms. Precise data on stomach contents are scanty but suggest that acorns are regularly eaten in autumn—Neal recorded that one animal in September contained 'a very large number broken up into fairly large pieces'[25]. Badgers do not hibernate completely but they put on a considerable amount of fat in autumn and are relatively inactive during the winter. Acorns could therefore play an important part in fattening and winter survival.

Other carnivores

Formerly in Britain, and now in only a few small refuges in Europe, the brown bear, *Ursus arctos,* is another omnivorous member of the order Carnivora that makes extensive use of the acorn crop[7]. The brown bear hibernates rather more completely than does the badger and lays down a very thick layer of subcutaneous fat in autumn.

Two recent introductions to Europe behave similarly. These are the racoon dog, *Nyctereutes procyonoides* (Gray), introduced in eastern Europe from eastern Asia, and the American racoon, *Procyon lotor* (L.), now feral in Luxembourg and adjacent regions. The racoon dog is unique amongst members of the dog family in hibernating (but only lightly, like the badger) and it fattens on fruit and acorns in autumn; the racoon comes from a family of omnivores and likewise hibernates lightly after fattening on acorns, grain and fruit.

Ways in which oak is exploited

Different parts of the tree are used in various ways by the species of oak-feeding mammals.

Buds

Buds are a major source of food for squirrels throughout the spring after the mast crop has run out and before animal food becomes abundant. Other species probably make only minor use of buds as such—those within reach will be included in the browse consumed by deer whilst a very small proportion may be taken by arboreal mice, especially yellow-necked mice, where they occur. But other species of hardwoods whose buds enlarge earlier in spring probably suffer more severely since by the time oak buds are attractive there is a much greater variety of alternative food available.

Leaves

Britain, like other regions of temperate deciduous forest, lacks any mammalian species specialised for the arboreal, leaf-eating niche. After the leaves have expanded they are practically immune from consumption by mammals unless they happen to be within reach of browsing ungulates. All the species of deer in Britain will browse on oak in summer but there is no evidence of any strong preference for it and where oak is young enough to offer much browse within reach there is generally an abundance of shrub and herb species to share the pressure. Cattle, sheep and goats will also browse on oak and other hardwoods, producing a clear browse line in oaks growing in pasture. Amongst their wild relatives the European bison, *Bison bonasus,* browses extensively on hardwoods including oak[4] as does the mouflon, *Ovis ammon musimon* (Pallas), which has been extensively introduced in European forests.

Acorns

The acorn crop is of major importance for most of the mammalian species considered here. Although the erratic nature of the crop precludes any one species being entirely dependent upon it, most species show a strong preference for acorns and the size of the crop has an important effect upon winter survival. Squirrels, and especially the grey squirrel, are the chief mammalian consumer of acorns, before they fall, although, as with buds, wood mice, yellow-necked mice and dormice also take a small proportion of the growing crop. But unless the crop is very small even the squirrels have little effect on the number that fall to the ground and it is the fallen crop that is exploited by squirrels, mice, bank voles, deer, badgers and rabbits; and formerly in Britain, and still in parts of the continent, by wild bears and brown bears.

In all these species acorns play a part in autumn fattening but this is especially important in the brown bear and badger, prior to complete or partial hibernation, and in the wild boar. The other species use the crop more evenly throughout the winter. The acorns buried in the litter by grey squirrels are often scratched up by deer and rabbits, but the underground caches of voles and mice are likely to be more secure from such misappropriation. Beech mast is used in a similar way by all of these species. It has a higher calorific value than acorns (6.7 kcal/g dry matter for beech, 4.07 kcal/g dry matter for oak according to Turcek) and in good years crops even more heavily[33].

Bark
Bark of most species of tree is liable to be eaten by deer, rabbits, hares, squirrels and voles, especially in winters when the mast crop has failed or when snow makes other food difficult to obtain. However, smooth-barked trees suffer more in this way than does oak and only young trees are vulnerable except to squirrels which may extensively bark the distal branches of mature trees. Squirrels are also liable to eat bark in early summer as well as in winter. Outside Britain a minor and local hazard to young trees is felling by beavers with the object of consuming bark and twigs from those branches that cannot be reached from the ground.

Winter twigs
Twigs in winter, if within reach, can normally be considered mainly as hard-weather browse for deer, rather than a preferred food. However it has been found in North America that hardwood trimmings (not including oak) were even more acceptable to white-tailed deer, *Odocoileus virginianus,* and equally nutritious, when cut after leaf-fall then when cut in leaf [1]. In the case of saplings and shoots feeding pressure in winter is considerable, mainly from deer, rabbits and hares, but also from voles and mice.

Seedlings
Seedlings generally suffer heavily from mammals, from voles and rabbits to deer. In sessile oak woodland in North Wales Shaw found that few seedlings survived more than four years, probably due mainly to voles[27 28].

Insects
The rich insect fauna of oak trees is undoubtedly exploited by both bats and shrews, the latter feeding upon Lepidoptera falling to the ground to pupate as well as on the permanent members of the leaf litter fauna. Of more direct concern to us here is the use made of insects by wood mice, and to a lesser extent voles and squirrels, especially in early summer, but also in winter in the form of the larvae and pupae of gall wasps.

Conclusions
Most species of mammal are versatile feeders, able to change their tactics to exploit the available resources. In summer there is gross overlap in the diet of most of the species dealt with here. It is in winter that a much higher degree of specialization emerges and competition is reduced. But cutting across these specializations is the erratic supply of mast and every species of woodland mammal with any vegetarian tendencies is sufficiently adaptable to make extensive use of a good crop of acorns and thereby protect itself against the equally erratic hazards of winter weather.

REFERENCES

1. ALKON, P. V. 'Nutritional and acceptability values of hardwood slash as winter deer browse'. *J. Wildl. Mgmt*, **25** (1961), 77–81
2. ASHBY, K. R. 'Prevention of regeneration of woodland by field mice (*Apodemus sylvaticus* L.) and voles (*Clethrionomys glareolus* Schreber and *Microtus agrestis* L.)'. *Q. Jl For.*, **53** (1959), 228–36
3. ASHBY, K. R. 'Studies of the ecology of field mice and voles (*Apodemus sylvaticus, Clethrionomys glareolus* and *Microtus agrestis*) in Houghall Wood, Durham'. *J. Zool., Lond.*, **152** (1967), 389–513
4. BOROWSKI, S., KRASINSKI, Z. and MILKOWSKI, L. 'Food and role of the European bison in forest ecosystems'. *Acta theriol.*, **12** (1967), 367–76
5. CADMAN, W. A. *The fallow deer*, Forestry Commission Leaflet no. 52 (1966)
6. CHABRECK, R. H. 'Beaver-forest relationships in St Tammany parish, Louisana'. *J. Wildl. Mgmt*, **22** (1958), 179–83
7a. CORBET, G. B. 'Provisional distribution maps of British mammals'. *Mammal Rev.*, **1** (1971), 95–142
7b. COUTURIER, M. A. J. *L'ours brun*, Ursus arctos L., Grenoble (1954)
8. DANSIE, O. *Muntjac* (Muntiacus *sp*), British Deer Soc. Publ. no 2 (1970)
9. DARLING, F. F. *Natural history in the Highlands and Islands*, London (1947)
10. DAVISON, V. E. 'Selection of foods by gray squirrels'. *J. Wildl. Mgmt*, **28** (1964), 346–52
11. DUVENDECK, J. P. 'The value of acorns in the diet of Michigan deer'. *J. Wildl. Mgmt.* **26** (1961), 371–9
12. DZIECIOLOWSKI, R. 'Winter food of red deer *Cervus elaphus* as determined by tracking techniques'. *Ekol. pol.*, **15A** (1967), 285–305
13. GORECKI, A. and GEBCZYNSKA, Z. 'Food conditions for small rodents in a deciduous forest'. *Acta theriol.*, **6** (1962), 275–95
14. HANSSON, L. 'Small rodent food, feeding and population dynamics'. *Oikos*, **22** (1971), 183–98
15. HOLISOVA, V. 'Food of an overcrowded population of the bank vole *Clethrionomys glareolus* Schreb. in lowland forest'. *Zool. Listy*, **15** (1966), 207–24
16. HORWOOD, M. T. and MASTERS, E. H. *Sika deer* (Cervus nippon), British Deer Soc. Publ. no 3 (1970)
17. JENSEN, P. V. 'Food selection of the Danish red deer (*Cervus elaphus* L.) as determined by examination of the rumen content'. *Dan. Rev. Game Biol.*, **5** (3) (1968), 1–44
18. JONES, E. W. 'Biological flora of the British Isles: *Quercus* L.'. *J. Ecol.*, **47** (1959), 169–222
19. MATUSZEWSKI, G. 'Studies on the European hare. XIII. Food preference in relation to tree's branches experimentally placed on the ground'. *Acta theriol.*, **11** (1966), 485–96
20. MELLANBY, K. 'The effects of some mammals and birds on regeneration of oak'. *J. appl. Ecol.*, **5** (1968), 359–66
21. MILES, J. 'Experimental establishment of seedlings on a southern English heath'. *J. Ecol.*, **60** (1972), 225–34
22. MILLER, R. S. 'Food habits of the wood-mouse, *Apodemus sylvaticus* (Linne, 1758), and the bank vole, *Clethrionomys glareolus* (Schreber, 1780), in Wytham Woods, Berkshire'. *Säugetierk. Mitt.*, **2** (1954), 109–14
23. MOHR, E. *Wilde Schweine*, Wittenberg Lutherstadt (1960)
24. MOORE, B. 'Oak woodlands on clay in south-western England and scarcity of natural regeneration of oak'. *Forestry*, **7** (1933), 85–92
25. NEAL, E. *The badger*, London (1948)
26. NOVIKOV, G. A. and TIMOFEEVA, E. K. 'The ecology of hare (*Lepus europaeus* Pall.) inhabiting fields and oak forests'. *Vest. leningr. gos. Univ.*, **9** (1964), 26–34

27. SHAW, M. W. 'Factors affecting the natural regeneration of sessile oak (*Quercus petraea*) in North Wales. I. A preliminary study of acorn production, viability and losses'. *J. Ecol.*, **56** (1968), 565–83
28. SHAW, M. W. 'Factors affecting the natural regeneration of sessile oak (*Quercus petraea*) in North Wales. II. Acorn losses and germination under field conditions'. *J. Ecol.*, **56** (1968), 647–60
29. SHORTEN. M. *Squirrels*, London (1954)
30. TANTON, M. T. 'Acorn destruction potential of small mammals and birds in British woodlands'. *Q. Jl For.*, **59** (1965), 1–5
31. THOMPSON, H. V. and PLATT, F. B. 'The present status of *Glis* in England'. *Bull. Mammal Soc. Br. Isl.*, **21** (1964), 5–6
32. TURCEK, F. J. 'Eichengallen als "Ersatznahrung" der Mäuse'. *Z. angew. Zool.*, **48** (1961), 215–20
33. TURCEK, F. J. 'Cycling of some forest tree-seeds with special reference to small mammals and the animals in general', in Petrusewicz, K. (ed.), *Secondary productivity of terrestrial ecosystems*, Warsaw (1967)
34. VIETINGHOFF-RIESCH, A. F. VON 'Der Siebenschläfer (*Glis glis* L.)'. *Monogrn Wildsäugetiere*, **16** (1960), 1–196
35. WATT, A. S. 'On the causes of failure of natural regeneration in British oakwoods'. *J. Ecol.*, **7** (1919), 173–203
36. WATTS, C. H. S. 'The foods eaten by wood mice (*Apodemus sylvaticus*) and bank voles (*Clethrionomys glareolus*) in Wytham woods, Berkshire'. *J. Anim. Ecol.*, **37** (1968), 25–41
37. WATTS, C. H. S. 'The regulation of wood mouse (*Apodemus sylvaticus*) numbers in Wytham Woods, Berkshire'. *J. Anim. Ecol.*, **38** (1969), 285–304
38. WHITEHEAD, G. K. *Deer and their management in the deer parks of Great Britain and Ireland*, London (1950)

THE BIRDS OF OAK WOODLANDS

J. J. M. Flegg and T. J. Bennett

British Trust for Ornithology, Tring, Herts

Introduction

The two species of oak may account for perhaps one quarter of British high-forest trees, and indeed dominate deciduous woodland over much of our countryside. As they are of such spatial importance, it is surprising to discover how few ornithologists have published results of their studies of them, and their birds, in real detail.

Yapp[1] and Simms[2] have each studied a series of such woods, and Beven[3] (1951 et seq) and his team carried out very detailed work at Bookham Common over a number of years. This assessment draws on the findings of these authors, and on the results of woodland areas in the British Trust for Ornithology's Common Birds Census, which has been operating since 1961/2.

Our conclusions are at variance with both Yapp and Simms, who have indicated a definite pattern to the distribution and frequency of oak woodland birds. In view of the complexity of the reasons for our disagreement, the seasonal use of a variety of oak habitats in one woodland in southeastern England (studied for some twelve years by J.J.M.F.) is considered first, to indicate the ways in which woodland structure affects bird populations, and how the various niches are exploited by the birds present. The word 'typical' has not been used, as our thesis is that it is inappropriate.

Northward Hill Vegetation

Within the boundaries of Northward Hill (High Halstow NNR), Kent, lies an area of some 25 hectares (62 acres) of oak woodland. The wood lies draped round a low promontary in the ridge of London clay forming the southern margin of the valley of the estuarine reaches of the River Thames. Adjacent to the oaks are areas of scrub and some stands of English elm, *Ulmus procera*, developed from old hedgerow trees and their suckers, giving way to a village, and the arable and fruit farmland and grazing marsh that characterise the Grain peninsular. With organisms as mobile as birds, these surrounding areas are of considerable importance.

Whilst the oak woodland contains almost exclusively *Quercus robur* (there is a single, planted, specimen of Turkey Oak, *Q. cerris*), there are considerable differences within the wood. Few of the trees are apparently more than 100 years old, and over about one third of the area all are standards 15–20 m (50–65ft) high. Another third of the area contains a mixture of clearings filled with bracken, (*Pteridium aquilinum*), bramble (*Rubus* spp) or scrub and standard oaks in small clumps, best described as a patch-work pattern and here called 'gladed'. The remaining third consists of oaks coppiced during the 1914–18 war and left untended since. The three areas, while of dissimilar shape, are each considered to form a coherent enough whole to be compared to one another. Other than the coppicing, little or no timber management had been carried out until the last three years, when some elms infected with Dutch elm disease were felled.

One consequence of this lack of timber management has been an abundance of dead and decaying branches, softened timber, holes and lifting flaps of bark. If anything, the coppiced area (with trees 10–12 m. high) shows proportionately more signs of decay than the area containing discrete standard trees. Fallen branches have been left in situ.

From an ornithological point of view, it is also important to describe briefly the vegetation of the three areas. The structural significance of the layers of vegetation will become apparent as the various bird populations are discussed.

1. *Coppice*

In the coppiced area stools are rarely more than a few metres apart and usually only two or three. Each stool gives rise to between one and four stems, usually two or three. These slender trunks rise to form a canopy with very few perforations, but because of their closeness, side branches are few and poorly developed. The canopy area relative to the plan area of the coppiced region is obviously lower than in the standards and much lower than in the isolated clumps, where the lower branches may spread to within one metre of the ground. With the continuous canopy other vegetation is sparse. The ground is largely covered to a depth of several centimetres in leaf litter, penetrated only by very occasional spindly elder bushes (*Sambucus nigra*), and by occasional patches of dog's mercury (*Mercurialis perennis*) and yellow archangel (*Galeobdolon luteum*). In spring about 50% of the coppice floor is covered with bluebells (*Endymion non-scriptus*).

2. *Standards*

As in the coppiced area, the canopy is complete, but if viewed from above it has a much more irregular appearance as adjacent canopies are dome-shaped rather than flat, increasing the surface area very considerably. Relatively speaking, the supporting branches are both more numerous and much more robust. Trunks are usually spaced at 10–15 m (33–50ft). Once again the shrub layer is elder, sparse and spindly as under the coppice canopy. The ground is leaf-litter covered, and only rarely do stands of bluebell or dog's mercury break this monotony.

3. *Gladed*

From an inspection of aerial photographs, oak canopy occupies less than half the plan area of the gladed area. Most of the oaks are discrete or in clumps of two or three, with very little vegetation beneath them. The open areas of the patchwork are filled with a variety of shrubs, herbaceous plants and grasses. Even in an area so floristically impoverished as High Halstow, several dozen species are represented (compared with the handful under closed canopy) and only a selection of those apparently of marked food or structural value are mentioned. The list includes gorse (*Ulex europaeus*), bramble and rose (*Rosa* spp), blackthorn (*Prunus spinosa*) and haw-thorn (*Crataegus monogyna*), bracken and a variety of vetches, composites and umbellifers. There are some areas of short rabbit-cropped turf.

Northward Hill birds

1. Coppice

Because of the lack of branches (especially at low level) and poor understorey development the numbers both of species and of individuals breeding within this area are poor. Mistle thrushes (*Turdus viscivorus*) can place their nests in the angles of major branches, but are only exceedingly rarely a high-density breeding species. The paucity of ground flora presumably limits invertebrate food to some extent—perhaps considerably—and the blackbird (*T. merula*) and song thrush (*T. philomelos*), which do not have the habit of the mistle thrush of flighting out to feed in neighbouring areas, suffer both from this and from the scarcity of nest sites. They and the chaffinch (*Fringilla coelebs*) and spotted flycatcher (*Muscicapa striata*) are limited to excrescences of small twigs on otherwise branchless trunks. The ephemeral nature of the ground vegetation, and the absence of ivy, greatly restrict nesting possibilities for the wren (*Troglodytes troglodytes*) and the robin (*Erithacus rubecula*). The peeling sheets of bark on decaying trunks do allow several pairs of treecreeper (*Certhia familiaris*) to nest, despite the small mean trunk diameter.

The generally high proportion of decaying timber allows both good feeding and abundant nesting possibilities for the great and lesser spotted woodpeckers (*Dendrocopus major* and *D. minor*) and in the coppiced area the small diameter of most branches favours the lesser rather than the greater. Neither species occurs at high density. Generally speaking, a number of species benefit at second hand from the single-season occupancy usual for woodpecker nests: the starling (*Sturnus vulgaris*) and the great and blue tits (*Parus major* and *P. caeruleus*). The starling requires holes bored by the great spotted, and is thus scarce in this region, and the exploitation of smaller holes, both natural and artificial, by the tits is less than would be expected, or than is the case elsewhere in the wood. It may be that the relatively small canopy area, carrying the winter moth caterpillar population that is the prime food of the nestlings, cannot support more. In most seasons fewer than six pairs of the two species nest, and the nests are relatively unproductive. Table 1 gives rough comparative figures of breeding numbers.

TABLE 1

Breeding birds in three oak woodland areas, Northward Hill, Kent
(approximate range of numbers of pairs)

Species	Coppice	Standards	Gladed
heron	0	10–100	0
mallard	0	0	0–2
shelduck	0	0	0–5
sparrowhawk	0–1	0–1	0
woodcock	0	0–2	0
stock dove	0	15–25	15–25
woodpigeon	5–10	25–40	25–40
turtle dove	0–5	5–10	35–50
cuckoo	0	1–5	5–10
barn owl	0	0	0–1
little owl	0	0–1	0–3
green woodpecker	0	0–1	0–3
great spotted woodpecker	1–2	1–5	1–5
lesser spotted woodpecker	2–5	1–2	1–2
carrion crow	0	1–2	1–2
jay	1–2	2–5	5–10
great tit	2–5*	5–20*	5–20*
blue tit	2–10*	20–40*	20–40*
willow tit	2–5	0	2–5
treecreeper	2–5	2–5	1–2
wren	2–5	5–10	15–20
mistle thrush	2–5	2–5	1–2
song thrush	2–5	2–5	15–20
blackbird	2–5	5–10	20–30
nightingale	0	0	5–10
robin	2–5	2–5	5–10
blackcap	0	5–10	10–20
garden warbler	0–2	1–5	5–10
whitethroat	0	0	0–5
lesser whitethroat	0	0	5–10
willow warbler	1–2	5–10	20–30
chiffchaff	1–5	5–15	5–10
spotted flycatcher	0–1	2–5	0
dunnock	0–1	2–5	30–50
starling	5–20	5–20	5–20
greenfinch	0	0	0–5
goldfinch	0	0	5–10
linnet	0	0	5–10
redpoll	0	0	0–2
bullfinch	0	0–2	10–20
chaffinch	5–10	5–10	5–10
yellowhammer	0	0	2–5
tree sparrow	5–10*	20–40*	20–40*
Total no species	23	31	39

* artificial nest sites available

In winter the coppiced area is relatively unproductive so far as bird numbers are concerned. Flocks of tits work the trunk bark and twigs for overwintering insects, but the leaf litter apparently contains less to interest the thrush flocks than either of the other two areas.

Finches are almost entirely absent as feeding birds presumably because of the absence of seeds on ground layer plants. Roosting sites, too, are scarce except for those species (eg tits) that frequently roost in holes. The lack of low vegetation, and the sparseness of that which does occur, must deter most of the smaller birds, and the poor twig framework of the canopy allows perching space for only a few woodpigeons (*Columba palumbus*).

2. *Standards*

Table 1 shows clear increases, both in species richness and in the number of individuals recorded, when comparing the breeding birds of the standards area to those within the coppiced trees. There are a number of probable reasons for these differences.

The proportion of decaying timber in the standards area differs little from that in the coppice, but the size of the branches when they fall or split allows species like the stock dove (*Columba oenas*) and little owl (*Athene noctua*) to appear. Great spotted woodpeckers become more abundant than lesser for the same reason. The greater structure of branches beneath the expanded, and uneven, canopy provides an increased number of nesting sites for woodpigeons, turtle doves (*Stretopelia turtur*) and for some thrushes. The height and strength of the canopy allows large nests to be built, such as those of the carrion crow (*Corvus corone*), and it is in these trees that part of the heronry is situated. Well-established nests of the heron (*Ardea cinerea*) may be up to one metre in diameter and of similar depth, and may be at a density of four or five to a tree. Occasionally one or two pairs of woodcock (*Scolopax rusticola*) will nest in more open leaf-litter areas, where their plumage characteristics camouflage them well.

Most insectivorous species must benefit from the considerably increased canopy area, the tits being a good example, and for these limitations are probably imposed by a lack of suitable nesting sites in the absence of a well-developed understory. The blackcap (*Sylvia atricapilla*) and chiffchaff (*Phylloscopus collybita*) are two of the warblers well adapted to exploiting such conditions.

The most conspicuous (and locally unpopular) feature of the standards area in winter is the size of the overnight woodpigion roost, which may on occasion exceed 10,000 birds. As in the other two areas, flocks of tits and associated species will work the trunks and twigs, and ground surface, for food. The leaf-litter for some reason, perhaps the greater spacing of the trees, and consequent improvement in predator perception, attracts flocks of thrushes, including blackbird and song thrush, fieldfare (*Turdus pilaris*), and redwing (*T. iliacus*). Such flocks may reach several hundreds of birds when surrounding farmland is snow-covered or deeply frost-bound. The standard oaks produce many more acorns than do those in the coppice, and these serve as a source of food for woodpigeons and especially jays (*Garrulus glandarius*). Jays moving out, acorns in beaks, to bury them in surrounding fields are a common early winter sight. Regrettably, agricultural practices usually deprive the jays of any benefit from this activity.

Late in winter herons roost in the standards but the area has little roosting potential for passerine species that do not roost in holes.

3. *Gladed*

Table 1 shows that generally speaking eight more species may be expected in the gladed area than under the standard oaks, and this richness of species, together with the numbers of pairs likely to be supported, offers a means of assessing the ornithological 'value' of this zone. Increases in numbers are most apparent in the thrushes, warblers and the finches, there being at least twice as many of all three in the gladed area compared with the standards. These increases are clearly attributable in the main to two features: the greatly increased structural diversity of the habitat in a physical sense, and the increase in both animal and vegetable food materials consequent on an increased diversity of plant species. Additionally, as there was an increase of vegetational surface area from coppice to standards, so there is an even greater one when glades are introduced amongst standard trees. Thus here is found the maximum nest site and food availability within the Northward Hill oak woodland—an indication of the benefits of both edge-effect and 'scrub' to bird populations.

In the context of this particular account it should be noted that the actual *oak* canopy area is smaller than in the standards. The effect of this reduction, not so much of oak foliage but of the insect fauna that it carries, is difficult to assess. It should influence only those species dependent in a major way on oak (for example, great and blue tits on caterpillars of the winter moth, but birds are mobile creatures, generally catholic in food preferences, and may have easy recourse to adequate other supplies.

Not unnaturally, the winter situation is similar, and again numerically it is apparent that the thrushes and finches derive most benefit from habitat of this gladed nature. The appearance of a variety of raptors and owls, able both to hunt mammals, insects and birds in the open glades and to prey on an increased biomass, and scarce species like the green woodpecker (*Picus viridis*) should also be noted.

Nor, too, should the dual use of this well-structured habitat pass without mention. Besides the winter food, numerous and well-sheltered roosting sites are available in the lower vegetational layers, and Batten (personal communication) has indicated that for blackbirds the midwinter overnight weight loss may be reduced by up to 80% by the choice of a sheltered roosting site during bad weather. For many species these roosts may be used throughout the winter, but for others the period of peak use may be quite short— perhaps less than one month—and this, of course, detracts not at all from their usefulness: indeed they may be the more vital for such birds as an 'ultimate refuge' in times of severest stress. Much the same argument may be applied to the winter food resources.

Situation summary for Northward Hill

Tables 1 and 2 show the changes in the size and species richness of the avifauna of three similar-sized but structurally very different

TABLE 2

Wintering birds in three oak woodland areas, Northward Hill, Kent
(approximate order of numbers: 1–9=**1**, 10–99=**2**, 100–999=**3** etc
R=roosting, F=feeding)

Species	Coppice	Standards	Gladed
sparrowhawk	0	1 F	1 F
kestrel	0	0	1 F
moorhen	0	0	1 R
woodcock	1 F+R	1 F+R	1 F+R
stock dove	0	2 R	0
woodpigeon	2 R	2–5 F+R	2–3 F+R
barn owl	0	0	1 F+R
little owl	0	1 F+R	1 F+R
long-eared owl	0	1 F	1–2 F+R
green woodpecker	0	0	1 F+R
great spotted woodpecker	1 F+R	1 F+R	1 F+R
lesser spotted woodpecker	1 F+R	1 F+R	1 F+R
carrion crow	0	1 R	1 R
jay	1 F	1–2 F+R	1–2 F+R
great tit	2 F+R	2 F+R	2 F+R
blue tit	2 F+R	2–3 F+R	2–3 F+R
coal tit	1 F	1 F+R	1 F+R
willow tit	1 F+R	1 F+R	1 F+R
treecreeper	1–2 F+R	2 F+R	1 F+R
wren	1 F+R	2 F+R	2 F+R
mistle thrush	0	1 F+R	1 F+R
fieldfare	0–1 F	0–4 F+R	0–4 F+R
song thrush	1–2 F	1–3 F+R	1–3 F+R
redwing	0–1 F	0–4 F+R	0–4 F+R
blackbird	1–2 F	1–3 F+R	1–3 F+R
robin	1–2 F+R	1–2 F+R	1–2 F+R
goldcrest	1–2 F	1–2 F+R	1–2 F+R
dunnock	1 F+R	1–2 F+R	1–2 F+R
starling	1 R	1–2 R	1–5 R
hawfinch	1 F	1 F+R	1–2 F+R
greenfinch	0	1 F	1–3 F+R
goldfinch	0	0	1–3 F+R
linnet	0	0	1–3 F+R
redpoll	0	0	1–2 F+R
bullfinch	0	1 F	2 F+R
chaffinch	1 R	1 R	2 F+R
brambling	0	1 R	1 R
yellowhammer	0	0	2 F+R
reed bunting	0	0	1 F+R
tree sparrow	1 R	2 F+R	2 F+R
Total no species	22	31	39

areas of oakwood in Northward Hill. They clearly demonstrate that throughout the year in this south-east English wood oaks with a canopy sufficiently complete to all but exclude other vegetation are a considerably poorer habitat for birds, in terms both of numbers and species richness, than oaks with a broken canopy and well-developed undergrowth. It may well be that the diversity of physical structure provided under broken canopy is at least as important to the bird population in all seasons as is the increase in food variety (and perhaps quantity) inevitably associated with this condition.

Under the closed canopy dead or decaying timber, loose flaps of bark, and holes or splits left by falling branches are of considerable importance both in providing a supply of food at all seasons and in furnishing nest sites in the lower strata. Thus, forestry hygiene is not beneficial to the health of the bird population.

Northward Hill is relatively small, and isolated in a considerable area of mixed farmland. Thus its value in winter as both a roosting and feeding area (and, in times of severe stress, a refuge) may be over-emphasised. Nevertheless, the decisions affecting the choice and management of reserve or conservation areas are based too frequently on breeding season data, which may not necessarily reflect the true values of the area under discussion.

Oak woodland in other areas

Two points arise from the consideration of Northward Hill that can be used as a basis for the introduction and discussion of data from other areas. First, at least three species are, to the 'surprise' of local ornithologists, missing from the list of breeding species. The redstart (*Phoenicurus phoenicurus*) has bred probably only twice in the last twenty years, the tree pipit (*Anthus trivialis*) probably not at all during that period, and the nuthatch (*Sitta europea*) has only occurred twice, never breeding. Yet these species are all apparently catered for so far as their ecological requirements can now be assessed; all breed within ten miles of Northward Hill and all are widely, if irregularly or thinly, distributed breeding birds in this part of England. Subsequent discussion will deal with the gross patterns of bird distribution and how they influence the possibilities of defining a 'typical' oak avifauna, but these lesser vagaries of distribution should not be forgotten.

Secondly, whilst uniform techniques of survey are available for breeding species that allow justifiable comparisons to be made between areas, no such techniques have been developed satisfactorily for wintering birds. Data are thus restricted to those in the detailed and personal studies already cited, and to the crude figures presented in table 2. A technique for survey during the winter as satisfactory as the Common Birds Census (CBC) would be a most desirable development, but the difficulties to be surmounted are considerable. It seems best, therefore, to omit further discussion of wintering populations.

The CBC has been running since 1961/62. Details of methodology and analysis have been fully described elsewhere[4][5][6]. A series of visits (preferably more than ten) is made to the survey plot, and on each occasion the locations of all birds showing any defined kind of behaviour associated with breeding are plotted on a large-scale map. These visit maps are collated, species by species, at the end of the season, and most records fall into well-defined clusters

representing territories. Objective standards for detailed analysis
were laid down by the International Bird Census Committee in
1969[7].

For the comparisons in fig 1, the several dozen oak woodland
plots available were reviewed and those better described as "mixed
woodland with oaks" or "scrub with oaks" were discarded. Also
discarded were all plots where habitat data were insufficient, or
where some bird species had for any resaon been excluded. The
CBC is an extensive survey designed to produce a population *index*
from the work of many observers, and can use data from plots
with observer bias. In this intensive study plots were only included
from observers whose past consistency had been checked. Finally,
because of the extreme population changes that can occur from year
to year for a variety of reasons (see below) the use of mean populations over a number of years was discarded, and only plots
censused in 1972 included. This rather strict selection procedure
reduced the plots available for consideration to ten, but they

FIGURE 1

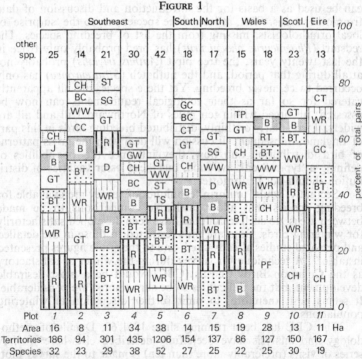

Plot	1	2	3	4	5	6	7	8	9	10	11	
Area	16	8	11	34	38	14	15	19	28	13	11	Ha
Territories	186	94	301	435	1206	154	137	86	127	150	167	
Species	32	23	29	38	52	27	25	22	25	30	19	

Percentage species composition of breeding bird communities in eleven woodland
plots. B blackbird. BC blackcap. BT blue tit. CC chiffchaff. CT coal tit. D
dunnock. GC goldcrest. GT great tit. GW garden warbler. J jay. PF pied
flycatcher. R robin. RT redstart. SG starling. ST song thrush. TD turtle dove.
TP tree pipit. TS tree sparrow. WR wren. WW willow warbler.

nevertheless serve our purpose. For comparative purposes, the Killarney plot has been included although it was surveyed in 1973.

In all cases the woodpigeon, a bird with an extended and a typical breeding season and difficult to census, has been eliminated from consideration. This does not imply that the association of this economically important bird with oakwoods does not merit discussion—rather that it necessitates a detailed individual study. A brief description of each of the selected plots follows.

1. *Eastern Wood, Bookham Common, Surrey*

This 16 hectare (40 acre) wood has been the subject of a study for some 26 years by the Ecological Section of the London Natural History Society. It is a typical semi-natural pedunculate oakwood growing on a damp clay soil, surrounded by similar woodland, but demarcated by a series of footpaths and rides. Six fairly distinct zones were identified within the plot by Beven[3] and although a certain amount of thinning and coppicing has taken place since then, it is considered that the wood as a whole has changed very little over the years.

First, there is a zone where the hawthorn shrub layer is sparsely scattered with bracken (dense in places) and occasional brambles and roses. About equal proportions of young and mature oaks exist here. Second, there is a zone containing a greater proportion of hawthorn with a little hazel (*Corylus avellana*); the oaks are predominantly young. This area accounts for over a third of the total plot. Third, there is a zone, of dense continuous hawthorn thickets, with brambles and honeysuckle *(Lonicera periclymenum)* abundant and very little bracken. The fourth zone contains more hazel with some birch (*Betula* sp) and hawthorn among the mainly young oaks. The fifth zone contains sparse mature oaks with a dense hazel understorey and little ground vegetation. Finally, there is a small area of mostly young oak with the wood floor almost bare. In addition there are two small ponds at the southern boundary with human habitation within 92 m (100 yards) of one corner.

2. *Chiddingfold, Surrey*

This eight hectare (20 acre) plot is described as a 'closed woodland of oak' with a fair amount of ash (*Fraxinus excelsior*) also present. It has a hazel understorey with sparse ground cover.

3. *Perivale Wood, Ealing, Middlesex*

This eleven hectare (27acre) wood is bounded by a canal to the north, a factory and warehouses to the west, meadowland and gardens to the south and another stretch of meadow to the east. The wood itself is mostly of closed canopy oaks with occasional ashes. There is a well developed shrub layer of hazel with varying amounts of hawthorn and occasional blackthorn thickets. The field layer is on the whole dense and predominantly of bramble. There are several small clearings in the wood, where the ground flora tends to be much denser. In addition to the canal there are two small ponds within the wood itself with a stream running along the western side. There are nestboxes in position.

4. *Ham Street Woods NNR, Ashford, Kent*

The reserve is some 96 hectares (237 acres) but the census plot, which is typical of the area, covers 34 ha (84 ac). It is essentially an area of coppice-with-standards, most of the standards being oak, but several other species are occasionally found. The distribution of the oaks is not uniform because of unplanned felling during the last war. Over half the plot contains fewer than 50 standards /ha (20/ac) and the other half has from 52–148/ha (21–60/ac). In the past the whole area was subjected to a standard coppice rotation of several species, mainly hornbeam (*Carpinus betulus*) with less of sweet chestnut (*Castanea sativa*), hazel and oak. Nowadays much of the area is managed as 'high forest' whilst other parts are periodically thined. To the north it is bordered by similar woodland, to the south by gardens and by grassland on the other sides.

5. *High Halstow NNR, (Northward Hill), Kent*

This is the area described in the first part of this paper. The results for the whole census plot are included in the figures.

6. *Knightwood, Chandler's Ford, Hampshire*

Oak is dominant over the 14 hectare (35 acre) plot as a whole, but is co-dominant with other species such as beech (*Fagus sylvatica*), yew (*Taxus baccata*), ash and birch in certain parts. There is a well-developed secondary shrub layer of hazel with occasional patches of holly (*Ilex aquifolium*) and hawthorn and a fairly dense field layer of bracken and bramble throughout. The plot is entirely surrounded by rough grazing land.

7. *Hirst Wood, Shipley, W. Yorkshire*

This 15 hectare (37 acre) plot is surrounded by the R. Aire, a canal, railway lines and roads. The dominant tree is oak but beech, sycamore (*Acer pseudoplatanus*) and birch trees are also quite frequent. The shrub layer variously consists of regenerating oak, hawthorn, holly and willow (*Salix* spp). There is also a well developed field layer of bracken and brambles.

8. *Ogmore Vale, Bridgend, Glamorgan*

This predominantly pedunculate oak woodland plot has areas of both open and closed canopy and covers some 19 hectares (47 acres). The NW corner consists of a closed larch plantation of about 1½ hectares (4 acres). The secondary layer is poorly developed and consists of hawthorn and birch where it is present. The field layer is very sparse except in open areas where it is dominated by bracken. The plot rises from about 175 m (575 ft) to nearly 275 m (900 ft) in the north. The southern boundary is formed by a busy main road. To the north the wood gives way to marginal hill country.

9. *Dinas Hill, Carmarthenshire*

The 28 hectare (70 acre) plot of sessile oaks rises from 180 m (600 ft) to over 305 m (1000 ft). Near the highest part of the plot the oaks are unable to develop beyond the scrub stage. Most of the canopy is closed, but there is a large open canopied area in the south-western part. There is no understorey and the field layer is confined to grass and bracken, which is very dense in places. In the south of the plot are one or two patches of birch. It is surrounded by marginal farmland except in the NW where the hill opens out. There is a large number of nestboxes to supplement the natural holes.

10. *Arrochymore, Loch Lomond, Stirlingshire*
The main part of this oak wood is on a low hill on the shore of Loch Lomond. The 13 hectare (32 acre) plot is bounded by a road and the shore-line. The sloping west side has rocky outcrops and wet patches, becoming very boggy by the shore, and here supporting alder (*Alnus glutinosa*), willow and birch. The floor is mainly of grass and is well grazed. There is a fairly large clearing in the middle, and two small artificial pools fenced to protect stock. Coppicing took place regularly to the end of the First World War, and explains the dominance of the introduced pedunculate species.

11. *Derrycunihy Wood, Upper Lake, Killarney, Co. Kerry*
This was the least grazed of three oakwood plots censused by a BTO expedition to the area in May 1973, these results being the first and only comparable results existing for Ireland. The eleven hectare (27 acre) plot was bordered on two sides by similar stretches of woodland and on the other two by open grassland with much dwarf gorse (*Ulex gallii*) and ling (*Calluna vulgaris*). There are several boggy areas and small streams trickle down to the lake. The dominant oaks are of varying age but there is now virtually no regeneration. There is a fairly prolific understorey of holly with a sparse field layer. The most noticeable feature of the wood is the rich bryophyte community both on the rocky ground and along the branches of the trees.

Discussion
1. *Gross factors influencing bird distribution and numbers*
Britain and Ireland are offshore islands. Compared with continental Europe their climate is unstable and their countryside extremely varied in geology, vegetation and management. Their mild winters encourage a wide variety of migrants fleeing the continental winters to stay, and their land-management, both historically and at the present, is so diverse as to encourage both generalist and specialist species, although depressingly few large tracts of specialised habitat now remain. It is generally argued today[7] that island avifaunas aree numerically more closely related to the island area than to the proximity of the 'home' continent: thus Ireland possesses only 60% of the breeding species in Britain. Other factors do play their part, and an inspection of the information in Parslow[8] shows that 53% of the passerine and near-passerine species breeding in Britain and Ireland have a predominantly south-eastern breeding distribution, compared with 20% showing a north-westerly one. The latter are frequently associated with areas of high ground, which are similarly disposed. Clearly, the avifaunas of western and northern oakwoods are more severely influenced by the absence of species such as the nightingale (*Luscinia megarhynchos*) (which is

limited to the south-east of England) than are woodlands in south-eastern England which are outside the range of species such as the pied flycatcher (*Ficedula hypoleuca*).

With the patchwork of habitats and numbers of species on the fringes of their range, several species occur regularly in what can be considered as secondary or marginal habitat. Indeed, on a grander, continental scale, it could be argued that the greater proportion of these islands consists of marginal habitats. Fig 2 shows one such woodland bird, the garden warbler (*Sylvia borin*) and its greater population fluctuations in the secondary habitat (farmland), and the reverse situation for the yellowhammer (*Emberiza citrinella*), primarily a bird of open scrubland, when it enters woodland.

FIGURE 2

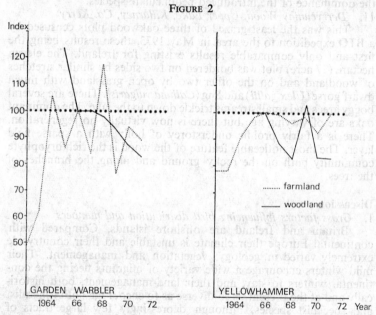

Abundance of garden warbler and yellowhammer in farmland and woodland, 1962-1972.

It is generally recognised that populations of birds are sensitive enough to be used as indicators of biological or ecological changes in the environment. This sensitivity, and the violent fluctuations it produces, is illustrated for two species, the wren and the white-throat (*Sylvia communis*), in fig 3. The magnitude of the impact of the 1962/63 cold winter on the population of the wren—a resident throughout the year—can be clearly seen, as can the only slightly less rapid recovery. In the case of the whitethroat, it seems likely that a climatic reversal south of the Sahara prevented most of this migratory species from successfully crossing the desert in spring 1969. Since that time, the southwards extension of the desert area may have inhibited any recovery. The impact of events such as these on the species and numerical composition of avifaunas can obviously be great even though two extremes have been selected for illustrative purposes.

FIGURE 3

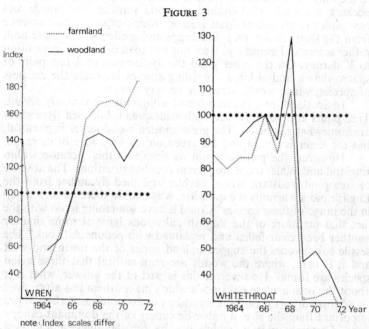

note: Index scales differ

Abundance of wren and whitethroat in farmland and woodland, 1962–1972.

Habitat selection by birds in Britain and Ireland, and perhaps largely elsewhere, seems most often to be a matter of degrees of catholicity. In the British woodland avifauna there are very few specialist species like the crossbill (*Loxia curvirostra*), which is largely restricted by its feeding adaptations to seed-bearing coniferous woods. The actual differences in success or productivity for species like the treecreeper, coal tit (*Parus ater*) and goldcrest (*Regulus regulus*), which are generally considered to be birds of coniferous woods when breeding in deciduous woodland, have not been assessed adequately, but seem unlikely to be great. Relatively few species of bird can cope with the seeds of oak because of their size and strength: the jay and woodpigeon are two examples, but both capitalise on acorns when available rather than specialising in them. Similarly, both great and blue tits have apparently adapted admirably, with a well-timed single large brood, to the sudden brief flush of winter moth caterpillars, but both species seem to thrive equally well in a wide variety of other habitats, including conifers, where they are usually double-brooded.

2. *Comments on the selected woodlands*

The most obvious feature resulting from a comparison of such widely scattered plots is the importance of their location in relation to the range of a particular species. Marsh and willow tits, the woodpeckers, nuthatch, pied flycatcher, wood warbler, nightingale and tree pipit are all absent from Ireland, which explains their absence from the Derrycunihy plot. Blackcaps and garden warblers are both rather scarce in Ireland and were not recorded during the expedition to Killarney. On the other hand the appearance of a few pairs of sparrowhawk and siskin as breeding species increases the richness of species, which would otherwise be very low.

In Scotland, too, the marsh and willow tits are virtually absent. Tree pipits and redstarts are both widespread, but pied flycatchers are somewhat restricted. The great spotted woodpecker is plentiful, but the lesser is absent and the green on the very edge of its range.

However, the picture is not as simple as this, because within England and Wales there are several peculiar situations. The absence of tree pipit, redstart, wood warbler and pied flycatcher from the English plots warrants the question, why should there be such a gap in the range of these species? Could it have something to do with the fact that far more of the English oakwoods have at some time or another been clear felled and replanted with pedunculate oak? The sessile oak favours the rugged upland zones of the north and west and it is here, where the woods are semi-natural that these avian species are found. However, if this is part of the answer, what is it about the pedunculate oakwoods which makes them less attractive?

Most authors regard the secondary understorey as perhaps more important than the size, number or variety of the dominant canopy trees. Certainly plot 4, which has by far the thickest and best developed understorey is the only one on which the *Sylvia* warblers and the nightingale show well. Stuttard & Williamson[9] have demonstrated the preference for certain coppice species that the nightingale has.

A dense ground layer can be either favourable or restrictive depending on its species composition. Much of plot 3 is covered by a very dense layer of brambles. Here the dunnock becomes an important member of the community. Presumably the scrubby areas of plot 5 also favour the dunnock sufficiently for it to become co-dominant.

The great variation and 'jig-saw' pattern of plot 5 accounts for the great diversification of species, considerable density and corresponding lack of any truly dominant species. Plot 5 and plot 4 are the most south-easterly, which may also enhance species richness. The chaffinch, a relatively unimportant bird in English plots, becomes sub-dominant in Wales and dominant in Scotland and Ireland. The willow warbler behaves in a similar way, except that there is a very surprising absence from the Killarney plot. Williamson explains its abundance in Scotland as depending on the amount of regeneration and pioneer growth and, as English woods tend to be closer to the climax state, with fewer open areas, the populations may be lower.

Robin and wren tend to be the dominant birds of the pedunculate woodlands, the absence of the former from plot 9 being interesting, and probably caused by the lack of understorey and ground layer. A similar situation would be expected for the wren, but its recent enormous population increase probably accounts for its overall good showing.

The almost unprecedentedly high numbers of the goldcrest in Killarney, where it seems to appear as a substitute for the *Phylloscopus* warblers, is possibly related to the unusual understorey of holly, which is used for song-posts, with some indication that the ivy-covered trunks are used for nest sites.

Holes are obviously very important for the tits, starlings, pied flycatchers and tree sparrows, so that the age of of the trees and incidence of disease must be important. Lack of holes for nest sites can be overcome by the provision of nestboxes. At Perivale this has resulted in the blue tit becoming the dominant species. At Dinas Hill, where there are nestboxes, the pied flycatcher is clearly dominant whilst on the nearby Gwenffrwd Reserve, with no nestboxes, they form less than 10% of the total bird population.

Conclusions

The many factors causing changes in bird distributions and bird numbers, on either a national or a local scale, are at present imperfectly understood, but they are sufficiently well-known to allow meaningful comparisons and a simple assessment of oak woodland as a habitat for birds to be made. Perhaps the need is greatest for a much increased knowledge of the availability of both plant and animal food and, more important, their selection and utilisation by bird communities.

Densities of breeding populations (in territories/km²) in the census plots studied range from a sparse 450 to 2700 and 3100—amongst the greatest and most diverse recorded for any habitat in Britain—but no strikingly characteristic species are recorded.

Certainly it appears that in any given area, the oak woodland is likely to be at least a satisfactory habitat for birds and given that its physical structure includes open glades and well-developed secondary vegetation which provide as full a range of feeding and nesting sites as possible, it can be a very rich habitat indeed, with a well-diversified fauna. Such a structure can be achieved relatively easily by management, but the importance of dead timber must be stressed.

There is an urgent need for more detailed information on oak woodland as a habitat for birds in *winter*. Such studies as are available indicate that its value to bird populations at this time may be considerable, especially in times of severe climatic stress.

REFERENCES

1. YAPP, W. B. *Birds and woods,* London (1962)
2. SIMMS, E. *Woodland birds,* London (1971)
3. BEVEN, G. 'The bird population of an oakwood in Surrey (Eastern Wood, Bookham Common)', *Lond. Nat.,* **30** (1951), 57–72
3a. BEVEN, G. 'Further observations of the bird population of an oakwood in Surrey', *Lond. Nat.,* **32** (1953), 51–77
3b. BEVEN, G. 'Further observations on the bird population of an oakwood in Surrey', *Lond. Nat.,* **35** (1956), 21–32
3c. BEVEN, G. 'The feeding sites of birds in dense oakwood', *Lond. Nat.,* **38** (1959), 64–73
3d. BEVEN, G. 'Population changes in a Surrey oakwood during fifteen years', *Br. Birds,* **56** (1963), 307-23
3e. BEVEN, G. 'Survey of Bookham Common. 25th year. Progress report for 1965. Birds', *Lond. Nat.,* **45** (1966), 52–5
3f. BEVEN, G. 'Survey of Bookham Common. 26th year. Progress report for 1966. Birds', *Lond. Nat.,* **46** (1967), 112–15
4. WILLIAMSON, K. 'Bird census work in woodland', *Bird Study,* **11** (1964), 1–22
5. WILLIAMSON, K. and HOMES, R. C. 'Methods and preliminary results of the common bird census, 1962–63', *Bird Study,* **11** (1964), 240–56
6. TAYLOR, S. M. 'The common bird census—some statistical aspects', *Bird Study,* **12** (1965), 268–86
7. LACK, D. 'The numbers of bird species on islands', *Bird Study,* **16** (1969), 193–209
8. PARSLOW, J. L. F. *Breeding birds of Britain and Ireland,* Berkhamsted (1973)
9. STUTTARD, P. and WILLIAMSON, K. 'Habitat requirements of the nightingale', *Bird Study,* **18** (1971), 9–14

Note: Comprehensive references to birds in woodlands are given by Yapp and Simms (references 1 and 2).

ECOLOGICAL ASPECTS OF OAK WOODLAND CONSERVATION

D. T. STREETER

School of Biological Sciences, University of Sussex

Introduction

It is now no longer necessary to emphasise the point that conservation is a subject that comprises a synthesis of three separate disciplines; ecology, economics and sociology. Here I am concerned with only the ecological component.

In this country most ecological conservation has as its major objective the maintenance of whole ecosystems, rather than the protection of populations of individual species. Coppice, and other forms of managed woodland, represent one of the richest of our wildlife habitats, from both the floristic and faunistic point of view. Furthermore, the conservation of semi-natural ecosystems is as important for their archaeological significance as it is for their scientific merit. The landscapes produced by past generations and past cultures can often provide a more explicit statement of contemporary social conditions than the evidence of more tangible remains. However, in this paper I intend to confine myself to a consideration of high forest, that is woodland comprising maiden trees and displaying little evidence of past management.

Deciduous high forest holds a unique place in British ecology as it is generally accepted that it represents the natural climatic climax vegetation of much of Britain. Estimates vary as to the actual proportion of the land formerly occupied by forest, but most agree on a figure between 70–75%, that is, all parts below the tree line, except for those areas of western Britain where ombrotrophic mire forms the climatic climax, some coastal areas, steep cliffs and rapidly eroding or accreting river banks. A high proportion of native plants and animals will therefore be essentially forest species and as natural climax ecosystems are normally regarded as supporting one of the highest total species diversities of a particular climatic region, then it is not unreasonable to expect high forest to possess an unusually rich flora and fauna. Woodland of this kind should therefore claim the special attention of conservationists for the two related reasons of intrinsic ecological interest in its relation to the climatic climax and in its general diversity of wildlife.

With only 8% of the country now covered by woodland of all kinds[1], Britain is the third least wooded country in Europe after Ireland and Holland. Of this, only about 13% is oak woodland[2].

Therefore, only a fraction over 1% of Britain is occupied by vegetation in any way approaching its natural climatic climax. With such a small area involved, the importance of the identification and conservation of the best examples is self-evident. At the beginning of 1973 there were 278,392 acres of National Nature Reserves of which about 12,235 acres were woodland or 4.4% of the total reserve area[3]. The proportion of woodland nature reserve in which oak plays a prominent part is not accurately known but is probably not more than 6,000 acres. This means that only about 1% of the oak woodland in Britain is at present protected by National Nature Reserve status. There are in addition a further 4,000–5,000 acres included in Forest Nature Reserves by agreement with the Forestry Commission and a not inconsiderable area of oak woodland in reserves managed by the County Trusts for Nature Conservation. For instance in Sussex there are 470 acres of oak-dominated high forest nature reserves.

Criteria for identifying best sites

One of the first requisites of any conservation policy is to establish criteria for identifying the most satisfactory examples of different types of ecosystem. It is therefore necessary to be able to assess the ecological value of a woodland as an example of high forest. As 5,000 years of continuous modification of the British landscape by Man has effectively ensured that no vestige of original forest remains, all that one can hope to achieve is the identification of those examples of woodland that most closely approximate to the primeval forest. An obvious difficulty here is that as no-one has actually seen an example of our primeval high forest, views on the subject are necessarily somewhat subjective. What are the most objective criteria that can be used? I suggest that there are three that could be developed, all of which should be potentially capable of quantitative comparison with a theoretical numerical value and none of which involves a consideration of species composition.

1. *Age structure*

Climax ecosystems are by definition self-perpetuating and the pollen record demonstrates that woodland dominated by oak did indeed persist over most of lowland Britain for 3000–4000 years before the period of extensive de-forestation[4]. Furthermore, species characteristic of mature ecosystems should theoretically possess an age-structure characteristic of stable populations. Therefore, populations of trees in natural high forest should not only exhibit all stages of the regeneration cycle, as shown in fig 1, but should also possess an age structure characteristic of a stable tree population. The age structure of the tree population of a woodland can be determined by sampling and the shape of the age-class frequency histogram examined. It should be possible to determine to what extent the structure differs from that expected from a stable population. The difficulty is that it is at present not clear what the detailed

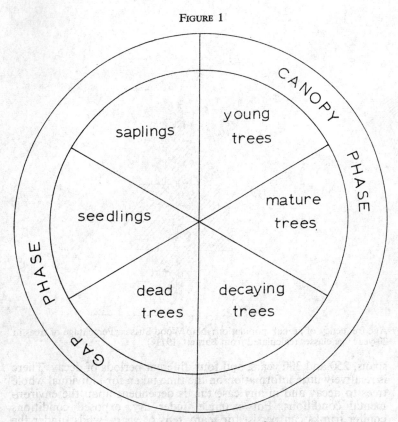

The woodland regeneration cycle.

shape of the frequency histogram of a stable tree population should be. However, for example, fig 2 is the age-class frequency histogram of the oak population from Nap Wood, Sussex and it can be clearly seen that there is a deficiency in the younger age-classes, perhaps indicating insufficient recruitment to the population, and fewer mature individuals than would be expected in a stable population.

2. *Dead wood*

Ecologists frequently complain that managed woodlands are deficient in dead and decaying wood, whilst undisturbed woods are richer in this resource. Few woods contain any number of whole dead trees. How many dead trees should we expect in undisturbed forest? It should be possible to calculate this provided one knew the length of time it took for a dead tree to decay to the point that it was no longer readily recognisable as such, and also the life span of the tree. Table 1 sets out the number of dead trees that could be expected on theoretical grounds per 100 trees for two different life

FIGURE 2

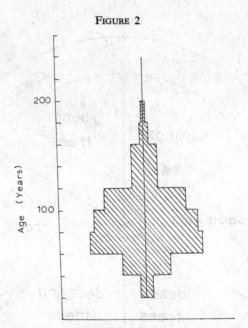

Age frequency of an oak population: Nap Wood Sussex. Percentage of trees in 20-year age classes (calculated from Barnett, 1971[5]).

spans, 250 and 300 years, and four different periods of decay. There is relatively little information on the time taken for individual whole trees to decay and in any case this is dependent upon the environmental conditions. For example under dry, exposed conditions conifer trunks can persist for many tens of years, whilst under the mild moist conditions of the deciduous woodland floor decomposition may be more rapid.

TABLE 1

Theoretical number of dead oaks per 100 trees

	Time taken to decay (years)	No of dead trees per 100 trees
a. Assuming life span of 300 years ..	5	1.6
	10	3.2
	20	6.2
	50	14.3
b. Assuming life span of 250 years ..	5	2.0
	10	3.8
	20	7.5
	50	16.7

From table 1 it can be seen that assuming a life span of 300 years (Peterken and Tubbs recorded values well in excess of this in the New Forest[6]) and a decay time of only 10 years one might expect on average 3–4 trees in every hundred to be dead. Under some conditions a decay period of up to 50 years might be more realistic, in which case about 1 tree in 8 would be dead. In either case the figures are much in excess of those for most of our woodlands. However, some parts of the unenclosed woodland of the New Forest certainly possess dead trees of the lower frequency. The main difficulty in using this feature of woodlands is in determining when a tree is actually dead as the normal pattern is for parts of the canopy to progressively die and shed branches over a long period of time. Some arbitrary value, such as when 75% of the canopy was dead or shed, would have to be used. However, in spite of the drawbacks, the frequency of dead trees does seem to provide a potentially quantitative property that could be numerically compared with a theoretical value for undisturbed woodland, once the parameters had been standardised and realistic values for the decay time determined.

3. *Species diversity*

It has become almost a tenet of conservation dogma that high species diversity is desirable and low species diversity undesirable. Smith and Streeter[7] have previously pointed out that the over-rigid application of this principle is not only unjustified on ecological grounds but the deliberate diversification of a site to encourage an increase in species can in some instances actually reduce the ecological value of the area. There are many natural ecosystems that are characterised by a low species diversity and some of these are accorded a very high priority in conservation terms, such as reed-beds. However, being the natural climatic climax over much of Britain, forest is a highly mature ecosystem and as such possesses a high species diversity. It is important to remember here that when talking about ecosystem diversity reference is being made to the total species diversity and not simply to one or two taxonomic groups that happen to be easy to identify. For instance it is easy to gain the erroneous impression that high forest is less diverse in

TABLE 2

Species diversity of some oak woodlands

Site	All trees		Trees > 20 cm diametre	
	No of spp	Diversity	No of spp	Diversity
Nap Wood, Sussex ..	8	1.55	5	0.97
Great Wood, New Forest	9	0.71	4	1.36
Felsham Hall Wood, Suffolk	11	1.72	11	1.72

Index of Diversity, $I = -\Sigma (Pi. \log_e Pi)$

species than some other kinds of ecosystem, for instance limestone grassland, by only considering the plant species or alternatively by looking at a piece of woodland that is not really a true example of natural type high forest, perhaps because it is deficient in some of the stages of the regeneration cycle. However, previous papers should have done enough to demonstrate that as soon as one has an ecosystem containing both oak trees and decaying wood, the faunistic diversity is likely to exceed that of most other West European ecosystems as a result of these two elements alone.

Misleading as a consideration of floristic composition alone may be, I suspect that the rather low species diversity of trees that most of our old high forest woodlands shows, is largely a result of past interference. For instance the pollen record has now made clear that elm and lime were selectively removed in prehistoric times, possibly to the point of near extinction in some parts of the country. There is no means of knowing what the tree species diversity of completely natural forest would be today as we have no example left in Britain. The nearest that we can probably get is to look at some of the old coppice woodlands of East Anglia, such as those described by Dr Rackham[8]. These, he has suggested, have more or less retained their primeval species structure. It might therefore be possible to use the tree species diversity of such woodlands as yardsticks, against which to compare the diversity of other sites. As an example, table 2 compares the species diversity of Felsham Hall Wood, Suffolk, one of the ancient coppice-with-standards woodland described by Dr Rackham, one of the old unenclosed woodlands of the New Forest given an Index of Ecological Continuity value of 85 by Dr Rose[9], and an area of Nap Wood, Sussex, showing little evidence of past coppicing, but having the tree age structure shown previously in fig 2.

If one takes those trees exceeding 20 cm in diameter, so as to decrease the effect of the understorey of dense small holly in Great Wood, then Felsham Hall Wood has the highest value and number of species, next Great Wood and finally Nap Wood. As pointed out by Rackham[8] the density of oak in Felsham Hall Wood is now lower than would be expected, so that diversity index for the wood will be on the low rather than the high side. In addition the figure for Felsham Hall Wood will have been further distorted by the differential effects of long term coppicing on different species.

Much attention has been paid to establishing the degree of continuity of present day woodlands with the primeval forest. The assumption behind this approach is that many forest species are dependent for survival upon some unique feature of the forest environment, in particular micro-climatological, and that any disruption in woodland continuity will result in their extinction. Reinvasion when woodland conditions are re-established becomes progressively less probable as general clearance increases in the vicinity. Woodland continuity in this context, implies continuity of high forest. The kind of continuity postulated for some of the East

Anglian coppice woodlands, and already referred to, would not be expected to result in the survival of these high forest 'indicator' species, even though the actual species composition of the tree flora did exhibit true continuity with the primeval forest.

A number of different kinds of evidence are frequently used to assess the historical continuity of woodland, including stratigraphic, archaeological and documentary evidence and an analysis of the fauna and flora. Pollen analysis is rarely of use in interpreting the history of individual woods although the soil pollen analyses that are increasingly being carried out as routine procedures in archaeological excavations are beginning to throw valuable light on woodland history where soil conditions are favourable. For instance the pollen analyses made by Prof Dimbleby on samples from J. H. Money's excavations at High Rocks on the Kent/Sussex border have revealed intresting fluctuations in the woodland composition of the site during the latter part of the Iron Age from about 100 BC into the first half of the first century AD[10].

Rackham has reviewed the various kinds of documentary and archaeological evidence that can be used to elucidate the history of woodland[8]. Where available, he has shown that these sources probably provide the most reliable and satisfactory guide to land use history, but unfortunately different parts of the country vary in the richness of their documented history and frequency of archaeological remains. Furthermore documented history is never continuous and gaps in the record of a few hundred years might well mark land use changes of major ecological significance.

The use of plant indicator species is the technique most frequently used to assess the antiquity and historical continuity of woodlands. Apart from any other consideration, the composition of the flora and fauna is the only kind of evidence that is available in all situations. For instance, Rackham uses *Primula elatior, Sorbus torminalis, Tilia cordata, Campanula trachelium, Mercurialis perennis* and *Platanthera chlorantha* as indicators of old woodland in East Anglia but makes the important point that little reliance should be placed on the occurrence of a single species. Similarly, the association of *Sorbus torminalis, Crataegus oxyacanthoides* and *Malus sylvestris* on the clays of the Weald is normally indicative of ancient woodland.

Rose first drew attention to the possible ecological significance of a group of woodland species showing a markedly disjunct distribution between western Britain and the woodland gills of the central Weald, which he called 'forest relict species of Oceanic type'[11]. This group includes species such as *Dryopteris aemula, Hymenophyllum tunbrigense, Festuca altissima, Wahlenbergia hederacea* and *Sibthorpia europea* and Rose attributed their occurrence in south-east England to their continued persistence in suitable micro-climatic conditions from the Atlantic 'climatic optimum', when presumably they were more widespread, to the present day. These conditions were particularly well satisfied where the deep, steep-sided stream ravines of the Hastings Beds had enjoyed a continuous history of tree cover providing the necessary moist, frost-free conditions of an oceanic-like climate. The implication was that if the tree canopy had at any time been destroyed, then the microclimate of the habitat would have dried out and the sensitive species lost. Indeed, it is all too often possible to see this very thing happening today; desiccated mats of *Hymenophyllum tunbrigense* peeling away from dried-out rock surfaces following large-scale woodland felling. The converse argument then inevitably follows. Where a number of these sensitive Atlantic species occur together in south-east England there must have been an almost continuous tree canopy from the Atlantic period to the present day. It is tempting to take the argument further and assume an inverse relationship between the number of such species present in a woodland and the amount of disturbance to which the wood has been subjected in the past. To the list of vascular plants showing such disjunct patterns of distribution can be added a much longer list of Bryophytes, the geographical affinities of which have been discussed in detail by Ratcliffe[12].

Rose has now considerably developed the concept of indicator species in relation to the epiphytic flora of the woodland trees and has suggested that a number of species of lichens that are at present faithful to old woodlands should be regarded as relics of the ancient forest epiphyte flora[9]. As such they can be regarded both as historical indicators of lack of environmental change over a long period of time and as ecological indicators of the existence of a particular type of forest environment at the present time.

Relatively little similar work appears to have been carried out with woodland faunas, but Morris made the point that a major element in those woods known to be of importance for rare species of invertebrates is the presence of old and decaying trees[13]. Cameron has suggested that the present distribution of the gastropod *Helicodonta obvuluta* in south-east England is correlated with those old scarp-face woodlands of the South Downs with much fallen timber[14]. Other woodland molluscs normally regarded as being indicative of little disturbance include *Limax cinereoniger, Acicula fusca* and *Hygromia subrufescens*. I suspect that detailed work on the faunas of old woodlands will reveal species associations even more significant than those of the plants in the interpretation of forest history.

However, for the purposes of assessing the conservation value of a woodland site as an example of a high forest ecosystem, the use of indicator species in isolation, unsupported by different kinds of evidence, can be very misleading. For example, some of the wooded stream valleys crossing the open heathland of Ashdown Forest, Sussex contain a number of these Atlantic indicators suggesting that the valleys may have been more or less continuously wooded from pre-historic times; but as most of them are less than 10 m wide they would hardly be considered as good examples of woodland ecosystems. Similarly, the richest wood for these species in the central Weald, Chiddingly Wood, contains large numbers of exotic conifers and a great deal of *Rhododendron ponticum* and on any other criteria would not be highly rated as an example of mature oak woodland. The same caution needs to be used in interpreting the data from other groups. For instance some of the sites supporting the highest values of Rose's Index of Ecological Continuity, such as Eridge Park with the second largest number of lichen epiphytes of any site in England and an Index of Ecological Continuity value of 85, is not high forest at all, but parkland. Thus, although the concept of ecological continuity remains valid, it seems that the assemblage of species cannot always indicate the existence of a forest environment at the present time. On the other hand the high IEC values of the unenclosed woodlands of the New Forest clearly substantiate the historical and other ecological evidence of a continuous history of forest conditions. The important point seems to be that a site that is highly rated as a habitat for forest indicator species is not necessarily one that would be highly rated as a good example of a mature forest ecosystem.

Size of sites

With land values at a premium, information on the ideal size of nature reserves is becoming of increasing economic as well as ecological concern to conservation organisations. The ideal size of a nature reserve depends upon the conservation objective of the reserve. If we accept the approach set out at the beginning, that we are concerned with the conservation of whole ecosystems rather than with individual species, then the ideal size will depend on the nature of the ecosystem under consideration. The question then defines itself as, what is the smallest area that can support a viable example of the particular kind of ecosystem under consideration? One of the properties of woodland systems that has already been discussed is its high species diversity and it would therefore seem reasonable to examine the relationship between area and species numbers. There is a considerable, body of information on this aspect of theoretical ecology and its relation to the size of nature reserves has been fully discussed by Hooper[15]. Accepting the log-normal distribution of individuals between species, he shows that the value of the exponent 'k' in McArthur and Wilson's equation relating to island faunas[16] will be about 0.27.

$$S = CA^k \text{ where } S = \text{number of species}$$
$$C = \text{density/unit area}$$
$$A = \text{area}$$

It then follows that, if this relationship is applied to a nature reserve, an increase in the area of a reserve tenfold should almost double the number of species. Hooper therefore concludes that a number of small reserves, each of a different habitat would be best in terms of numbers of species conserved. However, this argument does not necessarily lead to an estimate of the ideal size of a nature reserve for a specific kind of ecosystem.

Another approach has been discussed by Moore[17], arising from his work on the fragmentation of the Dorset heaths and its effect on the distribution of certain heathland species. He bases his argument on the premise that in any ecosystem the species can be separated into 'key' or 'essential' species and inessential ones. He defines a key species as one which if removed from an ecosystem results in a radical change. He then defines the smallest viable size of a *habitat* (not an ecosystem) as the smallest that will support a viable population of its weakest key species. On this definition heather on heathland and trees in a wood are clearly key species, whilst Dartford warblers and wood warblers are not. I suggest that what is needed is some idea of the smallest area that can support a viable example of the particular kind of *ecosystem* (not habitat) under consideration. All ecosystems possess a characteristic trophic structure and if any element of this is missing then it will clearly be rated less highly than a comparable example possessing a more or less intact food web typical of that ecosystem. The ideal size for a reserve will therefore be that which will support a viable population of all those species regarded as being characteristic of the ecosystem concerned. This must depend on the territory sizes of the species with the largest territories. These will normally, but not always, be the species occupying the end of the food chain. It is therefore possible to define the optimum size of a nature reserve as the smallest area that will support a viable population of the species character-istic of the end of the food chain (or alternatively having the largest territories) of the particular ecosystem concerned. Table 3 sets out the territory sizes of some forest species that fall within this definition. Using this criterion the minimum size would appear to be in excess of 100 acres. For comparison fig 3 represents the size frequency histogram of all British woodland nature reserves. If should be noted that almost all the >600 acre class would disappear if the Scottish forests, largely of pine, were omitted.

TABLE 3

Territory sizes of some forest vertebrates

	Acres
Sparrowhawk	96–1280[18] [19]
Tawny Owl	20–30[20]
Woodcock	15–50[21]
Pine Marten	220–640[22]
Red Deer	1 deer per 120 } Forestry Commission[23]
Fallow Deer	1 deer per 70 } figures of 'acceptable' density

A further important criterion related to size, is the shape of the woodland. Woodland edge represents conditions transitional between the open country and the true forest, particularly in relation to micro-climate. The width of this edge varies with aspect, topography and density of trees but clearly, however large in terms of acres, if the wood is long and narrow there is a possibility that much of the wood will be edge and little of it true woodland. There is little information on the actual width of the woodland edge, but Geiger[24] quotes a figure of 30 yards for light intensity.

FIGURE 3

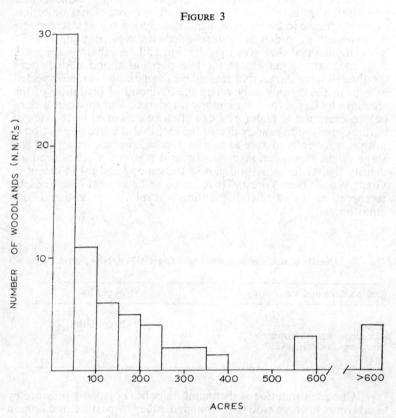

Size-frequency histogram of woodland National Nature Reserves.

Management implications

The ecological effect of most woodland management is to artificially remove the late-mature and decaying elements of the regeneration cycle (fig 1) and also to increase the frequency of the gap phase both in space and time by coppicing and selective felling. This inevitably results in a decline in those species characteristic of later stages of the regeneration cycle and an increase in the frequency of species of the gap phase. The rich and colourful ground vegetation of areas of young coppice are a good illustration of this.

In contrast, if the forest management objective is to produce something resembling a climax ecosystem, then the management prescription can be established from the fundamental relationship between ecological theory and conservation management. This can be stated as 'the intensity of management is inversely proportional to the maturity of the ecosystem being managed'. As climatic climax ecosystems are fully mature, the proper and only management prescription must be one of non-intervention. One objection frequently made to this management prescription is that intervention is necessary in order to ensure adequate regeneration. Shaw[25] has demonstrated that acorn production and germination are more than adequate to perpetuate the tree population and both he and Gradwell[26] have shown that reasonable regeneration can be expected in gaps in the canopy only where the liklihood of predation of the seedlings by larvae from the canopy is reduced. The apparent lack of oak regeneration in high forest can often be explained by the lack of natural gaps in the canopy due to the fact that the tree population is not yet sufficiently mature as to have reached the true decay and gap stage of the regeneration cycle. Table 4 sets out a set of seedling density figures for a natural gap in the canopy 350 m^2 in extent in Great Wood, New Forest. There seems to be no real case to assist regeneration by artificial planting except in exceptional circumstances.

TABLE 4

Density of oak seedlings and trees: Great Wood, New Forest

Oak seedling and tree density	Nos per ha
Trees	78 (20 cm DBH)
Seedlings beneath canopy	17
Seedlings in clearing (350m^2)	314

One such situation is the unnaturally heavy grazing pressure by herbivores in some woods surrounded either by pasture or common grazing. Some of the ancient, unenclosed woodlands of the New Forest illustrate this situation, where regeneration is being prevented by excessive grazing by deer and ponies. Exclusion of the animals by fencing would appear to be the answer in this kind of situation.

Conclusion

The acquisition and management of further areas of oak high forest should be a high conservation priority. The number of woodlands where the primary objective of management is to achieve true high forest conditions is at present too low and many of those that do exist are too small. If the objective of management is to produce something approaching mature forest then the management prescription should be unequivocally one of non-intervention. This will necessarily produce an ecosystem of zero net-productivity, probably a woodland of low aesthetic value and one which possibly would provide some surprises for ecologists in the final composition of its tree canopy !

REFERENCES

1. DEPARTMENT OF THE ENVIRONMENT. *Sinews for Survival,* 'A report on the management of natural resources', London (1972)
2. PENISTAN, M. J. 'Growing oak', in Morris, M. G. and Perring, F. H. (edit.) *The British Oak: its History and Natural History* (1974)
3. NATURE CONSERVANCY. (personal communication).
4. GODWIN, H. and DEACON, J. 'Flandrian history of oak in the British Isles', in Morris, M. G. and Perring, F. H. (edit.) *The British Oak: its History and Natural History* (1974)
5. BARNETT, C. *The study of age and distribution of the oak trees of Nap Wood, near Frant, Sussex.* Unpublished B.Sc. thesis, University of Bristol (1971)
6. PETERKEN, G. F. and TUBBS, C. R. 'Woodland regeneration in the New Forest, Hampshire, since 1650'. *J. Appl. Ecol.,* 2 (1965), 159–70
7. SMITH, A. E. and STREETER, D. T. 'The role of the County Trusts in the national strategy for nature reserves'. SPNR County Trusts Conference Proceedings, 1970
8. RACKHAM, O. 'Historical studies and woodland conservation', in Duffey, E. A. G. and Watt, A. S (edit.) *The Scientific Management of Animal and Plant Communities for Conservation,* Oxford (1971), 563–80
9. ROSE, F. 'The epiphytes of oak', in Morris, M. G. and Perring F. H. (edit.) *The British Oak: its History and Natural History* (1974)
10. MONEY, J. H. 'Excavations in the Iron Age hill-fort at High Rocks, near Tunbridge Wells, 1957–1961'. *Suss. Archaeol. Coll.,* 106 (1968), 158–205
11. ROSE, F. 'The importance of the study of disjunct distributions to progress in understanding the British Flora', in Lousley, J. E (edit.) *Progress in the Study of the British Flora* (1957)
12. RATCLIFFE, D. A. 'An ecological account of Atlantic bryophytes in the British Isles'. *New Phytol.,* 67 (1968), 365–439
13. MORRIS, M. G. 'Oak as a habitat for insect life', and Morris M. G. and Perring, F. H. (edit.) *The British Oak: its History and Natural History* (1974)
14. CAMERON, R. A. D. 'The distribution of *Helicondonta obvoluta* (Mull.) in Britain'. *J. Conch., Lond.,* 27 (1972), 363–9
15. HOOPER, M. D. 'The size and surroundings of nature reserves', in Duffey, E. A. G. and Watt, A. S. (edit.) *The Scientific Management of Animal and Plant Communities for Conservation,* Oxford (1971) 555–61
16. MACARTHUR, R. H. and WILSON, E. O. *The Theory of Island Biogeography,* Princeton, N.J. (1967)
17. MOORE, N. W. 'The heaths of Dorset and their conservation'. *J. Ecol.,* 50 (1962), 369–91
18. NEWTON, I. 'Birds of prey in Scotland'. *Scott. Birds,* 7 (1972), 5–23
19. YAPP, W. B. *Birds and Woods,* London (1962)
20. SOUTHERN, H. N. and LOWE, V. P. W. 'The pattern of distribution of prey and predation in tawny owl territories'. *J. Anim. Ecol.,* 37 (1968), 75–97
21. TESTER, J. R. and WATSON, A. 'Spacing and territoriality of woodcock *Scolopax rusticola* based on roding behaviour'. *Ibis,* 115 (1973), 135–8

22. HAWLEY, V. D. and NEWBY, F. E. 'Marten home ranges and population fluctuations'. *J. Mammal.*, **38** (1957), 178–84
23. SOUTHERN, H. N. (edit.) *The Handbook of British Mammals,* Oxford (1964)
24. GEIGER, R. *The Climate near the Ground,* Harvard (1959)
25. SHAW, M. W. 'The reproductive characteristics of oak', in Morris, M. G. and Perring, F. H. (edit.) *The British Oak: its History and Natural History* (1974)
26. GRADWELL, G. 'The effect of defoliators on tree growth', in Morris, M.G. and Perring, F. H. (edit.) *The British Oak: its History and Natural History* (1974)

APPENDIX I

EXHIBITS STAGED AT THE CONFERENCE

Fourteen exhibits were staged throughout the Conference in the Common Room of Lancaster House. Some illustrated papers which were presented in the lecture theatre, but others had been specially prepared to illustrate aspects of the oak and its importance not otherwise dealt with. They were an invaluable, integral part of the proceedings.

THE INFLUENCE OF THE STRUCTURE OF OAK TIMBER ON ITS PROPERTIES AND USE

Forest Products Research Laboratories, Princes Risborough, Buckinghamshire

Three main types of oak timber were demonstrated:

1. White oak, produced by Section Leucobalanus, and including *Q. robur* and *Q. petraea*.
2. Red oak, produced by Section Erythrobalanus (in part), including *Q. rubra*.
3. Evergreen oak, produced by Section Erythrobalanus (in part), including *Q. ilex*.

Only 1 and 2 are important sources of timber.

If grown vigorously oak produces a high proportion of fibres to vessels giving a dense tough timber. At a slow rate of growth the proportion of fibres to vessels is lower and a light-weight, weaker and brittle timber results.

In red oaks the vessels are largely open so that heartwood is permeable and has a low durability. White oaks have vessels occluded with tyloses resulting in a non-permeable and durable heartwood.

ESTIMATING THE AGE OF BIG OAKS

A. F. MITCHELL

Forestry Commission, Alice Holt Lodge, Wrecclesham, nr Farnham, Surrey

As all big oaks are hollow they cannot be dated by ring-counts. However the girth increases annually until death. Current girth (at 5 ft) will give the age only if the rate of growth is estimated. This can be done by making two measurements at an interval.

Dated young trees show rapid growth for at least 80 years. None is below one inch/year and a few are above two inches/year. These have been plotted as a graph.

Trees with girths from 10–20 feet and full crowns mostly show annual increases of one inch with a few one and a half inches and a few nearer half an inch.

Trees over 20 feet in girth usually show some dieback in the crown and annual increase diminishing to half an inch, but some maintain one inch.

Trees of 30 feet in girth mostly maintain half an inch a year, but some remain at one inch whilst a few pollards with little crown grow at a quarter of an inch.

From the above, age/girth curves can be drawn. The first 80 years are fixed by the data from trees of known age. These can easily show four rates of growth, rapid, moderately rapid, mean and slow. The undated data for later years continues these curves remarkably well, indicating that the old trees have, in fact, grown in youth in the way the curves show. Therefore the recent increases in girth plotted with the first measurement as datum ('zero') and showing a slope from previous girth to present girth, when superimposed on these derived curves, should fit quite closely the appropriate place on the graph and hence show the age of the tree.

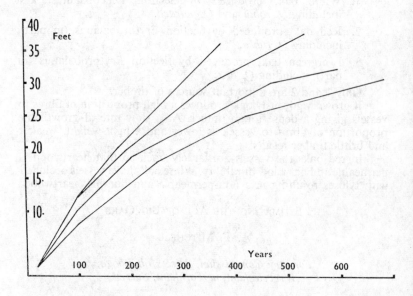

The exhibit included pictures of some of the largest oaks in Britain, including the largest of all, the oak at Bowthorpe Farm, Lincolnshire, with a girth of 39 ft.

The Oak in Pharmacy

Mrs Mary Briggs

White Cottage, Slinfold, Sussex

With the use of illustrations and texts from books and manuscripts, including Gerard's Herbal, the importance of oak in pharmacy down the ages was demonstrated.

The Reproductive Characteristics of Oak

M. W. Shaw

Merlewood Research Station, Grange-over-Sands

The experimental methods used in studying the problem, which was the subject of his paper, were illustrated.

Wistman's Wood—A Problem Oakwood

J. F. Archibald

Nature Conservancy Council, Taunton

During the last few years a series of photographs of the wood has been taken in, as far as possible, exactly the same position as some taken by R. J. Lythgoe for Tansley's *British Islands and their Vegetation* in the 1930s. Trees and boulders were refound and used as markers.

A study of the photographs past and present makes it clear that Wistman's Wood has increased in size during the last 40 years. This creates a problem for the Nature Conservancy Council which manages the wood as a National Nature Reserve and has as an object of management 'to maintain the wood as far as possible in its present state'. When this was written in 1961 the dynamism of of the situation was not appreciated.

Ring Widths of English Oak

J. M. Fletcher

Research Laboratory for Archaeology and the History of Art, University of Oxford

Materials used in establishing dendrochronological curves for Britain were exhibited, which illustrated further certain aspects of his paper.

EPIPHYTES OF OAK

F. ROSE

Dept. of Geography, King's College, Strand, London

Many species of lichen which occur as epiphytes on oak in the British Isles were exhibited, and served to illustrate his paper.

OAK WOODLAND NATURE RESERVES IN SUSSEX

D. T. STREETER and R. M. TITTENSOR

Sussex Trust for Nature Conservation,
Woods Mill, Henfield, Sussex

The history and development of oak woods owned or managed by the Sussex Trust were exhibited with particular attention to those being visited during the excursions. Nap Wood of 110 acres includes on shallow plateau soils an area of old oak coppice which is an unusual feature in south east England. Both species of oak occur and numerous intermediate specimens can be found. The valley bottom is rich in 'Atlantic' species of ferns and bryophytes, including *Dryopteris aemula* which is characteristic of woodlands in the centre of the Weald.

The Mens covers 360 acres which has been continuously wooded since the earliest known maps of the 16th and 17th centuries and probably from much earlier times. Because it was common land normal woodland management has been restricted and it remains one of the finest examples of high forest in England. This provides plenty of dead wood for rare beetles and woodpeckers.

MACROFUNGI IN OAK WOODS

R. WATLING

Royal Botanic Garden, Edinburgh

The intimate relationship between higher fungi and trees in woodlands was illustrated. The importance of this mycorrhizal development was demonstrated: the root hairs of the tree are suppressed and their function is taken over by the fungal mycelium which acts as an absorptive sponge. The tree benefits from the association with the fungus by gaining extra nutrients and water from the soil: in return some of the carbohydrate manufactured by the tree is absorbed by the fungus.

Many fresh specimens of macrofungi found in oak woods were exhibited.

OAK IN THE LANDSCAPE

Dept. of Landscape Architecture, Thames Polytechnic, Woolwich

The importance of the oak in the past and present life of the British people was illustrated by a series of over twenty specially designed posters. After dealing with the oak in history, superstition, mysticism, tourism and literature, the exhibit turned to consider the problems of the oak amidst the growing conflict for space and productivity in the second half of the 20th century, and finally posed the question do the English as a nation now care enough about oak to ensure its survival?

ENGLISH OAK IN EVERYDAY LIFE

C. J. VENABLES

Castletown Sawmills, Stafford

Many fine examples of modern domestic and church furniture made at Castletown Sawmills were exhibited. They served to show that oak timber is still in demand and that there are craftsmen available to turn it into objects of beauty, utility and durability.

LITERATURE OF OAK

Forestry Commission, Alice Holt Lodge, Wrecclesham, nr Farnham, Surrey

Over 20 volumes and papers illustrating the taxonomy and history of oak were kindly loaned by the Librarian of the Forestry Commission Research Laboratory at Alice Holt Lodge.

THE SPREAD OF ANDRICUS QUERCUSCALICIS IN BRITAIN

A. DARLINGTON

Dept. of Biology, Malvern College, Worcestershire

A map showing the spread of this gall in Britain and a quantity or recently collected material were exhibited which illustrated one aspect of his paper.

BLACK POPLAR SURVEY

E. MILNE REDHEAD

43 Bear Street, Nayland, Suffolk

A map was exhibited showing the progress of this Botanical Society Network Research Project which aims at obtaining accurate information regarding the distribution of Black Poplar in the British Isles. Many field botanists fail to recognise this handsome tree and fail to distinguish it from the more numerous hybrids which have been planted during this century. Black Poplar, *Populus nigra,* is a native tree of the flood-plain of lowland rivers, though even in this locality it has usually survived by planting.

When mature and well-grown Black Poplar is a tree of 80 ft or more with arching lower branches and a generally rounded crown. It is slow-growing relative to the hybrid poplars. In spring it is in green leaf when the leaves of *P.* × *serotina* are still bronze. The leaf of a mature shoot has a more attenuate tip than the hybrids, the length of the midrib being longer than the greatest width. The trunk develops large bosses.

APPENDIX II

EXCURSION to the WEALD and DOWNLAND OPEN AIR MUSEUM on Friday, 21 SEPTEMBER

Most of the B.S.B.I. members and other participants in the Oak Symposium took the opportunity to visit this well-known open air museum on the afternoon of Friday, 21st September. Situated in its own attractive 35–acre site at Singleton Park, near Chichester, the museum, which has been open to the public only since May, 1971, gives an unusually vivid impression of rural life during the past ten centuries or so. The importance of wood and timber in building, in all forms of craftsmanship, and indeed in nearly every aspect of life before the industrial revolution, is not readily appreciated in the latter half of the twentieth century. Hence the visit to Singleton Park was of particular relevance to the participants in a symposium on oak.

The preparation of oak timber was well demonstrated in the woodcraft area. The importance of pit-sawing in an age without power saws could easily be appreciated, but it came as a surprise to many that sawing, which is slow and prodigal of labour when done by hand, was often unnecessary as cleft timber could be used for so many purposes, at least until the seventeenth century.

Many of the exhibits at the museum are buildings and although a large number are built predominantly of timber not all are made, even in part, of oak. The Littlehampton Granary, for instance, is largely constructed of brick and stands on stone staddles. Its timber is 80% elm, with a mixture of oak and chestnut forming the battens. However, the largest and finest building, Bayleaf Farmhouse, uses large quantities of oak, particularly for the beams and braces. Such is the difficulty in finding good oak timber nowadays that six months were spent during the period of reconstruction in searching for suitable curved oak members for the braces which support the central truss. Bayleaf Farmhouse was undoubtedly one of the chief attractions of the museum, not least because of the wealth of speculation it gave rise to. The origin and purpose of 'jettying', position of the hearth, construction of the garderobe, nature of the floor and composition of the infilling between the oak framework were just a few of the problems raised by this intriguing fifteenth-century house.

It was of great interest to discover that the anvil of a hammer forge was supported by a massive block of oak embedded in the ground. Although the anvil used with the tilt-hammer on display weighed less than one ton others are known to have been as much as four tons in weight. The oak blocks supporting such anvils provided the elasticity to prevent neither hammer head nor anvil from shattering on impact.

Although not specifically concerned with oak as timber many other aspects of life in the past were recalled by the remaining exhibits. The Beeding Toll Cottage brought to mind the turnpikes of eighteenth and nineteenth century England, the Catherington Tread Wheel, used for raising well-water, focussed attention on the problems of primitive water supply, and the charcoal burners' camp and Southwater forge reminded us of ancient ways of life which have vanished for ever.

Nearly everyone visiting the museum mentally resolved to return for further examination of the exhibits, which are continually being added to. All the visitors were grateful for the vision and enthusiasm of all those concerned in the organisation of this unusual and fascinating museum.

APPENDIX III

THE EXCURSIONS on SUNDAY, 23 SEPTEMBER

Excursions were arranged to a number of areas of oak woods in Sussex, with leaders to demonstrate Forestry, Flowering Plants, Mosses and Liverworts, Lichens, Fungi, Insects or General Woodland Ecology.

There were two coaches, each containing two parties. The first coach went to Saxonbury Hill. The party led by Dr F. Rose went into Eridge Park (by kind permission of the Marquess of Abergavenny). Eridge Old Park is one of the most interesting and ancient examples of a Deer Park in England enclosed, probably from the primeval wilderness, some 800 years ago. Today the deer have been removed to the Home Park, with the result that much ecological succession is taking place over the former open parts of the remaining parkland. Interest for this party however focussed on the relics of ancient woodland in the ravines which carry the second richest epiphytic lichen flora known in England for an area of comparable size (c 2 sq km) including many species, formerly widespread, now very rare relics of the ancient forest of SE England.

The second party led by D. T. Streeter first visited Nap Wood, an oak wood nature reserve of 110 acres (45 ha) managed by the Sussex Trust for Nature Conservation and owned by the National Trust. On the shallow soil of the plateau old oak coppice, an unusual feature in SE England, was examined. Mixed populations of *Quercus robur* and *Q. petraea* were examined and numerous specimens showing intermediate characters were found. In the valley bottom a fine colony of *Dryopteris aemula* provided a nice example of the 'Atlantic' element characteristic of Central Wealden woodlands.

In the afternoon these two parties under Dr Rose and Mr Streeter joined forces to visit Saxonbury Hill, a woodland providing an interesting contrast with a greater proportion of beech and yew. In sheltered spots on the massive outcrops of Tunbridge Wells Sandstone *Hymenophyllum tunbrigense* was of special interest together with more *Dryopteris aemula* and such bryophytes as *Bazzania trilobata*.

The second coach took an excursion of mixed interest to 'The Mens', a large woodland reserve of 360 acres (145 ha) recently acquired by the Sussex Trust. Ruth Tittensor led a party interested in woodland history and management through The Cut where they noted the earthen enclosure banks, into Hammond's Wood where they noted *Carex strigosa* growing by a stream, and passed Terry's Meadow, an ancient enclosure in the middle of the wood where birch has grown up since the cessation of grazing. In Fence Piece and near Bedham several fine beech trees were seen, and the morning ended with a very steep climb up the sandstone escarpment to Bedham itself where Dr Rackham pointed out the date 1838 cut into the largest beech tree in The Mens.

The afternoon was spent in Idehurst Hurst where they noticed a huge parkland oak and a huge pollarded beech. The excursion finished at a large specimen of *Sorbus torminalis* near Hawkhurst Court.

Mycologists led by Dr R. Watling and entomologists led by Dr M. G. Morris followed the same route, if occasionally some distance in the rear. Unfortunately the long drought of the late summer of 1973 did nothing to encourage the fruiting of the higher fungi. Nevertheless the party had reasonable success, and collected several of the species referred to in the formal part of the symposium including the uncommon *Boletus pulverulentus* and the true *Lycoperdon echinatum*. Species of *Russula* and *Lactarius* were few in number even though The Mens is noted for many rarities in these genera, particularly *Russula*. Some help was given to the entomologists who often have difficulty in making a correct determination of the substrate on which their insects are found.

With this assistance Dr R. C. Welch, who accompanied Dr Morris, recorded seventeen species of beetle and their fungal hosts in The Mens. Five further species were identified which occurred under bark or in dead wood, and Dr Morris was able to demonstrate a wide variety of galls on fallen leaves and twigs. With a beating tray he worked a small amount of oak foliage in Crimbourne Wood and although Heteroptera were conspicuously absent a number of leaf hoppers characteristic of oak were recorded. In Crimbourne Wood also the common *Blepharidopterus angulatus* (Fall.), Black-kneed Capsid, was beaten from birch, and the weevils (Coleoptera) *Rhynchites caeruleus* (Deg.) and *Rhynchaenus fagi* (L.) from their respective foodplants, crab apple and beech.

INDEX

For plants and animals included in the text by both scientific and English names all references to a species will be found under either name. For plants and animals included in the text by only a scientific or an English name no cross reference is given.

No attempt has been made to index Quercus petraea or Q. robur: most entries in the index imply a relationship between the subject or the species with these trees.

Names of places, other than the more prominent ones, are not included but may be found by referring to the country in which they occur.

Abscission, 185, 202, 206
Acari, 279
Acer, 121, 204, 256, 268, 316
  campestre, 135, 136, 251
  platanoides, 317
  pseudoplatanus, 12, 102, 120, 121, 135, 143, 241, 256, 314, 334
  saccharum, 179
Acicula fusca, 348
Acorn, see also Regeneration
  collection, 103, 104
  disease, 235, 236, 242, 247
  dispersal, 103, 128, 129, 165
  fall, 143, 177
  frost resistance, 210
  growth, 21, 163, 165, 168, 177, 204, 206, 207, 210, 315
  insect feeders, 283, 284, 310
  morphology, 17, 22, 27, 128
  predation, 103–105, 162–165, 177, 312, 314–321, 328, 337
  production, 18, 103, 111, 162–164, 177, 206, 237, 315, 320, 328
  provenance, 101, 106
  sowing, 104–105, 317
  storage, 31, 104, 207, 236
Acreage, 98–101
Acrobasis consociella, 287
Actinomycetes, 149
Adela reamurella, 283
Aedes geniculatus, 291
Aesculus, 196
Age classes, 100, 101, 109, 110, 342–344
Agriopis leucophaearia, 186, 188
Agrostis canina, 135
  tenuis, 135
Alder, 51, 54, 59, 60, 80, 126, 316, 335
Aleyrodidae, 286
Allium ursinum, 136
Alnus, 28, 126, 316
  glutinosa, 51, 54, 59, 60, 80
Alternation of generations, 301, 302
Amanita caesarea, 226
  phalloides, 225
  rubescens, 222, 231
Ambrosia beetles, 290
American racoon, 319

Andricus curvator, 305
  fecundator, 304, 305
  kollari, 308–310, 316
  lucidus, 316
  quercuscalicis, 283, 303, 309, 310, 359
  quercusradicis, 303
  rhizomae, 303
  testaceipes, 305
Anemone nemorosa, 136, 143
Aneurus, 290
Anglo Saxon, 53, 61, 81, 93, 94, 123
Annual rings, 51, 69, 74, 80–95, 119, 177, 184, 240
Anopheles plumbeus, 291
Ants, 291
Anthocoris, 288
Anthoxanthum odoratum, 135
Anthus trivialis, 331
Anyphaena accentuata, 288
Apatura iris, 276
Aphids, 149, 286, 298, 300
Apion, 289
Apis mellifera, 283
Apocheima hispidaria, 183
  pilosaria, 182
Apodemus, 314, 315
  flavicollis, 312–314, 320
  sylvaticus, 169, 312, 314, 321
Apple, 126, 279, 282, 316, 317, 347
Aradus depressus, 290
Araneae, 275, 279, 288
Arctiidae, 279
Ardea cinerea, 328
Area, 98–101
Argyrotoxa albicomana, 239, 240, 299
  semipurpurana, 240
Armillaria mellea, 229, 239, 240, 243
Arrhenatherum elatius, 135
Art, 127–128
Arthonia didyma, 256, 264
Arthopyrenia fallax, 268
Arum maculatum, 135
Ascomycete, 289
Ash, 54, 75, 80, 102, 120, 135, 136, 143, 167, 241, 255, 259, 260, 265, 267, 268, 279, 317, 333
Aspen, 226, 316

Asterodiapsis variolosa, 281, 299, 300
Asterolecanium, 281, 299, 300
Athene noctua, 328
Attelabus nitens, 274, 287, 292
Auchenorhyncha, 285, 286, 298
Aureobasidium pullulans, 238, 239
Aureoboletus cramesinus, 231
Austria, 237

Bacteria, 149
Badger, 312, 319, 320
Bank vole, 169, 312–315, 317, 320
Bark, 15, 143, 152, 153, 159, 239–242, 247, 256, 257, 265, 267–269, 271, 278–280, 286, 290, 299, 314, 316–318, 321, 327
Bark beetles, 289
Bark-lice, 279, 287
Bazzania trilobata, 363
Beaver, 313, 316, 321
Beech, 54, 102, 120, 126, 129, 136, 196, 197, 203, 206, 223, 225, 226, 230, 231, 236, 237, 244, 256, 257, 259, 278, 279, 313–315, 319, 320, 334
Beef Steak fungus, 229, 244, 245
Bees, 283, 291
Beetle-mites, 279
Betula, 51, 54, 60, 136, 142, 143, 163, 173, 179, 230, 231, 279, 289, 316, 333
  pubescens, 232
  tortuosa, 226
  verrucosa, 232
Bilberry, 133, 135, 168, 250
Biorhiza pallida, 302, 304
Birch, 51, 54, 60, 136, 142, 143, 163, 137, 179, 226, 230–232, 279, 289, 316, 333
Birds, 241, 280, 291, 324–339, 350
  list of species, 327, 330
Bison, 313, 320
Bison bonasus, 313, 320
Biston betularia, 280
Blackbird, 124, 326
Blackcap, 328
Black-kneed capsid, 364
Black mulberry, 126
Black poplar, 360
Blackthorn, 135, 326
Blepharidopterus angulatus, 364
Blossom underwing moth, 286
Bluebell, 133, 136, 143, 235
Blue tit, 326
Boarmia roboraria, 280
Bog-oak, 51, Plate I
Boletus, 228, 231, 233
  list of species, 224
  chrysenteron, 225

Boletus—cont.
  luridus, 226
  parasiticus, 225
  porosporus, 226
  pseudosulphureus, 225
  pulverulentus, 225, 364
  rubinus, 223
  subtomentosus 225
Bos primigenius, 313
Brachypodium sylvaticum, 135, 143
Bracken, 142, 147, 148, 152, 168, 325
Bramble, 114, 135, 143, 314, 318, 325
Branches, 143, 145, 208, 229, 245, 257, 278–280, 286, 290, 316, 326, 328
  epicormic, 76, 106, 202
Breckland, 62
Bronze Age, 53, 61
Brown bear, 313, 319, 320
Brown tail, 182
Browsing, 60, 73, 105, 110, 111, 165–169, 176, 177, 180, 182, 312, 317, 318, 320, 321
Bruchidae, 292
Brussels lace moth, 280
Bryophytes, 133, 134, 136, 137, 165, 231, 250, 251, 255, 261–263, 266, 272, 335, 348, 358, 363
  list of species, 251, 261, 262
Bucculatrix ulmella, 284
Buds, 143, 153, 183, 185–189, 194–202, 206, 210, 281, 282, 302, 304, 309, 314–316, 320
Buellia canescens, 268
  punctata, 268
Buff tip, 182
Bugs, 290
Buildings, 53, 64–72, 114, 117, 121, 129, 361, 362

Caecilius flavidus, 287
Caenorhinus aeneovirens, 282
  aequatus, 274
Caesar's mushroom, 226
Calasoma inquisitor, 288
Caliroa, 287
Callirhytis, 283
Calluna vulgaris, 168, 318, 335
Calocoris quadripunctatus, 282
Cambium, 200, 201, 204, 209, 240, 242, 314
Campanula trachelium, 347
Camptothecium sericeum, 271
Canals, 117
Capreolus capreolus, 313, 317, 318
Capsid bugs, 185, 364
Carex strigosa, 363
Carnivora, 319

Carpinus betulus, 54, 55, 60, 75, 136, 334
Carrion Crow, 328
Castanea, 201
  sativa, 15, 136, 225, 226, 229, 236, 237, 246, 256, 274, 314, 361
Castor fiber, 313, 316, 321
Caterpillar, 86, 90, 93, 110, 148, 156, 157, 164, 169–177, 179, 182–192, 237, 239, 240, 298, 299
Catkins, see also Flowering, 143, 153, 185, 235, 282, 283, 304, 310
Cattle, 266
Cecidomyiidae, 185, 282, 284, 287, 300, 301
Cedar, 119
Cerambycidae, 289, 290
Ceratocystis, 236
  fagacearum, 209
Cercopis vulnerata, 286
Certhia familiaris, 326
Cervus elaphus, 313, 317, 318
  nippon, 313, 317
Cetraria glauca, 267
Chalcidoidea, 285, 288
Chamaecyparis lawsoniana, 107
Charcoal, 53, 116, 127, 159, 231, 362
Chenopodium, 299
Cherries, 316
Cherrywood, 119
Chiffchaff, 339
Chinese water deer, 318
Chromosomes, 28–30, 46
Chrysopa flava, 288
Ciboria batschiana, 230, 236
Cicadellidae, 286
Circaea lutetiana, 136
Cixius, 286
Cladonia, 271
Clearance, see also Cropping and Felling, 60, 61, 66, 69, 72, 136, 137, 149, 237, 263, 265, 292
Clearings, 177, 325, 326, 329, 339
Clematis, 122
Cleorodes lichenaria, 280
Clethrionomys glareolus, 169, 312–315, 317, 320
Climate, see also Desiccation, Frost, Light, Rainfall and Temperature, 12, 56–60, 93, 131, 281, 291, 321, 335, 336, 344, 346–348, 351
Climax vegetation, 18, 54, 74, 75, 142, 179, 180, 341, 342, 345, 352
Clinodiplosis, 283
Clubiona brevipes, 279
Coal tit, 337
Coccidae, 278
Coccinellidae, 288
Coccoidea, 286
Cockchafer, 299

Coeliodes, 282
  dryados, 282
Coffins, 117, 119
Coleophora, 281, 285
  lutipennella, 281
Coleoptera, 120, 263, 275, 284, 287–290, 292
Collembola, 149, 290
Collybia, 229
  peronata, 222, 230
Colpoma quercinum, 241
Columba oenas, 124, 328
  palumbus, 103, 315, 328
Common Birds Census, 324, 331, 332
Common dormouse, 312, 316
Competition, 167, 168, 177–179
Concealment, 280, 282, 284
Conifers, 98, 99, 106, 107, 118, 130, 186, 192, 201, 207, 209, 210, 222–233 passim, 238, 239, 242, 243, 245, 246, 257, 279, 313, 316–318, 337, 338, 344, 349
Coniothyrium quercinum, 236
Conocybe, 231
Conopodium majus, 136
Conservation, 77, 98, 110, 111, 180, 272, 293, 331, 341–353
Contarinia, 283
  amenti, 282
Coppice, 21, 63, 99, 101, 110, 136, 138, 158, 159, 194, 197, 202, 205, 237, 244, 257, 260, 265, 292, 308, 325–328, 333, 335, 338, 341, 346, 347, 351, 358
Coppice-with-standards, 20, 68, 82, 88, 99, 110, 136, 138, 237, 259, 260, 265, 333, 334, 346
Coprinus radiatus, 231
  sylvaticus, 229
Coriolus versicolor, 229
Cortinarius, 222, 229
Corvus corone, 328
Corydalis claviculata, 135
Corylus avellana, 20, 54, 55, 57, 58, 60, 65, 135, 136, 143, 226, 275, 285, 333
Cotyledons, 27
Crabonidae, 290
Crataegus, 123, 135, 143, 168, 287, 317
  monogyna, 287, 326
  oxyacanthoides, 347
Cronartium quercuum, 238
Cropping, see also Clearance and Felling, 158, 159
Crossbill, 337
Cryptocline cinerescens, 238
Cryptostigmata, 279
Cultivation, 98–112
Curculio glandium, 283
  venosus, 283

Cydia splendana, 283
Cylindrocarpon destructans, 242
  radicicola, 242
Cyllecoris histrionicus, 281
Cynipidae, 185, 278, 282–284, 287, 288, 292, 301–305, 309, 321
Cynips divisa, 287
Cytology, 27–30
Czechoslovakia, 222, 239, 315, 316

Daedalea quercina, 229, 289
Daldinia concentrica, 289
Dama dama, 136, 313, 317, 318
Damage, see also Defoliation, 110, 168, 176, 184, 192, 197, 200, 202, 206, 209, 210, 235–247, 278–284
Dasyneura squamosa, 283
Dasyscyphus niveus, 230
Dead wood, see also Dieback, 229, 230, 243, 255, 278, 284, 289–291, 325, 326, 328, 331, 339, 343–345, 348, 358
Death watch beetle, 115
Deer, 74, 110, 176, 177, 182
Defoliation, 86, 88, 90, 93, 110, 148, 156, 157, 164, 169–177, 179, 182–192, 237, 240, 298, 299, 352
Dendrochronology, 80–95
Dendrocopus major, 326
  minor, 326
Denmark, 84
Deraeocoris lutescens, 281
Dermatina quercus, 256
Deschampsia flexuosa, 135, 142, 165, 167, 168
Desiccation, 235, 236, 240
Diaea dorsata, 288
Diaporthe leiphaemia, 241
Dichonia aprilina, 279
Dieback, 91, 102, 236, 237, 239, 240, 243, 244, 356
Diplolepis rosae, 308
Diplopoda, 149
Diptera, 279, 284, 286, 288, 289, 291, 299, 300
Disease, 69, 86, 104, 110, 169, 209, 229, 235–248
Distribution, 11, 12, 18–24, 56–61, 128
Diversity,
  species, 148, 292, 293, 341, 345–349
  structural, 276, 293, 329, 330, 335, 339, 342, 343
Dog's mercury, 135, 136, 325, 347
Dogwood, 135
Dolichopodidae, 279
Dormancy, 194, 196–201, 207
Dorytomus, 283

Douglas fir, 118
Dryas, 226
Dryinidae, 286
Dryophilocoris flavoquadrimaculatus, 298
Drytopteris aemula, 347, 358, 363
  dilatata, 135, 250
  filix-mas, 135, 250
  pseudomas, 135
Dung, 231, 247, 267
Dystebenna stephensi, 278

Earthworms, 149
East Anglia, 51, 59, 61–77, 102, 110, 128, 262, 264, 346, 347
Economics, 109–111,
Ecosystem, 141–160 *passim,* 345
Ectoedemia, 285
Ectopsocus briggsi, 287
Elateridae, 290
Elder, 135, 325
Elm, 28, 54, 58, 60, 75, 102, 117, 120, 136, 251, 255, 257, 268, 317, 324, 346, 361
Emberiza citrinella, 336
Empicoris vagabundus, 279
Empidae, 279
Endymion non-scriptus, 133, 136, 143, 235
Ennominae, 280
Epiphytes, 133, 279, 280
  non-vascular, 231, 250–272, 335, 348, 349, 363
  vascular, 134, 250
Epirrita dilutata, 186, 188
Erannis, 186
  defoliaria, 182
Eriophyidae, 282
Eriosoma lanigerum, 300
Erithacus rubecula, 326
Eucosma, 186
Eudonia, 280
  murana, 280
Eulecanium cliatum, 278
Euproctis chrysorrhoea, 182
Eurhadina concinna, 285
  kirschbaumi, 285
  pulchella, 285
Eutrophication, 267, 268
Evarcha falcata, 288
Evernia, 271

Fagus, 196, 236, 237
  sylvatica, 54, 102, 120, 126, **129**, 136, 197, 203, 206, 223, 225, 226,

Fagus—cont.
230, 231, 244, 256, 257, 259, 278,
279, 313–315, 319, 320, 334
Fallow deer, 136, 313, 317, 318
Fat dormouse, 312, 316
Felling, see also Clearance and
Cropping, 119, 316, 338, 348
Fencing, 64, 110, 116–118, 121, 180
Fertility, 29, 30, 32
Festuca altissima, 347
Fibres, 355
Ficedula hypoleuca, 336
Fieldfare, 328
Field layer, 130–136, 142–160 *passim,*
351
lists of species, 131–133
Field maple, 135, 136, 251
Field vole, 313
Fire, 61, 231
Firewood, 116, 127
Firs, 107
Fistulina hepatica, 229, 244, 245
Flies, 279, 284, 286, 288, 289, 291, 299,
300
Flooding, 210
Flowering, see also Catkins, 163, 205,
206
Flushing, 86, 156, 157, 167, 171–174,
178, 183, 188, 192, 194–202, 206,
209, 237, 282
Fomes annosus, 243
Forest of Dean, 81, 88, 90, 92, 102,
109, 111, 239
Forestry, 98–112
Forestry Commission, 98–109, 118,
130, 342
France, 11, 80, 92, 119, 196, 260
Fraxinus excelsior, 54, 75, 80, 102, 120,
135, 136, 143, 167, 241, 255, 259,
260, 265, 267, 268, 279, 333
Fringilla coelebs, 326
Frost, 12, 90, 110, 111, 210, 235, 236,
244
Fungal pathogens, 69, 86, 104, 110,
169, 184, 209, 229, 235–248
list of species, 247–248
Fungi, 149, 222–234, 287, 289, 290,
358, 364
list of species, 233–234
Furniture, 11, 121
Fusarium oxysporum, 236

Galeobdolon luteum, 325
Galerina, 231
hypnorum, 231
Gall-midges, 185, 282–284, 287, 300,
301
Gall mites, 282

Galls, 169, 238, 281, 283, 284, 287, 288,
298–310, 316, 364
Gall-wasps, 185, 278, 282–284, 287,
288, 292, 301–305, 308, 309, 321
Ganoderma applanatum, 246
lucidum, 243, 245
Garden warbler, 336
Garrulus glandarius, 103, 128, 165,
315, 317, 328
Gastropoda, 348
Genetics, 27–49
of gall wasps, 301
Geometridae, 280, 315
Germany, 11, 20, 80, 84, 91–94, 119,
147, 194, 196, 241
Germination, see Acorn, growth
Geum urbanum, 135, 136, 166
Girth, 355–356
Glaciation, 53
Gleditschia, 208
Glis glis, 312, 316
Gloeosporium quercinum, 236, 238
Gnomonia veneta, 238
Gnorimus variabilis, 290
Goat willow, 105, 135
Goldcrest, 337
Goosefoot, 299
Gorse, 168, 326, 335
Gracillariidae, 285
Graphis, 266
Grazing, 74, 135, 136, 165–169, 180,
231, 267, 317, 318, 352, 363
Great oak beauty moth, 280
Great prominent, 182
Great tit, 326
Greenland, 226
Green oak tortrix, 86, 148, 156, 157,
182, 188, 239, 240, 299, 300
Green woodpecker, 329
Grey squirrel, 110, 312–314, 320
Grifola frondosa, 229, 246
Growth, 194–210, 355–356
Guignardia fagi, 239
Gypsy moth, 183
Gyrophaena strictula, 289
Gyroporus castaneus, 223

Hare, 182, 313, 317, 321
Harpocera thoracica, 291
Hawthorn, 123, 135, 143, 168, 287,
317, 326, 347
Hazel, 20, 54, 55, 57, 58, 60, 65, 135,
136, 143, 226, 275, 285, 333
Heather, 168, 318, 335
Hebeloma crustuliniforme, 226
Hedgerow oaks, 23, 73, 101, 102, 117,
301, 306, 308

Helicobasidium purpureum, 242
Helicodonta obvuluta, 348
Heliozela sericiella, 284
  stanneella, 284
Hemerobius humulinus, 288
  lutescens, 288
Hemiptera, 149, 263, 282, 285, 286, 298, 300
Hemiptera-Heteroptera, 298
Hemiptera-Homoptera, 278, 298
Hemlock, 107
Heracleum sphondylium, 135
Herbivores, 148, 156, 160, 168, 176, 180, 182, 190, 192, 257, 266, 267, 312–321, 352
Hercospora taleola, 241
Heron, 328
Heterobasidion annosum, 243
Heteroptera, 274, 281, 282, 285, 286, 288, 291
Hevea, 196
High forest, 21, 138–140, 237, 257–266, 324, 326, 334, 341–353, 358
History, see also Medieval
  Flandrian, 51–61, 130, 250
  Historic times, 62–77, 113–119, 347
Holcus mollis, 168
Holland, 341
Holly, 133, 135, 299, 334
Honeybee, 283
Honeydew, 287
Honey fungus, 229, 239, 240, 243
Hormones, 197–208
Hornbeam, 54, 55, 60, 75, 136, 334
Hornet, 291
Horse, 107, 113, 266
Hybrids, 16–18, 23–24, 29–46 *passim*
Hydnellum scrobiculatum, 230
Hydnum repandum, 230
Hydrocybe, 223
Hydropotes inermis, 318
Hygromia subrufescens, 348
Hygrophorus, 228
  chrysodon, 228
Hymenochaete rubiginosa, 229, 245
Hymenophyllum tunbrigense, 347, 348, 363
Hymenoptera, 284–286, 288, 290, 291
Hymenoscyphus phyllogenus, 230
Hyphodontia quercina, 229
Hypholoma fasciculare, 229
Hypnum cupressiforme var. *filiforme,* 271
Hypogymnia physodes, 271

Iassus lanio, 286
Identification, field characters, 47–49

Ilex aquifolium, 133, 135, 299, 334
Index of Ecological Continuity, 258, 259, 263–265, 346, 349
Indicator species, 258, 259, 263–265, 346–349
Inocybe, 229
  list of species, 227
  pusio, 232
Inonotus dryadeus, 243, 245
  hispidus, 245
Insect fauna, 12, 274–293, 314, 321, 364
  distribution, 291, 292, 307, 308
  habitats, 275–293
  melanism, 280
  requirements, 274
Interglacials, 53–55
International Biological Programme, 142
Introgression, 18, 20, 23, 24, 32–49
Ireland, 30, 59, 134, 231, 266, 292, 313, 333, 335, 338, 339, 341
Iron Age, 51, 53, 347
Isothecium myosuroides, 271
Italy, 240
Ivy, 135, 318

Jack o' Lantern, 229
Janus femoratus, 281
Japan, 119–121, 238
Japanese larch, 107
Jays, 103, 128, 165, 315, 317, 328
Juniper, 168

Kermes quercus, 278
  roboris, 278

Laccaria amethystea, 232
  laccata, 230–232
Lacewings, 288
Lackey, 182, 286
Lactarius, 228
  list of species, 227
  fuliginosus, 223
  glyciosmus, 231
  vietus, 231
Ladybirds, 288
Laetiporus sulphureus, 69, 244–246
Lake District, 20, 35–49 *passim,* 59, 60, 86, 134, 141–160 *passim,* 163, 165, 222, 232, 238, 261, 265, 271
Lammas shoots, see Flushing
Lampronia oehlmanniella, 285
Landscape, 107, 111, 261, 263, 341, 359

Larch, 107, 109, 118, 316
Largest oak, 356
Larix decidua, 107
  × *eurolepis,* 107
  kaempferi, 107
Lasiorhynchites cavifrons, 281
  olivaceus, 281
  ophthalmicus, 281
Laspeyresia, 283
Lawson cypress, 107
Leaf, see also Defoliation, Flushing and Litter
  characters, 33–49 *passim,* 201
  decay, 135, 230
  disease, 86, 104, 169, 236–239, 247
  feeders, 278, 284–289, 298–301, 306–308, 314, 316–318, 320
  folding, 18
  growth, 166
  miners, 284 285, 287, 299
  petiole, 284
  pubescence, 16, 17, 127
  retention, 202
  tannin content, 189, 190, 284
Leafhoppers, 285, 286, 298
Lecanactis premnea, 264
Lecanora conizaeoides, 267, 271
Leccinum aurantiacum, 226
  crocipodium, 223
  quercinum, 225, 226
Lecidia limitata, 268
Ledra aurita, 286
Legends, 123–129
Lejeuneaceae, 266
Lepidoptera, see also Defoliation 279, 280, 282–286, 292, 321
Lepiota, 230
Leptodon smithii, 251
Leptonia, 230
Lepus capensis, 182, 313, 317, 321
Lesser celandine, 136
Lestodiplosis, 283
Lichens, 134, 136, 251–272, 348, 349, 363
  list of species, 252–255, 261, 262
Light, 166, 169, 173–179, 204–207, 232, 244, 257, 265, 290, 351
Limax cinereoniger, 348
Lime, 59, 136, 225, 241, 287, 317, 346, 347
Lithocolletinae, 285
Lithocolletis, 285
Lithosiinae, 279
Litter, 143–156, 165, 168, 230, 238, 301, 305, 306, 321, 325, 328
Little owl, 328
Lobaria, 271
  laetevirens, 133, 271
  pulmonaria, 133, 264, 271
  scrobiculata, 264

Longevity, 98, 100, 179, 202, 342–344, 355, 356
Lonicera periclymenum, 135, 333
Loricula elegantula, 279
Loxia curvirostra, 337
Lumbricidae, 149
Lunar double-stripe moth, 292
Luscinia megarhynchos, 335
Luzula sylvatica, 135
Lycoperdon echinatum, 364
Lyctus, 120
Lymantria dispar, 183
Lymantriidae, 280

Macrodiplosis dryobia, 300
  volvens, 300
Malacosoma neustria, 182, 286
Malus, 274
  sylvestris, 126, 279, 282, 316, 317, 347
Mammals, 312–321
Management, see Woodland management
Mangifera, 196
Maple, 121, 179, 316, 317
Mast, see Acorns and Pannage
Master trees, 276
Meconema thalassinum, 280, 288
Medeterus, 279
Medieval, 53, 65–74, 76, 80–95, 126–128
Megacoelum infusum, 281, 291
Meles meles, 312, 319, 320
Melolontha melolontha, 299
Mercurialis perennis, 135, 136, 143, 325, 347
Meristem, 200
Merveille du Jour moth, 279
Microlepidoptera, 284–286, 299
Microsphaera alphitoides, 104, 169, 237, 239, Plate VII
  hypophylla, 237
Microtus agrestis, 313
Millepedes, 149
Minucia lunaris, 292
Miridae, 279, 281, 282, 298
Mirid bugs, 279, 281, 282, 298
Mistle thrush, 326
Mistletoe, 124–126
Mites, 149, 275, 282, 289, 290, 298
Modern times, 80–95
Molinia caerulea, 135
Mollusca, 348
Mompha, 278
Monodiplosis liebeli, 301
Mortality,
  of acorns, 86

Mortality—*cont.*
  of insects, 187–192
  of seedlings, 174, 176, 177
  of trees, 162, 184, 205, 210, 239, 240, 245, 289
Mosquitos, 291
Mottled umber, 182
Mouflon, 320
Mouse, 104, 169, 312–315, 317, 320
Muntiacus reevesi, 313, 317
Muntjac, 313, 317
Muscardinus avellanarius, 312, 316
Muscicapa striata, 326
Mycena galopus, 230
  hiemalis, 231
  inclinata, 229
  mucor, 230
Mycoblastus sanguinarius, 271
Mycosphaerella maculiformis, 238
  punctiformis, 238
Mucor polyadelpha, 230
Mycorrhiza, 154, 168, 178, 205, 223–233 *passim,* 358
  list of species, 224, 227
Myxomatosis, 110

Nathanica fulviceps, 288
National Nature Reserves, see also Wistman's Wood, 163–165, 324–331, 334, 338, 342, 351, 357
Nature Conservancy, 141, 357
Nature reserves, size, 349–351
Nectria coccinea, 241, 242
  ditissima, 241
  galligena, 241, 242
  mammoidea var. *rugulosa,* 242
Nematodes, 149
Neolithic, 51, 53, 60, 61
Nephrocerus flavirornis, 286
Nephroma laevigatum, 264
Nepticulidae, 285, 299
Nests, 291, 326–328, 331, 339
Neuroptera, 288
Neuroterus, 305, 306
  albipes, 305–308
  numismalis, 305, 307, 308
  quercusbaccarum, 305, 307, 308
  tricolor, 305–308
Neurotomus mandibularis, 287
New Forest, 20, 81, 88, 91, 92, 105, 111, 256, 260, 263, 265, 271, 292, 318, 349, 352
Nightingale, 335
Nolanea, 230
Norman, 53, 61, 94, 127
North America, 12, 31, 80, 119–121, 183, 184, 226, 230, 238, 240, 242, 244
Norway spruce, 107

Notodonta, 182
Nurse crops, 106–109
Nuthatch, 331
Nutrients, 141–160, 167, 171, 173–176, 197, 257
Nyctereutes procyonoides, 319

Oak-apple gall wasp, 302, 304
Oak-artichoke gall wasp, 304, 305
Oak bush-cricket, 280, 288
Oak leaf roller, 239, 240, 299
Oak-leaf spangle gall wasp, 305, 306
Oak-marble gall wasp, 308–310, 316
Oak mildew, 104, 169, 236, 237, 239, Plate VII
Oak timber,
  disease, 241, 244–246, 248
  price, 66, 70, 71, 118, 119
  quality, 15, 23, 102, 103, 113–122, 355, 359
  structure, 53, 355
  uses, 11, 53, 64–77, 111, 113–122, 361, 362
Oakwoods, 23, 53–61 *passim,* 62–77 *passim,* 111, 130–140, 141, 222–234 *passim,* 275, 276, 312–320, 324–339, 341–353, 357, 358, 363, 364
Ochrolechia androgyna, 271
  tartarea, 271
Odocoileus virginianus, 318, 321
Omphalotus olearius, 229
Opegrapha, 266
  lyncea, 256, 264
Operophtera brumuta, 182, 184, 186–192, 281, 326, 329, 338
Oporinia, 186, 188
Orthosia miniosa, 286
Orthotrichum, 266
  lyelli, 271
Orthotylus marginalis, 274
Oryctolagus cuniculus, 110, 114, 176, 177, 182, 312, 317, 320, 321
Ovis ammon musimon, 320
Oxalis acetosella, 143, 250
Oxlip, 136, 347
Oxythrips quercicola, 286

Pale brindled beauty, 182
Pammene fasciana, 283
  juliana, 283
Pamphilius, 287
  sylvarum, 287
Panaeolus semiovatus, 231
Pannage, 18, 73, 111, 127, 129, 135, 308, 312, 319
Pannaria pityrea, 264
  rubiginosa, 264

Parasites,
  fungal, see also Fungal pathogens, 223, 237, 238
  insect, 298–310
  of insects, 286, 288, 303
Parkland oaks, 66, 74, 101, 117, 244, 258–266, 317, 349, 363, 364
Parmelia aspera, 266
  caperata, 267, 268, 271
  glabratula, 267
  laevigata, 271
  physodes, 266–268, 271
  subaurifera, 267
  sulcata, 267, 268
  taylorensis, 271
Parmeliella plumbea, 133, 264, 271
Parus ater, 337
  caeruleus, 326
  major, 326
Paxillus involutus, 222, 225
Pealius quercus, 286
Peduncle, 13–15, 22
Peniophora quercina, 229
Pennines, 60
Peppered moth, 280
Peridea anceps, 182
Periodicity, 194
Perrisia, 283
Pertusaria, 271
Pestalotia, 236
Petioles, 230
Phaeographis, 266
Phaeolus schweinitzii, 243
Phalera bucephala, 182
Pharmacy, 357
Phellinus ferreus, 229
  robustus, 245
Phialina puberula, 230
Phigalia, 182
Phoenicurus phoenicurus, 331
Phomopsis, 236
  glandicola, 236
  quercella, 236
Photoperiodism, 196–205, 210
Photosynthesis, 207–209
Phyllobius, 287, 298
  argentatus, 278
Phyllonorycter, 285
  harrisella, 285
  quercifoliella, 285
Phylloscopus, 339
  collybita, 328
Phyllosticta maculiformis, 238
Phylloxera quercus, 298
Phylogeny, 30
Phylus melanocephalus, 298
Physiology, 194–211
Phytocoris, 279, 285
  populi, 279
Phytophthora, 242

Phytophthora cactorum, 242
  cinnamomi, 242
Picea abies, 54, 55, 107
  sitchensis, 99, 130, 176
Picus viridis, 329
Pied flycatcher, 336
Pigs, 73, 117, 127, 129, 135, 308, 312, 319
Pine, 51, 54, 58, 60, 99, 107, 130, 207, 210, 222, 226, 230, 239, 257, 279, 317
Pinus pinea, 239
  sylvestris, 51, 54, 58, 60, 99, 107, 130, 226, 279
  taeda, 207, 210
Pipunculidae, 286
Place names, 123, 124
Plagiochila spinulosa, 271
Plantations, 105, 106, 137, 260, 263, 265
Planting, 22, 31, 76, 77, 104–106, 178, 338
Platanthera chlorantha, 347
Platanus, 238
Pleistocene, 53, 231, 274, 275
Plesiocoris rugicollis, 274
Ploughing, 61
Poland, 11, 222, 318
Pollards, 63, 73–75, 244
Pollen, 18, 20, 27, 29, 51, 53, 56–61, 76, 130, 282, 283, 346, 347
Pollination, 205
Pollution, 231, 257, 260, 267
Polydrusus, 287
  cervinus, 278
Polypodium vulgare, 250
Polyporus betulinus, 289
  hispidus, 241
Poplar, 316, 317, 360
Populations,
  of insects, 182
  of oaks, 342–345, 352
Populus, 28, 283
  nigra, 360
  × serotina, 360
  tremula, 226
  tremuloides, 226
Poria andersonii, 245
Portrait paintings, 94, 95
Potash manufacture, 159
Potentilla erecta, 135
Powder-post beetles, 120
Primrose, 136
Primula elatior, 136, 347
  vulgaris, 136
Prionocyphon serricornis, 291
Prionus coriarius, 278
Private woodlands, 138–140
Privet, 135
Procyon lotor, 319

Productivity, 106, 107, 109, 111
Profenusa pygmaea, 285, 299
Prunus spinosa, 135, 326
Psallus, 285
  perrisi, 281
Pselaphidae, 290
Pseudotettix fusculus, 286
Psocoptera, 279, 287
Psychidae, 279
Psyllids, 286
Pteridium aquilinum, 142, 147, 148, 152, 168, 325
Purple emperor butterfly, 276
Purple hairstreak butterfly, 282
Pyralidae, 280, 286

Quadraspidoitus zonatus, 286
Quercus agrifolia, 28
  alba, 31, 39, 41, 202, 206, 207, 210
  borealis, 27
  cerris, 28, 29, 194, 198, 237, 239, 309, 310, 324
  cerris × *suber*, 28–30
  chrysolepis, 31
  coccifera, 28
  coccinia, 240
  conferta, 30, 31
  dunni, 31
  falcata, 199, 316
  frainetto, 198, 239
  gambellii, 31
  × *hispanica*, 28, 29, 194
  ilex, 28, 30, 210, 238, 355
  infectoria, 200
  lanuginosa, 30, 31
  lucumbeana, 28, 194
  lyrata, 207
  macrocarpa, 199
  margaretta, 31
  nigra, 199
  palustris, 199
  pedunculiflora, 30, 31
  petraea var. *laciniata*, Plate VI
  phellos, 199
  prinus, 31, 39, 41
  prinus × *alba*, 41
  pubescens, 28
  robur × *petraea*, 28, 30, 33, 46
  robur var. *tardissima*, 196
  rubra, 197–199, 201, 203–205, 207, 208, 240, 283, 355
  × *saulii*, 39, 41
  suber, 28, 29, 194, 205, 206
  undulata, 31
  velutina, 27, 28
Quercusia quercus, 282

Rabbit, 110, 114, 176, 177, 182, 312, 317, 320, 321
Racoon dog, 319

Radiocarbon dating, 51–61 *passim*, 94
Railways, 117
Rainfall, 81, 82, 88, 93, 142, 143, 145, 159, 231, 237, 266, 290, 291
Ramalina, 266
Ranunculus ficaria, 136
Rats, 104
Red barnacle gall wasp, 305
Red deer, 313, 317, 318
Red squirrel, 312–314
Redstart, 331
Redwing, 328
Regeneration, 68, 69, 162–180, 237, 342, 343, 346, 351, 352
  acorn, 69, 76, 110, 111, 128, 205, 317
  pollarding, 63, 73, 74
  stump, 69, 76, 110
Regulus regulus, 337
Rhizoctonia crocorum, 242
  solani, 242
Rhizophagus, 290
Rhododendron ponticum, 349
Rhynchaenus avellanae, 275, 285
  fagi, 364
  pilosus, 285
  quercus, 275, 285, 299
Rhynchites caeruleus, 281, 364
Robin, 326
Robinia, 208
Roe deer, 313, 317, 318
Roosts, 328, 329, 331
Roots, 150, 167, 176–178, 203–205, 209, 210, 239, 278, 303, 358
  diseases, 242–244, 247, 248
Rosa, 122, 326
Rose, 122, 326
Rosellinia necatrix, 242
  quercina, 242, 243
  thelena, 242, 243
Rot-holes, 290, 291
Rove beetle, 289
Rozites caperata, 226
Rubus, 114, 135, 143, 314, 318, 325
  vestitus, 143
Russula, 228, 364
  list of species, 227
  claroflava, 231
  ochroleuca, 231
Rusts, 236, 238
Rutstroemia, firma, 230

Salicaceae, 282
Salix, 75, 274, 283, 316, 317, 334
  atrocinerea, 105
  caprea, 105, 135
  repens, 226
Sallow, 136
Sambucus nigra, 135, 325
Sanicula europaea, 135

Saprophytes, 223, 228
Sarcodon imbricatum, 230
Sawfly, 281, 285, 287, 299
Sawing, 11, 64–68, 94, 113–115, 118, 120, 361
Scale-insect, 281, 299, 300
Scandinavia, 21, 80, 84, 222, 237, 265, 318
Sciurus carolinensis, 110, 312–314, 320
  vulgaris, 312–314
Scleroderma citrinum, 225
Sclerotinia candolleana, 230, 238
Scolopax rusticola, 328
Scolytidae, 289
Scoparia, 280
  ambigualis, 280
  basistrigalis, 280
Scopariinae, 280
Scotland, 20–24, 30, 31, 42, 47, 59, 60, 98, 130, 134, 139, 223, 225, 226, 229, 230, 237, 260–264, 266, 271, 292, 312, 313, 335, 338, 339
Scots pine, 51, 54, 58, 60, 99, 107, 130, 226, 279
Scrub, 99, 111, 138–140, 301, 306, 308, 312, 329, 338
Seasoning, 113–115, 120
Seed, see Acorn and Regeneration
Seedlings, 104, 165–179, 182–184, 194, 197, 205, 208, 210, 236, 242, 317, 321, 352
Sematophyllum demissum, 133
Senescence, 201
Septoria, 238
Sheep, 135, 176, 177, 231
Shipbuilding, 11, 22, 53, 68, 74, 102, 114
Shoots, see Twigs
Sibthorpia europea, 347
Sika deer, 313, 317
Silver fir, 55
Sitka spruce, 99, 130, 176
Sitta europea, 331
Small brindled beauty, 182, 183
Small-leaved lime, 136, 347
Snails, 348
Soil, 21, 35, 51, 54, 75, 81, 82, 93, 111, 131–133, 141–159 *passim,* 165–168, 174, 177, 179, 205, 222, 226, 227, 232, 242, 275, 302, 305, 333
Song thrush, 326
Sorbus torminalis, 347, 364
Sphaerophorus globosus, 271
Sphagnum, 51
Spiders, 275, 279, 288
Spotted flycatcher, 326
Springtails, 149
Spruce, 54, 55, 107, 245, 315, 316
Squirrels, 110, 291, 312–314, 317, 319–321

Stachys sylvatica, 135
Stag-headedness, see Dieback
Standards, 63, 67, 74–77, 105, 324, 325, 328, 329
Starling, 326
Stereum frustulatum, 246
  gausapatum, 69, 110, 229, 244, 245
  hirsutum, 244
  rugosum, 241
  spadiceum, 244
Sternorhyncha, 286
Sticta, 271
  fuliginosa, 133
Stigmella, 285
Stockdove, 124, 328
Stomaphis, 278, 286
Stomata, 208
Strepsiptera, 286
Stretopelia turtur, 328
Stropharia semiglobata, 231
Strophosomus melanogrammus, 278
Strumella coryneoidea, 241
Sturnus vulgaris, 326
Succession, 54, 58–61, 75, 135, 283, 284, 289–292
Sugar maple, 179
Sulphur tuft, 229
Sus scrofa, 313, 319, 320
Sutton Hoo, 93
Sweet chestnut, 15, 136, 225, 226, 229, 236, 237, 246, 256, 274, 314, 361
Switzerland, 237
Sycamore, 12, 102, 120, 121, 135, 143, 241, 256, 314, 334
Sylvia, 338
  atricapilla, 328
  borin, 336
  communis, 336
Sympherobius elegans, 288
  pygmaeus, 288
Synanthedon vespiformis, 278
Synergus clandestinus, 283

Tachinidae, 288
Tachydrominae, 279
Tannin, 27, 51, 189, 190, 314
Tanning, 113, 159, 308
Taphrina caerulescens, 237
Taxonomy, 13–18
Taxus baccata, 119, 126, 334
Temperature, 76, 81, 93, 197, 203, 206, 225, 237
Thamnotettix dilutior, 286
Thanatephorus cucumeris, 242
Thea, 196
Thelephora anthocephala, 230
Thelopsis rubella, 264
Thelotrema lepadinum, 264
Thelypteris limbosperma, 135

Theridion pallens, 288
Thrips minutissimus, 286
Thuja plicata, 107
Thysanoptera, 285, 286
Tilia, 59, 225, 241, 287, 317, 346
   cordata, 136, 347
Timber, see Oak timber
Tortricidae, 235, 283, 286
Tortrix viridana, 86, 148, 156, 157, 182, 188, 239, 240, 299, 300
Transpiration, 209
Treecreeper, 326
Tree pipit, 331
Tricholoma acerbum, 228
   sulphureum, 228
Trioza remota, 286
Troglodytes troglodytes, 326
Trunk, 145, 229, 250, 278–280, 326–328
Tuber magnatum, 226
Turdus iliacus, 328
   merula, 124, 326
   philomelos, 326
   pilaris, 328
   viscivorus, 326
Turkey oak, 28, 29, 194, 237, 239, 309, 310, 324
Turtle dove, 328
Tussock moths, 280
Twig-cutting weevil, 281
Twigs, 143, 145, 152, 183, 185, 186, 188, 194–210, 229, 237, 240–242, 247, 256, 266, 280, 299, 302, 304, 316, 321, 326–328
Tyloses, 209
Typhlocybidae, 285, 286

Ulex europaeus, 168, 326
   gallii, 335
Ulmus, 28, 54, 58, 60, 75, 102, 117, 120, 136, 143, 251, 255, 257, 268, 317, 346, 361
   procera, 324
Ulota, 266
Underwood, 64–77
Uredo quercus, 236, 238
Ursus arctos, 313, 319, 320
Urtica dioica, 135
Urus, 313
U.S.A., see North America
Usnea, 266
U.S.S.R., 184, 194, 210, 317

Vaccinium, 28
   myrtillus, 133, 135, 169, 250
Variability, 16, 30–33, 46, 47, 76, 77, 178
Vehicles, 116
Veneers, 119, 121
Vessels, 200, 355

Viburnum, 28, 207
Vikings, 94
Viola odorata, 135
Vole, 169, 312–315, 317, 320

Wahlenbergia hederacea, 347
Wales, 20, 30, 59, 60, 98, 102, 109, 123, 128, 130, 134, 140, 163–177 *passim,* 261, 271, 312, 334, 338, 339
Wasps, 291
Water,
   and beavers, 316
   in galls, 306
   storage, 210
   transport, 209, 210
Wavy hair-grass, 135, 142, 165, 167, 168
Weald, 344–349, 358, 361–364
Weevils, 185, 235, 274, 275, 278, 281–283, 285, 287, 292, 298, 299, 364
Western red cedar, 107
Wheat, 135
White-tailed deer, 318, 321
Whitethroat, 336
Wild boar, 313, 319, 320
Willow, 75, 105, 135, 226, 283, 316, 317, 334
Wilting, 209
Windsor, 225, 256, 292
Winter moth, 182, 184, 186–192, 281, 326, 329, 338
Wistman's Wood, 33–49 *passim,* 134, 184, 357
Wood anemone, 136, 143
Wood avens, 135, 136, 166
Woodcock, 328
Woodland management, 64–77, 130–140, 244, 263, 265, 351–353
Wood mouse, 169, 312, 314, 321
Woodpecker, 241, 329
Woodpigeon, 103, 315, 328
World War,
   I, 72, 115–118
   II, 72, 116–119
Wren, 326
Wych, elm, 60, 143
Wytham Wood, 86, 183–192

Xerula fusipes, 229
Xylem, 200, 202, 209, 355
Xylocoris cursitans, 290
Xylodon versiporus, 229

Yellow archangel, 325
Yellowhammer, 336
Yellow-legged clearwing, 278
Yellow-necked mouse, 312–314, 320
Yew, 119, 126, 334
Yugoslavia, 30, 86

Zeiraphera isertana, 186, 188